CHRONOLOGY, CONQUEST AND CONFLICT IN MEDIEVAL ENGLAND

CAMDEN MISCELLANY
XXXIV

CHRONOLOGY, CONQUEST AND CONFLICT IN MEDIEVAL ENGLAND

CAMDEN MISCELLANY
XXXIV

CAMDEN FIFTH SERIES
Volume 10

CAMBRIDGE
UNIVERSITY PRESS

FOR THE ROYAL HISTORICAL SOCIETY
University College London, Gower Street, London WC1E 6BT
1997

Published by the Press Syndicate of the University of Cambridge
The Edinburgh Building, Cambridge CB2 2RU, United Kingdom
40 West 20th Street, New York, NY 10011–4211, USA
10 Stamford Road, Oakleigh, Melbourne 3166, Australia

First published 1997

A catalogue record for this book is available from the British Library

ISBN 0 521 63109 2 hardback

SUBSCRIPTIONS. The serial publications of the Royal Historical Society, *Royal Historical Society Transactions* (ISSN 0080–4401), Camden Fifth Series (ISSN 0960–1163) volumes and volumes of the Guides and Handbooks (ISSN 0080–4398) may be purchased together on annual subscription. The 1997 subscription price (which includes postage but not VAT) is £50 (US$80 in the USA, Canada and Mexico) and includes Camden Fifth Series, volumes 9 and 10 (published in July and December) and Transactions Sixth Series, volume 7 (published in December). Japanese prices are available from Kinokuniya Company Ltd, P.O. Box 55, Chitose, Tokyo 156, Japan. EU subscribers (outside the UK) who are not registered for VAT should add VAT at their country's rate. VAT registered subscribers should provide their VAT registration number. Prices include delivery by air.

Subscription orders, which must be accompanied by payment, may be sent to a bookseller, subscription agent or direct to the publisher: Cambridge University Press, The Edinburgh Building, Shaftesbury Road, Cambridge CB2 2RU, UK; or in the USA, Canada and Mexico: Cambridge University Press, 40 West 20th Street, New York, NY 10011–4211, USA.

SINGLE VOLUMES AND BACK VOLUMES. A list of Royal Historical Society volumes available from Cambridge University Press may be obtained from the Humanities Marketing Department at the address above.

Printed and bound in the United Kingdom by Butler & Tanner Ltd, Frome and London

CONTENTS

I

The *Brevis Relatio de Guillelmo nobilissimo comite Normannorum*, Written by a Monk of Battle Abbey Edited with an Historical Commentary

by Elisabeth M. C. van Houts

In memoriam Edmé Renno Smits (1950–1992)

CONTENTS

FOREWORD

For the historical commentary I have benefited greatly from the notes of the late Professor R. H. C. Davis, whose unpublished papers on the *Brevis Relatio*, dated to 1959, were generously passed to me by his literary executors Miss Barbara Harvey and Dr John Blair. My greatest debt, however, must go to Dr Martin Brett to whom I owe the suggestion that the Battle manuscript of the *Brevis Relatio* is the author's copy, and who also gave much valuable advice on the Sussex background of the text.

This edition was meant to have been edited by myself in collaboration with Dr Edmé Smits, my former colleague at the Department of Medieval Studies in Groningen (Netherlands). In 1992, however, Edmé died tragically as a result of a heart attack and consequently our project laid still for a few years. As a token of our friendship and in commemoration of his short career as a Latinist of the medieval period I dedicate this edition to his memory.

E.M.C. v. H.
Emmanuel College, Cambridge

ABBREVIATIONS

Battle Chronicle	*The Chronicle of Battle Abbey*, ed. E. Searle (Oxford, 1980)
Dudo	*De moribus et actis primorum Normanniae ducum auctore Dudone sancti Quintini decano*, ed. J. Lair (Caen, 1865)
Gesta Guillelmi	*The Gesta Guillelmi of William of Poitiers*, ed. R.H.C. Davis (†) and M. Chibnall (Oxford, 1998)
GND	*The Gesta Normannorum Ducum of William of Jumièges, Orderic Vitalis and Robert of Torigni*, ed. E.M.C. van Houts, 2 vols (Oxford, 1992–5)
GRA	*Willelmi Malmesbiriensis monachi, De gestis regum Anglorum*, ed. W. Stubbs, 2 vols, Rolls Series (London, 1887–9)
HH	*Henry, archdeacon of Huntingdon, Historia Anglorum, The History of the English People*, ed. D. Greenway (Oxford, 1996)
'Hyde' Chronicle	*Chronica monasterii de Hida iuxta Wintoniam*, in: *Liber Monasterii de Hyda*, ed. E. Edwards, Rolls Series (London, 1866), 283–321
OV	*The Ecclesiastical History of Orderic Vitalis*, ed. M. Chibnall, 6 vols (Oxford, 1969–80)
Roman de Rou	*Le Roman de Rou de Wace*, ed. A.J. Holden, 3 vols (Paris, 1971–3)
TRHS	*Transactions of the Royal Historical Society*

INTRODUCTION

i Contents

The *Brevis Relatio*, as this text is commonly known, is a short history of Normandy and England from c. 1035 to the battle of Tinchebrai in 1106. Although it is called a history of Duke William who conquered England, it covers much more ground because it gives details of the end of his father's reign, in particular Duke Robert's pilgrimage to Jerusalem, and goes on well into the reign of his youngest son Henry I. The contents can be divided roughly into three sections. The first comprises paragraphs 1 to 9 which contain Robert the Magnificent's decision to go on pilgrimage to Jerusalem and the appointment of William as his successor and heir [par. 1], an anecdote illustrating his generosity of mind during the journey to Jerusalem [par. 2] and the troubles of William's minority following his father's death in Nicaea [3]. From there we jump to the story of the Norman conquest of England, the single most important theme of the text, covering five paragraphs [4–8]. The first section ends with William's death in 1087 [9].

The second section is devoted to the troubled reigns of Robert Curthose (1087–1106, d. 1134) in Normandy and William Rufus (1087–1100) in England and their ultimate, triumphant replacement by Henry I after the battle of Tinchebrai in 1106 [10–11]. In par. 12 the author emphasizes that Henry I represents the seventh generation after Rollo and that the future will tell what lies in store for England and Normandy. Paragraph 13 lists the burial places of the six dukes and gives the three monastic foundations of William the Conqueror: the Norman abbeys of Caen where he was buried and Battle which he had meant to turn into one of the richest monasteries in England, but was prevented from doing so by death. The author hopes that no one is displeased by what he has written about the dukes on the basis of what he has learned from others.

In the third section, comprising paragraphs 14 to 21, the author turns back to the past of the early dukes of Normandy and narrates a miscellaneous series of anecdotes in roughly chronological order. There are two paragraphs on Rollo [14, 15], one on the pact between the Normans and the French following the death of William Longsword and detailing the obligations between the duke and the king [16], a story about Duke Richard II and the theft of the plough shares [17], this duke's generosity to the monasteries of Fécamp [18] and Jumièges [19], and a brief reference to the story how shortly after his birth Duke William grabbed the straw, which was lying around his cradle, and put his hands full of straw on his breasts [20]. The final paragraph [21] contains a eulogy on Henry I.

ii Manuscripts

The *Brevis Relatio* survives in four medieval manuscripts and one seventeenth-century copy.

O: Oxford, Bodleian Library, MS e Museo 93 is the oldest and best known manuscript of the *Brevis Relatio*.[1] It consists of one quire of four folios which originally belonged to Hereford Cathedral Library, MS P.v.1.[2] Both sections formed one codex written at Battle Abbey in the 1120s. As a result of the break-up of the original manuscript in the sixteenth century two parts are still missing: a text of Nennius and an early history of the monastery of Battle Abbey.[3] The contents of the complete Battle codex can be reconstructed as follows: Lanfranc's *Monastic Constitutions* (Hereford, P.v.1, 1r-26v), St. Augustine's *Contra Felicianum* (*idem*, 27r-28v), the now lost copy of Nennius, Bede's *Historia Ecclesiastica* (Hereford, P.v.1, 29r-150v), St. Cuthbert's *Epistola* (*idem*, 151r-152r), a list of the archbishops of Canterbury updated till 1161-2 (*idem*, 152v), the now lost *De constructione ecclesiae Belli*, the *Brevis Relatio* (Oxford, e Museo, ff. 1r-7v, pp. 1-14), a charter dated 1177 as space filler (*idem*, ff. 7v-8r, pp. 14-15) and the *Ship list* of William the Conqueror (*idem*, f. 8v, p. 16).[4]

The *Brevis Relatio* begins with the rubric, written on top of a partially erased earlier rubric, followed by the first words 'Pater huius Willelmi fuit' and it ends on f. 7v, p. 14 in the middle of the first column with par. 20 '. . . pectus suum apposuit'. The text of the *Brevis Relatio* contains a fair number of erasures and rewritten passages, all in the same hand as that of the original scribe. It contains the best text (see **iii**), which is contemporary with the date of the contents (see **iv**). The scribe can be identified with a monk of Battle on the basis of his activity in the mid-1120s in other Battle manuscripts. He wrote London BL, Ms Cotton

---

1 F. Madan, H. H. S. Craster, *A Summary Catalogue of Western Manuscripts in the Bodleian library at Oxford*, 7 vols (Oxford, 1895–1953), ii, 712.

2 A. T. Bannister, *A Descriptive Catalogue of the Manuscripts in the Hereford Cathedral Library*, ed. M. R. James (Hereford, 1927), 147–9.

3 For the history of this manuscript and all relevant literature, see E. M. C. van Houts, 'The Ship list of William the Conqueror', *Anglo-Norman Studies* x (1987), ed. R. A. Brown (Woodbridge, 1988), 165–67, 177 (Appendix 2).

4 For my edition, see *ibidem*, p. 176 (and a photograph on 175).

Nero D ii, 238–41, which is the autograph of the *Annals of Battle Abbey*,[5] as well as London BL, Ms Royal 4 C xi, 1–222r which contains a text of Hieronymus. Since the contents clearly point to a strong Battle interest (see **v**) we have in O the autograph manuscript of the *Brevis Relatio*.

A: Aberystwyth, National Library of Wales, MS Peniarth 335A (previously Hengwrth 239), 61v–75v.[6] It is a late fourteenth-century manuscript with a large variety of texts, some of which show interest in Scottish affairs. It cannot be assigned to a particular scriptorium. The *Brevis Relatio* text begins on 61v with a rubric 'De Willelmo', followed by the opening words 'Pater Willelmi conquestoris fuit'. The text ends on 75v with par 21 and the words '... cum sanctis omnibus in eternam gaudeat. Amen.' This manuscript has not previously been used in any edition of the *Brevis Relatio*.[7]

S: London, British Library, MS Sloane 3103, 116v–121v. It comes from the Norman abbey of Saint-Sauveur-le-Vicomte (114v, 116r), where it was probably written by a mid twelfth-century hand, but after 1145, the date of Bernard of Clairvaux's letter 238 to Pope Eugenius III (121v–122, with one folium missing).[8] It is possible that either this manuscript or its immediate exemplar was actually copied at the nearby monastery of Cerisy-la-Forêt, because the *Brevis Relatio* contains an interpolation naming Duke Robert the Magnificent as the founder of

5 A. G. Watson, *Catalogue of dated and datable manuscripts c. 700–1600 in the Department of Manuscripts of the British Library* (London, 1979), i, no. 543.

6 *Handlist of Manuscripts in the National Library of Wales*, i (Aberystwyth 1943), 2. I am most grateful to Dr Daniel Huws, former Keeper of Manuscripts at the National Library of Wales, for letting me consult his description of the manuscript. The manuscript comprises ff. 192 written in one hand in the 'anglicana formata' of the mid-fourteenth century. The contents are 3–61 *Secretum secretorum Aristotelis* (ed. R. Steels (Oxford, 1920), 36–172); 61v–75v *Brevis Relatio*; 76–90 *Generacio regum Scocie*. A list of Scottish kings followed by a collection of documents relating to the years 1291–1301; 91–130v Pope Innocent III, 'De contempu mundi' (ed. Migne *PL* 217, 701–46 and ed. R. E. Lewis (1980); 131–182v several apocryphal bible texts followed on 182–186v by a collection of miscellaneous verses.

7 However, the last paragraph, 21, was edited from this manuscript by T. D. Hardy, *Descriptive Catalogue of Materials relating to Great Britain and Ireland*, 3 vols (London, 1862–71), ii, 6–7.

8 *Sancti Bernardi Opera*, ed. J. Leclerq, H. Rochais, viii (Rome 1977), no. 238. Detailed descriptions of this manuscript can be found in A. Wilmart, 'Eve et Goscelin', *Revue Bénédictine*, 50 (1938), 42–83 at 51–55 and C. H. Talbot, 'The Liber confortatorius of Goscelin of Saint-Bertin', *Analecta Monastica*, 3rd s. Studia Anselmiana, 37 (Rome 1955), 23–5. As the titles of these articles imply, the most significant text other than the *Brevis Relatio* is the unique copy of Goscelin of Saint-Bertin's *Liber Confortatorius* addressed to the recluse Eve, formerly a nun at Wilton, but now at Saint Laurent at Angers (1–114v.) Then follows a series of short texts written in the thirteenth century on the murder of Thomas Becket, which is incomplete due to the loss of one folium; on 115 follow a text on the martyrdom of St. Catherine and an antiphon with notes in honour of St. Bartholomew. 116 contains a hymn on St. Catherine.

this monastery.[9] The Saint-Sauveur manuscript, or its Cerisy exemplar, was used by Wace for his *Roman de Rou*.[10] The *Brevis Relatio* begins with a rubric which is identical to the original one in ms O, followed by the words 'Pater huius Guillelmi'. The text ends on 121v with par. 13 and the words '. . . et uoluntas et possibilitas'. Then follows a genealogy of the kings of England, starting with 'Ine regnauit.xxx.vii.annis. post eum regnauit Athelbardus annis .xiiii. . . .' and ending with Henry I: '. . . Henricus frater eius [sc. William Rufus] .xxxv. annis et .iiii. mensibus et duobus diebus regnauit.'[11]

L: London, Lambeth Palace, Ms 99, 219r–224r. The manuscript dates from the late fourteenth century and has a contemporary owner's mark from St. George's Chapel at Windsor.[12] The *Brevis Relatio* contains a gap in the text due to the loss of one folio between ff 221v and 222r covering most of the paragraphs 7–11. The text begins on 219r with a rubric that, although slightly different from the ones in O and S, is clearly modelled on the original rubric. The Lambeth manuscript is with A the only one to contain par. 21, though altered to suit the post 1135 circumstances, which ends with the words '. . . cum sanctis omnibus in eternam gaudeat. Amen.' It has not been used for an edition before.

The seventeenth-century manuscript of the *Brevis Relatio* is Oxford, Bodl. Lib., Ms Ashmole 865 which as a faithful copy of the Battle Manuscript, e Museo 93 has no independent value for the reconstruction of the text.

iii Text development

The *Brevis Relatio* has survived in a fair copy, O, made by the author of his draft, which consisted of wax tablets or parchment.[13] That it is the author's fair copy and not a working copy is shown by the following observations. Several times the author missed out a word which he wrote in the margin accompanied by a sign which corresponds with a

9 Par. 12 note k. *Recueil des actes des ducs de Normandie de 911 à 1066*, ed. M. Fauroux (Caen, 1961), no. 64 contains the foundation charter of Duke Robert for Cerisy dated 12 November 1032.

10 E. M. C. van Houts, 'Wace as historian', *Family Trees and the Roots of Politics: Britain and France from the Tenth to the Twelfth century*, ed. K. S. B. Keats-Rohan (Woodbridge, 1997), 103–32 at 115.

11 Printed by Giles as an appendix to his edition of the *Brevis Relatio* (London, 1845), 22–23.

12 M. R. James, C. Jenkins, *A Descriptive Catalogue of the Manuscripts in the Library of Lambeth Palace* (Cambridge, 1931), no. 99; N. R. Ker, *Medieval Libraries of Great Britain* (London, 1964), 203.

13 For a study of different types of autograph manuscripts of historians, see M. C. Garand, 'Auteurs latins et autographes des xie et xiie siècles', *Scrittura e Civiltà*, 5 (1981), 77–104, esp. 97–8.

similar sign in the text where the word has to be inserted. He also occasionally transposed words and again used small signs to indicate that the word order should be reversed. On one occasion, in par. 15 in the sentence *Tunc ille remandauit comiti quia in crastino eum usque ad primam expectaret. Ille autem in crastino ...*, due to an haplography from *in crastino* to *in crastino*, he skipped one line in his draft, omitted it accidentally, then discovered his mistake and inserted the missing words *eum usque ... in crastino* in the margin. Finally, in par. 16, note x, he erroneously wrote the word *ad* twice. I consider these lapses as scribal lapses made by the author while copying his draft into a final text. None of these mistakes had any consequences for the textual tradition. Moreover, O provides the best text without any of the omissions which can be observed in the other manuscripts which render certain passages unintelligible. After November 1120 (see **iv**), when β, the ancestor of A, S and L, had been made, the author altered the rubric and the sentence on William Adelin, by including a reference to the young prince's death, in par. 10.

As is clear from the critical apparatus there are numerous occasions which show the text in O as different from the text in A, S and L, due to the alterations introduced in their common exemplar, β. Its scribe altered prepositions, e.g. *uero* for *igitur* (par. 3 note a) and pronouns, e.g. *eum* for *illum* (par. 6, note u); he also exchanged the French sounding vocabulary and preferred more classical Latin words, e.g. *laneis uestibus* for *langis* (par. 14, notes e and i),[14] *sulcos* for *reias* (par. 15 notes y and f), *lignulum* for *fussellum* (par. 15 note d; par. 19 note i). Occasionally, β's scribe corrected the tense: e.g. *occubuisset* became *occumberet* (par. 10, note u), *factum habemus* became *fecimus* (par. 13, note o), *perditum habemus* became *perdidimus* (par. 14, note j) and *interfectum habuissent*, became *interfecerunt* (par. 16, note h). Though these were clearly attempts by β to correct the original text he twice made a mess by omitting phrases due to haplography: from *pius* to *pius* (par. 1, note g) and from *si* to *si* (par. 13, note m). Where S is lacking, that is for paragraphs 14–21, the opposition between O on the one hand and A, L on the other is

---

14 The alteration of 'langis' into 'laneis uestibus' can be explained in two ways, both of which point to the author being influenced by the French vernacular. Either 'langis' stands for the Latin word 'lanis', the verb in the ablative used as a substantive noun, from 'lanio', to tear, to grieve (W. von Wartburg, *Französisches Etymologisches Wörterbuch,,* 5 (Bonn, 1950), 164–5, s.v. 'laniare'). Written by a French speaking person the word could easily be spelled as 'langis' (or indeed 'lagnis'). Subsequently, it was misinterpreted in French as deriving from 'lange' (wool) and hypercorrected back into Latin as 'laneis uestibus', woollen garments (A.J. Greimas, *Dictionnaire de l'ancien français jusqu'au milieu du xive siècle*, 2nd ed. Paris, 1968), 356 s,v, 'lange'). Alternatively, von Wartburg s.v. 'lange', wool (*Idem*, 159–60) has a note explaining that in Old French 'langis' occurs often as a noun/substantive in conjunction with 'nuz piez' meaning an informal garment. I am most grateful to Professor Giovanni Orlandi for guidance in this matter.

maintained. For this reason I assume that it is the scribe of β who was responsible for the text of par. 21 which occurs in A and L, but not in O or S. It is possible that β represents corrections by the author himself. If so, one might have expected β instead of ms O to have survived at Battle.

A, S and L do not always go together and on several occasions a split can be observed between A, going together with O, versus S and L, which shows that the latter two share a common exemplar γ. A few examples will illustrate the divide: *uenire* (O, A) left out by S, L (par 2, note d) and *exheredare* (O, A) versus *exhereditare* (S, L in par. 3, note 1). The dividing line between O and A on the one hand and S and L on the other can also be observed in the historical updating of the text due to the scribe of γ (see **iv**).

If we now turn from groups of manuscripts to individual manuscripts, other than O, we can make some more interesting observations. There are two lacunae of a few words in A which strongly suggest a link with O and which shows that β must have had a similar lay-out as O. On the dividing line of paragraphs 1 and 2 there are five words missing, *similia contigerunt. Libet uero memorie*, which in Ms O (p. 1, f.1rb) happens to fit precisely into one line across one column.[15] In par 10, a similar gap occurs and A misses the words *inuadiaret et tunc fratri suo*.[16] In O these words straddle the last line of p. 7, f.4r and the first line of p. 8, f.4v. Since β did not have the second occurrence of the words *regi Anglorum* in the same sentence, the words missing in A could well have fitted on the last line of the page in β and omitted by accident. Both lacunae strongly suggest that A's exemplar had the same lay-out as O, namely written in two columns of exactly the same width as in O, which twice caused the scribe of A to 'jump' one line of text.

Where the texts of both S and L survive, their variants are very similar. This similarity suggests that where L is missing, as for example in the big lacuna in par 7–11, the text of S can be used to reconstruct the missing part.

iv Date

The original version was written after 1114 but before 1120. In 1114 Henry I's daughter Matilda married Henry V of the Holy Roman Empire, an event that is mentioned in par. 10.[17] The *terminus ante quem* for the *Brevis Relatio* is William Adelin's death in the White Ship disaster

15 See paragraphs 1–2, notes x ... x.
16 See par. 10, notes q and r: the missing words are *inuadiaret et tunc Henricus fratri suo regi Anglorum*.
17 *GND*, ii, 218; M. Chibnall, *The Empress Matilda* (Oxford, 1991), 15–17, 24–7.

of November 1120, an event that clearly had not happened at the time of writing, for in par. 10 the author expresses his wish that William live a long life.[18] The revisions that followed cannot all be dated precisely and only one can be attributed directly to the author. He revised the text in O after William Adelin's death, and after the scribe of β had already taken his copy. At this stage he too, presumably, altered the rubric and removed the reference to William the Conqueror's hereditary claim. The β scribe, however, also updated the passage on William Adelin's death, but independently from O. Moreover, he added the text of paragraph 21 eulogizing Henry and describing him as still alive. Therefore, β's activity, which can be traced in A, can be dated between 1120 and 1135. After King Henry I's death β's text was copied by the scribe of γ who altered all references to Henry I as still alive in paragraphs 10, 11, 12 and 21. His work, datable to a period shortly after 1135, can be followed in S (available until the end of par. 13[19]) and L. Finally, the scribe of S alone updated the text by omitting the words 'until now' (*adhuc*) which the author had used to indicate that the count of Mortain, captured in 1106, was still held captive. There is evidence which shows that he was released from the Tower of London in 1118, still held by the king in 1130 and not set free until he became a monk at Bermondsey in 1140.[20] The following diagram illustrates the evidence as set out in **iii** and **iv**.

18 *The Anglo-Saxon Chronicle*, trl. G. N. Garmondsway (London, 1972), 249.

19 The matter is complicated because the *Brevis Relatio* text in S ends with the one but last sentence of par. 13 and thus omits paragraphs 14 to 21. Clearly the monk of Saint-Sauveur-le-Vicomte was interested in the eleventh and early twelfth-century sections and not in the anecdotes about the early dukes of Normandy.

20 His release from the Tower of London is mentioned in the *Annals of Bermondsey*, which according to Martin Brett's reconstruction, go back to a series of now lost London annals, M. Brett, 'The annals of Bermondsey, Southwark and Merton', *Church and city 1000–1500. Essays in honour of Christopher Brooke*, ed. D. Abulafia, M. Franklin, M. Rubin (Cambridge, 1992), 298: 'Et eodem anno miraculose uirtute sancte crucis liberatur Willelmus comes Moritonie de turri Londonie.' The annal of 1140, in the same collection, tells of the count's entrance into the community of Bermondsey (*ibidem*, 299). However, the annals of Bermondsey need to be used with care due to the number of demonstratively erroneous entries. According to Henry of Huntingdon, William had been blinded at the orders of King Henry I (HH, x. 1, 698–9). The *Pipe Roll of 1130* (ed. J. Hunter, London 1833, p. 143) shows him to be in the king's custody. I am very grateful to Warren Hollister and Martin Brett for help with this note.

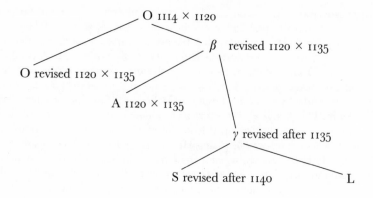

v Author

The author was a monk of Battle, whom at present cannot be identified. He was almost certainly a Norman judged by his exclusive interest in the dukes of Normandy, Duke William's conquest of England and lack of attention to England outside Sussex. Battle is mentioned as the Conqueror's only foundation in England and the author is unique in claiming that King William wished to turn it into one of his wealthiest monasteries in England [par. 13], but was prevented from doing so by death: 'From this we learn that he acts wisely who plans to do good as quickly as he attempts to execute it. Nobody knows whether alive today he shall be able to see tomorrow and therefore he acts wisely who does the good he is planning for tomorrow, if possible, today. It is safer to rejoice in the good we have done than in the good we mean to do but have not done. If often happens to some people that while they postpone doing the good they wish to do, they lack the will and the means.' No historian, except a monk of Battle acutely aware of the monastery's relative poverty, would regret the Conqueror's pro-crastination so explicitly. As a recent foundation Battle had none of the wealth of the Anglo-Saxon foundations. In fact, the author of the *Battle Abbey Chronicle*, using this very tradition, bemoans the lack of his monastery's endowment more than once.[21]

The anonymous Battle author wrote during the latter part of Abbot Ralph's abbacy (1107–24). Born in 1040 Ralph may have been a monk of Le Bec before he went to Caen.[22] In 1070 he came with Lanfranc to England, where after a probable stint at Christ Church, Canterbury

21 *Battle Chronicle*, 46–7, 68–9, and in particular 94–5 which read as a paraphrase of par. 13.
22 For Abbot Ralph, see *Battle Chronicle*, ed. Searle, 130–2 and R. W. Southern, *Saint Anselm: A Portrait in a Landscape* (Cambridge, 1990), 372–6.

he was a royal chaplain. In that capacity he acted as a go-between for William in Normandy and Lanfranc as justiciar with regard to Fawkham, a lost estate of Rochester.[23] This particular business may have led to his appointment, the date of which is unknown, as prior of Rochester. In 1107, after a vacancy of five years, he became abbot of Battle. Abbot Ralph was eighty four when he died in 1124, an age which made him a younger contemporary of both William the Conqueror and Lanfranc, whom he both knew personally. Although he was probably not an eyewitness of the invasion, battle of Hastings or any of the subsequent military campaigns, as one of the Norman monks sent out to the English monasteries he experienced at first hand the practical results of the conquest with regard to church property but also with regard to the secular affairs of the royal court. His position as royal chaplain brought him into direct contact with those who were implementing the Conqueror's wishes in England. Thus although the author of the *Brevis Relatio* for the moment at least must remain obscure, there is no doubt that he used Abbot Ralph's testimonies about the Norman conquest.

Presumably, it was due to Abbot Ralph's inspiration, which itself was based on his experience at Rochester, that the first chronicles of the monastery were being written.[24] In fact, manuscript O is a perfect record of the place Battle occupied in British history: covering the past from the sixth century (Nennius) to the foundation history of the monastery which itself was so completely tied up with the battle of Hastings. For the monastery was founded, as the author of the *Brevis Relatio* tells us twice, 'on the site where the Lord gave him victory over his enemies' (par. 13) and 'in memory of that victory and for the absolution of the sins of all those who were killed there' (par. 6). The author, as we have seen above (see **ii**), also wrote the *Annals of Battle* and was one of the monks who updated this text for 1124 and 1125. Whether he too is the author of the now lost foundation history of Battle is extremely likely though impossible to verify. The chronicle was in existence and indeed formed part of Ms O by the mid-1120s, a date which strongly supports the hypothesis for our man's authorship, but at present we cannot go further than that.

23 *The Life of Gundulf, Bishop of Rochester*, ed. R. Thomson (Toronto, 1977), 78 and L. Musset, 'La formation d'un milieu social original: les chapelains normands du duc-roi au xie et au début du xiie siècle', *Aspects de la société et de l'économie dans la Normandie médiévale (xe-xiiie siècles)*, ed. L. Musset, J. Bouvris, V. Gazeau (Caen, 1988), 106.

24 For record keeping, legal interest and historical writing at Rochester, see P. Wormald, 'Laga Eadwardi: the *Textus Roffensis* and its context', *Anglo-Norman Studies* xvii (1994), ed. C. Harper-Bill (Woodbridge, 1995), 243–66 and M. Brett, 'Gundulf and the cathedral communities of Canterbury and Rochester', *Canterbury and the Norman Conquest. Churches, Saints and Scholars 1066–1109*, ed. R. Eales, R. Sharpe (London, 1995), 15–26.

vi Historical value and sources

The value of the *Brevis Relatio* as a historical source lies primarily in its account of the battle of Hastings, based on the reports collected during his life by Abbot Ralph of Battle. They, in fact, resemble the conquest stories as told by William of Poitiers and William of Jumièges who stress that Harold had promised fealty and homage to Duke William but later broke his promise by seizing the English throne; this perjury justified Duke William's use of force to take back what was rightfully his. William is presented as King Edward's kinsman, a link that was necessary to explain William's hereditary right. Some details, however, cannot be found in the early sources. The author of the *Brevis Relatio* is the earliest surviving authority for the description of the relics on which Harold had allegedly sworn three oaths on 'a reliquary also called the oxe's eye' [*oculo bovis*], a statement which was repeated by the author of the so-called 'Hyde Chronicle' and Wace [par. 4].[25] These relics, as I have suggested elsewhere, were part of the collection of amulets which William the Conqueror on his deathbed had bequeathed to Battle Abbey, where the monks would have known their size and shape, even though they may have exaggerated the number of oaths promised by Harold in 1064 or 1065.[26] The amulets had been sold by Abbot Ralph's predecessor Henry under pressure from William Rufus in order to pay for a cope for the monks of Saint Germer at Fly (Vexin). The loss of the 1066 souvenirs may have been one of the reasons for the Battle monk to record the monastery's history, it also served to remind the monks that not amulets nor magic, but God had destined the Norman duke to win and subsequently found their monastery. Hence, the attention paid to the famous episode of the duke's reversed hauberk as told, originally, by William of Poitiers.[27] Moreover, The *Brevis Relatio* is the oldest literary source to refer to the location of Harold's standard [*standart*], a word otherwise employed only by Henry, archdeacon of Huntingdon, some two decades later.[28]

The author is also alone in making the unlikely claim that Harold

25 *'Hyde' Chronicle*, 283–321 at 290: 'Infinitam namque sanctarum multitudinem reliquiarum deferri jussit, superque eas filacterium gloriosi martyris Pancratii, quod oculum bovis vocant, eo quod gemmam tam speciosam, quam speciosam in medio sui contineat, collocavit, certissime sciens tantum martyrem nulla temeritate posse deludi.' *Roman de Rou*, ii, 98 (IIIe p., ll. 5601–4): 'desus out mis un filatiere,/tot le meillor qu'il pout eslire/ e le plus chier qu'il pout trover,/ oil de boef l'ai oi nomer./

26 For a discussion of the amulets of the Conqueror at Battle, see my 'The memory of 1066 in oral and written tradition', *Anglo-Norman Studies* xix (1996), ed. C. Harper-Bill (Woodbridge 1997), 167–9.

27 *Gesta Guillelmi*, 124.

28 *HH*, vi. 30; 394–5 and see p. cvi, where it is suggested that Henry is the earliest authority to use the French word, taken from a lost *chanson*. Note that the scribe of O wrote 'standart' but then corrected it to 'standarum' (par. 6 note w].

was crowned in St. Paul's Cathedral instead of Westminster Abbey [par. 4]. Although none of the contemporary sources explicitly mentioned the site of Harold's coronation they all imply that he was crowned where King Edward was buried.[29] The author of the *Miracles of St. Edmund's* written at the request of Abbot Baldwin of Bury St. Edmunds, who was the king's physician and presumably an eyewitness of the funeral and the coronation, adds that Harold was crowned promptly after the king's burial: 'After he [King Edward] was buried in royal manner before the Epiphany Day's mass immediately during the 'introitus' of the mass Harold Godwineson was enthroned on the royal seat, assuming government through cunning politics'.[30] This clearly implies the same venue for both occasions. Either the *Brevis Relatio* author was wrongly informed by his oral informants, or, less likely, he erroneously wrote St. Paul's instead of St. Peter's at Westminster.

The moralising tone of the conquest account in the *Brevis Relatio*, the fully developed 'perjury' story and the exploration of Bible quotations denouncing Harold's presumption, vanity and madness elaborate on the same themes in the contemporary Norman chronicles.[31] In contrast there is no sign of the growing empathy with the English as expressed by the second generation of Conquest chroniclers like Orderic Vitalis in his version of the *Gesta Normannorum Ducum* and William of Malmesbury, who were both of mixed Anglo-Norman descent.[32] The *Brevis Relatio* is also the first text to contain the germ for the later story developed at Battle that William the Conqueror vowed to found a monastery even before the battle had started. The author does not give the story of the vow, but says that William founded Battle out of

29 *Anglo-Saxon Chronicle* 'A', 'C', 'D', 'E', trsl. Garmonsway, 192–5. *The Chronicle of John of Worcester*, ed. R. R. Darlington, P. McGurk, J. Bray, ii (Oxford, 1995), 600–601; *Gesta Guillelmi*, 100; *GRA*, i, 280; *The Bayeux Tapestry*, ed. D. Wilson (London, 1985), plate 31.

30 *Heremanni Miracula sancti Edmundi*, ed. F. Liebermannn, in *Ungedrückte Anglo-Normannische Geschichtsquellen* (Strassburg, 1879), 245–6: 'Quo regali tumulato more ante diei missam, Theophaniorum die, statim cum introitu misse inthronizatur in solio regni Haroldus filius comitis Godwini, callida vi veniens ad regnum.' For the author, see now A. Gransden, 'The composition and authorship of the 'De miraculis Sancti Eadmundi' attributed to "Hermann the archdeacon"', *Journal of Medieval Latin*, 5 (1995), 1–52. See also George Garnett's commentary in his 'Coronation and propaganda: some implications of the Norman claim to the throne of England in 1066', *TRHS*, 5th s, 36 (1986), 90–116 at 93 n. 12.

31 The strong language used against Harold reflects the vocabulary of Guy of Amiens in the *Carmen de Hastingae Proelio*, see G. Orlandi, 'Some afterthoughts on the Carmen de Hastingae Proelio', *Media Latinitas. A Collection of Essays to mark the occasion of the retirement of L. J. Engels*, ed. R. I. A. Nip, H. van Dijk and E. M. C. van Houts, Instrumenta patristica, 28 (Turnhout, 1996), 117–27 at 119–22.

32 For recent discussions of the changing attitudes in Normandy and England to the conquest at the beginning of the twelfth century, see A. Williams, *The English and the Norman Conquest* (Woodbridge, 1995), 155–86 and E. M. C. van Houts. 'The memory of 1066', 167–79.

gratitude for his victory and for the absolution of the sins of those who were killed (par. 6 and 13). In itself it is not impossible that William had indeed made such a promise.[33] There are certainly continental parallels of princes founding monasteries as a result of victory in war: Count Fulk Nerra of Anjou founded the monastery of Beaulieu-lès-Loches in commemoration of the battle of Conquereuil in 992 and within one decade after the battle of Cassel (1071) Count Robert the Frisian of Flanders had established a monastery near the site of bloodshed.[34] In both these cases the monasteries were not actually built and endowed until almost a decade after the battles took place, a delay which corresponds with the obscure history of Battle before the mid 1070s.

The author's interest in Lanfranc is most significant. The presence at Battle of Ralph of Caen, who knew Lanfranc so well is the most obvious explanation for the author's eulogy of Lanfranc, his reforms at Canterbury and his insistence on Canterbury's primacy.[35] No other source gives us the, rather spurious, etymology of Lanfranc's name, meaning apparently that he carried a large heart (*ferentem cor largum*) This, however, is not to say that he was not generous. His immense generosity, as illustrated by his establishment of hospitals and care for the poor is a theme which his obit, written at Christ Church, Canterbury sets out in great detail.[36]

There is an extra element of developing sentiments that can be traced in the Battle copy of the *Brevis Relatio*. Its author revised the rubric and erased the reference to the hereditary right by which William claimed the English throne.[37] Although there is no date attached to this action, I presume the revision to date from the same moment that the author altered the reference to William Adelin's death at a date after 1120 but before 1135. It is a subtle reminder of a changing perception at Battle that perhaps the hereditary, and thus kinship, claim was less powerful than was once thought. The justification of conquest as a result of battle clearly was preferred at the Conqueror's own foundation.

Despite its primary preoccupation with Battle Abbey, the *Brevis Relatio* illustrates the author's attachment to Normandy, the dukes and some of the Norman monasteries endowed by them. Fécamp is mentioned as the place of burial for Richard I and II [par. 12] and as the recipient of Richard II's generosity [par. 18], but so is Jumièges [par. 19]. Rouen

33 E. Searle argues that the story of the vow was invented by the Battle monks in the mid-twelfth century, see *Battle Chronicle*, 17 and 'The abbey of the conquerors', *Proceedings of the Battle Conference* ii (1979), ed. R. Allen Brown (Woodbridge, 1980), 154–64.

34 B. Bachrach, *Fulk Nerra the Neo Consul 987–1040* (Berkeley, 1993), 130–6 and *Actes des comtes de Flandre 1071–1128*, ed. F. Vercauteren (Brussels, 1938), no. 6.

35 I am grateful to Martin Brett for pointing this out to me.

36 M. Gibson, *Lanfranc of Bec* (Oxford, 1978), 227–9.

37 See par. 1, note a.

cathedral is mentioned only as the resting place for Rollo and William Longsword [par. 12], while Saint-Ouen features in the Longpaon anecdote of Rollo [par. 14]. This lack of concern with the Norman capital makes nonsense of an earlier suggestion in favour of Rouen as the place of origin for the *Brevis Relatio*.[38] Caen is mentioned for its ducal foundations [par. 9], while Caen and Bayeux occur together in the context of the 1105–6 campaigns of Henry I [par. 11]. Neither place stands out in the text.[39]

The interest in Fécamp deserves our attention because of the availability of the *Ship list* at Battle. The most likely place where this document, listing the most important donations of ships to the 1066 campaign, was drawn up was Fécamp, where William spent the two most important Easter festivals of his life: in 1066 preparing the conquest and in 1067 celebrating his victory.[40] Information connected with Fécamp reached Battle either directly or through Fécamp's priory at Steyning not far away in Sussex.

The importance of the section on the sons of William lies in the eulogy of Henry I, the legitimisation of his acquisitions of Normandy and England on the basis of the fact that he was born to the purple, and in some details of Henry's dealing with his brothers. Henry is said to have received £5000 from his father's inheritance [par. 9]; the author accuses Robert Curthose and William Rufus of not having treated Henry as was fitting a son of a king [par. 10] and there is the reference to the almost complete destruction of Bayeux in 1105 [par. 11]. At Battle Henry I was certainly admired much more than his brother, though not perhaps as much as his father. Even so he embodied the only hope for the Battle monks to fulfil his father's procrastination of making gifts. This wish was unfortunately not realized, as the author of the *Battle Chronicle* later acknowledged, due to Henry's foundation of a new monastery for which he reserved his greatest generosity.[41] The irony of the matter cannot have escaped the monks of Battle, because Reading had formed part of the Conqueror's endowment to Battle. As far as the battle of Tinchebrai is concerned, the author interestingly omits to name the count of Mortain. The omission presumably reflects the fact that at the time of writing the dispossessed William of Mortain was still in captivity and the new count Stephen of Blois, later King Stephen, had not been appointed, an event that is usually dated to c. 1113.[42]

38 *The Chronicle of Robert of Torigni*, ed. R. Howlett, *Chronicles of the reign of Stephen, Henry II, and Richard I*, 4 vols, Rolls Series, iv (London 1889), p. xxxvi–vii.

39 The complete disregard for Bishop Odo of Bayeux may well be due to Abbot Ralph's partisanship for Lanfranc who had campaigned so hard on behalf of the monasteries to regain land wrongfully held by Bishop Odo as earl of Kent.

40 E. M. C. van Houts, 'The Ship list', 168.

41 *Battle Chronicle*, 122–4.

The historical value of the anecdotes narrated in the last paragraphs [par. 14–21] is uneven. Only two anecdotes [par. 15 and 16] have a strong contemporary resonance. Par. 15 contains the curious story of a man from Rennes who in Rollo's time claimed to have walked across the River Seine during his journey to Rouen. Towards the end of the story the man is asked by his host about the future of Normandy, and in particular, what will happen after the seventh generation of rulers. The man from Rennes prophesies that after the seventh generation the realm ('imperium') will either collapse or experience great troubles. Since this anecdote occurs in the earliest version of the text it must be dated to the period 1114 × 1120. Contemporary opinion accepted Henry I as the Norman duke of the seventh generation and his very position as seventh ruler may have caused fears about his succession.[43] Though such feelings were entirely understandable and justified after William Adelin's death, they are more difficult to understand prior to November 1120. There is, however, some evidence related by Orderic Vitalis on the basis of stories from Queen Matilda I's servant Samson, who tells that the queen, worried about the future of her sons, consulted a prophet in Germany.[44] Orderic does not say that Matilda's concern was fuelled by thoughts about the seventh generation. However, the consultation with the German soothsayer may not be unconnected to the location of the first written source mentioning the seventh generation as the limit for peace, which comes from Saint-Valéry-sur-Somme in Ponthieu neighbouring Matilda's home territory of the Low Countries.[45] Also, the fact that the *Brevis Relatio* was written while Robert Curthose and his son William Clito were still alive must have kept the, highly theoretical, possibility open that one day the conflict between the brothers might resume.

Perhaps, the anecdote represents general unease caused by the idea propagated by the Church that beyond the seventh generation history stops. What the Church meant was that looking back in time the seventh generation meant the end of kinship claims and therefore, in dynastic terms, the end of a family's history.[46] If one projects the story

---

42 R. H. C. Davis, *King Stephen* (London, 1977), 7; C. Warren Hollister, 'The aristocracy', *The Anarchy of Stephen's Reign*, ed. E. King (Oxford, 1994), 37–66 at 42.

43 Strictly speaking he was not the seventh, but the ninth, ruler of Normandy. By counting Duke Richard III (1026–7) and his brother Duke Robert the Magnificent (1027–35) as one generation, and Robert Curthose and Henry I as another one, the author achieves his numbering of generations. See also the similar listing in par. 12 where Duke Richard III is left out.

44 OV, iii, 104–8.

45 '... et postea heredes tui [sc. Hugh Capet] usque ad septimam generationem possidebunt gubernacula torius regni' (Ex historia relationis corporis s. Walarici abbatis, *Recueil des Historiens de France*, ed. M. Bouquet, ix, 147–8).

46 J. Goody, *The Development of the Family and Marriage in Europe* (Cambridge, 1983), 134–46 on the prohibited degrees of consanguinity which covered seven generations.

into the future, as the author of the anecdotes does, from Rollo to Henry I, one may by the same token conclude that there is no future for any dynasty. There are parallels from other dynasties, in particular the Capetians, where there were worries about the family's future couched in exactly the same terms.[47]

Par. 16 traces the origin of the mutual obligations of the Norman duke and the French king to an alleged pact set up and agreed in the mid-940s with help of Danish troops. This story is well known from the Norman chroniclers Dudo of Saint-Quentin and William of Jumièges, both of whom lack the specificity claimed by the author of the *Brevis Relatio*.[48] Clearly the details of the 940s 'pact' were concocted to suit the situation of c. 1114. According to the story, the duke of Normandy owed homage and fealty to the king of France for his life and earthly honour. He did not, however, owe (military) service to the king for the duchy. If the king wished to receive (military) service he would need to provide the Norman duke with a fief (other than Normandy) in France. The question of the 'feudal' arrangements between the duke and the king had become urgent again in 1106 when for the second time a duke of Normandy had become king. As kings, Henry I and Louis VI were equals, but with regard to Normandy Henry I was subordinate to the French king. Henry I refused to do homage and fealty to the king and in 1114/15 circumvented the problem by offering to send his son William Adelin in his place. This never happened even though the Norman magnates had done their homage to William, whom they accepted as Henry's heir and successor to the duchy of Normandy. None of this is discussed in the *Brevis Relatio*, but the importance of the alleged pact of the early 940s is clear. In the years 1114–1120 King Henry not only refused to provide military support for expeditions in France on the basis of the alleged agreement arranged two hundred years before, he went much further and denied any subordination to France. This led to four years of warfare culminating in the battle of Brémule in 1119, which was won by Henry I.[49] He

47 Robert of Torigni, inspired by the *Brevis Relatio*, renumbered the eight books of the *Gesta Normannorum Ducum* so that the eighth and last one on Henry I became the seventh. He also explained in his prologue to Book VIII that Henry represented the seventh generation of Norman rulers (*GND*, ii, 200–3). For the Capetians, see E. A. R. Brown, 'La notion de la legitimité et la prophetie à la cour de Philippe Auguste', *La France de Philippe Auguste. Le temps des mutations*, ed. R. H. Bautier (Paris 1982), 77–111 at 91–3.

48 The story goes back to the troubled years of Duke Richard I's minority after the murder of his father William Longsword in 943, when the Normans managed to hang on to their semi independence from Louis IV with the support of Danish troops. The Danes probably came from the Norman Cotentin and represented descendants of Danish settlers, rather than Viking support from Denmark (Dudo, 239–45; *GND*, i, 110–13).

49 This paragraph, as part of Robert of Torigni's *Gesta Normannorum Ducum* version, has been discussed in the context of the feudal arrangements between Normandy and France by F. Lot, *Fidèles ou vassaux?* (Paris, 1904), 231–5 and J. F. Lemarignier, *Recherches*

negotiated an agreement with Louis VI which allowed him not to do homage or fealty and yet acknowledged his son William Adelin as his heir and successor in Normandy. The sensitive and fragile arrangement collapsed when the king's son died in the White Ship disaster of November 1120.[50]

Some of the other anecdotes are historiographically interesting in that they were stories about the early dukes [par. 14, 18 and 19] that circulated in Normandy outside the official canon of the works of Dudo and William of Jumièges. Others clearly derive from these chronicles but also lived a life of their own and in the process became slightly distorted. Par. 16 on the 940s pact we have already discussed, but par. 17 concerning the duke and the theft of the plough shares is another good example. It is told by Dudo and William of Jumièges about Rollo instead of Richard II.[51]

The inclusion of unofficial stories and the distortion of official ones raises the question of the author's sources. Twelve times the author claims oral tradition or rumours for the stories he is writing down (par. 1, 4, 5, 6, 7, 8, 12, 13, 14, 15, 16, 20), but he never specifies his informants by name nor does he give any more details about their standing. Above we have already discussed the likelihood that Abbot Ralph was one of his informants for the conquest period. Having been born in 1040 he may also have carried with him stories about the dukes as they circulated in Normandy by the middle of the eleventh-century. The narrative of the Norman conquest bears great resemblance to William of Poitiers and William of Jumièges but there are no verbal echoes, let alone any verbatim quotes. The lack of verbal borrowing and the piecemeal stringing together of stories strongly suggests a predominantly oral tradition. The brevity of the text combined with the mediocre literary style and repetitive language, representing a syntax that is closer to Old French than to literary Latin, suggest that the author was writing for an audience that wished to be informed of the facts, rather than be instructed by a sophisticated rhetorical narrative. In Battle, as elsewhere in England under Norman domination, there emerged a demand for chronicles explaining the link with Normandy. Apart from the *Brevis Relatio*, the *Quedam Exceptiones*, written almost certainly in England shortly after 1102, and the so-called *'Hyde' Chronicle*, spring to

---

sur l'hommage en marche et les frontières féodales (Lille, 1945), 96–100; C. Warren Hollister, 'Normandy, France and the Anglo-Norman regnum', *Speculum*, 51 (1976), 202–242, esp. 229–31 correctly identified Robert of Torigni's source, but misled by Giles's edition dated the paragraph one decade too late.

50 For a discussion of the sources and interpretation, see Hollister, 'Normandy, France and the Anglo-Norman regnum', 228–9.

51 Dudo, 172–3; *GND*, i, 68–71. Wace followed the *Brevis Relatio* version but substituted Longueville-sur-Scie for Longpaon (now Darnétal, Seine Mar.), see *Roman de Rou*, i, 56 (IIe p, l. 1236).

mind as parallels. All three chornicles are short, factual, written from a Norman perspective and centred on the conquest of England: the *Quedam Exeptiones* was written by someone with links to the FitzOsbern family and in particular Bishop Osbern of Exeter,[52] while the Warenne family is the focus of the 'Hyde' chronicler's concerns.[53]

vii Reception of the *Brevis Relatio*

The earliest use of the *Brevis Relatio* can be traced to Robert of Torigni, monk at Le Bec in Normandy, who c. 1139 quoted the section on William the Conqueror's sons and transferred the series of anecdotes [par. 14–20] almost in its entirety to the *Gesta Normannorum Ducum*.[54] Le Bec had by then received a copy close to either the β or the γ version, which was clearly considered a reliable authority for both sections. Two decades later the Bayeux canon Wace consulted the *Brevis Relatio* for his vernacular *Roman de Rou*. He used the anecdote of Robert the Magnificent's generosity of mind and added the information that the incident took place during the duke's pilgrimage while still in Burgundy, somewhere south of Langres and Besançon.[55] He also changed the duke's answer to his men who wished to take revenge for the beating he had received. The *Brevis Relatio* gives the burlesque version according to which the duke said that he was much more pleased with the beating 'through the wind of my stomach [per animam ventris]' than if he had given me a large sum of money'. Clearly the blows on his back had resulted in him releasing (abdominal) wind. Wace, in the vernacular *Roman de Rou*, changes this to a much less physical and more abstract version, which reads that the duke had received penance for his sins.[56] Wace also describes the relic on which Harold is supposed to have sworn his oath as an oxe's eye and he gives the-baby-William-playing-

52 *GND*, ii, 292–304.

53 The 'Hyde' Chronicle was undoubtedly written by someone connected to the Warennes. What is still not clear is whether the author wrote in Lewes priory or whether he wrote from Normandy. I hope to return to this matter when I publish my new edition of this chronicle, see C. P. Lewis, 'The earldom of Surrey and the date of Domesday Book', *Historical Research*, lxiii (1990), 329–36; J. Gillingham, 'The Hyde chronicle', appendix to his 'Henry of Huntingdon and the twelfth-century revival of the English Nation', *Concepts of National Identity in the Middle Ages*, ed. S. Forde, L. Johnson and A. V. Murray (Leeds, 1995), 90–1 and van Houts, 'The memory of 1066', 177–8.

54 *GND*, ii, 194–5, 202–7, 216–23, 280–9.

55 *Roman de Rou*, i, 272–4 (IIIe p., ll. 2987–3036).

56 *Ibidem*, i, 273–4 (IIIe p., ll. 3025–36): 'Baruns,' dist il, 'eirez, eirez!/Leisiez le fol, ne l'adesez!/ pelerins sumes, ne devum/ moveir medlee ne tençun;/ mal fait ki medlee cumence,/ tut recevom en pacïence,/ mult devriom noalz sufrir/ pur noz pechiez espeneïr./ se li pautonier me feri/asez ai noalz deservi;/ mielz aim le cop k'il m'a duné/ ke tute Ruem ma cité.'/

with-straw anecdote, which he might have read in the *Brevis Relatio* or in William of Malmesbury.[57] Of the two English historians who indubitably consulted the *Brevis Relatio*, William of Malmesbury is of lesser importance, because he used the anecdote on William the Conqueror as a baby. The other one is the author of the *Battle Chronicle*, who, as we have seen, quotes lengthy sections of the text for his account of the Norman conquest.[58]

viii Editions

The *Brevis Relatio* has been edited twice before. The earliest is a seventeenth-century edition by Silas Taylor as an appendix to his *The History of Gavelkind* (London, 1663), pp. 182–210 on the basis of the Oxford manuscript. The one used by most scholars is, however, the 1845 edition produced by J. A. Giles as volume 3 of the *Publication of the Caxton Society*, which consists of a conflated text of the Oxford and Sloane manuscripts without variants. By printing the *Ship list* and the Sloane genealogy as appendices to the *Brevis Relatio* he created the erroneous impression that these texts formed an integral part of the chronicle. The edition which follows is based on manuscript O. I have followed its text, except for the duplication of the word *ad* discussed above in **iii**. All variants from the other three manuscripts are included, except for purely orthographical ones. The division into paragraphs occurs in the manuscripts, but the numbering is mine, as is the punctuation.[59]

---

57 For the oxe's eye reference, see above note 25; the baby William reference (*Roman de Rou*, i, 268 (IIe p., ll. 2869–86) is closer to William of Malmesbury (*GRA*, ii, 285: ipso quoque momento quo partu laxato, in vitam effusus pusio humum attigit, ambas manus junco, quo pavimenti pulvis cavebatur, implevit, stricte quod corripuerat compugnans. ostensum visum mulierculis, laeto plausu gannientibus; obstetrix quoque fausto omine acclamat puerum regem futurum.) than the *Brevis Relatio*.

58 M. Brett's review of E. Searle's edition of the Battle Abbey Chronicle, *Medium Aevum*, 150 (1981), 319–22 at 322; *Battle Chronicle*, 34–6.

59 As far as a translation of the text is concerned, I shall publish a translation of the paragraphs 1–10 in my *The Normans in Europe* (forthcoming, Manchester Medieval Sources in Translation series). Most of the text of the paragraphs 11–20 can be found in *GND*, vol. ii as part of Robert of Torigni's work.

INCIPIT QVEDAM BREVIS RELATIO DE GVILLELMO NOBILISSIMO COMITE NORMANNORVM, QVIS FVIT ET VNDE ORIGINEM DVXIT, ET QVO HEREDITARIO IVRE ANGLIAM SIBI ARMIS ADQVISIVIT.[a]

1. Pater huius[b] Willelmi[c] fuit Rodbertus dux Normannorum uir omni probitate conspicuus,[d] erga[e] superbos ferus,[e] sed[f] erga pauperes largus atque pius,[g] sed quanuis ergo omnes pauperes misericors et pius.[g] Maximam uero compassionem, semper habebat de his quos elefantiosus morbus[h] uexabat, ita ut ipsi elefantiosi sepius eum fratrem uocarent ob nimiam pietatem quam de miseriis eorum habebat. Hic[i] autem Rodbertus sicut quidam dicunt dux Normannorum extitit in quinta generatione ab illo Dano qui Rollo uocatus terram que modo uocatur Normannia armis cepit. Ab isto itaque Rodberto comite uiro tam nobili tamque pio egenis progenitus est iste Willelmus de quo loqui institui. Dilexit autem eum pater suus multum partim quia nullum habebat filium nisi illum[j] partim[k] quia secundum suam etatem idem filius suus multum erat strenuus atque decorus. Eodem uero tempore Rodbertus comes, mente compunctus, fecit uotum eundi in[l] Ierusalem et uidere locum illum[m] ubi Dominus suus crucifixus fuit[n] mortemque pro pec-

---

a *This rubric can be found in* O *before erasure and in* S; O *after erasure reads* Incipit quedam brevis relatio de Guillelmo nobilissimo comite Normannorum quis fuit et unde originem duxit et quam multitudinem ducens Anglie regnum sibi armis adquisiuit. L *has* Incipit tractatus de Guillelmo comite Normannorum et conquestore Anglie et eius progenitoribus et quo hereditario iure Angliam sibi armis adquisiuit. A *has* De Willelmo conquestore.

b *om* A
c *add* Conquestoris A
d perspicuus L
e...e *om* L
f *om* SL
g *om* ASL
h elefantinus A
i Hi S
j ipsum L
k *add* par S
l *om* ASL
m *om* A
n *om* L

catoribus sustinuit. Paratis itaque[o] omnibus que ad huius[p] itineris negotium pertinebant antequam de Normannia recederet congregari fecit barones Normannie eisque commendauit Willelmum filium suum ut nutrirent et custodirent illum donec sciret et posset[q] terram tenere et regere. Eum enim[r] heredem faciebat[s] post se de terra Normannie ut si casu aliquo ipse non rediret, filius suus Willelmus in paterna hereditate sine ulla contradictione succederet. Dispositis ergo omnibus que[t] illius uie necessitas poscebat et commendato Willelmo filio suo baronibus suis[u] quem heredem de Normannia faciebat perrexit Ierusalem comes Rodbertus, sed cum inde rediret in urbem que uocatur Nica[v] diem clausit extremum. In quo loco honorifice sepultus est et sicut postea quidam[w] retulerunt, ad sepulchrum eius quedam signa uirtutibus similia[x] contigerunt.

2. Libet uero memorie[x] tradere quoddam signum bonitatis Rodberti comitis[a] quod uice quadam in ipsa uia his qui[b] cum illo ibant ostendit ut ex hoc uno patenter cunctis manifestum sit quam humiliter iniurias que ei fiebant pro amore Dei pertulit. Quadam namque[c] die contigit eum uenire[d] ad quendam locum ubi musellas/p. 2, f. iv/ et tributum debebat pro se et pro pauperibus qui in eius comitatu erant, persoluere. Dum itaque ibi cum suis hominibus expectaret donec omnes pauperes quos secum ducebat transire fecisset quidam de paganis qui eas[e] musellas accipiebant[f] iratus contra eum, arepto fuste fortiter, supra[g] dorsum percussit illum.[h] Homines uero illius uidentes quid Rodberto comiti paganus fecisset mox illum uoluerunt percutere et percutiendo dominum suum uindicare. Rodbertus uero comes non parum letus de iniuria quam pro Dei amore[i] susceperat compescuit suos homines eisque[j] dixit: 'Nichil mali ei faciatis quia per animam uentris mei magis

o Paratisque A
p huiusmodi A
q p.e.s. A
r uero L
s f.h. L
t *add* huius S
u s.b. A
v Nicha A
w q.p. A
x...x *om* A
a c.R. SL
b his qui *written over an erasure* O, *om.* S, hiis AL
c autem A
d *om* SL
e easdem ASL
f accipiebat A
g eum supra [super L] SL
h *om* SL
i a.D. A
j atque eis A, eis S

sum letus de ista dorsata quam mihi dedit quam si mihi magnam[k]
pecuniam dedisset.'

3.   Vt ergo[a] ad id unde digressus[b] sum[c] redeam barones Normannie
ut[d] audierunt[e] Rodbertum comitem esse defunctum non paruas iniurias
Willelmo filio suo[f] facere ceperunt. Willelmus tamen iuuenis non
diffidens[g] de adiutorio et misericordia Dei sicut melius poterat secundum
tempus quod tunc erat se in omnibus habebat. Ad ultimum uero
postquam uidit quia[h] Normanni hereditatem suam ei auferre[i] uolebant
assumptis secum quibusdam Normannis qui ei[j] fideles erant, contulit se
ad regem Francie. Sed quam citius potuit in Normanniam rediens in
loco qui dicitur Valesdunas[k] contra Normannos illos qui eum exheredare[l] uolebant pugnauit quos et ibidem Dei[m] auxilio fretus pugnando
superauit. Quibus deuictis et[n] in fugam ire compulsis in breui post hec
totam hereditatem suam quam ei auferre conati sunt, ex integro
recuperauit. Deinde aliquanto tempore decurso accepit in coniugio
filiam Balduini comitis de[o] Flandria nomine Mathildam, mulierem
multum honestam et sapientem ex qua plures filios et filias generauit.
Quis uero facile referre possit toto illo tempore quo super Normannos
Willelmus comes dominium tenuit[p] quam strenue quam sapienter in
omnibus se habuit. Quos enim bonos et honestos uidebat cuiuscunque
ordinis essent non parum diligebat quos autem criminosos et inhonestos
esse audiebat, a consortio suo semper fugabat.[q]

4.   Eo itaque tempore dum Willelmus comes sic strenue et prudenter
regnum suum[a] gubernaret atque undique per circuitum terram suam
uiriliter protegeret, contigit ut Heraldus filius Goduini de Anglia naui-
gare uellet in Normanniam, sed uento flante in contrarium, non in
Normanniam sed in terram que uocatur Ponteium[b] deuenit. Quem

k *om* L
b degressus A
a uero A
c *om* S
d *om* S
e audirent A
f f.s. W A
g defidens A
h quod AL, quod quia S
i a.e. SL
j *om* A
k Valesdunans A
l exhereditare SL
m *om* A
n atque ASL
o *om* ASL, Flandrie ASL
p habuit A
q prefugebat A
a s.r. A
b Ponteum A

Wido comes eiusdem patrie cepit et in custodia tenuit donec industria Willelmi sapientissimi comitis Normannorum eum liberauit. Quem liberatum et ante se adductum[c] idem comes honorifice suscepit/p. 3, f.2r/ et susceptum aliquanto[d] tempore cum magno honore secum retinuit. Interim[e] uero dum cum eo conuersatus[f] est, ei homagium et fidelitatem fecit[g] Heraldus, et etiam[h] sicut multi dicunt tria sacramenta super filacterium quod uocabant oculum bouis quod ei fidem et promissionem quam ei faciebat,[i] bene custodiret. Peracto itaque negotio propter quod Heraldus uenerat in Normanniam quam citius potuit rediit[j] in Angliam. Post aliquantum uero temporis dum Edwardus rex Anglorum in Natali Domini festiuitatem corone sue Lundonie[k] apud Westmonasterium ageret, contigit ut tactus grauissima infirmitate uitam presentam finiret. Dicunt autem quidam quod tunc[l] Heraldus quasi oblitus sacramentorum que Willelmo comiti in Normannia fecerat antequam rex Edwardus obiret ad eum uenit[m] eumque rogauit ut ei coronam regni[n] Anglie concederet. Quo audito rex Edwardus non immemor quod Willelmo comiti[o] Normannorum cognato suo regnum Anglie iamdudum concessisset, respondit Heraldo hoc nullo modo[p] se posse facere, quia inde[q] Willelmum comitem[r] Normannorum[s] heredem fecerat. Veniens uero[t] rex Edwardus ad finem suum[u] diem clausit extremum. Adhuc autem erat corpus eius super terram sicut illi postea retulerunt, qui hoc se uidere dixerunt, cum[v] Heraldus quasi insanus atque postponens[w] quicquid Willelmo comiti de regno Anglie iurauerat, uidelicet quod ei fideliter illud[x] post mortem regis Edwardi seruaret,

c adductus L
d aliquot L
e Inde L
f conuersus L
g ferus L
h *om* S. *add* ei ASL
i facie *written on erasure* O
j *add* rediit L
k Londonie SL
l t.q. SL
m peruenit S
n *om* A
o comite L
p n.m.h. S
q *om* SL
r ducem L
s *add* idem S, inde L
t ergo ASL
u *om* ASL
v quum L
w postpotens L
x i.f. ASL

consentientibus sibi[y] ciuibus[z] Lundonie[a] multisque aliis insanie eius
fauentibus apud sanctum Paulum in ciuitate Lundonie[b] contra omnem
rectitudinem coronam regni Anglie arripuit.

5. Non longum uero tempus fuit quod iste rumor ad aures Willelmi
comitis Normannorum peruenit. Quod cum[a] audisset et pro certo
didicisset quod Heraldus in omnibus que iurauerat ei[b] periurus esset,
quam cicius potuit barones Normannie ad concilium conuocari fecit
eisque ostendit quomodo Heraldus coronam regni Anglie sibi impo-
suisset, de quo rex[c] Edwardus cognatus suus eum heredem fecisset[d] et
quomodo etiam[e] idem Heraldus de sacramentis que sibi in Normannia
fecerat, modo periurus existeret.[f] Normanni autem hoc audito non
parum irati de tanta contumelia quam Haraldus domino illorum et
sibi[g] fecisset, communiter ei consilium[h] dederunt ut de Haraldo periuro
suo se uindicare procuraret coronamque illi[i] iniuste[j] ademptam si aliter
non potuisset[k] per bellum[l] saltem[m] restitueret. Quo consilio[n] suscepto
precepit ut quamcicius possent omnes barones Normannie unusquisque
secundum suam possibilitatem[o] naues prepararent quibus ipse et omnis
militia quam secum ducturus esset[p] in Angliam transuehi posset.[q] Quas[r]
in ualde breuiori spatio quam unquam sperari posset preparatas adduci
precepit /p. 4, f.2v/ ad Sanctum Walericum in Summam que iuxta illud
castrum fluit. Dispositis itaque omnibus que ad huiusmodi[s] negotium
pertinebant, eisdem nauibus conscensis anno ab incarnatione Domini
millesimo sexagesimo sexto,[t] iiii kalendas Octobris cum magna alacritate

y igitur A
z ciuibus *written on erasure* O
a Londonie SL
b Londonie SL
a quum L
b e.i. ASL
c *om* S
d e.f.h. A, h.e.f. S
e *om* SL
f extitisset S
g illis S, *add* et illis L
h concilium L
i illi *written on erasure* O, sibi A
j *om* S
k posset A
l *add* sibi ASL
m *om* A
n concilio L
o ignobilitatem L
p erat S
q possent L
r Quias S
s huius AL
t sexagesimo sexto *om* L

animi Willelmus comes transiens in Angliam appulit[u] Deo[v] fauente ad castrum quod uocatur Peuenesel. Sed non diutius ibi moratus cum omni exercitu suo uenit ad alium portum non longe ab isto situm quem uocant Hastingas ibique omnem suam militiam[w] requiescere iussit. Interim uero dum ibi comes Willelmus[x] cum exercitu suo esset terramque Anglie ex illa parte inuaderet, nuncius ab Anglis ad Heraldum concite[y] missus est, qui eo tempore contra fratrem suum perrexerat, qui in altera parte[z] Anglie cum magna multitudine[a] pugnatorum intrauerat uolens Angliam super Heraldum fratrem suum[b] conquirere et conquisitam possidere. Pugnans uero Haraldus cum fratre suo interfecit eum[c] et eos qui cum illo uenerant.[d] Non parum itaque exultans[e] Heraldus de hac[f] uictoria ignorabat quid[g] in breui ei euenturum[h] erat.[i] Cum ergo audisset quod[j] Willelmus comes Normannorum cum exercitu[k] in Angliam[l] transsisset quam citius potuit Lundoniam[m] uenit, ibique loquens cum Anglis et Danis quos secum habebat contempnens et pro nichilo ducens quicquid Willelmo comiti in Normannia[n] iurauerat. Iussit omnes suos homines citissime preparari[o] ut Normannos cum duce suo[p] Willelmo antequam de Anglia fugerent inuenire posset. Putabat enim insania plenus quod Normanni non auderent eum expectare nec ad pugnam contra eum uenire. Sed aliter contigit et non solum[q] Normannos inuenit sed pugnando contra Normannos expertus est quod Normanni non propterea in Anglia transnauigassent, ut inde fugere uellent. Heraldus itaque cum omni exercitu suo exiens de Lundonia peruenit usque[r] ad locum qui nunc uocatur Bellum. Antequam uero

u applicuit AL
v f.D. A
w m.s. ASL
x c.W.i. SL
y concito L
z altera partem A
a m. magna A
b f.s.H. S
c illum l
d erant AS
e *om* S
f *om* A
g quod S
h uenturum AL
i esset A
j quid L
k *add* suo SL
l Anglia S
m Londoniam AL
n de Anglia A
o preparare A
p s.d. S
q solos S
r *om* L

ad hoc bellum peruenisset fertur dixisse quod nullam rem unquam amplius[s] libentius fecisset quam quod ad hoc bellum ueniebat. Ignorabat enim furore cecatus quam uerum esset quod[t] Scriptura dicit [*cf.* Prov. 16,18]: 'Ante ruinam exaltatur cor.' Ante ruinam enim exaltatum est cor Heraldi insani qui tam insipiens [*cf.* Ps. 13,1] et uanus [*cf.* Ps. 5, 10] fuit ut prouidere et sapienter intelligere non posset quod omnipotentis Dei iusticia superbos et[u] uanos nisi a maliciis suis resipiscant, semper humiliare et ad nichilum[v] deducere[w] solita sit.

6. Postquam uero[a] Willelmus comes et Normanni pro certo[b] intellexerunt quod Heraldus periurus[c] contra eos ad pugnam uenire[d] et ueniendo se auderet preparare, preparauerunt se et[e] ipsi ut melius potuerunt ex toto corde inuocantes Dominum ut eis nunc adiutor esset nec eos propter peccata sua in tante necessitatis articulo[f] despiceret. Peruenientes itaque usque ad collem unum[g] qui erat a parte Hastingarum contra illum collem in quo erat Heraldus et exercitus eius ibi ut[h] erant armati paulisper subsistiterunt[i] intuentes An/p. 5, f. 3r/ glorum exercitum. Dignum est autem[j] ut memorie literisque tradatur unum uerbum quod christianissimus comes Willelmus cum lorica sua indueretur dixisse fertur. Cum enim ei quidam eandem[k] loricam suam porrigeret, ut ex ea se indueret, ex improuiso ei[l] illam inuersam porrexit.[m] Quod ille animaduertens uultu placido quietoque animo militibus qui in circuitu eius erant dixit: 'Si ego in sortem crederem, hodie amplius in bellum[n] non introirem. Sed ego nunquam sortibus credidi neque[o] sortilegos amaui. In omni enim negotio quodcunque[p] agere debui Creatori meo semper me[q] commendaui.' Hoc[r] dicens atque

s *om* L
t uirq S
u *om* S
v illum A
w ducere A
a ergo AS
b pro certo *om* A
c perjures L
d ueniret SL
e *om* SL
f circulo L
g u.c. ASL
h non A, *om* S
i subtiterunt A, sustiterunt S
j *om* S
k *om* S
l *om* L
m p.i. S
n bello L
o nec S
p quodcuque AS
q *om* A
r hec S

in Creatorem suum sicut semper facere solitus erat[s] totam suam
fiduciam[t] ponens induit se armis suis. Armatus itaque et se totum
exercitum suum Domino commendans cepit inquirere a quodam milite
qui iuxta eum erat ubi Heraldum putaret esse. Respondit autem ille
quod putabat illum[u] esse in illo spisso agmine quod[v] erat ante eos in
montis summitate, nam sicut putabat Heraldi standart[w] ibi uidebat.
Tunc Willelmus comes[x] fertur dixisse: 'Credo in omnipotentis Dei
misericordia cuius iudicia etsi sunt[y] occulta sunt tamen iusta[z] quod
hodie iustitiam faciet mihi de Heraldo qui periurus existens hodie
contra me audet uenire ad pugnam.'[a] Hec dicens equum[b] super[c]
quem sedebat[c] calcaribus urgens super Anglos irruit unumque ex
illis percutiens interfecit. Non multum uero post quidam cuneus
Normannorum fere usque ad[d] mille equites ex altera parte Anglos
inuadentes super illos cum horribili impetu currere ceperunt quasi illos
percutere uolentes, sed dum illi[e] usque ad illos peruenissent quasi
timerent eos fugere se simulauerunt. Angli uero illi putantes eos[f] uere
fugere ceperunt post eos[g] currere uolentes eos si possent interficere.
Quod uidentes Normanni qui erant cautiores bello quam Angli mox
redierunt atque inter illos et agmen unde[h] se disiunxerant se immiserunt
omnesque illos mox interfecerunt. Atque hoc modo[i] Norhmanni et
Angli inuicem pugnare ceperunt. Pugnantes[j] itaque toto illo die fere[k]
usque ad uesperum[l] Northmannis[m] cum Anglis tandem Angli uicti
fugerunt et qui fugere non potuerunt extincti ibi remanserunt. Interfectus est autem in illa pugna[n] Heraldus et duo fratres eius et cum eis
maxima pars de nobilitate Anglorum. Facta est autem hec pugna pridie

s s.e.f. SL
t f.s. ASL
u eum AS, ipsum L
v qui A
w *add* uel standarum O, standarium AS, standarum L
x c.W. S
y sint S
z uera S
a a.p.u. S
b equm A
c...c que suum super que sedebat S, que super quem sedebat L
d *om* SL
e *om* ASL
f *om* S
g *om* SL
h *erased* S
i ergo ASL
j pugnatibus ASL
k f.d. S
l uesperam A
m Normannis ASL
n pungna A

idus Octobris in eo loco ubi Willelmus[o] comes Northmannorum postea
uero rex Anglorum abbatiam construi precepit ob memoriam huius
uictorie[p] et absolutionem peccatorum omnium[q] illorum qui ibi interfecti
sunt.[r] Victis uero[s] Anglis ad castra sua Willelmus comes rediit maximas[t]
omnipotenti Deo gratias reddens[u] qui ei per misericordiam suam
uictoriam concessit[v] de inimicis suis.

7. Non diutius uero ibi commoratus[a] uersus Lundoniam prin-
cipalem ciuitatem Anglie cepit ire et sic ipsam terram[b] Anglorum
conquirere. Deinde ad eum paulatim[c] ceperunt uenire Angli plurimi et
cum eo pacem facere. In breui itaque cum eo /p. 6, f. 3v/ maiori parte
Anglorum pacificata fidelitatem illorum suscepit et quibusdam eorum
suas terras reddidit, quibusdam[d] uero non reddidit[d] eo quod[e] illis
nondum se bene credidit.[f] Tandem ad Natiuitatem Domini Lundoniam
conuenientibus Francis et Anglis illisque omnibus concedentibus
coronam totius Anglie et dominationem suscepit. Constitutus itaque[g]
sapienter et cum magna discretione regnum quod acceperat disponere
cepit. Atque in ecclesiis Anglie in quibus pastores non erant, pastores
secundum Deum ponere curauit. Deinde post aliquantulum temporis
uxorem suam de Northmannia in Angliam uenire fecit atque reginam
de[h] comitissa esse constituit illaque iam regina filium genuit quem
Henricum uocari fecit. Quapropter sicut postea multi dixerunt iustum
fuit ut ipse rex Anglie post patrem suum fuisset[i] qui de patre rege et[j]
matre regina genitus extitisset.

8. Post hec autem Willelmus rex non immemor quam misericordiam
regno[a] Anglie sibi Dominus fecisset[b] cogitauit quia[c] Dorobernensem

o *add* tunc ASL
p *add* pugne S
q o.p. S
r *om* L
s ergo ASL, *add* ilis L
t magnas ASL
u reddentes L
v concesserat ASL
a *text of L breaks off due to loss of fol.; text resumes in* **11**, *see note* g
b t.i. S
c p.a.e. AS
d...d *om* S
e qui S
f credebat A, cedebat S
g *add* rex AS
h ex AS
i esset AS
j *add* de S
a misericorditer regnum AS
b contulisset A, tulisset S
c quod S

ecclesiam in honorem[d] Christi ab antiquo tempore constructam que prin-
cipatum et auctoritatem super omnes ecclesias Anglie tenebat secundum
uoluntatem Dei disponeret. Proinde non parum inde[e] cogitans si[f] in regno
suo inueniret[g] cui Dorobernensem ecclesiam utiliter committere posset[h]
tandem[i] inuenit Lanfrancum abbatem cenobii[j] sancti Stephani Cadomi
uirum ualde[k] religiosum et omni probitate conspicuum[k] et non solum de
his que ad honestatem et ad Deum[l] pertinent set etiam de his[m] que
secularia requirunt prudentem et cautum. Mittens itaque[n] propter illum[n]
in Normanniam fecit eum uenire in Angliam eique consensu et consilio
omnium baronum suorum omniumque[o] episcoporum et abbatum tot-
iusque populi Anglie commisit Dorobernensem ecclesiam ut eam sicut
melius sciret et posset[p] secundum uoluntatem Domini[q] et utilitatem plebis
cuius curam suscipiebat regeret. Quam utiliter uero ipsam ecclesiam
gubernauit quamdiu uixit et quantum in eius tempore ipsa ecclesia est
eleuata que per incuriam antecessorum non parum erat uilis et abiecta[r]
et fere ad magnam inopiam redacta omnes qui tunc fuerunt nouerunt.
Preter hec autem non est silentio pretereundum quod[s] largus fuit et erga
homines seculi et erga pauperes Christi et quomodo ipse exemplo sue
largitatis in Anglia multos[t] ad elemosinam accendit. Propter largitatem
itaque animi eius dicebant quidam eum merito[u] uocatum esse Lanfrancum, id est ferentem cor largum eo quod largus et bonus erga omnes
homines fuit. De rege uero Willelmo et Lanfranco archiepiscopo dicebant[v]
homines qui tunc uiuebant[v] quod tales duo simul in una terra non inueni-
rentur quales essent rex Willelmus et Lanfrancus suus archiepiscopus. Set
ut iam de Lanfranco dimittam et ad ea que de bono rege Willelmo cepi
redeam.

9.   Rex Willelmus ut uir prudentissimus Deumque ualde amans in
omnibus que et secundum Deum et secundum seculum agere disponebat

d honore AS
e *om* inde AS
f an AS
g inuenire posset AS
h committeret AS
i tandum S
j *om* AS
k...k *om* S
l Dominum O
m d.h. *om* S
n...n *om* AS
o omnium S
p p.e.s. S
q Dei S
r deiecta AS
s quam AS
t m.i.A. AS
u m.e. S
v...v multi qui tunc erant S, *om* A

diuinum semper auxilium[a] requirebat omnesque quos bonos et religiosos intelligebat non parum semper[b] diligebat quos autem praue agere uel turpiter uiuere omnino destruebat et nisi a maliciis suis resipiscerent /p. 7, f. 4r/ et honestatem diligerent eciam de regno suo expellebat.[c] Sed quicquid fecisset de aliis malefactoribus,[c] hereticos et quos exurgere uidebat contra usum et auctoritatem sancte eclesie omnino destruebat. Eius enim tempore expulsa est e Northmannia que[d] quosdam ibi[e] maculauerat clericos heresis Berengerii[d] conantis auferre ueritatem corporis et sanguinis Domini. Sed quis posset referre uel scribere omnia bona que bonus rex Willelmus fecit omnemque exaltationem sancte ecclesie que quamdiu ille[f] uixit in regno eius[g] durauit?[h] Quicquid uero fuisset in aliis regnis[h] in regno eius[i] pax semper[j] fuit nec erat ullus tam fortis uel potens qui pacem quam in terra sua posuerat auderet infringere uel si infregeret[k] in ea remanere. Nulla enim[l] alia redemptio de illo[m] esse poterat[m] qui pacem uel treuiam terre illius[n] uiolasset nisi ut exinde[o] exiret. Quamdiu itaque uixit carus et amabilis omnibus bonis hominibus fuit. Vixit autem postquam coronam regni[p] Anglie suscepit uiginti et uno anno. Quibus expletis presentem uitam finiuit in Northmannia apud Rotomagum quarto idus Septembris. Antequam uero finiret fecit heredem de Normannia,[q] Rodbertum filium suum de Anglia autem Willelmum alterum[r] filium suum. Qui quam citius potuit in[s] Angliam transiens post concessionem patris susceptus[t] ab Anglis et Francis sacratus[u] est rex Anglie a Lanfranco archiepiscopo Lundoniam[v] apud Westmonasterium in ecclesia beati Petri apostoli. Filio autem suo Henrico dedit rex Willelmus[w][x] cum

a a.s. AS
b *om* S
c...c Maxime uero AS
d...d quosdam clericos ibi maculauerat heresis Berengarii AS
e *om.* S
f *om* A
g suo S
h...h *om* S
i suo S
j s.p. S
k infringisset A, infegisset S
l est A
m...m *om* A
n i.t. A
o inde AS
p *om* A
q R.f.s.d.N. A
r alium S
s *om* S
t. *add* est AS
u sacratusque AS
v Londonie AS
w W.r. A

ad mortem uenit[x] quinque mille libras[y] de Anglicis denariis.[y] Defunctus
autem[z] rex Willelmus sicut ordinauerat Cadomi translatus est sepultusque
ante maius altare in ecclesia beati Stephani prothomartiris quam ipse
construxerat a fundamentis.

10. Fuit autem post hec non parua discordia inter Rodbertum
comitem Northmannie[a] et Willelmum fratrem suum regem Anglie.[b]
Tunc Henricus remansit in Northmannia cum Rodberto fratre suo qui
dedit ei quandam terram in Northmannia sed non diutius inde gaudium[c]
habuit. Non paruo[d] post tempore inuentis quibusdam uilibus[e] occasion-
ibus ei illam abstulit. Post hec autem aliquanto tempore transacto
concordiam adinuicem fecerunt Willelmus secundus[f] rex Anglie et
Rodbertus comes Normannie et cum fratrem suum Henricum debuissent adiuuare eique prouidere ut[g] honorabiliter inter illos[g] sicut frater
eorum[h] et filius regis posset uiuere[i] non hoc fecerunt sed[i] de tota terra
patris sui expellere conati sunt. Sed quanuis inde multum conati fuissent[j]
tamen non potuerunt facere sicut uoluerunt sed contra[k] uoluntatem
eorum tenuit castrum quod uocatur Danfrunt quod non parua industria
ceperat nec postquam[l] illud captum[l] habuit ei ulla ui[m] auferre potuerunt.
Dominus uero sicut multis uisum est adiuuabat Henricum de quo
postea disponebat de tota Anglia et Northmannia heredem facere
et dominum. Contigit uero postea ut Rodbertus comes Normannie
Ierusalem[n] iret Normanniamque totam[o] fratri suo Willelmo regi Anglorum inuadiaret et tunc[p] Henricus /p. 8, f. 4v/ fratri suo[q] regi
Anglorum[r] omnino se conferret atque cum eo ex toto remaneret. Dum
itaque cum eo esset post aliquantum temporis contigit ut quadam die

x...x iam moriturus AS, uenit *written on erasure* O
y...y Anglice monete AS
z ergo AS
a Normannorum S
b Anglorum S
c g.i. S
d multo S, *add* enim AS
e *om* S
f *om* AS
g *om* AS
h eius A
i...i *om* AS, u.p. S
j sunt AS
k extra A
l...l *om* AS
m ulla u.e. S
n *om* S
o totamque N. S
p *om* S
q fratrem suum S, inaudiaret ... suo *om* A
r r.A. *om* AS

rex Willelmus secundus[s] uenatum iret[t] ibique nescimus quo iuditio Dei
a quodam milite sagitta percussus occubuisset.[u] Quem statim Henricus
frater eius[v] Wintoniam deferri fecit ibique in ecclesia sancti Petri ante
maius altare sepulture tradidit. Quo sepulto Lundoniam uenit atque
apud Westmonasterium annuentibus cunctis Francis et Anglis coronam
regni Anglie suscepit cunctique letati sunt quod[w] modo regem natum
de rege et regina natum[x] et nuritum in Anglia habere meruissent.
Ordinatus autem[y] sicut intelligimus per uoluntatem Dei Henricus
Anglorum rex[z] cepit magnam iustitiam per[a] Angliam tenere et ut
legaliter uiueret accepit uxorem filiam regis Scotie de qua primum
unam filiam habuit quam postea imperatori[b] Alemannie in matri-
monium iunxit. Habuit etiam[c] de eadem uxore sua unum filium qui

A O [*before erasure*]	O [*after erasure*]	S [L *missing*]
ut credimus si ad	non diu uiuens huic	ut credimus sicut ad
perfectam etatem	uite finem fecit.	perfectam etatem
uenire poterit bonus		uenire potuisset
homo erit.		bonus homo fuisset.

11. Non longum autem tempus fuit postquam Henricus rex
coronam Anglie suscepit quod frater suus Rodbertus[a] de Ierusalem
rediit atque suam Northmanniam quam fratri suo Willelmo inua-
diauerat[b] recepit. Audiens itaque quod Henricus frater suus rex Anglorum esset constitutus cepit indignari aduersus[c] illum multumque ei[d]
minari quod regnum Anglie suscipere ausus fuisset non recte cogitans
neque intelligens quod Scriptura dicit[e] [*cf.* Rom. 13, 1]: 'quia[f] nulla
potestas nisi a Deo est.' Hac igitur de causa cepit nauigium preparare
quale potuit.[g] Quo preparato in Angliam transnauigauit. Henricus
autem rex[h] cuius fiducia tota erat in Deo magnam miliciam Anglorum

s *om* AS
t uenaret S
u occumberet AS
v f.e.H. AS
w qui S
x *add* de rege et regina S
y est A
z r.A. S
a *add* totam S
b imperator S
c autem S
a R.f.s. S
b inuadiaret S
c uersus AS
d *om* S
e diceret AS
f quod S
g *text of* L *resumes*
h r.a.H. L

congregans uelociter[i] aduersus eum uenit paratus eum[j] et omnes qui cum eo uenerant de terra Anglorum expellere. Quod profecto[k] annuente Deo in breui fecisset nisi[l] frater suus cum eo concordiam egisset. Facta itaque inter eos concordia[m] aliquanto tempore demoratus este comes Rodbertus in Anglia. In qua postquam tamdiu fuit quantum ei placuit in Normannia remeauit.[n] Non diu autem durauit inter eos ista concordia.[n] Robertus uero[o] comes plus iusto credens illis qui magis uolebant inter eos discordiam esse[p] quam pacem iterum cepit occasiones querere fratremque suum ad discordiam commouere. Rex autem Henricus non diutius hoc ferens quam citius potuit mare transiuit atque non multo post paruo exercitu congregato obsedit ciuitatem Baiocas eamque citius capiens fere omnem[q] destruxit. Deinde cepit Cadomum. Post aliquantum uero temporis cum obsideret quoddam castrum[r] comitis Moritonii quod uocatur Tenerchebrai[s] atque obsidendo laboret ut[t] illud caperet frater eius[u] Rodbertus comes et comes Moritonii cum magna multitudine militum putantes se de rege Henrico uindicare eumque omnino de terra[v] delere cum magno impetu irruerunt[w] super eum et super eos[x] qui cum illo[y] erant. Sed iudicio Dei super eos ueniente capti sunt /p. 9, f. 5r/ ambo et multi alii cum eis ab hominibus regis Henrici atque ante eum adducti. Finita itaque hac obsidione atque illis in captione sua retentis rex Henricus totam Normanniam et omnia castella comitis Moritonii in suum dominium suscepit. Atque ita omni terra sedata rediens in Angliam Rodbertum comitem fratrem suum[z] et comitem Moritonii et quosdam alios quos ei placuit secum adduxit eosque adhuc[a] in captione[b] tenere decernit.[c] Hic est autem[d] status

i v.c. SL
j illum SL
k profectu A
l si L
m c.i.e. A
n...n *om.* SL
o enim ASL
p e.d. ASL
q omnino L
r c.q. *add* ipsius domini L
s Techebray A
t quod L
u ei S
v d.t.o. S
w irruere L
x illos A
y eo ASL
z eius S
a *om* S
b *add* sua A
c decreuit ASL
d *om* S

Anglie et Normannie[e] ad presens.[f] Que autem post hec in his terris futura sint posteritas uidebit.[g]

12. Seriem uero huius[a] generacionis et ordinem, ab illo Dano qui Rollo uocatus terram que[b] uocatur Normannia super regem Francie conquisiuit et conquisitam ille[c] et heredes post eum possederunt usque ad Henricum regem,

AO	SL
qui modo eam regit et possidet,	qui diu eam rexit et possedit,

sic[d] quidam computare solent. Rollo, inquiunt, huius genealogie primus fuit.[e] Willelmus uero[f] filius eius qui uocatus[g] est[h] Longaspata secundus extitit. Ricardus uero huius Willelmi filius[i] tercius fuit. Ricardus huius Ricardi filius qui abbatiam Fiscanni construxit in quarto loco post Rollonem Northmannos rexit.[j] Rodbertus uero filius huius Ricardi qui[k] Ierusalem perexit sed dum[l] inde[m] reuerteretur[n] apud Niceam[o] uitam presentem finiuit huius generationis quintus comes Normannorum extitit. Willelmus uero huius Rodberti filius[p] qui non solum[p] Normanniam sed[q] etiam[r] Angliam possedit in sexto loco successit. Post illum autem in septimo loco fuerunt filii eius ex quibus solus Henricus

AO	SL
modo Normanniam et Angliam possidet.	tunc Normanniam et Angliam possedit.

Quis uero post eum has terras possidebit et possessas gubernauit generatio que tunc erit uidere poterit.

e N.e.A. L
f ad presens *om* S
g ibidit L
a *om* A
b *add* modo ASL
c illam A
d sicut S
e f.p. S
f *om* SL
g uocatur S, dictus L
h *om* S
i f.h.W. S
j regit L
k *add* abbatie Cerasii fundator extitit et S
l ut A
m *om* S
n *add* inde S
o *add* ciuitatem L
p...p qui non solum *om* S
q et S
r *om* S

13. Vbi sepulta iacent horum[a] corpora. Rollo et Willelmus filius eius iacent[b] Rotomagi in ecclesia beate Marie que est caput archiepiscopatus. Ricardus uero filius Willelmi et alius Ricardus iacent Fiscanni. Rodbertus uero filius Ricardi[c] qui rediens de Ierusalem uitam presentem finiuit in Nica ciuitate sepultus quiescit. Willelmus uero filius Rodberti iacet Cadomi in ecclesia beati Stephani quam ipse edificauit. Fecit autem iste Willelmus tres abbatias de suo dominio,[d] duas Cadomi, unam de monachis ubi ipse iacet,[e] aliam de sanctimonialibus ubi uxor eius Mathildis[f] regina sepulta est. Fecit autem et tertiam in Anglia in eo loco ubi ei Dominus[g] uictoriam[h] tribuit de inimicis suis que multo minoris precii est quam fuisset si eam dedicare potuisset.[i] Cum enim eam primum[j] incepit cogitauit eam facere unam de maioribus et ditioribus ecclesiis Anglie sed preuentus morte non potuit facere sicut cogitauerat.[k] Ex cuius rei euentu discimus[l] quod sapienter agit qui bonum quod agere disponit quam citius potest perficere satagit. Nullus enim nouit si[m] crastinum diem uidere poterit[n] et ideo prudentius agit /p. 10, f. 5v/ qui bonum quod in crastino agere disponit hodie faciat, si possit.[n] Securius enim gaudemus de bono quod[o] factum habemus[o] quam de bono quod facere disponimus[p] et nondum[q] fecimus.[k][r] Multotiens enim quibusdam accidit ut dum differunt bonum facere quod uolunt eis deficiat et uoluntas et possibilitas.[s] Que autem de his comitibus unde locutus sum a quibusdam soleant[t] referri si ego scribam fortassis quibusdam non displicebit.

14. Rollo qui huius generationis primus[a] extitit antequam Northmanniam cepisset sicut quidam dicunt paganus erat. Sed predicatione

a *add* comitum S
b *add* apud ASL
c R.f. ASL
d d.s. SL
e *add* et S
f Matilda L
g D.e. S
h D.u.e. L
i posset S
j p.e. L
k...k *om* S
l dicimus AL
m...m *om* AL
n...n *om* A, et ideo ... diponuit hodie facit L
o...o fecimus A, facimus L
p disponamus L
q dum L
r facimus L
s *end of* S
t solebant A
a p.h.g. L

cuiusdam archiepiscopi[b] Rotomagi[c] fidem Christi suscepit qui postquam baptizatus est. Leges christianas quamdiu uixit et ipse bene custodiuit et[d] omni populo suo[d] bene custodire fecit. Quante uero humilitatis fuit postquam fidem Christi[e] suscepit, ex una re quam fecit, patenter cunctis innotuit. Quodam tempore postquam pacificatus est[f] cum rege Francie uenientes ad eum homines[g] Rotomagi, ceperunt eum rogare ut de Francia faceret corpus sancti Audoeni redire, quod propter timorem eius illuc olim fuerat translatum antequam cepisset Normanniam. 'Tristes', inquiunt 'et multum dolentes sumus quod sic[h] archiepiscopum[i] nostrum[j] perditum habemus.[j] Hoc audiens comes mandauit regi Francie ut ei suum presbiterum[k] redderet quod si non faceret proculdubio sciret quod nullo modo pacem cum eo habere posset. Tunc rex Francie nolens ei de hac re facere contrarium[l] reddidit ei sicut petebat suum presbiterum. Tunc comes[m] precepit ut inde reduceretur sanctus Audoenus sueque[n] redderetur ecclesie unde fuerat asportatus. Monachi igitur[o] qui custodes[p] eius fuerunt[q] dum in Francia fuit reportauerunt eum usque ad quandam uillam que est ad unam leuuam[r] iuxta[s] urbem[t] Rotomagi. Ibi itaque cum peruenissent non parum de uia lassati manserunt in[u] illa nocte ut mane surgerent si possent sanctum Audoenum ad suum locum[v] reportarent. Cum itaque mane surgerent eumque ad ciuitatem portare uellent nullo modo potuerunt. Tunc tristes monachi nimiumque dolentes de hoc quod eis acciderat mandauerunt ciuitati[w] quod sanctum Audoenum nullo modo poterant mouere de illo loco ubi iacuerant[x] illa nocte. Quod cum comiti qui tunc erat[y] Rotomagum

b a.c. L
c Rotomagensis L
d...d omnem populum suum AL
e christianam L
f *om* A
g *om* A
h *om* L
i archiepiecopatum L
j...j perdidimus AL
k p.s. A
l molestiam AL
m Comes ergo AL
n et sue AL
o ergo AL
p *om* L
q fuae L
r leugam AL
s ab AL
t urbe AL
u *om* AL
v *om* A
w ciuibus AL
x iacuerunt L
y *add* apud AL

nunciatum fuisset respondit quia[z] merito hec tribulatio de corpore
sancti Audoeni eis[a] accidisset quia si recte cogitassent sensumque[b]
rectum habuissent[b] ad[c] processionem[d] et cum magna deuotione contra
eum uenire debuissent. Post hec precepit comes archiepiscopo omnique
populo Rotomagi ut in langis[e] et nudis pedibus cum eo a sanctum
Audoenum pergerent eiusque pietatem quam deuotius possent exor-
arent quatinus ad stultitias eorum uel negligentias non respiceret sed
propicius illis fieret[f] seque de loco[g] illo ad ciuitatem ubi archiepiscopus
fuisset[h] transferri permitteret. Tunc ipse comes primus sicut aliis preceperat in langis[i] /p. 11, f. 6r/ nudisque pedibus usque ad uillam ubi
sanctus Audoenus erat[j] peruenit. Quo cum peruenisset protinus cum
omni populo qui cum eo erat coram feretro eius prostratus hec orando
dixit: 'Sancte Audoene bone archiepiscope et aduocate noster permittite
uestrum corpus ad ciuitatem transferri ubi presulis officio functus fuistis
et sacras benedictiones sepius fecistis et ego do ecclesie uestre et uobis[k]
totam terram que adiacet ab isto loco usque ad menia ciuitatis. 'Tunc
continuo[l] comes et populus submissis humeris[m] feretrum in quo sanctum
corpus erat facillime deportare ceperunt et[n] sic usque ad ecclesiam
suam gaudentes et exultantes deportauerunt.[n] Ex huius[o] rei euentu
dixerunt quidam illam uillulam[p] uocari Longum Peanum[q] eo quod
comes illud tam longum iter nudis pedibus perexisset. Si quis hoc
factum non esse signum magne humilitatis asserit de eo ueraciter dici
potest quia quid[r] sit maxima[s] humilitas nescit.

15. Quiddam uero aliud dicitur[a] eidem comiti accidisse eo tempore
quo primum pacificatus est cum rege Francie quod non ideo scribo ut

z quod L, non A
a *om* A
b...b sensum non habuissent A
c cum AL
d processione AL
e laneis uestibus AL
f esset AL
g *om* L
h fuerat AL
i laneis uestibus AL
j fuit A
k *om* A
l comes c. A
m h.s. A
n...n *om* L
o cuius L
p uillam A
q Peonum A
r *om* L
s magna A
a dicunt A

certus sim[b] hoc uerum esse; sed quia a multis audiui hoc referri qui asserebant id ueraciter euenisse. Quodam die dum sicut dicebant erat idem comes[c] Rotomagum ad uesperam ipsius[d] diei stabant plurimi homines ante domos suas que erant iuxta ripam Sequane. Illic uero[e] cum essent eandemque aquam aspicerent uiderunt unum equitem transire super aquam quasi iret super terram et usque ad eos[f] peruenientem. Hac ergo de re non parum obstupefacti, cum ad eos peruenisset ceperunt inquirere ab eo quis esset et unde uenisset. Ille uero respondens: 'Videtis', inquit, 'quod ego unus homo sum et hodie multum mane[g] motus sum[g] de[h] Rethnis in Britannia. Abrincas uero ad sextam horam comedi, ad uesperam autem[i] hucusque sicut uidetis perueni.' Tunc mandauerunt comiti qui sicut dixi tunc erat in ciuitate de illo homine qui sic transierat super aquam sine ulla lesione. Comes uero audiens rem tam[j] insuetam mandauit ei ut illi loqueretur antequam hinc[k] recederet.[l] Tunc ille remandauit comiti quia in crastino eum usque ad primam expectaret.[m] Ille autem[n] in crastino mane surgens uiam suam tenuit et nichil locutus est comiti. Comes uero ut audiuit eum[o] recessisse dixit eum mentitum esse et ideo putate[p] eum aliquod fantasma esse qui sic eos uoluisset deludere. Tunc dixerunt quidam qui affuerunt quia sicut eis uidebatur non ei[q] mentitus esset quia non de prima comitis sed de prima sua ei[r] mandasset. Prima enim[s] eius multo citius esset[t] quam prima comitis et ideo uerum fuit quod dixit. Dum uero[u] in illa nocte sederet ad focum sui hospitis et suus hospes de multis eum[v] interrogaret et maxime de illo comite si generatio illa diutius maneret respondit illam diutius manere illudque imperium usque ad septimam generationem uiriliter durare. Cum itaque hospes inquisisset

b sum A
c *add* apud AL
d huius A
e ergo AL
f eo L
g . . . g discessi AL
h a L
i *om* L
j *om* L
k ille L
l procederet A
m expectarent A
n uerum A
o *add* ita AL
p putauit A
q *om* L
r *om* L
s uero L
t fuerat AL
u tamen AL
v *om* A

quid post septimam generationem futurum esset nichil uoluit /p. 12, f. 6v/ respondere sed de uno fussello[w] quem[x] manu tenebat cepit per cineres foci quasi reias[y] facere. Et cum hospes suus uehementer[z] ab eo[a] exigeret quid post septimam[b] generationem eueniret[c] de ipso fussello[d] quem[e] manu tenebat commiscuit reias[f] quas[g] in cineribus fecerat. Ex[h] quo[i] signo quod fecerat[i] arbitrati sunt quod post septimam generationem illud imperium[j] uel deficeret[j] uel magnas pateretur dissentionum tribulationes.

16. Willelmus uero filius eius sicut quidam dixerunt interfectus est[a] per traditionem a quodam comite in Ponteio. Quem cum interfectum Franci audissent mox eius filium[b] Ricardum ceperunt[c] et in Franciam in captionem duxerunt. Hic[d] Willelmus habebat unum[e] scriniolum de quo ipse[f] semper portabat clauiculam. Quod diffirmantes[g] postquam interfectus est nichil in eo aliud inuenerunt nisi unam staminiam quam solebat sicut dicebatur in Quadragesima uel in aliis diebus afflictionis portare. Dani autem audientes quod Franci[h] interfectum habuissent[h] Willelmum parentem illorum non parum irati[i] de hoc[i] quam citius potuerunt cum magna multitudine pugnatorum transnauigantes[j] in Normanniam ad portum Diue[k] arriuauerunt[l] contra quos rex Francie[m] cum non[n] parua multitudine militum uenit si forte posset[o] illos[p] pug-

---

w lignulo AL
x quod A
y sulcos A, fustos L
z s.u. *om* L
a illo A
b *om* A
c ueniret L
d lignulo AL
e quod A
f sulcos A, fustos L
g quos A
h Et L
i...i *om* AL
j...j non differet AL
a fuit A
b f.e. A
c *om* L
d *add* autem AL
e *om* A
f *om* L
g *om* AL
h...h interfecerunt AL
i...i *om* AL, *add* sunt L
j nauigantes L
k *om* A
l applicuerunt AL
m *om* L
n n.c. A
o i.p. A

nando de terra Normannie expellere. Veniens itaque fere usque ad illos timuit cum eis pugnare[q] sed quesiuit cum eis pacem facere illumque comitem qui Willelmum interfecerat cum eis concordare.[r] Dani autem ad horam finxerunt se illam concordiam suscipere sed ut uiderunt illum qui parentem illorum interfecerat[s] non curantes de concordia quam rex Francie querebat[s] impetum facientes super eum interfecerunt illum et plurimos de eis[t] qui cum illo uenerunt,[u] regem uero Francie fugere compulerunt, quem fugientem homines Rotomagi ceperunt atque captum[v] duxerunt Rotomagum. Postea uero communi decreto Franci et Dani talem concordiam inter se fecerunt ut Dani redderent regem Francie et Franci redderent Ricardum filium Willelmi Norhmannie. Tunc in illa concordia auxerunt[w] et augendo creuerunt[w] Norhmanniam Dani ad aqua que uocatur Andella usque ad[x] aliam aquam que uocatur Etta. Alii tamen dicunt ab Etta usque ad Isaram. Constitutum est etiam[y] et aliud[y] in illa concordia quod comes Normannie nullum seruicium faceret regi Francie de terra Normannie nec[z] ei aliter seruiret nisi rex Francie[a] feudium daret ei in Francia unde ei seruire deberet. Quapropter comes Normannie de Normannia tantummodo facit homagium regi Francie et fidelitatem de uita sua et de terreno honore suo.[b] Similiter et rex Francie[c] facit fidelitatem et[d] de uita sua et de suo terreno honore comiti Normannie et nichil aliud differt inter illos nisi quod homagium non facit rex Francie comiti Normannie sicuti[e] /p. 13, f. 7r/ comes Normannie regi Francie facit.[f] Hanc libertatem adquisierunt tunc Dani parentibus suis comitibus Norhmannie.

17. Post istum Ricardum alius Ricardus filius eius tenuit Normanniam. Hic Ricardus fuit pater patrie. Toto enim[a] tempore eius abundauit Normannia omnibus bonis et tanta pax fuit in Normannia eius[b] tempore ut nec eciam carrucarii de campis suis auderent ferra

p *add* illud A
q p.c.e. L
r conciliare A, consilare L
s...s *om* AL
t illis L
u uenerant A
v *om* L
w...w *om* AL
x *om* AL
y...y e.a. *om* AL
z neque A
a *om* L
b s.t.h. AL
c *om* A
d *om* A
e sicut A
f *om* L
a uero L
b eo A

carruce ad suas domos[c] reportare et si alicui furata fuissent preceperat
comes ut ad eum ueniret et quicquid furto[d] perdidisset ipse ei ex integro
totum redderet. Quod audiens uxor cuiusdam carrucarii probare uolens
si uerum esset quod hoc[e] comes iussisset. Quadam die furata est ferra
mariti sui. Carrucarius uero in crastino ueniens[f] ad carrucam suam, et
ferra sua[g] non inueniens uenit ad comitem eique retulit quod ferra
carruce sue ei furata essent. Tunc comes precepit ei dari[h] denarios
unde posset alia ferra emere. Ille itaque rediens domum retulit uxori
sue quid ei comes fecisset. Tunc dixit ei uxor ipsius quod modo bene
esset quia et ipse denarios et ipsa ferra haberet. Carrucarius uero[i] hoc
audiens ne infideliter ageret reportauit comiti suos denarios eique retulit
quid uxor sua[j] fecisset. Comes uero retinens carrucarium aliquanto
tempore misit et precepit ut uxori eius eruerentur oculi[k] propter furtum
quod fecerat. Cum itaque carrucarius domum suam[l] redisset inueniens
quod uxori eius oculi essent eruti cum indignatione dixit ei: 'Noli
emplius furari et amodo disce obseruare precepta comitis.'

18.   Hic comes edificauit ecclesiam Fiscanni illamque non parum
terris et ornamentis diuitem fecit. Hic erat solitus fere omni tempore
suam curiam in pascali solemnitate apud Fiscannum tenere et tunc[a]
quando ei placebat in ipsa solemnitate solebat unam tinam plenam
textis, turibulis, candelabris et quibusdam aliis ornamentis et coopertam
quodam optimo pallio ipse et uxor sua ante altare sancte Trinitatis
portare ipsaque pro suis peccatis ibi Deo offerre. Ipse uero die post
missas antequam ad curiam suam iret atque cum baronibus suis
comederet ueniebat cum duobus filiis suis Ricardo et Rodberto in
refectorio[b] monachorum et illi filii sui apportantes de fenestra coquine
scutellas sicut solent[c] monachi facere porrigebant patri suo et ipse per
se ipsum prima fercula ante abbatem et postea ante monachos ponebat.
Quod cum perfecisset[d] cum magna humilitate ueniebat ante abbatem[e]
et sic ab eo accepta licentia letus et gaudens ibat ad curiam suam.
Aliquando uero de sua mensa mittebat abbati scutellam argenteam

c d.s. A
d furati L
e hic A
f u.i.c. A
g *om* L
h dare L
i *om* L
j s.u. L
k *add* eius A
l *om* A
a *om* A
b refectorium L
c solebant A
d peregisset
e u.a.a. A

plenam piscibus et mandabat[f] ei ut eam retineret atque inde suam[g] uoluntatem faceret.

19. Iste bonus Ricardus non solum ecclesie Fiscanni multa dedit sed etiam aliis ecclesiis. Quadam uero nocte iacuit[a] apud Gemmeticum mane uero surgens /p. 14, f. 7v/ sicut sua consuetudo semper erat perrexit orare ad monasterium[b] qui[c] post orationem posuit[d] super altare unum[e] fussellum.[f] Recedente uero illo uenerunt secretarii ad altare putantes se ibi esse inuenturos uel marcam auri uel unciam uel aliquid huiusmodi, inuenerunt itaque fussellum[g] atque quid hoc significaret non parum mirari ceperunt. Ad ultimum inquisierunt ab eo quid hoc esset quod super altare illum[h] fussellum[i] posuisset. Tunc respondit eis quod hoc esset Vimonasterium[j] scilicet quoddam manerium quod ipse illis pro anima sua dabat. Hec de Ricardo comite dicta[k] sufficiant quamuis non possint[l] facile omnia bona que fecit referri.

20. De Rodberto uero comite filio eius et de Willelmo filio Rodberti comitis qui Angliam conquisiuit quia inde[a] iam satis diximus non est opus amplius quid dicere. De Willelmo tamen[b] hoc audiui quia cum natus fuisset[c] et super quoddam stramen quod ibi erat casu[d] poneretur ambas manulas suas super stramen proiecit easque illo stramine plenas super pectus suum apposuit.[e]

21. **A**	**L**
De rege autem Henrico huius Willelmi filio qui nunc gubernat Normannos et Anglos si uerum dicere uolumus nichil aliud dicere possumus nisi quia sit per Dei gratiam. In isto tempore uiuit de illis regibus uel principibus qui	De rege autem Henrico huius Guillelmi filio qui gubernauit et Anglos si uerum dicere uolumus nichil aliud dicere possumus nisi quod fuit per Dei gratiam. In illo tempore uiuit de illis regibus uel principibus qui utilius et honestius

f mandauit A
g s.i. L
a uenit L
b a.m. *om* L
c et A
d *om* AL
e *add* posuit A
f, g lignulum AL
h illud AL
i lignulum AL
j in misterium A
k *om* A
l possim A
a *om* A, *add* superius AL
b enim A
c esset AL
d forte A
e apparuit L, *end of* O

utilius et honestius et secundum Deum et secundum seculum suum populum regit atque disponit et propterea magna necessitas omnibus hiis super quos dominium habet incumbit ut longo tempore uiuat. Quamdiu enim uixerit nullus eos ut puto ultra racionem grauare poterit. Longam ergo uitam omnipotens Dominus ei tribuat qua tandem finita ad eternam felicitatem transeat ubi cum sanctis omnibus in eternam gaudeat. Amen.

secundum Deum et secundum seculum suum populum rexit atque disposuit et propterea magna necessitas omnibus hiis super quos dominium habuit incubuit ut longo tempore uixisset. Quamdiu enim uixerit nullus eos ut puto ultra rationem grauare poterit. Longam ergo uitam omnipotens Dominus ei tribuit qua tandem finita ad eternam felicitatem transeat ubi cum sanctis omnibus in eternam gaudeat. Amen.

II

De iniusta vexacione Willelmi episcopi primi per Willelmum regem filium Willelmi magni regis

Edited by
H. S. Offler (†)
Revised for publication by
A. J. Piper and A. I. Doyle

CONTENTS

PREFACE

William of St Calais, bishop of Durham from 1080 to 1096, ranks very high among the ablest occupants of the see. My acquaintance with the seemingly contemporary treatise about the 'unmerited harassment' inflicted on him by William Rufus in 1088 goes back to 1946. Just released from the Army, I was invited by David Douglas to help with the teaching of medieval history at Bristol. During the session Douglas was struggling with a bout of ill-health and asked me once or twice to stand in for him with his final honours candidates. They were offering the Norman Conquest as a special subject and among their set texts was *De iniusta vexacione*. Getting it up was an enjoyable and illuminating experience, though even then some aspects of it left me slightly uneasy. Removal next year to Durham, an ambience rich in monuments to Bishop William's impressive career, naturally stimulated my interest in the treatise. Dissatisfied with Thomas Arnold's edition, during the next few years I collated the surviving manuscripts and gradually formed opinions about the work's date and purpose divergent from those then current. In 1951 J. G. Edwards published my critique of *De iniusta vexacione* in *The English Historical Review* [reprinted in 1996 as VI in *North of the Tees*, preserving the original pagination]; considerations of space precluded printing a revised text.

My rather unorthodox views met with a mixed reception. If they pleased some (including V. H. Galbraith – but maybe that was just because they were unorthodox), others did not find them persuasive. But the consequences of setting even a not very pugnacious cat among the pigeons can be oddly persistent. On picking up this subject again in 1989 I was surprised – perhaps too a little pleased – to find how vigorously debate about *De iniusta vexacione* had continued. Meanwhile, Arnold's text had remained unamended. So it has seemed useful to seek a more adequate basis for discussion by presenting a revised text accompanied by the pretty full annotation it calls for. Since 1951 the mass of relevant secondary literature has grown prodigiously. I cannot claim to have mastered it all. But perhaps the notes will provide help as well as provocation to those grappling with the problems the treatise exhibits. Whatever they may come to conclude about its date and purpose, they will agree, I hope, that it is a notable document in the cultural history of Anglo-Norman England.

My thanks are due to all those who have allowed me access to historical manuscripts originating in Durham. I am particularly indebted to Dr A. I. Doyle and Mr Alan Piper for putting their up-to-date knowledge of these books at my disposal.

[H.S.O. completed the present contribution in March 1990, ten months before his death. A.J.P. and A.I.D have overseen its publication, making a very few additions, enclosed in square brackets.]

ABBREVIATIONS

ASC	*Anglo-Saxon Chronicle*, E Version, ed. Cecily Clark, *The Peterborough Chronicle 1070–1154*, 2nd edn., (Oxford, 1970)
Barlow, *EC*	Frank Barlow, *The English Church 1066–1154* (London, 1979)
Barlow, *WR*	Id., *William Rufus* (London, 1983)
Battle	*Proceedings of the Battle Conference on Anglo-Norman Studies*, ed. R. A. Brown, 1978 seq
Bishop & Chaplais, *ERW*	T. A. M. Bishop and P. Chaplais, *Facsimiles of English Royal Writs to A.D. 1100, presented to V. H. Galbraith* (Oxford, 1957)
Catt.vett.	*Catalogi veteres librorum ecclesiae cathedralis Dunelmensis*, ed. Beriah Botfield, SS 7 (1838)
C & S	*Councils and Synods with other documents relating to the English Church*, vol. I, part ii, ed. D. Whitelock, M. Brett, C. N. L. Brooke (Oxford, 1981)
Craster, 'Red Book'	H. R. E. Craster, 'The Red Book of Durham', *EHR* 40 (1925), 504–32
David, 'A tract'	C. W. David, 'A tract attributed to Simeon of Durham', *EHR* 32 (1917), 382–7
David, *RC*	Id., *Robert Curthose Duke of Normandy* (Cambridge, Mass., 1920)
DB	*Domesday Book, seu Liber Censualis Willelmi Primi Regis Angliae*, vols. i-ii, ed. Abraham Farley, 1783; vols. iii-iv, ed. Henry Ellis, 1816
DEC	*Durham Episcopal Charters 1071–1152*, ed. H. S. Offler, SS 179 (1968)
DIV	The treatise *De iniusta vexacione Willelmi episcopi Primi*
Doyle, 'Claxton'	A. I. Doyle, 'William Claxton and the Durham chronicles', in *Books and Collectors 1200–1700: essays presented to Andrew Watson*, ed. J. P. Carley and C. G. C. Tite, (London, 1997), 335–55
DCD	Muniments of the Dean and Chapter of Durham
DCL	Library of the Dean and Chapter of Durham
Eadmer, *HN*	Eadmer, *Historia Novorum in Anglia*, ed. M. Rule, *RS* 81 (1884)

EHD   *English Historical Documents*, vol. ii, *1049–1189*, ed. D. C. Douglas and G. N. Greenaway, (London, 1953; 2nd edn., 1981)

EHR   *The English Historical Review*

EYC   *Early Yorkshire Charters*, 13 vols., i–iii ed. William Farrer, iv–xii ed. C. T. Clay (Yorkshire Archaeological Soc., Record Series, Extra Series, 1914–65)

'Florence'   Florence of Worcester, *Chronicon ex chronicis*, ed. B. Thorpe (English Historical Soc.), 2 vols. (1848–9)

Freeman, WR   *The Reign of William Rufus and the Accession of Henry I*, 2 vols. (Oxford, 1882)

GEC   G. E. C[ockayne], *The Complete Peerage of England, Scotland, Ireland, Great Britain and the United Kingdom*, 12 vols. in 13 rev. edn., (1910–59)

Gibson, *Lanfranc*   Margaret Gibson, *Lanfranc of Bec* (Oxford, 1978)

HDE   See Symeon, *Opera*

Hinschius   *Decretales pseudo-Isidorianae et Capitula Angilramni*, ed. P. Hinschius, (Leipzig, 1863)

Hoffmann, 'Zur Echtheit'   Hartmut Hoffmann, 'Ivo von Chartres und die Lösung des Investiturproblems', *Deutsches Archiv für Erforschung des Mittelalters* 15 (1959), 373–440. Excurs: 'Zur Echtheit des Libellus de iniusta vexacione Willelmi episcopi', 435–40

HR   See Symeon, *Opera*

HRHEW   David Knowles, C. N. L. Brooke, Vera London, *The Heads of Religious Houses. England and Wales 900–1216* (Cambridge, 1972)

Loyd, *Origins*   L. C. Loyd, *The Origins of some Anglo-Norman families*, ed. C. T. Clay and D. C. Douglas, Harleian Soc. 103 (1951)

LV   Liber Vitae Dunelmensis (BL Cotton ms. Domitian VII); collotype facsimile, SS 136 (1923)

Malmesbury, GP   William of Malmesbury, *De gestis pontificum Anglorum libri quinque*, ed. N. E. S. A. Hamilton, *RS* 52 (1870)

Malmesbury, GR   William of Malmesbury, *De gestis regum Anglorum libri quinque*, ed. W. Stubbs, *RS* 90, 2 vols. (1887–9)

Mason, 'Roger of Montgomery'   J. F. A. Mason, 'Roger of Montgomery and his sons (1067–1102)', *Trans. Royal Historical Soc.*, 5th series, 13 (1963), 1–28

Mowbray Charters   *Charters of the Honour of Mowbray 1107–1191*, ed. D. E. Greenway, (London, 1972)

Mynors, *DCM*   R. A. B. Mynors, *Durham Cathedral Manuscripts to the end of the Twelfth Century* (Oxford, 1939)

North of the Tees   H. S. Offler, *North of the Tees. Studies in Medieval British History*, ed. A. J. Piper and A. I. Doyle, (Aldershot, 1996)

Offler, *Medieval Historians*   H. S. Offler, *Medieval Historians of Durham*, Durham, 1958; repr. as I in *North of the Tees*

Offler, 'Tractate'   H. S. Offler, 'The tractate *De iniusta vexacione Willelmi episcopi primi*', *EHR* 66 (1951), 321–41: repr. as VI in *North of the Tees*

Orderic   *The Ecclesiastical History of Orderic Vitalis*, ed. Marjorie Chibnall, 6 vols. (Oxford, 1969–80)

RAN   *Regesta Regum Anglo-Normannorum* i, ed. H. W. C. Davis and R. J. Whitwell, (Oxford, 1913); ii, ed. Charles Johnson and H. A. Cronne, (1956), pp. 390–413: Errata and Addenda to vol.i

RS   Rolls Series

Sanders, *Baronies*   I. J. Sanders, *English Baronies: a study of their origin and descent, 1086–1327* (Oxford, 1960)

Southern, *Anselm* (1963)   R. W. Southern, *Saint Anselm and his biographer* (Cambridge, 1963)

SS   Publications of the Surtees Society

Symeon, *Opera*   Symeon of Durham, *Historical Works*, ed. Thomas Arnold, *RS* 75, 2 vols. (1882–5)

    HDE   *Historia Ecclesiae Dunelmensis*, in vol. i

    HR   *Historia Regum* ascribed to Symeon, in vol. ii

INTRODUCTION

Structure and contents

DIV is not a homogeneous work. Of its two components by far the more important is a *libellus* recounting in detail Bishop William of St Calais's troubled relations with William Rufus between March and December 1088. This *libellus* is sandwiched between materials for a rudimentary *vita* of the bishop. The first part of the *vita* outlines his career until 1088: his beginnings as a cleric in Bayeux, his monastic profession at St Calais in Maine and his promotions there until he became abbot of St Vincent's near Le Mans, his translation thence by William the Conqueror to the bishopric of Durham in 1080, his journey to Rome to consult Pope Gregory VII, followed by his restoration of monastic life at Durham in 1083, and his initially amicable relations with the Conqueror's successor Rufus before discord broke out between them early in 1088. Then, after the interposition of the *libellus*, the *vita* concludes the treatise by sketching the bishop's fortunes after his return to England in 1091 from exile in Normandy, down to his death and burial in January 1096.

The *vita* portions of DIV (lines 3–28, 644–68) can confidently be taken as the work of someone other than the author of the *libellus*. Most of their substance and much of their wording are borrowed from Symeon's *HDE*. Whether a few pieces of information in the *vita* not coming from that source, but to be found in the later Durham compilation *HR*, indicate dependence of the latter on the *vita*, as C. W. David argued, or whether indebtedness may have been the other way round, as I suggested in 1951, is perhaps an insoluble problem.[1] The *vita* must have been composed after April 1109, since it refers to Anselm of Canterbury as *sancte memorie* (lines 659–60). It may have been put together long after that, unless we suppose that the date when *HR* was compiled, perhaps *c.* 1140, indicates a *terminus ante*.[2]

Vastly more original and interesting than the *vita* sections is the meat

---

1 David, 'A tract', 383–7; *id.*, *RC* 212–5; Offler, 'Tractate', 322–3.

2 Antonia Gransden, *Historical Writing in England c. 550 to c. 1347* (London, 1974), 122 and n. 113, while claiming that DIV was 'a remarkable piece of contemporary reportage', denied that the *vita* was a later addition to the *libellus*. These positions are difficult to reconcile. Since the *vita* is later than April 1109, if it and the *libellus* were composed at the same time, then all DIV must be later than that date. This seems incompatible with Dr Gransden's view that the treatise was a contemporary record of events in 1088.

in the sandwich provided by the *libellus*, which occupies more than nine-tenths of the whole treatise (lines 29–643). It describes the drastic consequences of Rufus's suspicion early in 1088 that Bishop William was party to the treasonable conspiracy against him by many of the great Anglo-Norman magnates. The *libellus* begins abruptly with Rufus's proclamation of the bishop's disseisin on 12 March and St Calais's flight to Durham from the king's presence. Its account of the energetic fencing between king and bishop during the next five months (lines 32–150) delineates firmly what was at issue. We are shown Rufus, convinced of the bishop's guilt and determined to bring him to trial in the king's court for gross breach of feudal obligation, exerting pressure by inciting his officers and lay vassals to action against the bishop's men and estates (at least those south of Tees). Bishop William's riposte, so the *libellus* represents, was based solidly on the privileges of his order: consistently declaring his innocence, he was willing to subject it to proof by legal process. But such process must respect his ecclesiastical character and ensure him a canonical trial by his fellow churchmen, with the prospect, if all else failed, of resort to Rome. Though not at this stage generous with precise dates, the *libellus* depicts the exchanges between king and bishop in lively detail, as if from first-hand information. It exhibits the text of three undated letters from St Calais to Rufus, skilful compositions at times verging on insolence, and reports an inconclusive meeting between them, presumably in southern England during June or July. Meanwhile Rufus had parcelled out the bishop's Yorkshire lands between Count Alan, lord of Richmond, and Count Odo of Champagne, lord of Holderness.

The *libellus* sets out these matters at a length which contrasts markedly with its brief account of how the bishop's resistance was at last broken (lines 150–4). In late August or early September (it must be assumed, since the *libellus* is not explicit about the date) Rufus sent a feudal host against the bishop, and he was forced to come to an agreement with its leaders, Counts Alan and Odo together with Roger le Poitevin, third son of Roger Montgomery, on 8 September (lines 155–209). St Calais now accepted that he must appear before the king's court, but, if we can believe the *libellus*, his capitulation was on terms subtly formulated in favour of his position. Even should he incur an adverse judgement irrefragable on his own principles of ecclesiastical privilege, if he was unwilling to accept it he was to be allowed safeconduct overseas. Analysis of this intricate document can hardly fail to suggest that if the two counts and Roger le Poitevin really did agree to it on the king's behalf, they must have been simple souls indeed.

The *libellus* does not explain why the hearing of the bishop's case was postponed from 29 September, the date originally envisaged, nor what St Calais's movements were during the next seven weeks after he had been expelled from Durham on 11 September (as the *vita*, not the *libellus* records: lines 649–50). It moves on to the bishop's appearance before the meeting of the king's court which opened at Old Salisbury on 2 November. This centrepiece of the *libellus* (lines 210–543) is so justly famous for its uniquely detailed and intimate report of proceedings in the Anglo-Norman *curia regis* that it can be treated briefly here.[3] As the *libellus* tells the story, St Calais defended himself with skill and guile and occasional resort to pathos and drama before an assembly whose membership seems almost wholly congruous with our knowledge of the upper ranks of Anglo-Norman society at this time. Thanks to the *libellus* we are allowed, as it were, to sit in the gallery and listen to the debate in person. There is Lanfranc, playing the role of moderate, reasonable statesman in a fashion capable of rousing the lay members to outbreaks of vocal approval; there are uninhibited interjections by some of those members; there is Rufus, obdurate in his intention to secure Durham castle, at times driven beyond endurance by the equal obstinacy on St Calais's part not to accept the jurisdiction of a lay court, though willing to purge himself from guilt canonically. The *libellus* presents the bishop as a superbly accomplished pleader, daring at last to appeal to Rome. But the odds against him were too great. The decision was that he must go into exile; only after Durham castle had been handed over to the king could he expect a royal safeconduct to his port of embarkation. According to the *libellus* the castle was surrendered and the bishop's disseisin completed on 14 November (lines 565–7). Nevertheless even when he had arrived at Southampton on 26 November he was still pursued by the king's rancour and harassed about alleged transgressions by his followers. A further appeal by the bishop to the three magnate guarantors of the agreement on 8 September was needed before he was allowed to proceed overseas, certainly not till well on in December or even the early days of 1089 (lines 580–643).

Sources, date and purpose

Discussion of these aspects of DIV will be almost exclusively with reference to the *libellus*. As has been seen, the source of most of the *vita* portions is readily identifiable. Their use of Symeon's *HDE* must be after April 1109; possibly, though not certainly, it was before *c.* 1140, for we cannot be really sure how soon they were put together to form a framework for the *libellus*.

The *libellus* itself presents much greater difficulties. At face value it seems the work of an author standing very close to the bishop during

3 See e.g. the narratives in Freeman, *WR* i, 95–120 and Barlow, *WR* 85–9.

his troubles in 1088, with access to his correspondence and present when he appeared before the king's court at Salisbury. Who else could possibly have been in a position to report what went on in court with such lively and detailed verisimilitude? Is the *libellus* not clearly a production by a contemporary on the spot, or at any rate 'based on copious notes taken during the actual proceedings'?[4] If we agree, we must grant it the authority of authentic testimony at first hand about events in a year of English history not richly served by the sources.

This view of the *libellus* has long been held by eminent scholars. In 1951 I ventured to challenge it as too easy. After repeated readings of the text while collating the manuscripts I had formed the opinion that it was less a straightforward report of events made as they occurred or shortly afterwards than a piece of *ex post facto* pleading. It was, I argued, an artful composition, designed to show Bishop William's relations with Rufus in the best possible light from the ecclesiastical point of view. Though doubtless written by someone to whom genuine information was available, it was not itself acceptable as a wholly faithful account of what really happened in 1088. Despite a high level of skill on the author's part, I contended, the *libellus* showed anomalies and anachronisms enough to suggest that it was composed no inconsiderable time after the events it purported to narrate. I concluded that in date it was probably posterior to Eadmer's *Historia Novorum* or even to William of Malmesbury's *Gesta Regum*.[5]

These views have not met with general approval. Among the first to take serious issue with them was Hartmut Hoffmann in 1959.[6] Regarding the *libellus* as a mere *Prozessbericht*, to him that character guaranteed its contemporaneity. He esteemed it a sort of aide-mémoire, drawn up by the bishop or some member of his entourage to help pursuit of his business at Rome, maybe, or in some other way to insure against eventualities. This approach seems to me completely to discount the quite outstanding literary qualities of the piece, most marked perhaps in the verbal exchanges at Salisbury and the adroit intercalation of canonistic learning throughout. Hoffmann's claim that the 'authenticity' of the *libellus* finds support in the terms of Urban II's letter to Rufus in April–June 1089 carries little weight.[7] Nor does his argument that a later author could not have resisted the temptation to report what went on in court at Salisbury on the occasions when the bishop retired from the king's presence. It is indisputable that whoever wrote the *libellus* was intelligent: intelligent enough, one may assume, if he were a later

---

4 As David Knowles supposed, *The Monastic Order in England* (Cambridge, 1949), 169, n.1.

5 Offler, 'Tractate', 321–41.

6 Hoffmann, 'Zur Echtheit', 438–40.

7 See the note 56 to DIV.

fabricator, not to destroy his own credibility by pretending to know what a follower of the bishop in November 1088 could not have known.

When R. W. Southern in 1963 rejected my suggestion as a 'desperate remedy' he based himself on the belief that 'the motives for falsification appear to be lacking'.[8] That seems questionable to me. Durham was immensely indebted to Bishop William; he had set on foot the building of its great new cathedral and established the monastic community there. But elsewhere the reputation of this preeminent innovator was not altogether savoury. The historiographical tradition developing in England at large, represented by Eadmer, the OE Chronicle, 'Florence' of Worcester and William of Malmesbury, disclosed two great blots in his copybook: his exile in 1088 for treason against Rufus and his bullying, opportunist opposition to Anselm at Rockingham in 1095. A certain unease about some aspects of Bishop William can be sensed, I think, even in the domestic Durham historians. In his *HDE* Symeon, as Hoffmann admits, glosses over the bishop's vicissitudes between 1088 and 1091; but even so, perhaps not without a nuance of ambiguity.[9] Later on, when the Durham compiler of *HR* came to 1088, he deserted his habitual source for this period, 'Florence', who has harsh things to say about St Calais; instead, he resorted to manipulating a version of *ASC* 1087 [1088] in order to let the bishop down lightly.[10] Though (*pace* Hoffmann) I am far from considering that the *libellus* was a *Panegyricus* of St Calais, it does not strike me as unreasonable (let alone 'desperate') to suggest that at some time well after 1088 the need was felt in Durham for a defence of the bishop against the aspersions being cast upon him. To present an image of St Calais guiltless of treason and consistently championing the principles of ecclesiastical liberty years before Anselm was put to the test in England: here surely was motive enough for confecting the *libellus*. Of course the author did not simply draw upon his own imagination for this purpose; he must have used at least some material collected in 1088.[11]

Tackling the problem head on in an appendix to her book on Lanfranc (1978), Dr Margaret Gibson, while accepting that the *libellus* was a *Tendenzschrift*, argued that it was 'written in the heat of the affair itself', or at any rate before St Calais's return to England from Normandy in 1091.[12] Her suggestion that its strongly canonistic flavour might have owed more to a Norman than an English background has its attractions. But was it so 'desperate' on my part as she supposes to have thought that it might have been composed much later than 1089–

8 Southern, *Anselm* (1963), 148 and n. 1.
9 Hoffmann, 'Zur Echtheit', 439; Symeon, *HDE* 132.   See note 98 to DIV.
10 *HR* 214–7.
11 Offler, 'Tractate', 341.
12 Gibson, *Lanfranc*, 220–1.

91 'by an unknown hand for an unknown purpose'? As has been said, palliation of St Calais's conduct during a murky episode in his career may well have seemed called for at Durham long after 1091. As for the 'unknown hand': it seems reasonable enough that an author going about to rewrite the historical record tendentiously should be at pains to keep his identity dark. The best efforts of modern scholars to uncover the names of ingenious twelfth-century forgers are not always successful.

Though Professor Frank Barlow admitted in 1979 that the *libellus* was 'an *ex parte* account, completely sympathetic to the defendant', he was unconvinced by my attempt to assign it to a comparatively late date.[13] Confident that 'it was at least based on an eye-witness account of the trial', like Hoffmann he took as a sign of 'authenticity' the fact that the author never reports what went on at Salisbury when the bishop was not in court. Barlow's narrative of the Salisbury proceedings in his study of William Rufus (1983) reflected his continued belief in the contemporaneity of the *libellus*.[14] I cannot agree that the excellencies of the work really rebut the suggestion of later fabrication, as Barlow claims they do: they merely testify to the undoubted skill of the author. Much more substantial is his contention that many of the apparent inconsistencies in the naming of the *dramatis personae*, which nourished my doubts about the *libellus*, can be explained 'by the faulty transmission of the manuscript and the erroneous extension of names abbreviated to initials'.[15]

There is some force in this. Abbreviating personal forenames to initials was a common practice with late eleventh-century scribes; examples of it can be found in the *libellus* itself (lines 300, 322, 443, 533, 593). No surviving manuscript of DIV is datable earlier than the middle of the fourteenth century; by then there had been plenty of time for minor scribal aberrations from the original. In this fashion might be explained why the Ralph Paynel of lines 53 and 81 has turned into the Roger Paynel of line 231 and, perhaps, into the Reginald Paynel of line 516. On the other hand, our primary witness of the text of the *libellus*, though late, does not give the impression of being bad, and if, in order to get round difficulties, we impute scribal error too freely, we run the risk of rewriting the text to suit our own convenience. Authors as well as scribes are capable of making mistakes, particularly when discussing events at some distance from their own experience. A classic difficulty in the *libellus* is its mention on five occasions of a *Hugo de Bellomonte* at Salisbury, for no likely member of the *curia regis* in 1088 with that name is identifiable. Barlow proposes to solve the problem by supposing that *Hugo* is repeated scribal error for *Henricus*: the man intended was Henry

13 Barlow, *EC* 281, n. 46; *id.*, *The Norman Conquest and Beyond* (London, 1983), 234, n. 7.
14 Barlow, *WR* 85–9.
15 *EC* 281, n. 46.

Beaumont, either already or just about to become earl of Warwick. I find it more convincing to assume that it was the author himself who got things wrong here; he meant to name Hugh Beauchamp, a thoroughly plausible character in this context, but confused *de Bello monte* with *de Bello campo*.[16] Again, if error is involved at all when the *libellus* refers to a Roger Mowbray, this seems quite as likely to be due to the author as to a scribe; Barlow's alteration of Roger to Robert is too peremptory.[17] The instance of Roger Montgomery's third son, Roger le Poitevin, a leading figure in the narrative, also demands comment. Sometimes the *libellus* calls him count, not so at other times. In fact Roger does not appear to have acquired that title until 1091, on the death of his brother-in-law, Boso count of La Marche.[18] When Barlow dismisses the references in the *libellus* to Roger as a count as 'a stylistic simplification', permissible 'since the use of the title at this time was chancy', I remain skeptical.[19] To me they suggest strongly that the *libellus* was completed after Roger had inherited the comital title from Boso by an author ignorant or forgetful of the fact that in 1088 he was not yet a count. When reading the *libellus* we must certainly be on the alert for the results of textual corruption, as Barlow has warned us. But by no means all the puzzles it presents can be explained away by a defective tradition of the text. Some of them, it can still reasonably be argued, are the consequences of error by an author who, however skilled, was at work well after 1088.

On the whole, then, despite my critics, I am prepared to abide by my opinion about the *libellus* expressed in 1951. Various apparent anomalies which aroused my suspicions then still await satisfactory elucidation; they are discussed further in the notes to the text. Whether Lanfranc's statement about the Conqueror's action against Odo of Bayeux in 1082, as reported in the *libellus*, depended on Malmesbury's *Gesta regum*, does now seem more problematical to me than it did in 1951. But Dr Chibnall's conclusion that the accounts of this incident in Malmesbury, Orderic and the 'Hyde Chronicle' appear independent of each other still, I believe, leaves it open to postulate a source for the *libellus* here other than the author's personal experience.[20] Certainly I continue reluctant to accept that the author had not found in Eadmer's *Historia Novorum* a case he thought necessary to answer. Perhaps judgement about the 'authenticity' of the *libellus* is fated to remain more a matter of temperament than of conviction on purely technical grounds. To some, anything as good as this must surely be true; to others it will

16 See note 45 to DIV.
17 Barlow, *WR* 77, n. 111, 89, 92, 168; see DIV lines 581–2 and note.
18 See note 28 to DIV.
19 Barlow, *WR* 85, n. 160.
20 Orderic iv, pp. xxvii–xxx; Offler, 'Tractate', 340–1. See note 57 to DIV.

always appear rather too good to be wholly true. Much of its content can be made to point either way. What could better guarantee the piece's 'authenticity' than the *dramatis personae* it puts on stage at the Salisbury court? With one or two exceptions, these are men to be found attesting Rufus's charters on great occasions; we need turn to no more than a couple of witness lists from early 1091 to identify a very high proportion of them.[21] But on the other hand, might not a later fabricator have used one or more genuine royal diplomas to muster a plausible cast before whom to bring Bishop William in November 1088?

Beyond all dispute, the *libellus* holds its ground as a significant historical source. What needs to be determined is the nature of the evidence it offers and the way in which that evidence is to be used. For those questions its date is crucial. To put the matter crudely, dare we swallow it holus-bolus as a trustworthy contemporary guide to events in 1088, as Freeman did in 1882 and as Professor Barlow, with some reserves, seemed still prepared to do a century later? Looking back over the decades since 1951, perhaps some shift in approach can be perceived, some disposition towards greater caution in handling the *libellus*. In 1981 the editors of the revised *Councils and Synods*, while rejecting my proposed dating, proved not wholly deaf to my doubts about the likelihood of an uncontested appeal to a pope from England in the circumstances of November 1088.[22] Quite obviously the author of the *libellus* demands our admiring attention for his literary ability and his grasp of canon law: they were first-rate. But what he produced is essentially less valuable for narrative than for other kinds of history. In my opinion the *libellus* should not be treated as a contemporary *procès-verbal*. Rather it was a skilled *plaidoyer* for Bishop William's conduct in 1088, drawn up in its existing form considerably later than that year.

Title

It is improbable that the treatise was originally known by its present title. In mid-twelfth century the Durham *Historia Regum* referred simply to a *libellus* about Bishop William's tribulations: the same word, picked up by the 'Durham Book', passed from there into Roger of Howden. When F, a manuscript of the later fourteenth century and the earliest surviving version of the treatise, was written it displayed no title or heading at all, but the original list of contents (f. vi^v) describes it as *De iniusta vexacione Willelmi episcopi primi per Willelmum Regem Filium Willelmi Magni Regis*; the entry for this book in the 1395 catalogue of the cloister

21 *RAN* i nos. 315, 319.
22 *C & S* I.ii, 635, n. 2; 855, n. 1.

library at Durham abbreviates the title to *De Injusta Vexacione Willielmi Episcopi primi*.[23] For his transcript made early in the sixteenth century William Todd devised what looks like a mere description (H, f. 224r): *Incipit vita Willelmi Karilephi episcopi Dunelmensis*. Later antiquaries followed the contents-list of F, adding the title *De iniusta vexacione* [etc.] in F (f. 207r), B (f. 66r) and D (f. 88r) in varieties of the late sixteenth-century archaizing script which Dr A. I. Doyle has identified as practised by the Durham antiquary William Claxton of Wynyard (d. 1597) and members of his circle.[24] Even later was the use of this title as a running headline to the text of D by Edward Rud (1677–1727).

Authorship

Nothing conclusive can be said about this. There is no guarantee and little likelihood that the biographical framework of the treatise and its kernel, the *libellus* concerned with the events of 1088, were both the work of the same author. The wealth of vivid detail in the *libellus* has often tempted scholars to suppose that it must have been written by some member of the bishop's entourage in 1088. Even if the validity of that hypothesis is doubted, it can hardly be denied that whoever did compose the *libellus* must have relied to some extent on information collected by such an intimate. So outstandingly able and active a prelate as William of St Calais will not have tolerated incompetent men in his service. Details about his *familia* are hard to come by, but something can be said concerning a few who belonged to it. The list must begin with that member of the Durham scriptorium (probably an Englishman) who has been identified by Dr Chaplais as the editor and main scribe of Great Domesday. The record of his efforts, Chaplais supposes, enables us to characterize William of St Calais as 'the man behind the Survey', so that the bishop's exile in 1088, accompanied by 'his favourite scribe', helps to explain why the Survey was left incomplete. If this contention be accepted, we have here alongside the bishop in the 1080s a highly accomplished monk-chaplain–scribe, well acquainted with the workings of government and the tenurial situation in England. But his very existence depends on a technical exercise in script-comparison, and he remains anonymous.[25]

On the other hand the monk Geoffrey, whom Symeon tells us St Calais appointed general manager or caretaker (*procurator*) of his bish-

23 DCL ms. B.iv.46, f. 21v = *Catt.vett.*, p. 55 entry P.
24 [Doyle, 'Claxton', 338–9, 344.]
25 Pierre Chaplais, 'William of St Calais and the Domesday Survey', in J. C. Holt (ed.), *Domesday Studies* (Woodbridge, 1987), 65–76; on the script, cf. Alexander R. Rumble, *ib.*, 82–5.

opric, figures quite prominently in the *libellus* itself.[26] His employment in administrative tasks somewhat resembles the uses to which later on at Canterbury Anselm put Baldwin the monk from Tournai. After St Calais had come to terms with the king's forces in September 1088, Geoffrey was left in charge at Durham castle; he was with the bishop again at Southampton in early December. Presumably he had quitted Durham in order to rejoin his bishop after the royal seizure of Durham castle on 14 November; he does not appear to have been present at the Salisbury court earlier in the month.

It is unlikely that Geoffrey was a Durham monk by origin. A third chaplain-scribe in St Calais's service almost certainly was. The William responsible for the fine calligraphy of Durham Cathedral ms. B.II.14 gives his name and expresses devotion to his bishop [during his exile] in verses on f. 200v;[27] he also wrote the text of Bede's *Ecclesiastical History* given by St Calais to his monks, now in ms. B.II.35.[28] He may well be the William whose name stands 35th in the list of Durham monks at the beginning of *HDE*, and 39th in *LV*. It has been claimed that this versatile penman worked 'indifferently' in the business of both bishop and priory, for his hand has been detected in genuine or purported grants by Scottish kings in favour of the latter.[29]

A final name is perhaps just worth mention: that of the monk-illustrator Robertus Benjamin, who has identified himself on f. 102 of Durham Cathedral ms. B.II.13, where a famous picture shows him kneeling at Bishop William's feet.[30] Conceivably one or other of these four talented monks may have had something to do with the genesis of the *libellus*. But it must be admitted that not a scrap of evidence has been found which points positively to any of them.

[Since HSO would have liked to give Symeon, the author of *HDE* or *Libellus de exordio* ..., 'more credit for the *Historia Regum* than as yet seems wholly safe',[31] it can be no accident that he made no mention of the possibility that Symeon played a part in the composition of DIV, but he might well have been persuaded to do so by recent work strongly suggesting that Symeon is to be identified with a Norman-trained scribe, very probably recruited by Bishop William during his exile, who became a monk of Durham shortly after the bishop's return and

26 See note 98 to DIV.

27 Printed by Thomas Rud, *Codd. mss. ecclesiae cathedralis Dunelmensis Catalogus* (Durham, 1825), 111; cf. Mynors, *DCM* no. 32, p. 35.

28 Mynors, *DCM* no. 47, p. 41. [For further examples of his work, see pp. 68–9 in M. Gullick, 'The scribe of the Carilef Bible: a new look at some late-eleventh-century Durham Cathedral manuscripts', in *Medieval Book Production: Assessing the Evidence*, ed. L. L. Brownrigg, (Los Altos Hills, 1990), pp. 61–83.]

29 Bishop & Chaplais, *ERW*, pl.viii(a) and note.

30 Mynors, *DCM* no. 31 and pl. 20.

31 Offler, *Medieval Historians*, 9.

remained active until at least 1128.[32] On a point of chronology, however, DIV and *HDE* are significantly at variance, see below note 117.]

Manuscripts and editions

Since 1951 no further manuscripts of DIV have come to light, though some of those then listed have been scrutinized more thoroughly for other purposes.[33] In chronological order they are:

F Oxford, Bodley, Fairfax 6.[34] This Durham book contains a wide range of hagiographical and historical material; it was put together shortly before 1375. DIV appears on ff. 207r-212r in its entirety as an independent treatise. It is prefixed to a version of the 'Gesta episcoporum Dunelmensium' down to 1334 in 184 chapters, comprising Symeon's *HDE* and his continuators followed by the chronicles of Geoffrey of Coldingham and 'Graystanes'.[35] DIV and the 'Gesta' are written in the same clear anglicana hand, 2 columns to the folio. The last seven lines of DIV have been written straight across the bottom margin of f. 212r by the text hand in a much reduced script. Since the preliminaries to the 'Gesta' begin on f. 212v, it looks as if some of this text was written before that of DIV and the space needed for the latter had been slightly miscalculated. While F presents DIV as a separate work, in the top margin of f. 207r the archaizing hand responsible for adding the title notes:[36] 'Haec quae sequuntur de Rege et episcopo interponenda sunt vt ordinem legas cap. 96 ad tale signum [*drawing of sign*]'. This sign does indeed appear in cap. 96 of the 'Gesta' on f. 242v, nearly at the end of Symeon's account of Bishop William, after the words 'in ecclesiam sancti Michaelis deportauerunt', with a note in the same pseudo-medieval hand as on f. 207r: 'Hic interlegendum est de iniusta vexacione Willelmi episcopi per Willelmum Regem filius Willelmi regis'.

Some ten misreadings or omissions in F's text of DIV have been corrected, presumably by reference to the exemplar, by a hand (F[2]) which is probably, though not certainly, distinct from F. There are also two or three small interventions by later hands (F[3]).

This manuscript was given the signature P in the 1395 catalogue of

---

32 M. Gullick, 'The scribes of the Durham cantor's book (DCL ms B.iv.24) and the Durham Martyrology scribe', in *Anglo-Norman Durham 1093—1193*, ed. D. Rollason, M. Harvey and M. Prestwich, (Woodbridge, 1994), 93‒109.

33 See Offler, 'Tractate', 323‒4.

34 Described in *Summary Cat.of Western MSS. in the Bodleian Library*, ii, pt. ii, no. 3886, pp. 773‒5.

35 Offler, *Medieval Historians of Durham*, Durham, 1958, 23, n. 39; repr. as I in *North of the Tees*.

36 See p. 13.

books in the cloister library at Durham.[37] The book entered immediately above it in this catalogue, signed O, had among its contents a 'Tractatus de Gestis Willielmi de Karilepho'.[38] O could hardly have been earlier than *c*. 1200, since it is reported to have contained Geoffrey's *Lives* of Godric and Bartholomew, written in the 1190s. Unfortunately it can no longer be found, so it cannot be verified whether F took its text of DIV from this source. Thus F remains the oldest surviving witness of DIV.

B Oxford, Bodley, Laud misc. 700. A Durham book, perhaps a couple of decades later than F, and commonly said to copy it, though that is not true of all B's contents.[39] After the Dissolution B was acquired by William Claxton of Wynyard, from whom it passed to John Richardson of Elvet (d. 1614), and then to Laud. B no longer shows DIV as an independent treatise; it has now been incorporated in the text of the 'Gesta episcoporum Dunelmensium' at ff. 66r-74v, precisely where the sixteenth-century note at F, f. 207r indicates it ought to stand. B's text of DIV is markedly inferior to that offered by F/F²; while the fifty variants it shows are mostly small, commonly they are for the worse. They seem due to carelessness in copying F; nothing suggests that B made reference to F's exemplar.

L London, Lincoln's Inn Library, Hale ms. 114. The relations between this version of Prior Wessington's historical compilation about the church of Durham with a draft of the same work, to be dated *c*. 1405– 15, now Bodley, Laud misc. 748, were investigated by Sir Edmund Craster in 1925.[40] He regarded ff. 1–133 of L as a fair copy of Laud misc. 748, perhaps made directly from it. But whereas the Laud ms. has copied out only an initial fragment of DIV and a few lines at the end (f. 33r: lines 36–66, 639–43 of the text), L, ff. 63r-75v gives the *libellus* complete, though adapting and abbreviating the biographical material enclosing it. Though there is clear evidence that Wessington drew on the contents of F when making his compilation,[41] L's text of the *libellus* exhibits a number of variants from F. Perhaps F was indeed L's source here, and these variants betoken no more than idiosyncratic liberties taken by the compiler for stylistic reasons. But possibly Wessington also consulted the exemplar on which F was based. L, f. 1r shows the hand of Thomas Swalwell, monk of Durham until his death in 1539 and monastic chancellor 1496–1500. The book was still at Durham late in the sixteenth century.

37 DCL ms. B.iv.46, f. 21v = *Catt.vett.*, p. 55.
38 *Catt.vett.*, 55, 81.
39 H. C. Coxe, *Catalogue of the Laudian mss.*, corrected reprint, Oxford, 1975, 580; cf. A. G. Watson (ed.), *Supplement* to N. R. Ker, *Medieval Libraries of Great Britain*, 2nd. edn. (London, 1987), 31, n. 3.
40 Craster, 'Red Book'; cf. R. B. Dobson, *Durham Priory 1400–1450* (Cambridge, 1973), 379–81.
41 Craster, 'Red Book', 518, n. 1.

C London, BL, Cotton ms. Claudius D.IV. This fine folio volume from the early fifteenth century containing Wessington's history was, Craster thought,[42] 'evidently written for the conventual library' at Durham. How Robert Cotton acquired it is not known. The book is later than L, compared with which it has been revised and expanded. But the text of DIV it presents on ff. 48r-54r (modern foliation) varies hardly at all from L's, to which it adds no authority.

H London, BL, Harley ms. 4843. A richly varied miscellany on paper of historical, hagiographical and devotional pieces mainly concerned with Durham, put together in the early sixteenth century by William Tode or Todd.[43] His hand is omnipresent in the collection; cf. f. 276v: Calamo Dompni Willelmi Tode pingitur iste libellus. He names himself also on ff. 67, 67v, 181v, 185v, 222v, 223v (initials only), 231v, 262 and 267, in the last two instances naming the year 1528, [and on f. 222v identifying himself as 'Monachus D'. There were two Durham monks of this name; one entered *c.* 1521 and his namesake some three years later. The older last occurs in November 1538.[44] It was almost certainly the younger who studied at Durham College Oxford for nine years, 1525-34 and] incepted as D.Th. Oxon. in 1538, going on to become the first prebendary of the fifth stall in the reformed cathedral at Durham.[45] Many items in this miscellany seem transcribed from F. H brings the text of DIV as a separate treatise on ff. 224r-31r. On the whole it is close to F, though agreeing on some dozen occasions with L and C against F, perhaps by reference to one or other of them, or even to a common exemplar other than F. H's repeated error, *Oxonia* for *Exonia* (lines 173, 436), is presumably a bit of academic jocosity.

D Durham, Bishop Cosin's Library ms. V.ii.6. This is the famous early manuscript of Symeon's *HDE*; its main text was written at the beginning of the twelfth century.[46] But after f. 87v, where gathering 13 ends, an extra quire of 10 folios was inserted in the second half of the sixteenth century. On this a version of DIV is written in a pseudo-medieval hand which may well be that of William Claxton of Wynyard, a Durham antiquary who died three years before 1600.[47] The intention

42 'Red Book', 513.

43 Described by B. Colgrave, *Two Lives of St Cuthbert* (Cambridge, 1940), 28–9; W. A. Pantin, 'Some medieval English treatises on the origins of monasticism', in *Medieval Studies presented to Rose Graham* (Oxford, 1950), 201–2.

44 [DCD, Bursar's Book L ff. 146v-147v, a list of monks serving chantries; they took turns in order of seniority in the community, making it possible to identify one of them as the older William Tode.]

45 A. B. Emden, *A Biographical Register of the University of Oxford A.D. 1501 to 1540* (Oxford, 1974), p. 570, [with the description of H misplaced under Todde, *alias* ? Smerthwaite, John, p. 569].

46 Mynors, *DCM* no. 88, pp. 60–1. Dr Doyle kindly allowed me to consult the detailed description he has prepared for his forthcoming catalogue of Cosin's mss.

47 [Doyle, 'Claxton', 344]

was to insert DIV into the text of *HDE* at the place where it occurs in B's version of the 'Gesta episcoporum Dunelmensium.' Accommodating the additional quire to the existing structure of the book caused problems. It was necessary to find space to complete DIV's text by erasing the first few lines of the original *HDE* text on the first page of the next gathering. Thus DIV now appears on ff. 88r-98r (line 9) of D; the major twelfth-century hand of *HDE* then immediately carries on that work until it ends on f. 98v. The lines in this hand erased from f. 98r are supplied at the head of f. 88r by the antiquary's hand. Interesting as all this is for the history of D as a book, its version of DIV contributes nothing to our knowledge of the text. It is a close copy of B (also known to have passed through Claxton's ownership), sharing B's errors and adding some of its own.

DIV was first published in 1732, as appendix i of Thomas Bedford's edition of *Symeonis Monachi Dunelmensis Libellus*, London, pp. 343-75. Starting with D, Bedford realised that it was corrupt and says that he frequently preferred F's readings, procured for him by a young Oxonian whose name he was not at liberty to disclose.[48] The hybrid text which resulted has the merit of indicating a number of variants. The nineteenth-century edition by Caley, Ellis and Bandinel of Dugdale's *Monasticon* i, London, 1817, repr. 1846, printed DIV from F alone, pp. 244-50; a translated abridgement from this appeared in M. M. Bigelow, *Placita Anglo-Normannorum*, Boston, 1881, appendix D, pp. 307-9. Thomas Arnold's edition of DIV in the *auctarium* to vol. i of his *Symeonis Monachi Opera Omnia*, RS 75 (1882), pp. 170-95 was again based on D and F only. Arnold owed a good deal to Bedford, but, unlike him, supplied almost no notice of variant readings. The whole treatise was translated by Joseph Stevenson, in *The Church Historians of England* iii, pt. ii, 1855, pp. 731-50, and again in D. C. Douglas and G. W. Greenaway (edd.), *English Historical Documents* ii, 1953, pp. 652-69; 2nd edn. 1981.

48 Preface, p. vii.

EDITORIAL NOTE

This edition is based on F as corrected by F². Whenever the text deviates from F, this is noted in the apparatus, which offers only an exemplary selection of variants from the other manuscripts. F's orthography, of course, follows fourteenth-century conventions: for instance, it invariably writes *e* on occasions when an eleventh- or twelfth-century version of the treatise would sometimes have shown the dipthong *ae* or an *e* with a cedilla. It has seemed sensible to tamper as little as possible with F's spellings, even though they do not remain wholly self-consistent; *c* and *t*, *cc* and *ct* have been retained indifferently, as they appear in F. One exception calls for mention. F's use of *u/v* is so disconcertingly haphazard as to incite intervention: the edition always renders the capital as *V* and the lower-case letter as *u*. In general it does not attempt to follow precisely F's lavish and indiscriminate spattering of capital and semi-capital letters.

F's punctuation has been handled rather more freely than its spelling. While F's grasp of the structure of sentences has been accepted, its frequent recourse to the *punctus elevatus* and median point has not been imitated. Moreover it has seemed desirable to remedy F's meagre articulation of the treatise as a whole, since throughout its length it exhibits no more than four clear paragraph marks or signs of division (at lines 32, 152, 185 and 223, all occuring on the first two folios). Following precedent, this edition breaks up the text into manageable sections as the logic of the narrative suggests.

Manuscripts collated. See pp. 100–01 below.

B   Oxford, Bodleian Library, Laud misc. 700
C   London, BL, Cotton Claudius D.IV
D   Durham, Bishop Cosin's Library, V.II.6
F   Oxford, Bodleian Library, Fairfax 6
F² Corrector of F
F³ Later hands in F
H   London, BL, Harley 4843
L   London, Lincoln's Inn, Hale 114

t   Consensus of BD
w   Consensus of CL

DE INIUSTA VEXACIONE WILLELMI
EPISCOPI PRIMI PER WILLELMUM
REGEM FILIUM WILLELMI MAGNI
REGIS

Anno[1] ab incarnacione domini millesimo octogesimo, interfecto a suis parrochianis Walchero episcopo,[2] post *sex mens*es *et decem die*s[3] ei successit in prelatum *Dunelmensis ecclesie Willelmus, electus quinto idus Nouembris,* *ordinat*us *a Thoma Eboracensi archiepiscopo die dominica tercio nonas Januarii* apud Glocestre,[4] *presente* Willelmo *rege, et tocius Anglie astantibus episcopis.* Ex *clero Baiocensis ecclesie in monaster*io *Sancti Karilephi monachico habitu suscepto, primo prior claustri, deinde maior prior,* postmodum abbas est effectus in monasterio Sancti Vincencii.[5] Postremo comperta *in rebus difficillimis* *eius industri*a, *rex* Willelmus eum *ad episcopatum* transtulit Dunelmensem. Erat namque acerrimus *ingeni*o, *subtili*s *consili*o, magne *eloquencie* simul et *sapiencie.* Et quia *in ecclesiastica gentis Anglorum historia* atque in *vita beati Cuthberti* legerat monachorum conuentum et ante patrem Cuthbertum et post multis annis in hac ecclesia deo de*seruisse,*[6] sed postmodum superuenientibus paganis cum omnibus pene ecclesiis et monasteriis deletum, antiquum eidem ecclesie sedulo meditabatur seruicium reparare. Iussu itaque regis Willelmi Romam adiit,[7] et domino pape Gregorio

5

10

15

---

1 Lines 3–28 are mostly quotation or paraphrase from Symeon, *HDE* 119–24, 127–8. But David, 'A tract', 385 erred in supposing that the author had no other source, since *HDE* does not give the place of St Calais's consecration nor the date of William II's. The latter could easily be found: cf. *ASC* 1086 [1087], 'Florence', ii, 20 and *HR* 214. Only *HR* 211 gives St Calais's consecration at Gloucester, though with the wrong date, 2 January.

2 Walcher was killed on 14 May 1080: Symeon, *HDE* 117.

3 sex menses et decem dies: i.e. $(6 \times 28) + 10 = 178$ days.

4 William was chosen bishop (*ab ipso rege electus*) on 9 November 1080, Symeon, *HDE* 119. For his consecration by Thomas of Bayeux, archbishop of York, assisted by suffragans of Canterbury, at the Council of Gloucester on 3 January 1081, see *C & S* I.ii, 629 and n. 2.

5 William's early career is discussed by Offler, 'William of St Calais, first Norman bishop of Durham', *Trans. Architect. & Archaeolog. Soc. Durham & Northumberland* 10 (1950), 260–5; reprinted as V, with unchanged pagination, in *North of the Tees*. He had become abbot of St Vincent-des-Prés at Le Mans by 1078.

6 St Calais's gift copy of Bede's *Historia ecclesiastica* to the priory is still at Durham: DCL ms. B.II.35, ff. 36–150; cf. Mynors, *DCM* no. 47, p. 41. A version of Bede's prose life of St Cuthbert written in Durham at this time is now in Oxford, Univ. Coll. ms. 165.

7 The date of the bishop's journey to Rome is uncertain, though it must have been between 1081 and early 1083. He witnesses with the king in Normandy on 5 September 1082, *RAN* i no. 146a, and in the same year at Downton in Wiltshire, *RAN* i no. 147.

qualiter antiquitus et qualiter nunc se Dunelmensis ecclesia habuerit,
20 ueraciter ostendit. Rediens cum precepto et auctoritate apostolica
monachicam circa corpus beati Cuthberti uitam restaurauit, quinto
kalendas Junii, *die sancto Pentecostes, tercio anno* sui *episcopatus* et septimo*decimo anno regni Willelmi.*[8] Quo defuncto, Willelmus filius eius sexto
kalendas Octobris in regem consecratur, a quo sicut et a patre magno
25 honori habebatur episcopus. Sed *orta inter* regem et primates Anglie
magna *dissensione*, episcopus ab inuidis circumuentus usque ad expul-
sionem iram regis pertulit. Quam rem sequens libellus manifestat ex
ordine.[9]

Rex Willelmus iunior dissaisiuit Dunelmensem episcopum de suis et
30 ecclesie sue terris quarto idus Marcii, et homines suos et omnes res
suas ubicumque potuit capi fecit.[10] Ipsum quoque episcopum capi
iussit et multas ei tetendit insidias. Quas dei nutu euadens episcopus
Dunelmumque ueniens, ipsa die qua Dunelmum intrauit legatum suum
cum huiusmodi litteris regi misit:[11] *Willelmo Anglorum Regi domino suo,*
35 *Willelmus Dunelmensis Episcopus salutem et fidele seruicium. Sciatis domine quod*
homines uestri de Eboraco et de Lincolnia homines meos in capcione detinent et
terras meas saisiuerunt et meipsum si possent capere uoluerunt,[12] *et per preceptum*
uestrum dicunt se fecisse hec omnia. Requiro autem uos inde sicut dominum meum

From May 1081 onwards Pope Gregory at Rome was under heavy pressure from hostile
imperialist forces.
  8 28 May 1083. This is indeed in the Conqueror's seventeenth regnal year, though
Symeon, *HDE* 122 says the eighteenth.
  9 sequens libellus: cf. *HR* 216–7: cujus ordinem causae libellus in hoc descriptus aperte
ostendit. Arnold's note is misconceived.
  10 The immediate effects of this royal proclamation of the bishop's disseisin on 12
March are difficult to estimate. Most vulnerable would have been his comparatively
small estates in Bedfordshire, Northamptonshire and Essex (*DB* i, 210b and 220; ii, 15b).
While his lands in Lincolnshire and Yorkshire were clearly affected, this seems much less
certain in respect of his possessions north of Tees; see below, lines 565–7, 609–10.
Assuming that the bishop had left the king's court just before the proclamation, he would
have been back in Durham by or shortly after the middle of March. These early dates
raise problems, as Freeman, *WR* i, 29 remarked. He concluded that there must have
been seditious movements in south-east England before the open revolt broke out after
Easter (16 April), as *ASC* 1087 [1088] and 'Florence', ii, 22 report; cf. Barlow, *WR* 75–7.
This is perhaps implied by the *libellus* itself, lines 487–91 below.
  11 If authentic, this letter is to be dated in late March or in April 1088. While noting
its somewhat insolent tone, Barlow, *WR* 83, regards it as 'written in impeccable chancery
style'.
  12 terras meas: before the Conquest the bishops of Durham held 7 manors totalling
81 carucates in the North Riding of Yorkshire: *DB* i, 304b. To them William I had added
two great areas in the East Riding: King Edward's manor of Howden and Morcar's of
Welton, *LV,* f. 50v. By 1086 Durham's Yorkshire lands amounted to more than 243
carucates, though much was uncultivated. For Durham's lands in Lincolnshire, see
Craster, 'Red Book', 529; C. W. Foster (ed.), *The Lincolnshire Domesday and the Lindsey Survey*
(Lincs. Rec. Soc. 19, 1924), 30–7.

ut homines meos et terras meas cum pecunia mea michi reddi faciatis sicut uestro homini et fideli, quem de nullo unquam forisfacto appellastis et qui uobis nunquam defendit iusticiam. Postea uero, si me de forisfacto aliquo appellaueritis, presto sum 40 *in curia uestra uobis iusticiam facere conuenienti termino, securitate ueniendi accepta. Precor autem uos diligenter ne per consilium inimicorum meorum me tam turpiter et inhoneste tractetis uel iniuste dissaisiatis. Non est enim omnium hominum episcopos iudicare, et ego uobis secundum ordinem meum omnem iusticiam offero. Et si ad presens uultis habere seruicium meum uel hominum meorum, illud idem secundum* 45 *placere uestrum uobis offero.* Rex uero, acceptis et auditis istis litteris episcopi, dedit baronibus suis terras episcopi uidente legato, quem sibi miserat episcopus. Remandauit autem episcopo ut ad eum tali condicione ueniret, quod si cum eo secundum uelle regis remanere nollet, liceret ei Dunelmum secure reuerti. Cumque episcopus auditis huiusmodi 50 responsis ad regem ire disponeret, premisit Eboracum ad uicecomitem querens ab eo pacem ad requirendum regem. Radulfus uero Paganellus, qui tunc erat uicecomes,[13] non solum episcopo sed et omnibus legatis et hominibus suis regem adire uolentibus pacem defendit. Ipsum quoque monachum episcopi, qui de rege redibat, accepit et equum suum ei 55 occidit, postea peditem abire permisit. Et super hec omnia precepit omnibus regis fidelibus de parte regis ut malum facerent episcopo ubicumque et quomodocumque possent.

Cumque episcopus per se uel per legatos suos regem non posset requirere et terras suas destrui et uastari absque ulla ulcione per septem 60 septimanas et amplius sustineret, tandem misit sibi rex abbatem Sancti Augustini mandans ei, ut sicut prius mandauerat, sibi ad curiam suam cum abbate ueniret.[14] Episcopus autem inimicorum suorum insidias cum regis ira metuens, sine bono conductu se non posse uenire respondit et legatos suos per abbatis conductum cum subscriptis litteris regi 65 misit:[15] *Domino suo Willelmo Anglorum Regi Willelmus Dunelmensis Episcopus salutem et fidele seruicium. Notum uobis est domine quod postquam ego de curia uestra ueni, statim legatum et litteras meas uobis misi, in quibus seruicium meum et omnium calumpniarum rectitudinem uobis ut regi meo et domino presentaui,*

13 Ralph Paynel: probably from the family which held Les Moutiers-Hubert (Calvados, arr. Lisieux, cant. Livart) and Hambaye (Manche, arr. Coutances, cant. Gavray): Loyd, *Origins*, 77. For his career in England, see C. T. Clay, *EYC* vi, 2–5, and 56–65 for the Paynel fee. Following William Farrer, *EHR* 30 (1915), 282–4, Clay accepted the evidence of the *libellus* that Ralph was sheriff of Yorkshire in 1088. But it should be noted that 'R. Painel' witnesses a charter of Duke Robert in Normandy during 1088: *RAN* i no. 299. If this was our Ralph, it was more likely to have been before than after the rebellion in England; cf. Barlow, *WR* 72.

14 For Guy (Wido), abbot of St Augustine's, Canterbury from 1087 to 1093, see *HRHEW* 36. St Calais witnesses royal writs in favour of Wido, 1087 × 1093: *RAN* i nos. 371,372. Wido appears as witness to a spurious charter of William I for Durham, *RAN* i no. *286, and to a spurious confirmation by Bishop William of a grant to the prior and convent of Durham, *RAN* i no. 318; cf. *DEC* no. *6 and pp. 48–53.

15 If this letter is authentic, its date can hardly be before early June.

70   *misericordiam quoque uestram requisiui ut homines meos et terras et pecuniam, que*
uicecomites uestri ubicumque poterant michi abstulerunt, scilicet [H]offedene et
Welletune,[16] *quas diuiserunt Odoni et Alano comitibus cum ceteris terris in*
Ewerwykscire sine racione aliqua de parte uestra michi facta,[17] *me semper offerente*
iusticiam, michi reddi faceretis sicut uestro homini et fideli, qui michi hoc fieri debere
75   *numquam forisfeceram sed fideliter seruieram uobis et seruire uolebam. Vobis uero*
uice illa non placuit mea michi reddere sicut ego requirebam et iustum michi
uidebatur, sed per breue uestrum pacem michi dedistis ad uos secure ueniendi et
uobiscum morandi et a uobis redeundi, et in eodem breui fidelibus uestris per totam
Angliam precepistis ut omnia mea in pace essent donec sciretis si uobiscum remanerem.
80   *Quod breue cum misissem Radulfo Paganello, non solum michi pacem negauit, sed*
eciam de parte uestra me diffidauit et in crastinum terras ecclesie nostre rapina
inuasit, predam distribuit, hominum uero quosdam uendidit, quosdam redimi permisit.
Monachum autem portantem breue pacis uestre homines Paganelli in capcione
miserunt et equum suum ei occiderunt. Super hec omnia dictum est michi uos dedisse
85   *partem terrarum mearum,*[18] *et cum ad uos pro hiis omnibus mittere uellem, defendit*
Paganellus legatis meis transitum per terram uestram. Nunc uero uestri gracia per
abbatem Sancti Augustini et litteras uestras michi mandatis ut ad uos secure uenirem.
Ego autem precor uos et requiro sicut regem et dominum ut mea michi reddatis, que
sine racione et iudicio michi abstulistis, et ego libenter ueniam in curiam uestram et
90   *secundum ordinem meum quicquid iuste iudicabitur uobis faciam. Si hoc apud uos*
impetrare ualeo, deo uobisque gracias inde referam. Si uero nec modo mea michi
reddere uobis placuerit, paratus sum tamen uenire in curiam uestram per talem
conductum, qui me saluum conducat usque ad uos saluumque reducat usque ad
ecclesiam meam, et uidentibus cunctis baronibus uestris me defendam quod de
95   *dampno corporis uestri uel terrarum uestrarum uel honoris uestri nulli fiduciam uel*
sacramentum feci uel ab aliquo recepi nec consilium uestrum alicui ad dampnum
uestrum me sciente detexi nec dampnum uestrum ut audiui quod uobis nocuum esset

16 For Howden and Welton, see note 12.

17 Odo (Eudes III, nephew of Thibaud I, count of Blois-Champagne), disinherited count of Champagne, was the third husband of Adelaide, sister or half-sister of William the Conqueror, and father of Stephen of Aumale; on him, see Orderic, ii, 264, n. 3 and iv, 182, n. 2; Barbara English, *The Lords of Holderness 1086–1260* (Oxford, 1979), 9–13; M. Bur, 'Les comtes de Champagne et la "Normanitas"', *Battle* 3 (1980), 29. Odo appears to have acquired his lordship of Holderness in Yorks ER in 1086/7: GEC i, 351– 2; *EYC* iii, p. 26. His only appearances in *RAN* I are as witness to royal charters issued overseas, nos. 30, 323. Complicity in Robert Mowbray's conspiracy in 1095 cost him his lands in Holderness, which were granted to Arnulf of Montgomery: Mason, 'Roger of Montgomery', 17.

The Breton count Alan Rufus, lord of Richmond and founder of St Mary's, York, was in the first flight of great post-Conquest landowners: J. F. A. Mason, 'The "Honour of Richmond" in 1086', *EHR* 76 (1963), 703–4. After the imprisonment of Morcar in 1071 William I had granted the western half of the North Riding to count Alan, who must be esteemed 'the greatest man in the north of England': Southern, *Anselm* (1963), 184.

18 partem terrarum mearum: thus the *libellus* does not make bishop William claim to have been disseized of all his lands.

celaui, sed quam cicius potui uobis uerbo uel legato uel litteris notificaui, usque ad eam diem qua nouissime de curia uestra ueni. Et hoc in ueritate uobis mando quod libenter cum hoc abbate uenissem, nisi plus inimicos meos et indoctam populi 100 *multitudinem timuissem quam de uestro breui et baronum uestrorum fiducia dubitassem. Precor igitur uos ut talem michi conductum mittatis, qui cum honore uestro et salute mea me ducat et reducat. Firmiter enim credo uerbo uestro quod per uoluntatem uestram nemo michi contumeliam inferret, sed si contra uoluntatem uestram michi fieret, parum com[m]odi sequens ulcio michi daret. Quod si dissaisitus* 105 *ad uos uenero, nullum aliud placitum preter purgacionis mee defensionem hac uice subintrabo.*[19]

Rex uero uisis hiis litteris misit conductum episcopo et bene affidauit eum per litteras suas quod per eum uel per suos homines nullum illi dampnum eueniret usquequo de rege rediens Dunelmum intraret. 110 Perrexit ergo episcopus ad regem et deprecatus est eum ut rectitudinem sibi consenciret sicut episcopo suo.[20] Rex autem respondit ei quod si laicaliter placitare uellet et extra pacem quam rex ei dederat se mitteret, hoc modo rectitudinem sibi consenciret, et si hoc modo placitare recusaret, Dunelmum faceret eum reconduci. Episcopus uero requisiuit 115 archiepiscopum Eboracensem[21] et episcopos qui aderant ut inde sibi consulerent. Ipsi autem responderunt regem sibi prohibuisse ne ei consulerent. Tunc episcopus archiepiscopum suum per debitum, quod ecclesie sue sibique debebat, summonuit ut sibi consuleret, cumque archiepiscopus regem inde requisisset, remandauit episcopo se non 120 posse consilium sibi dare. Precatus est ergo regem episcopus ut consilium archiepiscopi et primatis sui[22] et comparium suorum episcoporum sibi consenciret. Et hoc totum sibi rex deffendit. Tunc episcopus purgacionem sceleris et periurii regi optulit. Quam cum rex suscipere

19 Quod si dissaisitus: foreshadowing the appeal to the principle *spoliatus ante omnia restituendus* on which according to the *libellus* St Calais consistently based his resistance to a feudal judgement against him in 1088: Nam nec convocari ad causam nec diiudicari potest expoliatus vel expulsus, quia non est privilegium, quo expoliari possit iam nudatus (Pseudo-Isidore, Eusebius, *Decret. c. xii,* ed. Hinschius, 237; cf. *Actio quintae Synodi sub Simacho,* Hinschius, 676; Sixtus I, *Decret. c. vi,* Hinschius, 109; Sixtus II, *Decret. c. vi,* Hinschius, 192; Julius, *Decret. c. xii,* Hinschius, 468). On the extracts from Pseudo-Isidore concerning the *exceptio spolii* in Lanfranc's collection of canon law, see F. Joüon des Longrais, 'Les réformes d'Henry II en matière de saisine', *Rev. hist. de droit français et étranger,* 4th ser., 15 (1936), 548. Though William will not submit to trial before his possessions are restored, he offers to clear himself of guilt in the king's court by canonical purgation.

20 There is no other evidence for this meeting between Rufus and St Calais. If it took place, it was presumably in south-east England at some time during the summer, since from mid-April until early July Rufus was preoccupied in besieging Tonbridge, Pevensey and Rochester. Barlow, *WR* 83, n. 150 does not specify the 'several reasons' for supposing a date after the fall of Rochester in July.

21 Thomas of Bayeux, archbishop of York 1070–1100.

22 Lanfranc, archbishop of Canterbury and primate 1070–1089.

125 noluisset, Dunelmum rediit episcopus,[23] cui rex interim plus quam septingentos homines cum multa preda abstulerat. Misit autem episcopus iterum ad regem quemdam suum monachum cum subnotatis litteris:

Domino suo Willelmo Regi Anglorum Willelmus Dunelmensis Episcopus salutem
130 *et, si placet, fidele seruicium. Notum est uobis karissime domine quod ego sepius per litteras meas et legatos plures misericordiam uestram requisiui, offerens diligentissime de infidelitate et periurio me purgaturum in curia uestra recto iudicio mei ordinis. Quod quia sic impetrare non potui, idem requirens ad uos ueni, sed inimicorum meorum preualente consilio, parum michi profuit. Et quoniam dileccionem uestram*
135 *quam iniuste amisi recuperare cupio, mando uobis ut domino et regi meo quatenus intra securitatem pacis uestre rectitudinem de me ut de homine et episcopo uestro secundum rectum mei ordinis iudicium recipiatis. Et si adhuc in sentencia illa ut me purgare debeam laico more perseueratis,[24] de hoc prius paratus sum recto iudicio iudicari, ea quidem condicione ut si quis me iniusto iudicio opprimere uoluerit,*
140 *securitate predicte pacis conseruata, liceat michi contradicere secundum recta iudicia mei ordinis in eo loco ubi canonice iudicatum fuerit, et quicquid ibi recte iudicabitur ex toto profiteor me sequi, siue carcerali pena cruciari seu honoris dignitate priuari uel, quod concedat deus, ut iustum est dileccionis uestre solacio refoueri. Vnde conuenientem fiduciam presto sum dare uobis. Si uero hoc michi denegatis et ita*
145 *immutabiliter disposuistis quod nullam rectitudinem michi consentire uelitis, saltem in curia uestra liceat me purgare recto iudicio de calumpnia periurii et infidelitatis.[25] Nullam enim habeo uoluntatem tenere terram de uobis contra uoluntatem uestram. Talis enim dominus dedit michi terram quam habeo,[26] qui me eam et honorifice tenere permittebat et multa michi daturum promittebat.* Rex uero uisis litteris
150 monachum qui eas portauerat capi et custodiri fecit et exercitum suum misit super episcopum.[27] Et cum exercitus ille incendio et rapina terram

23 If Bishop William had returned to Durham during June, the letter which follows would have to be dated soon after that. But on Barlow's reckoning (note 20) it cannot be dated before July.

24 I take the sense of this convoluted passage (lines 138–42) to be: If Rufus insists that the bishop shall clear himself in lay fashion (i.e. from a charge of treason in the curia regis), the bishop is prepared to submit to a preliminary lawful finding (i.e. by ecclesiastics) on this issue, provided that, if he considers this ecclesiastical judgement unjust, he may, while remaining within the protection of the king's peace, appeal against it, as canon law demands, in that place where a canonical judgement is to be had (that is, at the papal curia; cf. lines 163–4 below). In effect, with subtlety and impudence the bishop offers to toss a coin with Rufus on the terms: 'Heads you lose, tails I win'. The *ubi canonice iudicatum fuerit* in line 142 should be compared with Anselm at Rockingham: me paratum inveniet ei sicut debeo, et ubi debeo, respondere, Eadmer, *HN* 61.

25 The bishop renews his offer to clear himself in the curia regis by canonical purgation (*recto iudicio*); cf. lines 107–08, 131–5.

26 Talis enim dominus: that intended further generosity by William the Conqueror towards Durham was frustrated by his death is suggested by Symeon, *HDE* 124.

27 exercitum suum misit: presumably after Rufus had overcome his troubles in southern England by mid-July. A date in August or early September seems indicated; see below, lines 156, 245–6, 649–50.

uastasset episcopi, locuti sunt barones cum episcopo et subscriptam
conuencionem per fidem suam firmauerunt:

Comes Alanus et Rogerus Pictauensis et comes Odo[28] dederunt fidem
suam Dunelmensi episcopo in natiuitate Sancte Marie quod eum sanum   155
et saluum ad curiam regis cum suis omnibus ea condicione conducerent
quod si rex ei nollet consentire rectitudinem secundum legem episcopi
per tales iudices, qui episcopum iuste iudicare deberent, tunc predicti
comites episcopum cum suis omnibus Dunelmum reducerent absque
mora, que contra uoluntatem episcopi fieret.[29] Si uero tale iudicium   160

28 For Count Alan and Count Odo see note 17. On Roger le Poitevin, third son of
Roger of Montgomery, earl of Shrewsbury, cf. Mason, 'Roger of Montgomery', 1–28;
Victoria Chandler, 'The last of the Montgomerys: Roger le Poitevin and Arnulf', *Historical
Research* 62 (1989), 1–14. By 1086 Roger le Poitevin had forfeited his lands in England, as
V. H. Galbraith, *The Making of Domesday Book* (Oxford, 1961), pp. 187–8, pointed out. It
is uncertain whether he was restored by the Conqueror, or by Rufus before 1088,
surviving his family's participation in the revolt against the king, or by Rufus immediately
after and despite the revolt: Mason, 16. Whether he was one of the two unnamed sons
of Earl Roger who according to *ASC* 1087 [1088] aided their eldest brother Robert of
Bellême against Rufus at the siege of Rochester is perhaps uncertain; it has been denied:
Mason, 'Roger of Montgomery', 16; C. P. Lewis, 'The King and Eye: a study in Anglo—
Norman politics', *EHR* 104 (1989), 572, 575–6. If he did dabble in rebellion in 1088, he
can hardly have been reconciled with Rufus before the surrender of Rochester, which is
probably to be dated in early July; cf. Dr Chibnall's note 1 to Orderic, iv, 134. About
Roger le Poitevin's title the *libellus* is inconsistent. Though Barlow, *EC*, 283 refers to
'three earls making the pact of 8 September', in fact the *libellus* here avoids calling Roger
comes. This seems correct, for Roger acquired the title of count only in 1091, on the death
of his wife's brother, Boso III, count of La Marche: Mason, 17; Chandler, 3. It is simply
as Roger le Poitevin that the *libellus* has him as a party to the pact of 8 September and
accepting the bishop's counter-assurances (line 181). Later on the *libellus* becomes confused
and perhaps anachronistic about Roger's title. Like his fellow guarantor, Count Alan, he
is called *comes* at line 268, and like Count Odo at line 443. While the *Rogerus comes* at
lines 282–3 may possibly be his father, the earl of Shrewsbury (as Mason, 16, n. 4), it
seems more likely that Roger le Poitevin was intended (cf. Barlow, *WR* 85, n. 160). At
lines 420 and 622 Roger seems to be included among the *comites* responsible for the pact
on 8 September. Lines 637–8 refer to the guarantors explicitly as *comites Alanum et Rogerum
et Odonem*, and here Roger le Poitevin must surely be intended. From these contradictory
instances it might be argued: (a) that the *libellus* must have been written at a date after
Roger acquired the title of count in 1091; or (b) that the author of the *libellus* was not
particularly well-informed about Roger's status and title in 1088; or (c) that to an author
in 1088/9 Roger's extensive holdings in England seemed to justify ranking him as a
count though he had not yet achieved that status officially. None of these inferences
carries complete conviction; the least likely seems the last.

29 These are extraordinarily favourable terms (lines 156–80) to have been granted to
a suspect and defeated traitor. Bishop William is indeed to appear before the curia regis.
But (a) he is to be allowed trial by churchmen, or be escorted safely back to Durham;
(b) if the judgement given in such a trial is considered by the bishop to be unjust, and
either the king or the (ecclesiastical) judges hinder his appeal to the pope, then the bishop
is to be returned to his castle at Durham; (c) if the bishop is unwilling or unable to
accept the judgement, he is to have a safe-conduct overseas with men and goods. The
date of this agreement was 8 September.

episcopo diceretur quod sibi uideretur iniustum et ipse contradiceret, et in rege uel in iudicibusad confirmandum iudicium illuc ire remaneret ubi contenciosa pontificum iudicia iuste debent terminari,[30] sicut supradictum est, ad castellum suum reduceretur episcopus. Et si rex
165   rectitudinem, que iuste contradici non posset episcopo consentiret, et nulla inde contradictio nasceretur, uel si nasceretur in rege uel in iudicibus non remaneret quin ibi iudicium suum confirmarent ubi huiusmodi iudicia iuste debent confirmari uel destrui, et episcopus rectitudinem illam intrare uel facere uel nollet uel non posset: tunc rex
170   inueniret episcopo sine aliqua detencione uel mora portum et naues quantum necesse esset sibi et suis omnibus, qui eum sequi uellent, ubi ipse eligeret ab Exonia usque ad Sanguichium, et securitatem et conductum regis episcopus et sui haberent donec ultra mare ad terram siccam cum rebus suis essent, et liceret eis per conductum regis secum
175   ducere et portare aurum et argentum, equos et pannos et arma et canes et accipitres et sua prorsus omnia, que de terra portari debent. Et quod nulla alia conuencia uel fiducia ab episcopo uel a suis ui uel ingenio exigeretur, uel aliud facere cogerentur quam ibidem episcopus et sui homines Rogero Pictauensi promiserunt.
180   Episcopus dedit fidem suam Rogero Pictauensi quod si ipse per prescriptam condicionem ad castellum reduceretur, et maior fortitudo in castello missa uel facta esset in hominibus uel in municione uel in castelli fortitudine quam eadem die ibi erat, episcopus totum illud destrui faceret, ita quod episcopus inde nullum proficuum haberet nec
185   rex dampnum. Et postquam episcopus intraret uiam ueniendi ad curiam non quereret uel reciperet dampnum regis, de quo male eum tractaret se sciente, usque ad festum Sancti Michaelis.[31] Preterea iurauerunt septem[32] ex precepto episcopi Rogero Pictauensi uice regis hoc suscipienti quod si episcopus rectam rectitudinem ut supradictum est
190   recusaret et transfretare eligeret, ipsi castellum Dunelmi regi redderent. Promisit autem episcopus fidem suam Rogero Pictauensi de parte sua convencionem istam se regi seruaturum quamdiu comitum conuencio sibi attenderetur, sine omni malo ingenio, excepto ingenio placiti quod facturus erat contra regem.
195   Comites uero promiserunt episcopo fidem suam regem sibi seru-

30 ubi contenciosa pontificum iudicia juste debent terminari: a reference to the papal curia, as in line 142. See Pope Gregory VII, *Reg.* viii. 21, ed. E. Caspar, MGH *Epp. sel.* ii,549: omnes maiores res et precipua negotia necnon omnium ecclesiarum iudicia ad eam [Romanam ecclesiam] quasi ad matrem et caput debere referri, ab ea nusquam appellari, iudicia eius a nemine retractari aut refelli debere vel posse. Cf. *Reg.* ii.55a (*Dictatus pape*), nos. 21 and 18, p. 206.

31 29 September 1088.

32 septem: presumably seven of the bishop's major tenants, men of the kind later to be known as 'barons of the bishopric'. Are they the same as the seven knights referred to in lines 286 and 347–8?

aturum conuencionem istam et quod incepcio placiti non differetur
ultra proximum festum Sancti Michaelis, nisi per consensum episcopi
uel per tales terminos, quales legales iudices dictis causis inter regem
et episcopum iuste poni debere decernerent, et si aliquem hominum
uel equorum episcopi contingeret egrotare, ipsi et eorum custodes   200
pacem regis haberent quamdiu eos infirmitas detineret, et postea ut alii
homines episcopi per conductum regis post episcopum ducerentur. Qui
uero uellent per consensum episcopi remanere et fidelitatem regi
facere, cum suis omnibus pacifice remanerent. Quod si rex prescriptam
conuencionem aliquo modo frangeret, in comitibus uel in suorum   205
quolibet per eorum uoluntatem uel consensum nullus ulterius proficuum
haberet donec episcopus sine ui uel ingenio eos inde gratanter abso-
lueret.

Accepta igitur fide ista, respectatum est utrimque placitum usque in
quarto nonas Nouembris.[33] Ea uero die uenit episcopus Salisbiriam.[34]   210
Quem cum Vrso de Habetot unus ex seruientibus regis ad regem
intrare moneret,[35] premisit episcopus legatos suos ad regem et deprecatus
est eum ut liceret ei loqui cum quibusdam fratrum suorum episcoporum
qui aderant. Nemo enim illorum ut aiebant audebat eum osculari uel
alloqui,[36] quod episcopus iam de ipso metropolitano suo expertus erat.   215
Cumque rex hoc facturum se negasset nec eorum ullus hanc fraternitatis
uicem et legis sancte preceptum ei exhiberet, ingressus tandem episcopus
requisiuit ab archiepiscopis utrum reuestitus ingredi deberet dixitque
nichil se prorsus acturum ibi nisi canonice et secundum ordinem suum,
et sibi uidebatur quod ecclesiastica consuetudo exigebat ut ipse reuestitus   220
ante reuestitos causam suam diceret et causantibus canonice responderet. Cui Lanfrancus archiepiscopus respondens: 'Bene possumus'
inquid 'hoc modo uestiti de regalibus tuisque negociis disceptare. Vestes
enim non impediunt ueritatem.'

Episcopus ergo surgens precatus est regem ut episcopatum suum,   225
quem iamdiu sibi sine iudicio abstulerat, sibi redderet. Lamfrancus
uero rege tacente dixit: 'Rex de episcopatu tuo nichil tibi abstulit uel
aliquis per eum, neque breue suum uidisti, per quod te de episcopatu
tuo dissaisiret uel dissaisiri preciperet.' Et episcopus: 'Vidi' inquid

---

33 2 November 1088.

34 The court was probably held in the castle (or just possibly the cathedral) at Old
Salisbury: Barlow, *EC* 283, *WR* 85.

35 Urse, royal constable, sheriff of Worcester, despoiler of monks, active administrator
and judge on Rufus's behalf, came from Abbetot, Seine-Maritime, arr. Le Havre, cant.
Saint Romain. Loyd, *Origins* 1–2; see J. H. Round, *DNB* xx, 52; Emma Mason, 'Magnates,
Curiales and the Wheel of Fortune', *Battle* 2 (1979), 135–8; Barlow, *WR* 152, 185–9, 207–
11. He appears as witness to many royal charters, including two *spuria* for Durham, *RAN*
i nos. *281, 349.

36 See I Cor. 16,20. According to Eadmer, *HN* 63 Rufus asked the bishops at
Rockingham in 1095: nonne saltem ... fraternae societatis amicitiam ei abnegare potestis?

230 'Rogerum Paganellum,[37] quem hic uideo, qui ex precepto regis me
dissaisiuit de toto episcopatu meo, quem habeo in Eboracensi comitatu.
Cumque ego per litteras et legatos meos regem inde requisissem
deprecans ut res meas michi redderet, et si de qualibet causa me
calumpniari uellet, de me sicut de ipso suo episcopo plenam recti-
235 tudinem reciperet, rex michi nichil reddidit, sed baronibus suis terras
ecclesie prout sibi placuit distribuit. Postea uero,[38] cum per memetipsum
in curia sua regi plenam rectitudinem obtulissem et ipse eam penitus
michi denegasset, non solum quod prius abstulerat detinuit, sed quicquid
michi supererat auferri precepit misitque baronibus suis ad partes
240 nostras litteras sigillatas coniurans eos et precipiens ut quicquid mali
possent michi facerent. Et cum nec ista sibi sufficerent, misit comites
et barones cum exercitu suo et per eos totum episcopatum meum
uastauit, terras quoque et homines et pecuniam Sancti Cuthberti et
meam michi abstulit. Nostram eciam sedem me ad tempus abiurare
245 coegit.[39] Ipsi eciam casati ecclesie,[40] qui mei homines ligii fuerant et
quicquid habebant de casamento ecclesie tenebant, ex precepto regis
guerram michi fecerunt, et terras suas de rege tenentes pacifice, hic eos
cum rege uideo aduersum me conuenisse.'
   Lanfrancus autem dixit: 'Rex te inuitat ut rectitudinem sibi facias et
250 barones sui ad hoc te adduxerunt ut rectitudinem sibi faceres, et tu
requiris ut ipse tibi prior rectitudinem faciat. Fac sibi prius rectitudinem,
et postea require ab eo hoc quod modo requiris.' Cui respondens
episcopus ait: 'Domine archiepiscope, hoc quod modo dicitis, dicitis
pro consilio uel pro iudicio?' 'Certe' inquid 'non dico pro iudicio, sed
255 si rex michi crediderit, satis cito faciet inde iudicium fieri.' Tunc laici
huiusmodi uerbis Lanfranci tocius Anglie primatis[41] animati aduersus
episcopum exclamantes dixerunt iniustum esse quod rex episcopo
responderet, antequam regi fecisset iusticiam. Laicis uero hec et alia
multa declamantibus et iterantibus, facto silencio dixit episcopus:
260 'Domini barones et laici, permittite me queso que dicturus sum regi

37 Surely Ralph, not Roger, Paynel must be meant.
38 Presumably when they met in the summer; see note 20.
39 For the royal expedition against Bishop William, see lines 151–2. He was forced to
quit Durham on 11 September: lines 609–10, 649. The words *ad tempus* may suggest that
he returned there later. But the *libellus* throws no clear light on the bishop's movements
between 11 September and his appearance at Salisbury in November.
40 casati: tenants of the episcopal demesne seem intended.
41 tocius Anglie primatis: though s.a. 1066 'Florence' describes Stigand thus, i, 228,
this is not the title favoured by Canterbury under Lanfranc. Its archbishop was usually
(and programmatically) called *tocius Britannie primas*. For examples, see Eadmer, *HN* 12,
63 *The Letters of Lanfranc Archbishop of Canterbury*, ed. and trs. Helen Clover and Margaret
Gibson, (Oxford, 1979), pp. 3–4, 46, 72–4, 78, 152. This was the form normally used by
bishops in their professions to Canterbury, where the title *tocius Anglie primas* does not
appear until 1177/1180 (there are later examples of *tocius Britannie*): M. Richter (ed.),
Canterbury Professions (Canterbury and York Soc. 67, 1975), nos. 113–4.

dicere et archiepiscopis et episcopis respondere, quia nichil uobis habeo dicere, et sicut huc non ueni iudicium uestrum recepturus, ita illud omnino recuso, et si domino nostro regi et archiepiscopis et episcopis placuisset uos huic negocio interesse, nec me taliter obloqui decuisset.'

Tunc rex ait: 'Sperabam quod episcopus prius michi respondere   265
deberet de hiis, de quibus eum accusarem, et multum miror quod ipse aliud requirit.' Comes uero Alanus et comes Rogerus dixerunt:[42] 'Ad hoc adduximus episcopum ut ipse regi rectitudinem faciat.' 'Presto sum' inquid episcopus 'si michi canonice iudicatur, despoliatus respondere.[43] Nullo enim modo ordinis mei legem in hoc placito transgrediar.' Tunc   270
Rogerus Bigotus dixit regi:[44] 'Vos debetis episcopo dicere unde eum appellare uultis et postea, si ipse uobis uoluerit respondere, de responsione sua facite eum iudicari. Sin autem, facite inde quod barones uestri uobis consulerint.' Ad hec episcopus: 'Iam dixi et iterum dicam quod laicale iudicium et quicquid est contra canones prorsus respuo nec   275
aliquam accusacionem recipio, nisi prius de episcopatu meo inuestiar uel canonice michi iudicetur quod ante inuestituram debeam accusari et respondere et iudicari.'

Tunc Hugo de Bellomonte ex precepto regis surgens dixit episcopo:[45]

42 comes Rogerus: in this context Roger le Poitevin must surely be intended.

43 The bishop will plead before the king while still *despoliatus* only after an ecclesiastical judgement that he must.

44 Rogerus Bigotus: on him see GEC ix,575–9; Barlow, *WR* 61–2. The greatest lay tenant in south and east Norfolk, he acted as sheriff in that county and also in Suffolk. Though he witnessed royal charters at the beginning of Rufus's reign, *RAN* i nos. 290, 291, 295, 296, he appears to have taken some part in the feudal disorders in 1088: *ASC* 1087 [1088]; Malmesbury, *GR* ii,361; *HR* ii, 215. Possibly he was influenced by the example of Odo of Bayeux, whose tenant he was in England and Normandy: D. R. Bates, 'The character and career of Odo, bishop of Bayeux (1049/50–1097) ', *Speculum* 50 (1975), 11. But the extent of his involvement is difficult to estimate, Barlow, *WR* 81, n. 141, and soon after the capture of Rochester he must have made his peace with the king, for he witnesses *RAN* i no. 302. By 1091 he appears as royal steward, *RAN* i, p. xxiv, and in that year his name occurs as witness to a spurious Durham charter: *RAN* i no. 318; cf. *DEC* no. *6, pp. 48–53.

45 Hugo de Bellomonte: the problem of identifying a Hugh Beaumont at this date has baffled scholars from Freeman onwards, *WR* i,98, n. 2. For a Beaumont of this name we have to await Hugo *pauper*, third son of Robert of Meulan, for whom King Stephen may have tried to create an earldom of Bedford in 1138, and this Hugh was born after 1104: GEC vii,526, n. 2. The *libellus* repeats the name in full, lines 313, 383–4; the given name only, lines 291, 391. Barlow, *EC* 284 and *WR* 75, 77 n. 111, attempts to get round the difficulty by supposing error in the textual transmission of the *libellus*; he feels entitled to convert on five occasions Hugo into Henricus: i.e. Henry, the brother of Robert of Meulan, who does indeed attest twice for Rufus during 1088: *RAN* i nos. 302, 325. But would not Henry de Beaumont have been styled earl of Warwick by November 1088? It seems generally accepted that his promotion to earl occurred before the end of 1088; cf. G. H. White in GEC xii.2 app. A, pp. 2–3; David Crouch, *The Beaumont Twins* (Cambridge, 1986), 10; though Barlow, *WR* 93 says 'probably' in 1089. Some opinion inclines to a date in or shortly after July 1088: cf. Sally N. Vaughn, *Anselm of Bec and Robert of Meulan* (Berkeley and Los Angeles, 1987), 99; D. C. Douglas, *EHD* ii, 616 n. 1. Repeated scribal

280 'Rex te appellat quod cum ipse audiuit quod inimici sui super eum
ueniebant,[46] et homines sui, episcopus scilicet Baiocensis et Rogerus
comes et alii plures,[47] regnum suum pariter sibi et coronam auferre
uolebant, et ipse per consilium tuum contra illos equitabat, ipse te, me
audiente, summonuit ut cum eo equitares. Tu uero respondisti ei te
285 cum septem militibus[48] quos ibi habebas libenter iturum et pro pluribus
ad castellum tuum sub festinacione missurum, et postea fugisti de curia
sua sine eius licencia et quosdam de familia sua tecum abduxisti, et ita
in necessitate sua sibi defecisti. Et modo uult ut inde sibi facias quod
curia sua iudicabit, et si necesse fuerit, postea te de pluribus appellabit.'
290 Episcopus autem Hugoni respondit: 'Hugo dicas licet quicquid uolueris.
Non tibi tamen hodie respondebo nec accusacionem aliquam recipiam
uel placitum aliquod ingrediar, usquequo iuste iudicetur quod dispoliatus debeam placitare uel canonice de episcopatu meo inuestiar. Et
postea de quibuscumque rex me appellauerit, uoluntarie respondebo et
295 quicquid feci legaliter me fecisse monstrabo faciamque dictante iusticia
quod in nullo prorsus reus inueniar.'

Cumque multum tumultuantes laici, quidam racionibus, quidam
uero contumeliis aduersus episcopum decertarent et ipse eis nullo
modo respondere uellet, G. Constanciensis episcopus ait:[49] 'Domini
300 archiepiscopi, nos non oporteret diucius hec ita considerare, sed deceret
uos surgere et episcopos et abbates conuocare, quosdam eciam comitum
et baronum istorum uobiscum habere, et cum eis iuste decernere si

---

error, as postulated by Barlow, seems to me a less likely explanation of the difficulty than
sheer confusion on the part of the author of the *libellus*. May he not have written (and
continued to write) Hugo *de Bellomonte* by mistake for Hugo *de Bellocampo*? Hugh
Beauchamp (of Bedford), Domesday tenant in Bedfordshire, Hertfordshire and Buck-
inghamshire (in which county he was sheriff), is a wholly plausible participant at the
Salisbury curia; he witnesses Rufus's charters *RAN* i nos. 419, 446 (with Ralph Paynel),
477 (again with Ralph).

46 If the *libellus* be accepted as a faithful witness, it implies (lines 282–9) this chronology:
At the beginning of March or earlier Bishop William had advised Rufus to attack his
enemies, Odo of Bayeux and Roger Montgomery, earl of Shrewsbury. When summoned
to accompany the king, the bishop had agreed to do so with the seven knights he had
with him and to send to Durham for more. But then St Calais fled from the royal court
without leave, taking with him certain men of the royal household. All this must have
happened before the proclamation of disseisin on 12 March; cf. line 30 and note 10.

47 For the parts played in the conspiracy against Rufus by Bishop Odo and Roger
Montgomery, see *ASC* 1087 [1088]; 'Florence', ii,21–2; Orderic, iv,121–34; Malmesbury,
GR ii,360–1. Bates, 'Character and career' (as in note 44), 4, decries Orderic's account as
'garbled and uninformed'.

48 septem militibus: were these the same as those mentioned in lines 189 and 347–8?

49 For Bishop Geoffrey, see J. Le Patourel, 'Geoffrey de Montbray, Bishop of
Coutances, 1049–1093', *EHR* 59 (1944), 133–58. If Geoffrey's intervention amounted to
support of Bishop William's plea for clerical privilege, as Le Patourel claims, p. 154, it
was hardly forceful. Geoffrey himself had been involved in the revolt: *ASC* 1087 [1088];
'Florence', ii, 24.

episcopus debeat prius inuestiri uel ante inuestituram de querelis regis intrare in placitum.' Ad hec Lanfrancus archiepiscopus: 'Non est necesse' inquit 'nos surgere, sed episcopus et homines sui egrediantur, et nos remanentes tam clerici quam layci consideremus equaliter quid inde iuste facere debeamus.' 'Ego' inquid episcopus 'libenter egrediar, sed bene uobis dico archiepiscopi et episcopi ut quicquid in mea causa feceritis, ordinabiliter et canonice faciatis nec eos in uestro iudicio habeatis, quos ab episcoporum iudiciis decreta sequestrant et canones.'[50] 'Vade' inquit Lanfrancus archiepiscopus 'nos enim iuste faciemus quicquid fecerimus.' Hugo de Bellomonte dixit episcopo: 'Si ego hodie te et tuum ordinem iudicare non potero, tu uel tuus ordo numquam me amplius iudicabitis.' 'Videant' inquid episcopus 'qui in domo ista remanent et me iudicare disponunt ut et canonicos iudices habeant et canonice me iudicent. Si enim aliter agerent, eorum iudicia penitus recusarem.'

Egresso itaque episcopo cum suis, et rege cum suis episcopis et consulibus et uicecomitibus et prepositis et uenatoribus[51] aliisque quorumlibet officiorum in iudicio remanente, et post diutinas moras reuocato et reuerso episcopo, T. Eboracensis archiepiscopus ait: 'Domine episcope, dominus noster archiepiscopus et regis curia uobis iudicat quod rectitudinem regi facere debetis antequam de uestro feodo [te] reuestiat.' Et episcopus respondit: 'Inuestituram episcopatus mei michi reddi precatus sum. Despoliatus sum enim sine omni uocacione et iudicio. Et de episcopatu iudicandus exiui domum istam, et inde requiro iudicium, quia nullus michi hodie uel ego alicui de feodo feci uerbum.' Et idem archiepiscopus ait: 'Vobis iudicat curia ista quia de nulla re debet uos rex resaisire antequam sibi rectitudinem faciatis.' Et episcopus: 'Vellem' inquid 'michi canonoicam aliquam sentenciam demonstrari, per quam iudicium istud canonicum esse cognoscerem. Iudicium enim huiusmodi nec in ecclesiasticis usibus nec in lege christiana didici uel audiui, et si iudicium contra canones susciperem, in sanctam dei ecclesiam et in sanctum sacerdotalem ordinem grauiter peccarem. Quod enim ad presens me fortassis parum lederet, plures in posterum hoc exemplo confunderet. Ideoque certam michi queso monstrare sentenciam, per quam iustum hoc esse cognoscam.' Tunc Lanfrancus archiepiscopus ait: 'Iudicium istud iustum est et illud oportet te concedere et sequi uel contradicere.' Et episcopus: 'Vellem' inquit 'ex consensu regis et uestro cum quibusdam episcoporum istorum loqui et per eorum consilium facienda facere et dimittenda dimittere.' Et Lanfrancus archiepiscopus ait: 'Episcopi sunt iudices et eos ad consilium

---

50 Cf. Pseudo-Isidore, Felix II, *Decret. c.xii*, ed. Hinschius, 485: Ut nemo episcopum penes seculares arbitros accuset, sed apud summos primates.

51 et prepositis et uenatoribus: Croc the huntsman, a Domesday tenant-in-chief in Hampshire, certainly attests charters for Rufus: *RAN* i nos. 319, 359, 361.

tuum habere non debes.' 'Precor' inquid episcopus 'regem ut illos michi consenciat et eos ut michi fraterna consulant caritate.' Rex uero
345 respondit: 'Cum tuis tibi consule, quia de nostris in consilio tuo nullum prorsus habebis.' Et episcopus: 'Parum' inquid 'consilii in hiis septem hominibus[52] habeo contra uirtutem atque scientiam tocius huius regni, quam hic aduersum me uideo congregatam.'

Accepta tamen concilii licencia et egresso cum suis episcopo et in
350 placitum regresso, archiepiscopo ait: 'Iudicium quod hic dictum est, respuo quia contra canones et contra legem nostram factum est. Neque enim ego canonice uocatus sum,[53] sed coactus ui regalis exercitus assum et dispoliatus episcopio extra prouinciam meam absentibus omnibus comprouincialibus meis[54] in laicali conuentu causam meam dicere
355 compellor, et inimici mei, qui michi consilium et colloquium suum et pacis osculum denegant, postpositis dictis meis, de hiis que non dixi me iudicant et accusatores sunt simul et iudices,[55] et in lege nostra prohibitum inuenio ne tale iudicium suscipiam. Quod si ex fatuitate mea uellem suscipere, archiepiscopus et primas meus dei ordinisque
360 respectu ab huiusmodi presumpcione me deberent caritatiue compescere. Et quia per regis odium uos omnes aduersarios sencio, apostolicam sedem, Romanam scilicet ecclesiam, et beatum Petrum eiusque uicarium appello[56] ut ipsius ordinacione negocii mei iustam sentenciam

---

52 hiis septem hominibus: see lines 189, 286.

53 Lines 352–5 are redolent of Pseudo-Isidore. Cf. Julius, *Decret. c.xii*, ed. Hinschius, 469: Salva apostolicae aecclesiae auctoritate nullus episcopus extra suam provinciam ad iudicium devocetur, sed vocato eo canonice [*sic ed.*] in loco omnibus congruo tempore synodali ab omnibus conprovintialibus episcopis audiatur, qui concordem super eum canonicamque proferre debent sententiam, quondam si hoc minoribus tam clericis quam laicis concessum est, quanto magis de episcopis serviri convenit? Nam si ipse metropolitanum aut iudices suspectos habuerit aut infensos senserit, apud primates dioceseos aut apud Romane sedis pontifices iudicetur.

54 absentibus omnibus comprouincialibus meis: Freeman, *WR* i, 105, thought the bishop's complaint 'grotesque'; Hartmut Hoffmann, 'Zur Echtheit', 439, justifies it as pleader's guile, 'ein juristiche Trick'. At St Calais's own consecration suffragans of Canterbury had assisted Thomas of York; at that time only one bishop acknowledged York's authority, Ralph of Orkney, who had himself been consecrated by Thomas in 1073 with the aid of two Canterbury suffragans: *C & S* I.ii, 629–30; *Letters of Lanfranc*, ed. Clover and Gibson, nos. 12–13, pp. 78–85. It would be difficult to regard Fothadh, the last Celtic bishop of St Andrews, as even a nominal comprovincial of St Calais in 1088. There was indeed a later York claim that Fothadh professed obedience to Thomas of Bayeux: BL Harley ms. 433, f. 260r, edited for the Richard III Society by R. E. Horrox and P. W. Hammond, iii, (Gloucester, 1982), 84–5. But this seems very improbable.

55 et accusatores sunt simul et iudices: cf. Pseudo-Isidore, Damasus, *Decret.* c.xvi, ed. Hinschius, 504: Accusatores vero et iudices non idem sint, sed per se accusatores, per se iudices, per se testes, per se accusati, unusquisque in suo ordinabiliter ordine.

56 To whom as St Peter's vicar could St Calais appeal effectively in 1088? Since Gregory VII's death in 1085 neither William I nor Rufus had recognised any of the contenders for the papacy: Z. N. Brooke, *The English Church and the Papacy* (Cambridge, 1931), 145; Southern, *Anselm* (1963), 145. St Calais here exposed himself to the sort of

suscipere merear, *cuius dispositioni maiores causas ecclesiasticas et episcoporum*
iudicia antiqua apostolorum eorumque successorum atque canonum auctoritas 365
reseruauit.'[57] Tunc Lanfrancus archiepiscopus respondit: 'Nos non de
episcopio sed de tuo te feodo iudicamus, et hoc modo iudicauimus
Baiocensem episcopum ante patrem huius rege de feodo quo, nec rex
uocabat eum episcopum in placito illo sed fratrem et comitem.'[58] Et
episcopus ait: 'Domine archiepiscope, ego nullam feci hodie feodi 370
mencionem uel feodum habere me dixi, sed de episcopii mei dis-
saisicione conquestus sum et conqueror.' Et archiepiscopus: 'Si
numquam' inquid 'audiam te loqui de feodo, scio te tamen magnum
feodum habuisse et inde te iudicauimus.' Et episcopus: 'Domine archiepiscope, modo audio quod uos omnia dicta mea dimisistis et de 375

question from Rufus which Anselm was to hear in 1095 when he wished to go to the
pope to receive his pallium: 'A quo papa illud requirere cupis?', Eadmer, *HN* 52. Though
Brooke accepted that St Calais did appeal to Rome in 1088, he warned against regarding
this action 'too seriously. He was taking a very unusual step, but only to evade judgement,
not as a matter of principle' (p. 162). While the editors of *C & S* I.ii reject my views
about the date of the *libellus* (p. 855, n. 1), they nevertheless remark (p. 635, n. 2): 'It is
certainly strange that a contemporary account should lay so much stress on the bishop's
appeal to Rome without anyone on either side referring to the schism.' Though St
Calais, once across the Channel, did not proceed in person to Italy, he may have written
to Pope Urban II about his treatment by Rufus, though it seems unlikely that the *libellus*
was composed as an aide-mémoire for that purpose, as Hoffmann suggested, 'Zur
Echtheit', 440. Urban's letter to Rufus, datable perhaps to April-June 1089, printed by
S. Löwenfeld, *Epp. Pont. Rom. ineditae* (Leipzig, 1885), no. 129, p.65 (JL 5397), though it
confirms that St Calais's complaints had come to Urban's ears, offers no guarantee that
the *libellus* already existed, and there is no evidence that the letter ever reached Rufus;
cf. *C & S* I.ii, 635. A. Becker, *Papst Urban II* (MGH Schriften 19/1, 1964) i, 173–6 surmised
that Urban had heard about this affair from his legate in France, Cardinal Roger. Becker
dismisses St Calais's appeal as a mere formal step, which the bishop never pursued
seriously.

57 cuius dispositioni .... reseruauit: literally from Pseudo-Isidore, either Sixtus II,
Decret. c.ii, ed. Hinschius, 190, or Julius, *Decret.* c.xii, Hinschius, 467; cf. Sixtus I, *Decret.* v,
Hinschius, 108. All stem from Innocentius papa I, *Ep.* ii. 3 (Victricio Rothomagensi),
Migne, *PL* 20, 473; *ib.* 635.

58 On the face of it, this is the earliest account of how the Conqueror's action against
Odo of Bayeux in 1082 was justified. The story as told by Orderic, iv,42, writing between
1130/1 and 1133 (see editor's note, p. xix), does not record an intervention by Lanfranc.
Malmesbury however does impute responsibility for the reply to Lanfranc at *GR* ii,351,
though not at *GR* ii, 334. Orderic's editor, Dr Marjorie Chibnall, remarks, Orderic, iv,
xxvii-xxx, that Malmesbury, Orderic and the 'Hyde' chronicle appear to be independent
of each other; she thinks that their accounts of the incident 'tip the balance in favour of'
the distinction in capacities 'having been made, if not in 1082, at least shortly afterwards'.
But the 'Hyde' chronicle (post 1120), ed. Edward Edwards, *RS*, (1866), p. 296, is not very
specific here, and Dr Chibnall's conclusion that if Lanfranc 'did not make the distinction
in 1082, almost certainly he made it retrospectively in 1088' seems to postulate that the
story in the *libellus* was contemporary with the events it purports to describe. If that
cannot be sustained, then we may still envisage the *libellus* borrowing the distinction if
not from the first version of Malmesbury's *GR* (completed in 1125: R. D. Thomson,
William of Malmesbury (Woodbridge, 1987), pp. 3–4), then from Malmesbury's source.

uestra me consciencia iudicastis. Sed quia dei gracia sapientissimus et
nominatissimus estis, in hoc sapere uestrum tam sublime intelligo quod
paruitas mea illud comprehendere non potest. Sed apostolicam sedem,
quam ex necessitate appellaui, per licenciam regis et uestram adire
380 uolo.' 'Egredere' inquid archiepiscopus 'et rex cum suis habito consilio
dicet tibi quod sibi placuerit.'

Cumque episcopus egrederetur et uocatus regrederetur, Hugo de
Bellomonte surgens dixit episcopo: 'Domine episcope, regis curia et
barones isti uobis pro iusto iudicant quoniam sibi uos respondere non
385 uultis de hiis, de quibus uos per me appellauit, sed de placito suo
inuitatis eum Romam, quod uos feodum uestrum inde forisfacitis.' Et
episcopus respondit: 'In omni loco in quo non uiolencia sed iusticia
dominetur, de scelere et periurio me purgare paratus sum et hoc, quod
hic pro iudicio recitasti, in Romana ecclesia falsum et iniuste dictum
390 esse monstrabo.' 'Ego' inquid Hugo 'et compares mei parati sumus
iudicium nostrum in hac curia confirmare.' Et episcopus respondit: 'In
curia ista nullum ad presens placitum subintrabo, quia nichil ibi tam
bene dicerem quin fautores regis deprauando peruerterent, qui ipsam
eciam non reuerentes apostolicam auctoritatem post eius appellacionem
395 me iudicio non legali grauant. Sed dei et Sancti Petri postulans auxilium,
Romam uadam.'

Tunc rex ait: 'Modo uolo ut castellum tuum michi reddas quoniam
iudicium mee curie non sequeris.' Et episcopus respondit: 'Numquam
uobis in conuencione habui me castellum meum uobis redditurum, nisi
400 canonicum iudicium sequi nollem et si iudicii contradictio oriretur, illuc
ire ad contradicendum recusarem ubi contradictionis huiusmodi finalem
sentenciam juste deberem suscipere. Et ego presto sum iudicia michi
facta in Romana ecclesia contradicere, de qua pendet et pependit ab
apostolorum tempore et infra ordinis mei diffinitiua sentencia.'[59] Et rex
405 ait: 'Per uultum de Luca,[60] numquam exibis de manibus meis donec

59 See Gregory VII, *Reg.* viii.21, cited in note 30.

60 Per uultum de Luca: reported as an oath favoured by Rufus in the 1090s by
Eadmer, *HN* 30, 39, 101, 110 (cf. 116) and Malmesbury, *GR* ii,364, 375; *GP* 80, 83n. The
Volto Santo, a romanesque figured wooden crucifix of disputed date in the cathedral of
San Martino at Lucca, is illustrated by Gustav Schnürer and Joseph M. Ritz, *Sankt
Kümmernis und Volto Santo* (Forschungen zur Volkskunde, Heft 13–15, Düsseldorf, 1934), pls.
xi, xii, and by Barlow, *WR* pl. 4a, with discussion *ib.* 116–8. Diana M. Webbe, 'The Holy
Face of Lucca', *Battle* 9 (1987), 227–37, admits the difficulty that while 'the earliest
independent Italian evidence for the existence and cult of the Vultus' comes from the
episcopate of Rangerius, bishop of Lucca *c.* 1097–1112 (the legend, ed. Schnürer and
Ritz, 128–34, was written in the early twelfth century), Rufus's oaths in England 'seem
to furnish the earliest incontrovertible evidence' for the existence of the Vultus. Accepting
Eadmer's testimony (though not noticing the appearance of the oath in DIV), she inclines
to the conclusion (p. 237) that Rufus 'was bearing witness to the existence of a cult which
had grown from obscure roots, although in favourable conditions, over the twenty or
thirty years before 1090'. If the cult did indeed flourish as early as this, there would of

castellum habeam.' Et episcopus respondit: 'Domine mi rex, ego passus sum per tres seruientes uestros auferri michi terras et pecuniam ecclesie presentibus centum meis militibus,[61] et in nullo uobis prorsus restiti. Et cum nichil michi remanserit de episcopatu meo preter ipsam urbem in qua sedes est ecclesie, et eandem michi auferre uultis, nulla nisi dei   410
uirtute resistam uobis. Sed de parte dei et Sancti Petri et eius uicarii domini pape dico uobis ne eam michi auferatis. Paratus sum enim bonos obsides et fiducias dare uobis quod homines mei, quos ibi dum Romam uado uolo dimittere, in fidelitate uestra eam custodient et si uolueritis libenter uobis seruient.' Tunc rex ait: 'In ueritate credas   415
episcope quod nullo modo Dunelmum reuerteris et quod homines tui Dunelmi nullatenus remanebunt, nec tu manus meas euades donec castellum tuum liberum michi reddas.' 'Bene' inquid episcopus 'confido de fide, quam michi comites[62] promiserunt quod usque ad ecclesiam meam securus perducar, sicut inter nos condicio firmata est et ipsi   420
coram uobis in hoc placito cognouerunt.'

   Tunc Lanfrancus archiepiscopus dixit regi: 'Si episcopus amplius castellum suum uobis contradixerit, bene eum capere potestis, quia conductum quem hactenus habuit nunc dimittit, cum prior con-uencionem frangit et barones uestros probare appetit quod fidem suam   425
non bene seruauerint.' Tunc Radulfus Piperellus[63] et omnes laici unanimiter conclamantes dixerunt: 'Capite eum, capite eum, bene enim loquitur iste uetulus ligaminarius.'[64] Quod Alanus comes audiens,

course be little difficulty in suggesting how Rufus had come by his knowledge of it by 1088; a possible channel was his physician, Baldwin abbot of Bury (cf. Barlow, WR 117). But it should be borne in mind that the English evidence for Rufus's use of this oath in the 1090s is not strictly contemporary: Eadmer did not put together the first four books of HN until 1109–1115, according to Southern, Anselm (1963), 299; Malmesbury, who may well have borrowed from Eadmer, is some ten years later; and the date of DIV, whose authority here Barlow, EC 67, n. 76 and WR 116, n. 73, esteems as no more than 'probably' independent, can be regarded as still at issue. It may be relevant to remark that Eadmer, HN 112–4, was vastly impressed by the conduct of Bishop Rangerius of Lucca at the Roman Easter council in 1099.

   61 presentibus centum meis militibus: if the bishop's household and stipendiary troops are included, this claim is perhaps not much exaggerated. By 1135 the bishops of Durham had enfeoffed 64 knights: H. M. Chew, English Ecclesiastical Tenants in Chief (Oxford, 1932), 19, 119. The total sum to be accounted for from the aid levied on the bishopric's knights in 1129 was £58 6s. 8d., PR 31 Henry I, ed. Joseph Hunter, (Record Commission, 1835), 132; on the nature of this levy, see Judith A. Green, The Government of England under Henry I (Cambridge, 1986), 77. Assuming a rate of £1 per fee, this would amount to almost 60 fees.

   62 comites: presumably, though perhaps mistakenly, including Roger le Poitevin.

   63 Radulfus Piperellus: Ranulf Peverel, lord of Hatfield Peverel in Essex and also Domesday tenant in Berkshire, Oxfordshire, Norfolk and Suffolk, witnesses in early 1091 a royal charter and a royal confirmation in company with many others whom the libellus names as at Salisbury in November 1088: RAN i nos. 315, 319.

   64 uetulus ligaminarius: this has puzzled the translators. Joseph Stevenson, Church Historians of England III.ii (London, 1855), 743, offered 'old turnkey'; Freeman, WR i, 109,

surrexit et dixit: 'Ego eum interposita fide mea de castello suo eduxi et
ad regis curiam adduxi, ea condicione quod si rex nollet ei consentire
iusticiam que iuste contradici non posset sicut episcopo suo, ego eum
ad castellum suum cum suis omnibus sanum reducerem, et si rex ei
rectitudinem sicut episcopo suo que iuste contradici non posset offerret,
et ipse eam sequi uel nollet uel non posset, tunc rex sibi et suis omnibus
secundum uoluntatem episcopi ubi ipse eligeret ab Exonia usque ad
Sanguicium naues et portum inueniret, et liceret ei omnes homines
suos, quos ipse uellet et qui cum eo ire uellent, cum omnibus suis et
eorum pecunia secum ducere per securitatem et conductum regis
usquequo ultra mare ad siccam terram cum rebus suis essent. Et
multum precor dominum meum regem ne fidem meam inde faciat me
mentiri. Nullum enim proficuum in me haberet ulterius.' Cumque hoc
idem R.[65] et Odo comites precarentur, Lanfrancus archiepiscopus ait:
'Rex bene uos adquitauit. Plenam namque rectitudinem episcopo optulit
et ipse eam nobis audientibus recusauit. Regem quoque Romam iniuste
inuitauit. Recognoscat igitur episcopus nos iustum fecisse iudicium et
se illud sequi nolle, et rex sibi naues inueniet et conductum.'

Et episcopus: 'Bene' inquid 'uos moneo comites, qui promissa fide
uestra me ducendum suscepistis, ut me Dunelmum reducatis, quia rex
michi nullam rectitudinem consentit, et hoc paratus sum in Romana
ecclesia demonstrare.' 'Non est' inquid Lanfrancus 'iustum ut placitum
uel iudicium regis pro aliqua contradiccione longius procedat, sed
quociens in curia sua iudicium agitur, ibidem necesse est ut concedatur
uel contradicatur. Tu ergo iudicium nostrum uel hic concede uel hic
euidenti racione contradicito.' Ad hec episcopus: 'Hic' inquid 'optime
contradico et Rome, ubi debeo et ubi iusticia magis quam uiolencia
dominatur, huius contradiccionis sentenciam suscipere appeto. Et quia
nemo uestrum iudicando uel testificando dicere audet quod regi dis-
pliceat, cum alios testes non habeam, christianam legem quam hic
scriptam habeo[66] testem inuoco me Romam sicut dixi iuste posse
pergere et huius cause finalem sentenciam ex auctoritate Romani

n. 3, 'old gaoler'. Admitting that the meaning is uncertain, *EHD* ii,619 suggested 'this
trusty old liegeman'. Gibson, *Lanfranc of Bec*, 161, n. 1, perhaps by aid of the *Revised
Medieval Latin Word List* (1965), arrived at 'old bloodhound'. Possibly a shade of animus
can be detected in Frank Barlow's repeated rendering 'the old binder', *EC* 286; *The
Norman Conquest and Beyond* (London, 1983), 235. The variant *vitulus* for *uetulus* in two of
the mss. hardly helps. To me the form *ligaminarius* suggests 'lymerer', the man who
handled the leash or scenting hounds in a hunting pack.

65 R. et Odo comites: presumably Roger le Poitevin is intended.

66 christianam legem quam hic scriptam habeo: if St Calais was referring to a volume
of canon law held in hand, it may well have been that copy of Lanfranc's collection now
surviving in Cambridge, Peterhouse ms. 74. See Z. N Brooke, *English Church and the
Papacy*, 109, 162; Barlow, *EC* 286 and n. 52; Horst Fuhrmann, *Einfluss und Verbreitung der
pseudoisidorischen Fälschungen von ihrem Auftauchen bis in die neuere Zeit* (MGH Schriften 24/1,
1972) i,169, n. 61.

pontificis debere procedere.' Et rex ait: 'Dicas licet quicquid uelis, non tamen effugies manus meas nisi castellum prius michi reddas.' Et episcopus respondit: 'Cum uos non solum episcopatum, uerum et omnia mea iniuste abstuleritis, et ipsam modo sedem uiolenter auferre uelitis, pro nulla re quam facere possim capi me paciar.' Constituta est ergo dies,[67] qua episcopus urbem suis hominibus uacuaret et rex suos ibi poneret. 465

Tunc episcopus dixit regi: 'Domine mi rex, a uobis scire uolo si de episcopatu meo aliquid michi dimittetis unde saltem uiuere ualeam.' Et Lanfrancus archiepiscopus respondit: 'Tu pro regis dampno et omnium nostrorum dedecore uadis Romam, et ipse tibi terram dimitteret? Remane in terra sua, et ipse episcopatum tuum preter urbem tibi reddet, ea condicione quod in curia sua iudicio baronum suorum rectitudinem sibi facias.' 'Ego' inquid episcopus 'apostolicam sedem appellaui quia in curia eius nullum iustum iudicium audio, et nullo modo dimittam quin illuc uadam.' 'Si tu' inquid archiepiscopus 'sine regis licencia Romam perrexeris, nos dicemus ei quid de episcopatu tuo sibi sit faciendum.' Et episcopus: 'Vos' inquid 'ad presens ad opus meum nichil boni sibi dicitis, et quicquid uultis, satis libere dicere potestis. Sed antequam hinc discedam, paratus sum coram omnibus baronibus istis ab omni scelere et periurio me purgare, et modis omnibus me defendere quod dampnum regis de corpore suo uel de terra sua nullo modo me sciente feci uel quesiui et quod inde nulli fiduciam feci uel ab aliquo recepi, et cum prius hoc dampnum suum intellexi, eum inde quam citius potui premuniui et contra hostes suos fideliter eum iuui,[68] et hoc legaliter me fecisse monstrabo. Monstrabo enim quod Dorobernium et Hastingas, que iam pene perdiderat, in sua fidelitate detinui.[69] Londoniam quoque, que iam rebellauerat, in 470 475 480 485

---

67 Constituta est ergo dies: apparently 14 November; see lines 549-50.

68 Lines 484-7 are reminiscent of how Fulbert of Chartres defined the obligations of fealty in his *Ep*. li (to Duke William V of Aquitaine, before 9 June 1021), ed. F. Behrends, *Letters and Poems of Fulbert of Chartres* (Oxford, 1976), 90-2. The definition appeared in various canonical collections before finding its way into Gratian, *Decretum* C.22, q.5, c.18; cf. *Consuetud.Feud*. ii, tit.6. Durham DCL ms. B.II.11, which contains Fulbert's letters, may have been copied for St Calais, who left it to the library: Mynors, *DCM* 38.

69 Dorobernium et Hastingas, que iam pene perdiderat: if the claim is authentic, when did St Calais render these services? *ASC* and 'Florence', though admitting that the conspiracy against Rufus was prepared in Lent, place the outbreak of open hostilities after Easter (16 April), and St Calais must be assumed to have left the king's court before his first disseisin on 12 March; see note 10. Freeman, *WR* i,29, dated these efforts by St Calais 'at the latest in the very first days of March'; so too Barlow, *WR* 75-6. The only possible alternative would seem to be during the putative meeting between the bishop and Rufus in the summer of 1088 (see line 112 and note 20), though this would necessitate the hypothesis of a temporary reconciliation between them at that time. It is generally accepted that *Dorobernium* here means Dover, as for example it quite plainly does in Henry of Huntingdon, *Hist. anglorum*, ed. T. Arnold, *RS*, (1879), 218, though forms such as *Dubris, Dofra, Dofris, Doura, Doveria, Dovoria* and *Dovere* seem better witnessed. But just

eius fidelitate sedaui. Meliores eciam duodecim eiusdem urbis ciues ad
490 eum mecum duxi ut per illos melius ceteros animaret, et hoc ita me
fecisse per testimonium baronum suorum, si eis licenciam dederit,
demonstrabo.[70] Et multum precor eum ut purgacionem quam predixi
modo suscipiat et postmodum seruicium meum iuste me monstrare
permittat, et si ei placeret et benignam eis licenciam dare uellet,
495 ad hanc purgacionem faciendam plures episcoporum istorum testes
haberem.[71] Et cum hoc multum multociens deprecaretur episcopus et
rex omnino recusaret, Lanfrancus archiepiscopus ait episcopo: 'Melius
ageres si in misericordia regis totum te poneres, et ego ad pedes eius
libenter tui causa uenirem.'[72] Et episcopus: 'Misericordiam' inquid 'eius
500 obnixe deprecor ut pro amore dei et honore sancte ecclesie iudicia,
que hic ad detrimentum sancte dei ecclesie et confusionem sanctorum
ordinum et christiane legis ignominiam iniuste prolata sunt, legaliter
faciat emendari, et propter hoc libenter ei seruiam et de meo, si placet,
ei tribuam.' 'Ex toto' inquit archiepiscopus 'in misericordia eius te pone
505 et iudicio curie sue refragari penitus dimitte.' Et episcopus: 'Absit'
inquid 'ut iudicium contra canones, immo ad destruccionem canonum
suscipiam uel concedam.'

Tunc rex ait: 'Faciat michi episcopus fiduciam quod dampnum
meum citra mare[73] non querat uel recipiat et quod naues meas, quas
510 sibi inueniam, non detinebit frater meus[74] uel aliquis suorum ad
dampnum meum contra nautarum uoluntatem.' Et episcopus respondit:
'Domine, comites uestri fidem suam michi promiserunt quod nullam
fiduciam ego uel homines mei facere cogeremur ui uel ingenio super

possibly *Dorobernium* could be taken as a variant for *Dorobernia*, i.e. Canterbury. Both
'Florence', ii, 23 and Orderic, iv, 126 state that Canterbury and London were targets for
the rebels from Rochester (in May 1088 ?).

70 This seems the only record of unrest in London, though 'Florence', ii, 22 reports
that Rufus went there at an early stage in the revolt *belli tractaturus negotia*. In 1066 'all
the best men from London' had submitted to the Conqueror, according to *ASC* D version
and 'Florence', i, 228. But Liebermann's view, *Die Gesetze der Angelsachsen* II.i (Halle, 1906),
573, that the *XII meliores ciues* of DIV formed something like a permanent governing body
for London in 1088 must be treated with caution, though it is not explicitly rejected by
M. Weinbaum, *Verfassungsgeschichte Londons 1066–1268* (Stuttgart, 1929), 15. It seems just as
likely that the twelve were a chance *ad hoc* selection of prominent citizens; see James
Tait, *The Medieval English Borough* (Manchester, 1936), 266; C. N. L. Brooke and Gillian
Keir, *London 800–1216: the shaping of a city* (London, 1975), 248–9.

71 *Compurgatores* and their oath as to the credibility of the accused are discussed X
V.34.5, ed. Friedberg, col. 870.

72 Cf. the advice given by the bishops to Anselm in 1095, according to Eadmer, *HN*
56: Verum si, remote omni alia conditione, simpliciter ad voluntatem domini nostri regis
consilii tui summam transferre velles, prompta tibi voluntate, ut nobis ipsis, consuleremus.

73 citra mare: if Rufus was not looking at things from a Norman viewpoint, we must
postulate a heedless author writing on the continent. At this stage it would not have
made sense to demand further guarantees for the bishop's behaviour in England.

74 Duke Robert of Normandy.

fiduciam, quam eis Dunelmi fecimus, et hanc quam modo fiduciam
queritis nullo modo nisi coactus faciam.' Et Reginaldus Paganellus 515
ait:[75] 'Certe comites uestri promiserunt hoc quod dicit episcopus, et
conuenienter inde eos custodite.' 'Tace' inquit rex 'quia pro nullius
fiducia naues meas perdere paciar. Sed si episcopus inde se fiduciam
fecisse cognouerit, super illam aliam non requiro.' Et episcopus ait: 'De
multis rebus baronibus uestris fiduciam me fecisse cognosco et super 520
illam nec uos querere nec ego aliam facere debeo.' Tunc rex iratus ait:
'Per uultum de Luca, in hoc anno mare non transibis nisi fiduciam,
quam de nauibus requiro prius modo feceris.' 'Faciam' inquid episcopus
'hanc et multo maiorem si necesse fuerit fiduciam antequam hic in
capcione detinear, sed bene omnes audiant quod ea[m] inuitus faciam 525
et capcionis timore coactus.' Fecit itaque episcopus fiduciam et naues
et conductum quesiuit. Et rex ait: 'Nullum conductum habebis sed
Wiltone[76] moraberis donec ego uere sciam quod castellum habeam in
mea potestate, et tunc demum naues recipies et conductum.' Et
episcopus respondit: 'Cum quod uellem et deberem facere non ualeam, 530
hoc ipsum quod dicitis iniuste paciar et coactus.'

Tunc W. de Merlaio surgens dixit regi:[77] 'Domine, homines episcopi,
qui in castello suo sunt, abstulerunt domino meo Constantiensi episcopo
cc[ta] animalia in conductu uestro postquam episcopus modo uenit ad
curiam uestram, et dominus meus requisiuit eos ut sibi redderent 535
pecuniam suam et noluerunt. Postea uero precepit eis Walterus de

75 Reginaldus Paganellus: No contemporary Reginald Paynel appears in the Paynel
pedigree facing p. 1 of *EYC* vi (1939), or seems known otherwise. Possibly a mistake for
Radulfus; if so, it is uncertain whether the error is a scribe's or the author's. *Reginaldus*,
though common enough by *c.* 1130–1140, seems an unusual form for 1088; at that time
the name generally occurs as *Rain-* or *Reinaldus*.

76 Wilton, seat of a famous community of aristocratic nuns, struck Freeman as a
rather odd choice of place for the bishop's house arrest. He queried, *WR* i,112, n. 5:
'should it be *Wintonie*?'

77 W. de Merlaio: As John Le Patourel remarked, 'Geoffrey de Montbray' (as in note
49), 154, we would like to know if this was William, Bishop Geoffrey's steward, who was
his vassal in Bedfordshire, *DB* i, 210. Perhaps there was a connexion between this *W. de
Merlaio* in DIV and the later Merlay lords of Morpeth in Northumberland. Of these a
William de Merlay was charged on the *PR 31 Henry I* with a palfrey for his rights to his
brother's lands, ed. Joseph Hunter, (Rec. Comm., 1833), 36. This William, who died
before 5 September 1129, gave Morwick (par. Warkworth, Nb.) to St Cuthbert and his
monks at Durham; DCD Cart. II, f. 251r = Dugdale, *Monasticon* i,241. The suggestion
that the Merlay family was established in Northumberland by Geoffrey's nephew, Robert
Mowbray, while he was earl (*c.* 1086–95), seems plausible: see J. C. Hodgson in
Northumberland County History v, 1899, 345; W. P. Hedley, *Northumberland Families* i (Newcastle,
1968), 196–7. When and where this alleged depredation by St Calais's men from Durham
can have taken place is far from clear. The *libellus* offers no clue to Bishop William's
movements between his leaving Durham in early September and his appearance at
Salisbury in November. Where could Geoffrey's cattle have come within reach of the
Durham garrison during that time? Had he been attempting to restock his estates in the
south from Scotland or Northumberland?

Haiencorte[78] de parte uestra ut redderent pecuniam et noluerunt. Modo autem precamur uos ut faciatis domino meo reddi pecuniam suam.' Et rex ait: 'Videant barones isti si ego iuste possum implacitare episcopum'.

540 Et Lanfrancus archiepiscopus ait: 'Iniustum esset si amplius implacitaretis eum, cum de uobis nichil teneat et securum conductum habere debeat.' Recessit itaque illa die episcopus ad eligendum portum, rediturus in crastinum.

Die uero crastina[79] requisiuit comitem Alanum ut Hamptone sibi

545 naues et portum inueniret. Quod cum rex audisset, dixit episcopo: 'Bene scias episcope quod numquam transfretabis donec castellum habeam. Episcopus enim Baiocensis inde me castigauit.[80] Sed bene uide ut castellum Dunelmi homines mei habeant octauodecimo kalendas Decembris,[81] et si homines mei ea die castellum habuerint in mea

550 potestate, tunc sine ulla dubitacione uel mora habebis naues et conductum.' Precepit itaque Gilberto uicecomiti[82] audiente episcopo et Alano comite ceterisque baronibus suis ut undecimo kalendas Decembris[83] liberaret episcopo tot naues Hamtone quot sibi suisque ad transfretandum essent necessarie. Episcopus autem dixit Alano comiti:

555 'Domine comes uidete uos et socii uestri, per quorum fidem debeo conduci, ne ultra hunc terminum disturber, et dum in Anglia fuero habetote mecum unum bonum hominem, qui et hospicia michi inueniat et ab impedimento me defendat ut et uos de uestra fiducia salui sitis et ego non fatiger ulterius.' Et comes Alanus respondit: 'Hoc faciet uobis

560 rex per quemdam suum seruientem.' Remansit itaque episcopus Wiltone et Robertus de Comitis uilla[84] cum eo ut hospicia ei liberaret et eum

78 Walter of Aincourt (Ancourt, Seine-Maritime, arr. Dieppe, cant. Offranville: Loyd, *Origins*, 2), lord of Blankney in Lincolnshire, was also a Domesday tenant in Yorkshire, Northamptonshire, Derbyshire, Nottinghamshire and Cheshire. He witnessed a royal charter 1088–91: *RAN* i no. 325. His son William is said to have died while being brought up at Rufus's court: Barlow, *WR* 133–4.

79 Die uero crastina: 3 November 1088. The bishop chose Southampton as his port of departure.

80 Episcopus enim Baiocensis inde me castigauit: 'the bishop of Bayeux taught me a sore lesson about that sort of thing'. Presumably a reference to the complications about the surrender of Rochester a few months earlier: see *ASC* 1087 [1088], Malmesbury, *GR* ii, 562; Orderic, iv,126–38. As Dr Chibnall points out, iv, 126, n. 2, Orderic fails to mention 'the apparent trick by which he [Odo] entered Rochester on the grounds of negotiating its surrender.'

81 14 November 1088.

82 Gilberto uicecomiti: Gilbert of Bretteville was a Domesday tenant-in-chief in Hampshire, Berkshire and Wiltshire. He appears as sheriff of Berkshire 1090 × 1094: *RAN* i no. 359.

83 21 November 1088.

84 Though Robert count of Mortain could be called Robert de Conteville, he cannot be intended here. But it is naturally tempting to try to link this Robert in the *libellus* in some way with Herluin vicomte of Conteville (Eure, arr. Bernay, cant. Beuzeville), father by Arletta of Odo of Bayeux and Robert of Mortain. By his second wife, Fredesendis, Herluin had two more sons, Ralph and John, the former of whom may be the *Radulfus*

secure conduceret Hamptonam termino constituto ad recipiendas naues
et uentum expectandum.

Acceperunt ergo Yvo Taillesbosc[85] et Ernesius de Burone[86] castellum
Dunelmi in manus regis et dissaisiuerunt episcopum de ecclesia et de 565
castello et de omni terra sue octauodecimo kalendas Decembris[87] et
liberauerunt hominibus episcopi Helponem balistarium regis[88] et breue
regis deforis sigillatum hec uerba continens:[89] *Willelmus Rex Anglorum
omnibus fidelibus suis per totam Angliam salutem. Sciatis Dunelmensem episcopum
et omnes suos homines pacem meam habere per totum regnum Anglie et licencia et* 570
*pace mea mare transire. Ideoque defendo omnibus mee potestatis hominibus ne
aliquid mali eis faciant.* Cum autem sperarent homines episcopi securos
se esse per comitum fiduciam et per sigillum regis et conductum
Helponis, accepit Yvo Taillesbosc duos milites episcopi et coegit eos
placitare de animalibus Constantiensis episcopi, de quibus iudicatum 575
fuerat ante regem Dunelmensem episcopum non debere respondere.
Et iterum fecit auferri Yvo Taillesbosc cuidam militi episcopi equm
suum in predicto conductu.

Episcopus uero requisiuit Gilbertum et Robertum undecimo kalendas
Decembris[90] ut naues sibi liberarent et liceret ei transfretare cum Rogero 580

---

de Contivilla who held land in Somerset and Devon according to the Exon Domesday, or
the *Radulfus filius Herluini*, tenant of Roger Bigot in Norfolk: see Orderic, iv, 98, n. 1;
David R. Bates, 'Notes sur l'aristocratie normande', *Annales de Normandie* 23 (1973), 26,
29–33. Possibly the *Robertus* of DIV is author's or scribal error for *Radulfus*. But it must
be noted (a) that Robert of Mortain's second son was named Robert, and might
conceivably have been called de Conteville; and (b) that there are other Contevilles in
Normandy, not connected with Herluin at all.

85 Ivo Taillebois, first husband of Lucy of Bolingbroke, benefactor of Peterborough
and St Nicholas, Angers, and frequent witness to royal charters under William I and II,
appears as royal *dapifer* in 1091: see *RAN* i, p. xxiv and nos. 129, 143, 177, 229, 233–6,
288a, 302, 315, 319, 326, 328, 370, 386, 403–4, 406–10. Domesday tenant-in-chief in
Lincolnshire and Norfolk, and perhaps sometime sheriff of Lincolnshire, before his death
c. 1094 he had become established as a great landowner in northern England, on the
upper Eden and in a block of territory stretching from upper Ribblesdale to Lonsdale
and Kendal: see Sanders, *English Baronies*, 56; *Mowbray Charters*, p. xxii.

86 Erneis de Burun, sheriff of Yorkshire towards the end of the Conqueror's reign,
was perhaps succeeded in that office by Ralph Paynel under Rufus; see W. Farrer, *EHR*
30 (1915), 282 and note 13 above. Domesday tenant-in-chief in Lincolnshire and Yorkshire,
where he held in effect the barony of Hunsingore, that is Gospatric's former lands in
Nidderdale in chief and those in and about Masham from Count Alan, lord of Richmond;
see *EYC* x, 1–2, 23–30; Sanders, *English Baronies*, 56; *Mowbray Charters*, p. xxii.

87 14 November 1088.

88 Identified by Freeman, *WR* i, 114, n. 4 as Heppo the Balistarius, tenant-in-chief in
Lincolnshire, *DB* i, 369.

89 Calendared *RAN* i no. 298.

90 21 November 1088; for Gilbert the sheriff and Robert, see notes 82 and 84.

de Molbraio,[91] qui eodem termino transfretauit. Et illi responderunt se nullam sibi nauem liberaturos et dixerunt regem sibi precepisse ut bene seruarent episcopum ne de potestate regis exiret usquequo quid de eo fieri preciperet illis per suas sigillatas litteras remandaret. Seruauerunt
585 itaque episcopum usque sextum kalendas Decembris[92] et ea die adduxit eum Robertus Hamptonam. Quo cum uenisset episcopus, naues intrare uoluit, erat enim uentus bonus et omnia ad transfretandum prospera. Predicti uero seruientes regis defenderunt ei naues et transitum, et in crastinum,[93] cum uentum defecisse uiderent, dederunt episcopo
590 transfretandi licenciam et liberauerunt ei naues. Episcopus ergo dato naulo uentum necessarium expectauit.

Postea uenerunt ad eum O. Salesbiriensis episcopus[94] et Robertus de Insula[95] et Ricardus de Cultura[96] et summonuerunt eum de parte regis kalendis Decembris[97] ut in natiuitate domini esset Londonie ad curiam
595 regis et faceret ei rectitudinem de Gaufrido monacho suo,[98] qui post-

91 If the name has been transmitted correctly, this seems the only indication that Roger Montbray, brother of Geoffrey of Coutances and father of Robert earl of Northumberland, had been present in England in 1088, or had indeed survived so long. Roger, said to be a kinsman of Nigel of St-Sauveur, vicomte of the Cotentin, was among the Norman notables of 1066 eulogized by Orderic, ii, 140, and in that year was a benefactor of Holy Trinity, Caen: M. Fauroux, *Recueil des actes des ducs de Normandie de 911 à 1066* (Caen, 1961), no. 231, p. 445. His Norman estates were forfeited by his son Robert in 1095: C. W. Hollister, 'The greater Domesday tenants-in-chief', in *Domesday Studies*, ed. J. C. Holt, (Woodbridge, 1987), 229. Only very much later does the next Roger Mowbray appear in English records. He was the son of Nigel d'Aubigny and Gundreda de Gournay, and not born till *c.* 1119/1120: *Mowbray Charters*, p. xxvi and n. 1. Barlow, *WR* 89 and n. 171, 92, 168, attempts to get round the difficulty by proposing to read *Robertus* for *Rogerus*.

92 26 November 1088.

93 27 November 1088.

94 Osmund, bishop of Salisbury, 1078–99.

95 Robert de Lisle witnesses Rufus's confirmation of a Salisbury charter in 1091: *RAN* i no. 319. His relationship, if any, to Humphrey de Lisle, who witnesses the same document, is uncertain. Humphrey was a Domesday tenant-in-chief in Wiltshire: *DB* i, 64b, 70b.

96 Ricardus de Cultura: not identified. It may just be worth recalling that Richard *de Courceie* (Courcy) witnesses Rufus's charters at this time, *RAN* i nos. 310, 334, 349, 433; his name also appears on two spurious charters of William I for Durham, *ib.* nos. *205, *286.

97 1 December 1088.

98 Gaufrido monacho suo: No Geoffrey is named among the early monks at Durham in the list given in Durham UL, Cosin's ms. V.ii.6, ff. 7r-8v. But in the similar list in LV, f. 42r col. 2, after the entries for Bishops Walcher, William of St Calais and Rannulf and for Priors Aldwin and Turgot, *Gosfridus* has been interlineated before the next name in the original hand, that of the monk Aelfwius. Bishop William's high regard for Geoffrey is indicated, not perhaps wholly favourably, by Symeon, *HDE* 132. Here Symeon inserts into his history a kind of purgatorial vision by an episcopal knight called Boso, who claimed when in a rapture to have seen the bishop thrusting his head out of the doors of an iron building sited in the midst of a desolate waste, and to have heard him asking: ubinam Gosfridus monachus esset.... 'Hic enim', inquit, 'hic ad placitum mecum

quam episcopus ad curiam uenerat de dominicatu episcopi quingenta
et triginta nouem animalia acceperat et municionem castelli[99] abstulerat,
et de quibusdam suis aliis hominibus, qui unum hominem regis occi-
derant. Episcopus uero respondit eis: 'Per me nichil horum factum est,
et ego et homines mei conductum securum habemus et ad curiam eius   600
amplius ire non possum. Ipse[100] enim omnia michi mea abstulit et
equos meos iam uenditos manducaui. Sed si ipse me et meos homines
abire permiserit et fidem comitum quorum seruauerit, Romanam
ecclesiam, quam ex necessitate appellaui, deo miserante requiem. Sin
autem, antequam capiar me solum ab hiis omnibus, que meis hominibus   605
imponitis, hic coram uobis per sacramenta defendam quod per preceptum meum uel per conscienciam meam nichil horum factum est,
quamuis juste facere potuissem. Potui enim de meis facere quicquid
uolui usquequo de mea sede me dissaisiuit.'[101] Tunc ministri regis
dixerunt episcopo: 'Modo defendimus tibi naues.' Et episcopus   610
respondit: 'Rex omnem terram et pecuniam meam michi abstulit, et si
homines meos auferre uoluerit, pro nullo eorum in placitum intrabo,
sed solus, ei michi liceat, transfretabo.' Misit autem episcopus ad regem
quemdam suum militem et deprecatus est eum ut pro amore dei et
Sancti Petri eum Romam ire permitteret.   615

adesse deberet.' Boso's narrative continues: Hunc namque episcopus procuratorem sui
episcopatus constituerat. This clearly denotes Geoffrey's function as general viceregent
for managing business in the bishopric. The reference to *placitum* seems to betray the
presence of a calculated barb, for here the word most probably means trial, rather than
court (as Barlow, *WR* 356 translates). Perhaps brought to Durham by St Calais from a
Norman monastery, Geoffrey may well be the *G. Dunelmensis* who seems to have acted
as custodian of the temporalities of the see after the bishop's death: DCD I.I. Reg. 8,
illustrated as pl. x in Bishop and Chaplais, *ERW*, and printed *EYC* ii no. 930. On four
occasions between March and June 1088 the *libellus* shows St Calais using an unnamed
monk as his envoy to Rufus: lines 56, 84, 128, 151; whether this was Geoffrey is uncertain.
The *libellus* implies that Geoffrey was with the bishop in early December at Southampton,
whence he was to be sent back to Durham (line 619), but he does not appear to have
been at the Salisbury court a month earlier. Presumably he had been in charge of
Durham castle after the bishop had come to terms with Rufus's army in September (see
note 107) and had quitted Durham in order to rejoin St Calais after the royal seizure of
the castle on 14 November (lines 549–50). Though it cannot be proved, it is very tempting
to suppose that this Geoffrey is the monk of that name from St Calais (*cuidam monacho
sancti Carileffi Gausfrido nomine*) to whom Henry I gave custody of Battle abbey after the
death of Abbot Henry in June 1102. The Battle chronicler says that though Geoffrey
lacked learning, he was highly shrewd, prudent and skilled in worldly affairs, as he
showed in defending the monastery's temporal interests until his death on 16 May 1105:
The Chronicle of Battle Abbey, ed. & trans. Eleanor Searle (Oxford, 1980), 108–117.

99 municionem castelli: the castle's stores and provisions.

100 Ipse: Rufus.

101 The *libellus* thus makes St Calais argue that he was not disseized of his church,
castle and all his lands until 14 November (cf. lines 565–7), despite the disseisin from his
Yorkshire possessions on 12 March (lines 29–30). Yet the tractate in which the *libellus* is
framed reckons the date at which William was driven from his see as 11 September: lines
649–50 below.

Rex uero misit ei Wyntoniensem episcopum[102] et Hugonem de Portu[103] et Gaufridum de Traileio[104] et per illos sibi mandauit ut Gaufridum monachum ad placitandum de predictis forisfactis Dunelmum mitteret et ipse Londoniam iret ut in natiuitate domini de
620 hominibus suis ibi rectitudinem regi faceret. Quibus episcopus respondit: 'Ego semper ex quo conuencionem cum regis comitibus feci in regis custodia mansi, et comites michi fidem suam promiserunt quod si castellum Dunelmi regi traderetur, ego et homines mei, qui me sequi uellent, securum conductum haberemus et naues et portum absque
625 detencione uel mora per aliquem hominem contra uoluntatem meam michi facta. Et cum rex Dunelmum habeat, et nos per conductum regis et comitum ad portum uenerimus et naues per preceptum regis receperimus et precium pro eis dederimus et apostolicam sedem requirendo Romam tendamus, multum peccat qui nos ita detinet. Presto sum
630 tamen, si propter hoc me abire permiseritis sine dilacione, me purgare coram uobis quod nichil horum que dicitis per preceptum meum uel per consciencam meam factum est uel quod ego unius panis precium inde non habui uel expecto habere. Postea si homines meos retinuerit, sustineant quicquid eis fecerit, quia pro nullo dimittam quin Romam
635 uadam, si capcione ista ualeam liberari.' Tunc seruientes regis fecerunt episcopus die noctuque custodiri. Episcopus ergo tristis misit ad comites Alanum et Rogerum[105] et Odonem mandans eis impedimenta sua et coniurauit eos per eam fidem, quam in baptismo susceperant et quam sibi promiserant, ut eum de capcione ista liberarent et naues sibi et
640 portum et conductum sine mora inuenirent et impedimentum et dampnum, quod iniuste sustinebat, iuste sibi emendarent. Tandem illorum instancia rex permisit episcopo transitum.[106]

102 Walkelin, bishop of Winchester, 1070–1098.

103 Hugh of Port-en-Bessin (Calvados, arr. Bayeux, cant. Ryes: Loyd, *Origins*, 77) was a tenant-in-chief in Hampshire, Berkshire, Dorset and Cambridgeshire, and held lands in England and Normandy from Odo of Bayeux; he appears as sheriff of Hampshire: GEC xi, 316–7; *RAN* i nos. 143, 267, 270, 284, 379.

104 Geoffrey *de Traileio*, perhaps from Trelly (*Trailliacum*) in Normandy, (dép.) La Manche, cant. Montmartin-sur-Mer: Loyd, *Origins*, 106. Goisfridus de *Traillgi* or *Tralgi* appears as a Domesday tenant of Geoffrey of Coutances in Bedfordshire: *DB* i, 210. Presumably it was a descendant, also named Geoffrey, who married Albreda, sister and joint heir of Walter Espec, and so came into some of the lands in Bedfordshire held in 1086 by William Espec: Sanders, *English Baronies*, 133–4. Nicholas of Trailli, nephew of Walter Espec of Helmsley, occurs from *c.* 1143 onwards as canon of York: C. T. Clay, *York Minster Fasti* ii (Yorks. Arch. Soc. Record Series 124, 1959), 70–1.

105 Here Roger le Poitevin seems reckoned as a count.

106 transitum: on the evidence of the *libellus* this must have been well on in December. After receiving the royal sumons dated 1 December (line 595), St Calais had sent his knight to the king (lines 614–15); Rufus had dispatched Bishop Walkelin and his companions to St Calais (lines 617–20), causing him to appeal to Earl Alan and his fellow guarantors, who will have needed time to work on Rufus. Possibly the bishop did not reach Normandy before the new year opened.

Anno sui episcopatus octauo expulsus est ab Anglia, sed a Roberto
fratre regis comite Normannorum honorifice susceptus tocius Normannie curam suscepit.[107] Tercio autem anno repacificatus regi recepit 645
episcopatum suum,[108] ipso rege cum fratre suo totoque Anglie exercitu,
cum Scociam contra Malcolmum tenderent,[109] eum *in sedem suam
restitu*entibus, *ipsa* uidelicet *die qua* inde pulsus fuerat, *tercio idus Septembris*.[110] Secundo anno sue reuersionis *ecclesiam* ueterem, quam Aldunus

107 After the end of the *libellus*, this concluding section of DIV is mostly based on
Symeon, *HDE*: lines 648–56 *HDE* 128–9, and lines 658–68 on *HDE* 133–5. But *HDE*
does not give the information at lines 646–8 about the restoration of the bishop to
Durham by Rufus on 11 September 1091, nor that at lines 656–7 about the collaboration
of Malcolm king of Scots in laying the first stones of the new cathedral on 11 August
1093. These entries do appear, however, in the Durham *Historia regum*, 218, 220, as
additions to *HR*'s habitual source for this period, 'Florence' of Worcester. David, 'A
tract', 384 argued that here *HR* borrowed from DIV. Undoubtedly the compiler of *HR*
knew the *libellus*. But the framework of DIV (lines 3–28, 644–68) in which the *libellus*
proper is presented was probably composed separately; it is not impossible that it
borrowed from *HR*.

Anno sui episcopatus octauo: cf. *HR* 217. Calculating William's episcopal years from
his 'election' on 9 November 1080 (as the total length of his episcopate is calculated,
lines 664–5), this might imply that the bishop was driven out of England before 9
November 1088, which is plainly at variance with the *libellus*. Possibly *expulsus* refers to
the sentence of the Salisbury court early in November.

tocius Normannie curam suscepit: *HR* 216–7 has: a Rodberto comite totius provinciae
curam suscepit. But *HR* appears to have muddled the order of the last two sentences in
its entry for 1088, thus leaving a half-suggestion that Odo of Bayeux was being referred
to. The language of *ASC* 1087 [1088] on the eve of the conspiracy against Rufus is
similarly ambiguous: 'So generously did the king behave to that bishop that all England
was governed on his advice and direction.' Though the Waverley annals, ed. H. R.
Luard, *RS* (1865), 198 explicitly refer this to Bishop Odo, Dr Cecily Clark thinks that
ASC probably means St Calais, not Odo (*ASC*, 77); cf. 'Florence', ii,22 on St Calais's
influence early in Rufus's reign: eiusque consiliis totius Anglie tractabatur respublica;
Malmesbury, *GR*, ii, 360 tells the same story. Barlow, *WR* 61, n. 35 thinks it likely that
'Florence' and Malmesbury give the correct meaning of what *ASC* had garbled.

108 repacificatus regi: David, *RC* 59, n. 79 regards it 'as a plausible hypothesis' that
St Calais had something to do with bringing about peace between Rufus and Robert
Courthose at Rouen after Rufus's crossing to Normandy in February 1091; cf. Symeon,
HDE 128. According to the agreement between Rufus and Robert, those who had lost
their lands in England for supporting Robert were to recover them: *ASC* 1091; 'Florence',
ii, 27. Perhaps St Calais was regarded as included in these terms, but note Barlow's
skepticism about this, *WR* 282. It is not known precisely when the bishop returned to
England; Rufus came back in August 1091 according to 'Florence', ii, 28; Orderic, iv,
236.

109 For Rufus's expedition in company with his brother Robert against Malcolm III
(Canmore) of Scotland, see *ASC* 1091; 'Florence', ii, 28; Orderic, iv, 254, 268–70; Barlow,
WR 291–5.

110 As *HR* 218, which gives the same date, 11 September 1091. Perhaps DIV's claim
that St Calais had been driven from Durham on 11 September 1088 refers to the date
when he capitulated to Rufus's expedition against him; see note 101. Bishop William's
charter confirming the Allertonshire churches to the monks of Durham, often connected
with this episode because of its famous list of witnesses, which includes Rufus, Robert
Courthose and their brother Henry, is not authentic: *RAN* i no. 318; see *DEC* no. *6, pp.

650 quondam episcopus construxerat, a fundamentis *destru*xit, *et sequenti anno,* hoc est *millesimo nonagesimo tercio* ab *incarnacion*e *domini, aliam* meliori *opere incepit,* idest *anno* sui episcopatus *terciodecimo, ex quo autem monach*os *con*gregauerat *in Dunelmum undecimo.* Ipso namque anno ille *et qui post eum secundus erat in ecclesia, prior Turgotus, primos in fundamento lapides*

655 *posuerunt, tercio idus Augusti feria quinta.*[111] Aderat ibi tunc et rex Scottorum Malcolmus,[112] qui una cum eis in fundamento lapides cooperabatur. Tercio post inceptam ecclesiam anno *apud Wyndesoram ipso dominice natiuitatis die acr*ius solito *morbo corr*ipitur.[113] Vbi sepius a sancte memorie Anselmo Cantuariensi archiepiscopo[114] uisitatur et in confessione pec-

660 catorum eius absolucione et crebra benediccione perfruitur. Vbi et a *Thoma Eboracensi archiepiscopo* et *Walchelino Wyntoniensi et Johanne Bathoniensi*[115] inunctus et eukaristia confirmatus iiii° nonas Januarii noctu decessit,[116] xvi^{mo} anno suscepti episcopatus transacto et duobus mensibus minus duobus diebus,[117] hoc est *anno* ab *incarna*cione *domin*i m° xcui^{mo}, *ex*

665 *quo in Dunolmum monachi congregati fuerant terciodecim*o. Cuius corpus a Wyndesora perlatum Dunolmum *xvii*^{mo} *kalendas Februarii sepulture* est *tradi*tum in capitulo monachorum.[118]

1–34 om. CL which begin: Hac discordia durante dictus Willelmus Dunelmensis episcopus per inimicorum quorum machinamenta apud regem est accusatus quod parti inimicorum quorum faueret. Vnde rex Houeden et Welton cum [totis add. C] terris episcopi in Everwycschyre saisiri fecit quarto idus marcii et Odoni et Alano comitibus diuisit. Super quo episcopus sic regi scripsit Willelmo Anglorum regi [etc.] **1–2**. For this title in FBD see pp. 65–6 above. H gives: Incipit vita Willelmi Karilephi episcopi Dunelmensis **24** et *om. t* **39** meos *om. t* **44**

48–53, where the dating limits suggested should be corrected in the light of Barlow's criticisms, *WR* 287, n. 106: 294, n. 136.

111 Thursday, 11 August 1093.

112 Neither Symeon, *HDE* nor the tendentious rehandling of it in LV, f. 46v mentions Malcolm's presence. *HR* 220 does, and is followed by Chron. Melrose, f. 16r, facs. edn., 1936, p. 29. If indeed Malcolm was at Durham on 11 August, presumably he was on his way to attempt to see Rufus at Gloucester on 24 August: 'Florence', ii,31; Barlow, *WR* 309–10.

113 25 December 1095.

114 a sancte memorie Anselmo: Anselm died on 21 April 1109.

115 Thomas of Bayeux, archbishop of York, 1070–1100; Walkelin, bishop of Winchester, 1070–1098; John of Tours, bishop of Bath, 1088–1122.

116 Wednesday, 2 January 1096. *ASC* gives 1 January; 'Florence', ii,39, Wednesday, 1 January.

117 DIV's reckoning gives an episcopate of 16 years and 54 days $(2 \times 28 - 2)$ from William's 'election' on 9 November 1080 to 2 January 1096. This is better than Symeon, *HDE* 134–5, which says 15 years and 53 days.

118 Wednesday, 16 January 1096.

iniuste: inde *t* **47** istis: hiis *w* **48** legato: nuncio *w* **61** suas *om. t* **72** Hoffedene BF³: Offedene FH*w*; Hofden D. **73** Weltun *t*; Willentune L **74** racione: raciocinacione H*w* **83** predam: predictam *t* **88** mandastis H*w* **95** cunctis: omnibus *w* **102** quam: quod *codd.* **120** debeat F, *corr.* F² **127** abstulit *w* **139** more: modo *w* **141** recta *om. t* **155** Putauensis FBD, *as often* **170** illam: ullam *codd.* **173** Exonia: Oxonia H. Sandwicum *w.* et episcopus *add. t* **174** haberet FB. **175** siccam *om. t* **176** et pannos *om. t* **178** conuencio *w. As a form of* convenientia = covenant, conuencia, *though not quite unex-ampled, is rare and suspect.* **182** ad *add.* F³, *om.* F *t* **188** ad *om.* FD **190** est *om. t* **191** Dunelmie H; Dunelmense LD. regi *om. t* **210** utrumque *w, corr.* C **211** Saleysbyriam *w* **222–3** et causantibus ... responderet *expunct.* L; *om.* H **223** Lamfrancus *w*H **227** Lamfrancus *codd.* **236** rex uero *add. w* **250** autem: ergo *t* **252** tibi *ex corr.* F² **253** hoc *om. t* **260** facito F, *corr.* F² **269** faciat et rex sibi rectitudinem consentiat *add. w* **270** si michi canonice *rep.* F, *corr.* F² **283** suum *om.* F, *supra lin. add.* F³B **290** de *om.* F*t* **293** usquoque F **299** eis: ei FBHD **319** episcopis et *om. t* **322** T.: Thomas *w*D **324** te *om.* FBLHD, *add. manu recent.* C **337** monstrate *w* **338** quam: quod *codd.* **369** Boiocensem FB **371** feodi *om.* F*t* **385** quoniam: quando F*t* **395** reuertentes F **427** seruauerit FD. Piperellus *ex corr.* F² **429** vitulus LH **436** Exonia: Oxonia H. **437** Sandwicum w; Sangucium H **443** R.: Radulphus *w* **454** hic¹: sic *t* **466** possum *w* **481** hinc discedam: decedam *t* **516** Riginaldus C; R. H **526** eam: ea *codd.* **529** Wyltone B **533** W.: Willelmus *w.* Merlao D **538** Hainecorne B; Haiencorn D; Aiencorte *w* **545** Hamtone H **552** Gileberto C; Geleberto H **554** Hamptone *t*L; Hamptonis C **561** episcopus *om.* F, *supra lin. add.* F². Wyltone B **563** Hamptoniam L; Ham-tonam H **565** Ivo *w.* Erneisus *w*H **569** continentem FBHD **575** Ivo Taillebosc L; Ivo Tailbosc C; Yvo Tailbosc H **577** Dunelmensi episcopo *codd.* **578** Yvo Tailbosc L; Ivo Taillebosc; Yvo Taillebosc H **581** licet F, *corr.* F². eis *w* **582** Moulbreio *w* **586** Decembris *om.* F, *add. supra lin.* F². **587** Hamptoniam L; Hamtonam H **589** ei *om.* F, *add. supra lin.* F² **593** Salesbyriensis w; Salisberiensis H **597–8** quinquaginta et xxxix L; 89 D **601** et² *om.* F, *add. supra lin.* F². conductum securum [regis] *should perhaps be read* **609** potuissem: debuissem *w* **624** omnes homines *add. w*H **636** de capcione *add. w* **644** sui: vero H **645** *post* Normannorum: non ut exul sed ut pater *add. w* (cf. Symeon, *HDE*, 128). *post* susceptus: per tres annos quibus ibi moraturus est *add. w* (*as* Symeon, *HDE*,128) **645–6** Nomannie F. **646** suscepit: *here the* Tractatus *ends in w.* anno sui exilii *add.* H **652** ecclesiam aliam *add.* H **656–68** Aderat ... in capitulo monachorum: F *writes these lines in a much reduced script across the bottom margin* **658** Wyndehoram B; Winderesoram H; Windehoram D **662** Wintoniensi H **662–3** Bathanensi H **664** discessit H **666** Dunelmum *t*H **667** Win-deresora H; Windesora D. Dunelmum *t*H **668** monachorum et cetera *add. t*

INDEX

Abbetot, Urse d', 81
Aincourt, Walter d', 93–4, 101; his son William, 94 n. 78
Alan, count of Brittany, lord of Richmond, 59, 76 and n. 17, 79, 83, 89–90, 94, 95 n. 86, 98, 100; unnamed, 92–3, 97
Allertonshire, churches, 99 n. 110
Anglo-Saxon Chronicle, 62, 73–99 nn. 1, 10, 47, 69, 70, 80, 107, 109
Anselm, archbishop of Canterbury, 58, 62, 67, 78 n. 24, 86–7 n. 56, 92 n. 72, 100
Arnold, Thomas, 71

Baldwin, abbot of Bury, 88–9 n. 60
Baldwin, monk of Tournai, 67
Barlow, Prof. F., 63–5, 74–100 nn. 10–11, 13, 20, 28, 34–5, 45, 60, 64, 69, 91, 98, 107–09, 110, 112
Battle abbey, 96–7 n. 98
Bayeux, 58, 73, and see Odo
Beauchamp, Hugh, of Bedford, 64, 83–4 n. 45
Beaumont, Henry, earl of Warwick, 63–64, 83 n. 45; Hugh de, 63–4, 83–5, 88, and see Beauchamp; Hugh *pauper*, 83 n. 45
Bede, *Historia ecclesiastica*, 73; *Vita S. Cuthberti*, 73
Bedford, Thomas, 71
Bellême, Robert of, 79 n. 28
Benjamin, Robert, illuminator, 67
Bigot, Roger, 83, 94–5 n. 84
Boso, count of La Marche, 64
Boso, knight, 96–7 n. 98
Bretteville, Gilbert de, 94–5
Burun, Erneis de, 95, 101

Canterbury, 91–2 n. 69
Chartres, Fulbert of, *Ep.* LI, 91 n. 68
Chibnall, Dr M. M., 64, 87 n. 58, 94 n. 80
Claxton, William, of Wynyard, 66, 69–71
Conteville, Herluin of, 94 n. 84; Ralph *al.* Robert of, 94–6
Courcy, Richard de, 96 n. 96
Craster, Sir Edmund, 69–70
Cultura, Richard de, 96

David, C. W., 58, 73 n. 1, 99 nn. 107–08

Domesday Book, scribe, 66
Douglas, Prof. D. C., 53, 71
Dover, 91
Downton (Wilts.), 73 n. 7
Dugdale, Sir William, *Monasticon*, 71
Durham, 59–60, 67; castle, 60, 74–5, 77–80, 82 n. 39, 84, 88–91, 93–5, 96–7 n. 98, 97–8
Durham cathedral, 99 n. 107, 100; chapter-house, 100
Durham cathedral priory, 58, 62, 73–4; library, 65–6, 68–71, 73 n. 6, 91 n. 68; monks, see Symeon, Swalwell, Todd, Wessington

Eadmer, 61–2, 64, 78–92 nn. 24, 36, 41, 56, 60, 72
Espec, Walter, 98 n. 104
Exeter, 80, 90

Fothadh. bishop of St Andrews, 86 n. 54
Freeman, E. A., 65, 74–95 nn. 10, 45, 54, 64, 69, 76, 88

Galbraith, V. H., 53
Geoffrey, monk, 66–7, 96, 98
Gibson, Dr M. M., 62, 89–90 n. 64
Gloucester, 73
Gransden, A., 58 n. 2
Gratian, *Decretum*, 91 n. 68
Gregory, *Regesta*, 80 n. 30
Gregory VII, pope, 58, 73
Guy, abbot of St Augustine's, Canterbury, 75–6

Hastings, 91
Heppo *balistarius*, 95
Historia Regum, 62, 65, 73–99 nn. 1, 9, 107, 110
Hoffmann, Hartmutt, 61–3, 86–7 nn. 54, 56
Holderness (Yorks.), 76 n. 17
Howden (Yorks.), 74 n. 12, 76, 100–01
Howden, Roger of, 65
Hyde Chronicle, 64, 87 n. 58

John, bishop of Bath, 100

103

III

A 1301 Sequestrator-General's Account Roll For the Diocese of Coventry and Lichfield

Edited by Jill B. Hughes

CONTENTS

ACKNOWLEDGEMENTS

I am grateful to the Dean and Chapter of Lichfield for permission to publish the text offered here, LJRO, MS D30 M4. I wish to thank Mr M. S. Dorrington, archivist in charge, and his staff at Lichfield Joint Record Office for their assistance and co-operation. Thanks are due to Professor R. L. Storey, Dr A. K. McHardy, and Miss K. Major for their suggestions and encouragement. I owe special thanks to Professor D. M. Smith for his advice and constructive criticism during the preparation of the text, and to the Literary Director, Professor Michael Jones, for his support and helpful guidance.

ABBREVIATIONS

BL	British Library
BRUO	A. B. Emden, *A biographical register of the University of Oxford to A.D. 1500*, 3 vols. (Oxford, 1957–9)
CCR	*Calendar of Close Rolls*
CPL	*Calendar of Papal Letters*
CPR	*Calendar of Patent Rolls*
Fasti	John le Neve, *Fasti Ecclesiae Anglicanae, 1300–1541*, new edn. 12 vols. (London, 1968–77), x
Hughes, 'Episcopate'	J. B. Hughes, 'The episcopate of Walter Langton, bishop of Coventry and Lichfield, 1296–1321, with a calendar of his register (unpublished Ph.D. thesis, University of Nottingham, 1992)
Hughes, 'Clergy List'	Jill B. Hughes, 'A 1319 clergy list of the Tamworth and Tutbury deanery in the diocese of Coventry and Lichfield', *Staffordshire Studies*, 6 (1994), 1–25
JEH	*Journal of Ecclesiastical History*
Jenkins, 'Lichfield cathedral'	H. Jenkins, 'Lichfield cathedral in the fourteenth century' (unpublished B. Litt. thesis, University of Oxford, 1956)
Knowles & Hadcock	D. Knowles, R. N. Hadcock, *Medieval religious houses: England and Wales*, 2nd. edn. 1971 (reissue Harlow, 1994)
LJRO	Lichfield Joint Record Office
Reg. Sutton	*The rolls and register of Bishop Oliver Sutton, 1280–1299*, ed. R. M. T. Hill, 8 vols. (Lincoln Record Society, 39, 43, 48, 52, 60, 64, 69, 76, 1948–86)
Reg. Winchelsey	*Registrum Roberti Winchelsey Cantuariensis Archiepiscopi*, ed. R. Graham, 2 vols. (Canterbury and York Society, 51, 52, 1952–6)
Swanson, 'Episcopal income'	R. N. Swanson, 'Episcopal income from spiritualities in later medieval England: the evidence for the diocese of Coventry and Lichfield', *Midland History* (1988), 1–20
Taxatio	*Taxatio Ecclesiastica Angliae et Walliae auctoritate P. Nicholai IV circa A.D. 1291* (Record Commission, 1802)
VCH	Victoria History of the Counties of England

INTRODUCTION

The document printed here is in the collection of the Dean and Chapter of Lichfield preserved in Lichfield Joint Record Office: LJRO, MS D30 M4. It is a roll of six membranes, 12cm wide, recording the sequestrator-general's accounts in the diocese of Coventry and Lichfield for the period Epiphany (6 January) 1300/1 to Michaelmas (29 September) 1301 from the episcopate of Walter Langton, bishop from 1296 to 1321. The condition of the roll is good apart from membrane one where a contemporary, stitched, diagonal tear 11cm long extends upwards from the foot, around which the scribe has worked, and some staining also on this membrane has made the manuscript illegible in places as Lichfield Joint Record Office does not allow the use of an ultra-violet lamp. It has been written in normal early fourteenth century court hand, with a change of hands being evident from the seventeenth entry on membrane two; the first hand then resumed work at the beginning of membrane three, and completed the roll. The roll appears to be a fair copy, but there are some clerical errors, and the totals were subsequently checked and the few mistakes in calculation rectified, albeit erroneously in the case of the Derby sequestrations total on membrane six. It has been endorsed *annus primus* in another hand, but as a sequestrator-general's account for November 1297 to November 1298 is summarised in Langton's episcopal register,[1] presumably from such a roll, or rolls, as this, the endorsement may have been made because it is the earliest extant sequestrator-general's account roll for the diocese.

The account roll is complete and thus it seems to be a unique example of its type from the fourteenth century: three fragments of other rolls also survive from Langton's episcopate, two for the period April 1309 to Michaelmas 1310 and one which covers the years 1315 to 1317, while a fragment of a similar roll for 1314 from the diocese of Lincoln is preserved in Lincolnshire Archives Office, but there does not appear to be similar material in other dioceses, except from the sixteenth century.[2] The account roll and Langton's episcopal register

1 LJRO MS B/A/1/1, fo. 4v; Hughes, 'Episcopate', no. 86.
2 LJRO MSS D30 M9, D30 M5, D30 M7; Lincolnshire Archives Office, Lincoln, MS D & C/Bj/5/17(2). For a full discussion of income from spiritualities in the diocese see Swanson, 'Episcopal income', and pp. 2, 13–15, & nn. 1, 3, 4, 110; Hughes, 'Episcopate', i, 177–83. The dioceses of Exeter, Norwich and Worcester, for example, have sequestration material dating from 1500: Exeter Cathedral Library MS 3690; Norfolk and Norwich Record Office, Norwich, MSS DN/SUN/1a, DN/SUN/1b; Hereford and Worcester Record Office, Worcester, MSS 737.5 BA2487, and see R. N. Swanson, 'Episcopal income from spiritualities in the diocese of Exeter in the early sixteenth century, *JEH*, 39 (1988), 520–30.

supplement one another: the roll lists clergy and parishioners who would otherwise be unknown, and it records the income the bishop received from spiritualities, while the register clarifies the length of time that some benefices were sequestered, and both it and other sources provide information on individuals and institutions listed on the roll.

Although the diocese of Coventry and Lichfield was the third largest in medieval England,[3] Bishop Langton employed only one sequestrator-general. This was also the case in the diocese of Worcester, but the larger sees of York and Lincoln, and some others, often had one or two sequestrators-general with sub-sequestrators working under them in each archdeaconry.[4] No commission appointing a sequestrator-general has been recorded for Langton's episcopate, but the duties which generally fell to his office have been well-described: his primary function was as a bishop's chief collector of spiritual revenues and custodian of sequestrated property, whether benefices (which were sequestrated either as a matter of course whenever they fell vacant, or as a means of canonical coercion) or the goods of intestates, and he was often granted testamentary jurisdiction by his diocesan.[5] It was not unusual, however, for other diocesan administrators, chiefly archdeacons, their officials, or the rural deans, to be appointed *ad hoc* custodians of sequestrated property in the diocese.

As the fourteenth century progressed a sequestrator-general's duties were often extended which eventually led to his office being combined with that of commissary-general, a bishop's judicial officer. In the diocese of Coventry and Lichfield this may have been from 1360,[6] but

3 It covered an area of approximately 5,260 square miles and it was divided into five archdeaconries: Chester, Coventry, Derby, Shrewsbury and Stafford. Derby and Stafford archdeaconries largely followed the county boundaries; Chester comprised of Cheshire, Lancashire as far north as the Ribble, and part of north Wales; Shrewsbury contained the northern part of Shropshire; and Coventry part of Warwickshire: P. Hughes, *The Reformation in England* (London, 1950), i, 31–2; D. Robinson, *Staffordshire Record Office cumulative hand list, part 1: Lichfield Joint Record Office: diocesan, probate and Church Commissioners' records*, 2nd. edn. (Staffordshire County Council, 1978), 1.

4 By 1360, however, the diocese of Coventry and Lichfield had a sub-sequestrator working in each deanery, and the sequestrator-general was empowered to appoint and remove these officers at will: LJRO MS B/A/1/3, fo. 108; *The registers or act books of the bishops of Coventry and Lichfield. Book 5, being the second register of Bishop Robert de Stretton, A.D. 1360–1385: an abstract of the contents*, ed. R. A. Wilson (Wm. Salt Archaeological Society later Staffordshire Record Society, new series, 8, 1905), 93; *VCH Staffs.*, iii, 35.

5 R. M. Haines, *The administration of the diocese of Worcester in the first half of the fourteenth century* (London, 1965), 114–9, 123–4, and for examples of commissions appointing sequestrators-general see ibid, 335–6; R. L. Storey, *Diocesan administration in fifteenth century England* (Borthwick papers 16, York, 1959), 8–15; C. Morris, 'The commissary of the bishop in the diocese of Lincoln', *JEH*, 10 (1959), 53–8.

6 *VCH Staffs.*, iii, 36; Morris, 'Commissary of the bishop', 55–65; Storey, *Diocesan administration*, 15–16; *The registers or act books of the bishops of Coventry and Lichfield. Book 4, being the register of the guardians of the spiritualities during the vacancy of the see, and the first register of*

during Langton's episcopate, although each officer received similar types of *ad hoc* commission,[7] their primary duties remained separate, with the exception of testamentary jurisdiction from 1311. Then, each officer was granted the probate of wills of those with goods valued under £30, and the right to grant administrations and issue aquittances after examining the executors' accounts.[8] It has been suggested, however, that this may have been merely a personal grant made to the then commissary-general as no probate powers are mentioned again in commissions to that office until the late fifteenth century.[9]

The account lists gross episcopal revenue from spiritualities totalling £598 1s. 1 3/4d. This has been bolstered by £321 19s. 7d., apparently from visitation corrections, but this was not regular, annual income. Visitation receipts apart, after expenses such as the payment of administrators and collectors, and the charges sent to Rome of £10 5s. annually for Peter's Pence and Langton's common service tax, paid by instalments of perhaps 10 marks (£6 13s. 4d.) a year, it has been estimated that the bishop's net regular income from this source averaged about £150 a year. This was clearly a substantial element of the bishop's total income, particularly so when visitation receipts were included, and one that was vital when the temporalities of the see were seized when Langton was imprisoned on Edward II's orders in 1307–8. Nevertheless, Langton was personally deprived of even this income for more than fourteen months in 1302–3 when he was suspended from episcopal office and his see was sequestrated by Boniface VIII, a time when all the spiritualities and temporalities of the diocese were managed by papal administrators.[10]

The archdeaconry of Chester is excluded from the account except

Bishop Robert de Stretton, 1358–1385: an abstract of the contents, ed. R. A. Wilson (Wm. Salt Arch. Soc., new series, 10 (2), 1907), 7; *Reg. Stretton. Book 5, 3–4, 93*.

7 For example, to induct incumbents to benefices and to exercise the office of visitation on behalf of the bishop: Hughes, 'Episcopate', nos. 207, 342, 395, 473, 859, 1047, 1050.

8 At the same time the rural deans of the archdeaconries of Coventry, Derby, Shrewsbury and Stafford were granted the probate of wills of the deceased within their jurisdictions with goods valued below 100s., with the right to grant administrations to executors, while Robert de Donechirch, vicar of Lichfield, received a similar grant for wills up to 40s. with an additional clause enabling him to audit the accounts of executors. The rural deans of Chester archdeaconry were excluded from this grant because of the unique status of the archdeacon of Chester who had the probate of wills within his jurisdiction: Hughes, 'Episcopate', no. 719. For the archdeacon of Chester, see below n. 50.

9 *VCH Staffs.*, iii, 35.

10 Swanson, 'Episcopal income', 1, 4–5, 9, 13–15; Storey, *Diocesan administration*, 12; *Accounts rendered by papal collectors in England 1317–1378*, ed. W. E. Lunt, E. B. Graves (Philadelphia, 1968), 27, 37; A. Beardwood, 'The trial of Walter Langton, bishop of Lichfield, 1307–1312', *Transactions of the American Philosophical Society*, 54, pt. 3 (1964), 11–13; *CCR 1307–13*, 88; Hughes, 'Episcopate', i, 151, 186–97, 226–7, 257, 270–1, 328–35; no. 364.

for sequestrations, which pertained to the bishop by right, and for the £20 pension from the archdeacon. This is the first record of the pension which the archdeacon paid annually to the bishop in recompense for the semi-autonomous jurisdiction he exercised within his archdeaconry.[11] The charges listed under visitation corrections vary from 12d. to 60 marks (£40), with no explanations given for their levy. Some of the lesser amounts may be procurations, but the majority are probably fines for offences revealed at visitation. Others may be for non-appearance before the visitor, whether the bishop or his commissary,[12] or, in the case of clerics, perhaps for non-attendance at diocesan synods. Those paid by the three sets of executors may be connected with probate, while some of the larger sums, such as the 60 marks received from M. Jordan de Caunvill, rector of Clifton Campville, may represent first fruits of vacant benefices which Langton was entitled to receive by grant of Boniface VIII. Many others were probably paid for a variety of episcopal acts and dispensations.[13]

None can be identified as such with any certainty. Under Langton institutions were charged at 1/2 mark (6s. 8d.) and may have been collected at the following Michaelmas; this was still the customary fee in 1496.[14] The fees for other services such an induction, non-residence licences, letters dimissory, and perhaps ordination, may have been charged at this rate also, as in other dioceses, but Langton's register is silent on this except in one case. Then, a rector was granted licence to study for three years on condition that he paid 1 mark (13s. 4d.) annually to the bishop for his alms, but this amount is probably atypical.[15] Nevertheless, other entries in the register indicate it was not uncommon for fees to be relaxed by the bishop or his chancellor as a means of bestowing patronage.[16]

Langton frequently extended his fund of patronage by granting temporary custody of vacant benefices and their revenues to others; instructions were then issued to the sequestrator-general, or *ad hoc* custodian, to surrender them.[17] These custodies were granted either

---

11 See n. 50 below; Swanson, 'Episcopal income', 2, 14.

12 For Langton's visitations see Hughes, 'Episcopate', i, 280–93; Hughes, 'Clergy list'.

13 See n. 21 below; Hughes, 'Episcopate', no. 841.

14 Hughes, 'Episcopate', i, 179–80; nos. 3, 7, 8, 12, 187, 317, for example; *The register of John Morton, archbishop of Canterbury 1486–1500*, ed. C. Harper-Bill (Canterbury and York Society, 75, 78, 1987, 1991), ii, no. 432; Swanson, 'Episcopal income', 8.

15 *The register of Robert Hallum, bishop of Salisbury 1407–17*, ed. J. M. Horn (Canterbury and York Society, 72, 1982), nos. 1150–3; M. Bowker, *The secular clergy in the diocese of Lincoln, 1495–1520* (Cambridge, 1968), 40; see below M. Alexander de Vernon, n. 37; Hughes, 'Episcopate', no. 37 (entry duplicated no. 228). Under Bishop Stretton (1360–85) non-residence fees rose to 20s. a year, see *Reg. Stretton. Book 5*, 65, 68–9, 71, 77–8; Swanson, 'Episcopal income', 8–9, nn. 48, 57.

16 Hughes, 'Episcopate', nos. 5, 6, 8, 13, 31, 43, 46, 54, 82, 84, 109, 110, for example.

17 Hughes 'Episcopate', nos. 81, 405, 420, 441, 750, 826, 835, 897, 963, 1055, 1056, for

'during pleasure' or for a specific term, and often to the clerk presented and subsequently instituted to the living.[18] It is unclear whether the total receipts of £158 8s. 7 1/2d. from the sequestrations are just that, or if they represent clear profits after all expenses, including the payment of a chaplain, had been met. Four of the benefices listed in this section had been alienated for some of the accounting period: Ashover, Birdingbury, Sheinton, and Bangor. The receipts for Ashover, Sheinton, and Bangor relate to the period before alienation, whereas the autumn fruits of Birdingbury, amounting to 5 1/2 marks (£3 13s. 4d.), were sequestered by episcopal right after custody of the church had been granted to the presentee on 23 August 1301 and he had been instituted rector on 31 August.[19]

The contents of the account roll can be summarized as follows:

1. Visitation receipts from the archdeaconries of Coventry, Stafford, and Shrewsbury, with those from the archdeaconry of Derby being included in a composite section.
2. Probate of wills.
3. Synodals and perquisites at Easter term in each deanery of the archdeaconries of Coventry, Shrewsbury, Stafford, and Derby.
4. The £20 annual pension from the archdeacon of Chester.
5. Peter's Pence, synodals, and perquisites at Michaelmas term in each deanery of the archdeaconries of Coventry, Shrewsbury, and Stafford, with only Peter's Pence and perquisites being recorded for Derby archdeaconry.
6. Revenue from the vacant archdeaconry of Stafford.
7. Peter's Pence from prebends.
8. Revenue from sequestrated benefices in all five archdeaconries: Derby, Coventry, Stafford, Shrewsbury, and Chester.

example. The sequestrator-general's account in Langton's register for 1297–8 suggests that rural deans were appointed *ad hoc* custodians of sequestrated property, or as the bishop's financial agents, more often than is actually documented in the register, as were their contemporaries in the dioceses of York and Worcester: Hughes, 'Episcopate', nos. 80, 36, 668; Storey, *Diocesan administration*, 12; Haines, *Administration of Worcester*, 66, 71, 123–4.

18 Hughes, 'Episcopate', nos. 208, 298, 405, 413, 433 for 'during pleasure', for example; for fixed terms see nos. 9, 13, 52, 400, and for eventual institution, 44 (instituted 326), 53 (instituted 235), 208 with note of institution, 297 (instituted 300), 415 (instituted 288), for example. On one occasion the presentee to Buildwas, Salop., had his grant of custody revoked when the bishop committed this to another, even though the initial clerk was eventually instituted rector, see no. 464.

19 See nn. 62, 72, 79, 84 below; Swanson, 'Episcopal income', 14.

EDITORIAL PROCEDURE

The biographical details of individuals, of incumbents of named benefices, and information on other institutions listed on the roll, have been annotated to the text. This information has been taken chiefly from the episcopal register of Walter Langton, bishop of Coventry and Lichfield, 1296–1321, which was the subject of my University of Nottingham Ph. D. thesis; the relevant entry number quoted is that given both in the thesis and in my edition of the register to be published by the Canterbury and York Society. The valuation given to the sequestrated benefices, and to others, where appropriate, by the *Taxatio* of Pope Nicholas IV, which assessed clerical incomes in 1291, has been included in the footnotes to provide a bench-mark for the receipts listed. Arabic have been substituted for Roman numerals. Scribal peculiarities of spelling have been preserved. Scribal suspension marks have been preserved for place-names lacking one or more syllables. With the exception of rectors, vicars and chaplains, for those persons having names in addition to their first name, either a patronymic, or a territorial, occupational, or a descriptive name, these have been transcribed in the upper-case. Scribal suspensions of personal names have been preserved, with the exception of occupational names which have been extended, conjecturally, in round brackets. Other conjectural editorial extensions are also in round brackets. Square brackets indicate illegible words or figures, or supplied text. Marginal headings are printed in bold type.

A 1301 SEQUESTRATOR-GENERAL'S ACCOUNT ROLL FOR THE DIOCESE OF COVENTRY AND LICHFIELD

[LJRO, D30 M4, roll of 6 membranes, 12cm wide, the first of which is damaged. Endorsed (in a later hand) *Primus annus ... 1300*]

Exitus episcopatus Coventr' et Lich' a festo Epiphanie
Domini anno gracie MCCC usque ad festum Sancti
Michaelis proximo sequens
Archidiaconatus Coventr'
Corr(ectiones) vis(itaciones)

De abbate de Stonlee	40s.
De abbate de Cumba	100s.
De priore de Hertford[20]	60s.
De magistro Jordano de Caunvill rectore de Clifton[21]	6om.
De rectore de Berkeswell	20m.
De domino Thoma de [...] de Assho	60s.
De Galfrido de Stoke[... ?rector]e de Allesleye	40s.
De vicario de Gren[eberg]	40s.

20 The priory of Hertford received an annual pension of £1 6s. 8d. from Solihull church (Warw.), which was granted by Ralph de Limesi when he founded the priory before 1093. His endowment included a carucate of land in Itchington (Warw.), and tithes both there and in Ulverley in Solihull: *Taxatio*, 242a; *VCH Warwicks.*, iv, 218, 228; *VCH Herts.*, iv, 419; Knowles & Hadcock, 54, 67.

21 M. Jordan de Caunvill, rector of Clifton Campville church, with its dependent chapels of Harlaston and Chilcote, was a local man. In 1319 he was assisted by three parochial chaplains. In both 1291 and 1319 the parish was said to lie in the deanery of Tamworth and Tutbury, in the archdeaconry of Stafford, whereas the account roll lists it under the archdeaconry of Coventry. Jordan was granted custody of Clifton Campville church on 7 Dec. 1298 and he was instituted rector on 2 Jan. 1298/9, having been presented by Sir Geoffrey de Caunvill. He received licences to study for 5 years: twice for a two year period on 4 Apr. 1301 and from Michaelmas 1311, and a one year licence on 3 Mar. 1313/4. He appointed two attorneys on 3 Mar. 1315/6 as he was going 'beyond seas' for two years, perhaps to complete his education. He was presumably at least in subdeacon's orders while on study leave, but he does not appear to have proceeded to higher orders. Although he was probably charged the customary fees for his institution (1/2 mark) and licences for non-residence, the 60 marks (£40) receipted here may represent the first fruits of his benefice as the parish was assessed at £16 13s. 4d. p.a. by the *Taxatio*: Hughes, 'Clergy list', 9-10; Hughes, 'Episcopate', nos. 19, 95, 15, 434, 727, 967, 841; *CPR 1313-17*, 437; *Taxatio*, 243a; Swanson 'Episcopal income', 14-15, nn. 109, 111.

De magistro Roberto Tancard[22]	[. . .]
De magistro Ricardo rectore de Fennycompton	£10[. . .]
De domino Nicholao rectore de Franketon	20s.
De vicario de Neubold	40s.
De rectore[a] de Herdewyk[23]	1m.
De rectore de Wedinton	100s.
De priore de Canewell	1/2 m.
De Rogero Henr'	2s.
De domino Nicholao rectore de Herdebergh	10s.
De Roberto capellano de Shulton	1m.
De Johanne Doubeday	2s.
De Willelmo Clerico preceptore de Balsale[24]	[. . .]m.
De Henrico de Eyton juniore	[. . .]
De Ricardo Middyng apparitore	2s.
De Johanne capellano de Brughton	8s.
De fratre Willelmo de Alcrington	1/2 m.
De Roberto capellano de Milverton	1/2 m.
De Roberto de Bobenhull	1/2 m.
De Willelmo Godefrey de Wyllugby	1/2 m.
De Rogero le Yek de Salebrugg'	4s.

a *Sic* in MS

22 M. Robert Tancard was rector of Withybrook (Warw.) until his death on 17 Oct. 1313. He received a licence to study for one year from 2 Mar. 1299/1300: Hughes, 'Episcopate', nos. 406, 646.

23 Priors Hardwick church with its chapels and appurtenances had been appropriated to the prior and convent of Coventry (Warw.) by Bishop Roger de Meuland in 1260. A vicarage was ordained there and the *Taxatio* assessed it at £3 and the church at £18 p.a. The prior and convent exercised a peculiar jurisdiction in this parish and, although the bishop retained the right of institution, apparently it fell to the official of the peculiar to induct the vicars. However, the first recorded mandate to induct, dated 1 Feb. 1313/4, was addressed to the archdeacon of Coventry or his official, as were several others in the mid-fifteenth century. The first vicar to be mentioned in Langton's register was Roger Bacoun, who died on 17 Jan. 1313/4: William Dugdale, *Antiquities of Warwickshire* (Coventry, 1765), 372; *Taxatio*, 241b, 244a, R.N. Swanson, 'The priory in the later Middle Ages' in *Coventry's first cathedral. The cathedral and priory of St. Mary, Coventry: papers from the 1993 anniversary conference*, ed. G. Demidowicz (Stamford, 1994), 150–1; R.N. Swanson, 'The rolls of Roger de Meuland, bishop of Coventry and Lichfield (1258–1295), *Journal of the Society of Archivists*, 11 (1990), 37–8; Hughes, 'Episcopate', no. 651.

24 The manor of Balsall was given to the Knights Templars by Roger Mowbray, probably during the reign of King Stephen, and it became the site of a preceptory of the order, the remains of which stand to the west of Balsall church, which was also built by the order about 1290. Following accusations brought against the Templars in 1307–8, Edward II ordered the arrest of the English members of the order in 1308 and Balsall then reverted to John Mowbray, bishop of Coventry and Lichfield (1258–1295), who held it until his death in 1322. The preceptory and its possessions then passed to the Knights Hospitallers: *VCH Warwicks.*, iv, 86, 88; Knowles & Hadcock, 292, 293, 300, 301. For a history of the order see G. A. Campbell, *The Knights Templars* (London, 1937); H. Nicholson, *Templars, Hospitallers and Teutonic Knights: images of the military orders 1128–1291* (Leicester, 1993).

De vicario de Weston[25]	1/2 m.
De Willelmo de Milverton	1/2 m.
De Henrico le Bret domino de Ansteleye[26]	72[...]s. [...]
De Simone de Mancestr'	1/2 m.
De rectore de Fylungleye	100s.
De Johanne de Engham de Colleshull	1/2 m.
De rectore de Sekkyndon	[...]
De fratre Nicholao de Brewode	1/2 m.
De priore de Tykeford[27]	1m.

Summa £112 10s. 8d. probavit

Staff'

Corr(ectiones) vis(itaciones)

De abbate de Roucestr'	100s.
De abbate de Crokesden	10m.
De magistro Johanne rectore de Uttoxhather	60m.
De Willelmo rectore de Northbur'	£10
De rectore de Thorp juxta Tamworth[28]	100s.
De rectore de Bisshebur'[29]	2s.
De rectore de Blumshulf	1m.
De domino Johanne Basset rectore de Chedle	2m.
De vicario de Dulverne	2m.
De vicario de Chesewrth'[b][30]	10s.
De Willelmo de Seukworth	20s.
De vicario de Athelaston[31]	1m.

b *Sic* in MS

25 Thomas de Sutham is the first vicar of Weston under Wetherley to be recorded; he died on 26 Apr. 1316: Hughes, 'Episcopate', no. 675.

26 Henry le Bret, son and heir of William le Bret, was a minor when his father died in 1281. His wardship, and that of his two brothers, was sold to Gilbert, vicar of Nuneaton, by Sir John de Montalt. He held the manor of Bretts Hall, Ansley, and had a wife, Margaret: *VCH Warwicks.*, iv, 6; *CPR 1302–7*, 117.

27 Aston church (Warw.) was appropriated to Tickford Priory (Bucks.). The church had three dependent chapels, including Yardley. It was assessed at £26 13s. 4d. and the Dean and Chapter of Lichfield additionally received an annual pension of £13 6s. 8d. from it: *VCH Bucks.*, i, 361, n. 4, 364; *Taxatio*, 242a.

28 The first rector of Thorpe Constantine to be recorded is William de Neuton, who was an acolyte when he was instituted on 28 Oct. 1301, having been presented by Richard Constantyn, lord of Thorpe Constantine. In 1319 the church was also served by a parochial chaplain. This church was not assessed by the *Taxatio*: Hughes, 'Episcopate', no. 291; Hughes, 'Clergy list', 9, 17.

29 The rector of Bushbury at this date may have been Hugh, who was ordained deacon and priest on 18 Dec. 1305 and 19 Mar. 1305/6 respectively: Hughes, 'Episcopate', nos. 1295, 1296.

30 Perhaps this was John de Dunston, the first vicar of Cheswardine to be recorded, who died on 7 Aug. 1316: Hughes, 'Episcopate', no. 780.

31 Robert de Kenilleworth, chaplain, was instituted vicar of Ellastone on 6 Jan. 1298/9, having been presented by the prior and convent of Kenilworth (Warw.): Hughes, 'Episcopate', nos. 21, 279.

De Ricardo de Prestwod	1m.
De Is(abella) de Swynnerton	2s.
De Agnete Consutrice	2s.
De Alicia filia Galfridi atte Shawe	2s.
De Thoma Molend(inario)	2s.
De Johanne atte Barre	1m.
De Ada de Wedinton	5s.
De Nicholao capellano de Bromwych[32]	17s.
De Willelmo capellano de Aldestr'	1/2 m.
De Henrico Silvestr' capellano	4s.8[d.]
De Margeria Wodenotte	12d.
De Ricardo Herbert de Clyfton	2s.
De Willelmo filio Roberti[c] de Tappele	40d.
De Silvestro capellano de Lega	12s.
De Willelmo de Elynghal'	6s.
De Roberto capellano de Dulverne	8s.
De Ricardo Wyldegos capellano	1m.
De Ricardo de Stubbeley	3m.
De Willelmo Hereward capellano[33]	6s. 9d.
De Roberto capellano de Gayton in Weston	2s. 6[d.]
De Thoma Pistore de Farton	1/2 m.
De Roberto de Moeles capellano de Gnousal'	2s. 6[d.]
De Johanne de Elmynton capellano de Chekkel'	20s.
De Roberto Cundy de Chedle	2s.
De Philippo de Pencrich capellano de Northbur'	8[. . .]
De Ricardo de Sheldon manente in Middelton	1/2 m.[d]
De Ricardo Pyrie de Honeswrth'[e]	2s.
De Johanne Basset rectore de Chedl'	1/2 m.
De Willelmo de Rouhal' clerico	4s.
De Laurencio de Egemundon	1m.
De rectore de Blore	1/2 m.

c *Roberti* interlined
d *1/2m.* interlined
e *Sic* in MS

32 This may be the same Nicholas de Bromwich who was parochial chaplain of West Bromwich church in Jan. 1318/9, for although parochial chaplains were engaged for a year at a time, by contracts made at Michaelmas, many enjoyed continuous employment. The church was farmed in perpetuity to Sandwell Priory by the monks of Worcester for an annual payment of 6 marks. No vicarage was ordained there and so the cure of souls would have been committed to the parochial chaplain, who was assisted by three celebrants in Jan. 1318/19: Hughes, 'Clergy list', 4, 6, 14.

33 William Hereward may be the unbeneficed chaplain who was later ordained subdeacon, deacon and priest on 20 Dec. 1315, 5 June 1316 and 28 May 1317 respectively, having been presented by John de Swynnerton: Hughes, 'Episcopate', nos. 1313, 1315, 1318.

De domino Ada de Whetenhal'	20s.
De priore Beati Thome juxta Staff'	40s.

Summa £86 19s. 6d. probavit

Salop'

Corr(ectiones) vis(itaciones)

De Willelmo Bedel de Albrighton	4s.
[De] Willelmo Hod de Ideshal'	2s.
De Ricardo Spaynel de Neuport	40d.
De Hugone ad Aulam capellano Salop'	1/2 m.

[Membrane 2]

De Willelmo de Fennymor	3s.
De magistro Roberto de Preston[34]	5s.
De Matilda uxore Willelmi Gaypogge	2s.
De Willelmo filio Eve capellano	6s. 9d.
De Thoma filio Kenewreyk'	5s.
De Johanne capellano de Egemundon	1m.
De Waltero Madekyn de Kembrighton	3s.
De Ricardo Tyf de Benynton	3s.
De Ricardo capellano de Rokleye manente apud Wroxcestr'	5s.[f]
De Ricardo le Webbe de Baschirche	2s.
De Rogero filio Ricardi de Eyton	2s.
De Youkyno Molend(inario) de Loskesford	2s.
De Hugone de Roma de Drayton in Hales	40d.
De Hugone Coco	40d.
De Johanne Preposito, Thom(a) de Ruewothin, Johanne Forestar(io) de Betton subtus Limam	1/2 m.
De domino Roberto rectore de Tonge	20s.
De Hugone le Mortimer rectore de Stocton	40s.
De vicario de Welinton	40s.
De Thoma rectore medietatis ecclesie de Condovere[35]	100s.

f 5s. interlined

34 This may be the same Robert de Preston, acolyte, who was instituted rector of Fitz (Salop.) on 23 May 1315, having been presented by the abbot and convent of Haughmond (Salop.). He was accorded the title 'Master' when he was ordained both subdeacon on 20 Dec. 1315 and priest on 17 June 1318; his ordination to the diaconate has not been traced. He received two one-year dispensations for non-residence, holy orders, and to study on 3 Mar. 1315/6 and 25 Nov. 1316: Hughes, 'Episcopate', nos. 979, 1313, 1320, 985, 988.

35 Thomas de Charnes was instituted to moiety of Condover church on 31 Jan. 1299/1300. On 28 Feb. 1298/9 Langton commissioned his official to hold an inquiry concerning Thomas' presentation to the benefice by the abbot and convent of Shrewsbury. We then learn that the bishop knew of nothing to prevent his admission except that John de Shelton had been presented to the same moiety by a papal provision. The official was to ascertain the merits of this provision; if he established that John's opposition lacked force or truth, he was ordered to admit and induct Thomas, saving to the bishop

De Martino vicario Sancte Crucis Salop'	20s.
De vicario de Ercalewe	1m.
De magistro Henrico de Shavyngton	20s.
De rectore de Stirchesle	20s.
De rectore[g] de Nortone in Hales	100s.
De rectore de Nesse Extranea	2 1/2m.
De rectore de Stauntone	100s.
De Roberto de Warr' porcionario de Wroxcestr'[36]	1/2m.
De magistro Alexandro de Verdon[37]	1/2 m.
De rectore de Smethecote[38]	1/2 m.

g *rectore* interlined

the later institution. Afterwards, a letter ordered Thomas, 'who acts as rector of a moiety of Condover', to be at York on 21 June 1299 to discuss with the bishop business about himself and his position. To end the dispute over the moiety, an annual pension of 40s., or at least 20s., to be conferred by the abbot of Shrewsbury, was ordered to be provided to John de Shelton. Thomas was in subdeacon's orders when he was presented to the moiety, and he proceeded to the diaconate and priesthood without delay, on 4 June and 17 Dec. 1300 respectively. On 17 Dec. 1300 also he received the first of two one-year licences to study, the second of which was granted some years later, on 3 Feb. 1309/10. The 100s. receipted here may have been paid by Thomas for the satisfactory outcome of the disputed presentation, although it may have included some element for his first licence to study. Condover church was wealthy; the whole church was assessed at £23 6s. 8d. a year. Presumably Thomas would have been able to pay the charge from his half of the benefice without too much difficulty: Hughes, 'Episcopate', nos. 69, 77, 327, 416, 1285, 1286; *Taxatio*, 247b.

36 In 1155 Wroxeter church was divided into five portions, but by 1291 these had been reduced to three, the first of which was then assessed at 20 marks, the second at 10 marks, and the third at 5 marks p.a. The *Taxatio* additionally names two of the church's portionaries separately under a heading indicating that they were not beneficed elsewhere; Roger de Warro' and Roger Bernoc' then held the third and second portions respectively. Nicholas de Trokuesford (or de Troughford) had succeeded Roger de Warro' in the third portion before 29 June 1301, when he in turn was replaced by M. Walter de Clune, while Bellingar de Qwillino (or de Berenger de Quiliano) held either the first or second portion by 17 Dec. 1295, and on 18 Apr. 1301 custody of it was granted to Roland de Vinquiria (or de Viquiria), who was then instituted on 31 May 1301; Robert de Warr' thus occupied the remaining first or second portion of the benefice: *VCH Salop.*, ii, 63, 66; *Taxatio*, 247b, 245b; Hughes, 'Episcopate', nos. 444, 348, 414, 437, 335; see below nn. 75, 76.

37 M. Alexander de Verdon was rector of Biddulph (Staffs.); his inclusion in a Shrewsbury section of the account roll therefore appears to be erroneous. He had been granted custody of the sequestrated church on 31 Dec. 1299 until the next ordination service, which may have been the date he was ordained subdeacon on 4 June 1300, the first ordination service for which records have survived from Langton's episcopate. He was instituted rector of Biddulph on 2 July 1300, having been presented by Henry de Verdoun. The 1/2 mark receipted here may represent the fee for his first one-year licence to study. This was granted on 1 Feb. 1300/1, and he received a second licence from Christmas 1307. He later presented Roger Dobyn of Darlaston (Staffs.) to be ordained subdeacon and deacon on 23 Dec. 1318 and 22 Dec. 1319 respectively: Hughes, 'Episcopate', nos. 400, 1285, 285, 421, 498, 1321, 1324.

38 The first rector of Smethcott recorded in Langton's register is Roger de Smethecote, who was granted a licence to study for two years on 1 Jan. 1312/13. He was ordained

De Johanne Gillot de Salop'	1/2 m.
De Johanne de Upphavene rectore de Chetewynd	1/2 m.
De magistro Henrico de Shavington	1/2 m.
De magistro Galfrido Dogyn	3s.
De Hugone de Wloukeslowe	1/2 m.
De magistro Henrico de Shavinton	1/2 m.
De rectore de Kynardeseye	1m.

Summa £32 14s.[h] 9d. probavit

Item Staff'

Corr(ectiones) vis(itaciones)

De domino Henrico vicario de Alveton	40s.
De Philippo filio Ricardi ad Montem	2s.
De abbate de Cumbermere	100s.
De Agnete de Kinggeston	12d.
De priore Sancti priore Sancti[i] Thome juxta Staff'	40s.
De Matheo de Vilers	20m.
De vicario de Melewych[39]	1/2m.
De rectore de Northbur'[40]	1m.
De Ricardo de Perte	5s.
De Johanne de Cravenhung'	1/2m.
De Willelmo capellano de Hadenhale	4s.
De Johanna de Kington	2s.
De Osberto de Tamworth	10s.
De Ada filio Roberti le Hayward	40d.
De Johanne le Seler capellano	5s.
De vicario de Tuttebur'[41]	6m.
De Willelmo Fuody[j] capellano	5s.
De Willelmo de Aldustre capellano	1/2m.
De Willelmo capellano de Blithefeld	10s.
De Ricardo de Camera[42]	2s.

h *14s.* corrected
i *Sic* in MS
j *Sic* in MS

deacon and priest on 21 Dec. 1314 and 17 May 1315 respectively: Hughes, 'Episcopate', nos. 580, 1311, 1312.

39 The vicar of Milwich may have been Richard de Nonynton, who resigned on 26 Oct. 1315: Hughes, 'Episcopate', no. 769.

40 The rector of Norbury was previously listed as William, see p. 116 above.

41 Tutbury church, assessed at £7 13s. 4d. p.a., was appropriated to the prior and convent of Tutbury (Staffs.). The clergy list of Jan. 1318/19 records that John atte Cok was then the perpetual vicar, but he does not occur in Langton's register; he then had the assistance of nine unbeneficed chaplains: *Taxatio*, 243a; Hughes, 'Clergy list', 7, 19.

42 Richard de Camera was rector of Leigh (Staffs.), having been instituted on 9 Jan. 1298/9 at the presentation of Philip de Draicote. He was assisted by at least one chaplain named Silvester, who is also listed on the account roll above. The manor of Leigh and its possessions had been granted to Burton upon Trent Abbey in the 12th century and Leigh

De Sibilla filia Rogeri Clerici	1/2m.
De Willelmo sacrista de Wolrenhampton[43]	1/2m.
De Willelmo Hereward capellano	40d.
De domino Waltero de Beyci	1/2m.
De priore Sancti Thome juxta Staff'	100s.

Summa £36 12s. 8d.[k]

Item Salop' corr(ectiones) vis(itaciones)

De priore de Wombrugg'	5m.
De Thoma de Pesshale	10s.
De domino Roberto de Warr'[44]	20s.
De Editha Borre	5s.
De Johanne le Gaunter	1m.
De Johanne de Lilleshull	4s.
De rectore de Smethecote	1/2m.
De domino Philippo Flambaus	20s.
De Willelmo filio Rogeri de Anecot'	40d.
De Johanne filio Rogeri de Meleford	40d.
De Johanne Caperon	1/2m.

k *8d.* corrected from 6d.

church was mentioned in a confirmation of the abbey's possessions by Bishop Richard Peche of Coventry (1161–82). The abbey received 5 marks annually from the rector, but the payments were often in arrears and the abbot and convent had then to resort to law to receive their dues: Hughes, 'Episcopate', no. 277; *Collections for a history of Staffordshire* (Staffordshire Record Society, 1937), p. 41; nos. 408, 411, 420; *VCH Staffs.*, iii, 202–3.

43 The college of St Peter, Wolverhampton, was re-founded as a royal free chapel in 1203. The parochial duties fell to the sacrist. Following a dispute about their respective jurisdictions, the dean of Wolverhampton and Bishop Alexander Stavensby (1224–38) agreed in 1224 that the bishop should receive the dean's canonical obedience, while the dean should retain his customary power of conferring the prebends of his church, of institution, and of correction, except in cases of lapse after canonical monition, when the bishop should correct. The bishop was to receive 2s. annually for Peter's Pence and the oblations from the Pentecostal Procession were to be reserved for him, and matrimonial cases, cases of sacrilege, cases of appeal, and other difficult cases were to be referred to him. He was to be honourably received on his first arrival at the church after his consecration and could celebrate, preach, confirm, enjoin penances, give the oil and chrism, and, at the request of the dean and canons, canonically admit ordinands from their church, provided that he and his church were indemnified; he also undertook to protect the church in its rights and possessions. Nevertheless, the peculiar jurisdiction of the royal free chapels may have caused difficulties for Langton; this is suggested by the clause that clerks from royal free chapels in the diocese were not to be ordained without his special licence which has been included in statements preceding some ordination lists: Knowles & Hadcock, 419, 444; *VCH Staffs.*, iii, 326; J. H. Denton, *English royal free chapels 1100–1300: a constitutional study* (Manchester, 1970), 41–4; D. Styles, 'The early history of the king's chapels in Staffordshire', *Transactions of the Birmingham Archaeological Society*, 60 (1936), 85–6; *The great register of Lichfield Cathedral known as Magnum Registrum Album*, ed. H. E. Savage (Wm. Salt Arch. Soc., 1924), no. 587; Hughes, 'Episcopate', i, 68–9, 128–9; nos. 1313, 1320, 1321, 1323, 1324; Hughes, 'Clergy list', 6.

44 Portionary of Wroxeter, see n. 36.

De Isabella Logghe	1/2m.
De Ada Wattestach'	40d.
De sacrista de Ercalewe	10s.
De magistro Henrico de Swavington[l]	10s.

[Membrane 3]

De magistro Johanne de Uphavene	1/2m.
De Hugone de Wloukeslowe	2m.
De Johanne rectore capelle de Pemington	2m.
De uxore Radulphi Bercar(ii) de Longeford	1/2m.
De Hugone Gregori	40d.
De Johanne de Callerhal'	40d.
De Begoue[m] rectore de Froddesle	1/2m.
De Emma uxore Walteri Prat	2s.
De parochianis de Ordele	10s.
De Alicia Underwod'	1/2m.
De Bogoue rectore ecclesie de Froddesleye	60s.
De Petro Gentil	2s.
De Roberto Beaumeis	40d.
De Rogero filio Alani Pryde	40d.
De domina de Morton Corbet	100s.
De Nicholao capellano de Roulton	1/2m.
De Ada Fythelare	2s.
De hominibus de Upton	1m.
Summa £23 18s. 4d. probavit	

Corr(ectiones) vis(itaciones)[45]

De Willelmo Drinkewater	2s.
De Henrico capellano de Ilum	1/2m.
De Ada capellano de Clifton	1/2m.
De Ricardo Clerico de Clifton	40d.
De Willelmo de Pecco	1m.
De Gilberto Keys	10s.
De Roberto filio Bate Diacono[n]	2s.
De Thoma de Whytemor	2s.
De Thoma Teyt	12d.
De Ricardo de Wytton	40d.
De Johanne Dalke	2s.
De Johanne de Cornub'	2s.
De Ricardo capellano de Ochovere	10s.
De rectore de Kyrkolston	40s.

l *Sic* in MS *recte* ?Shavington
m *Sic* in MS
n *Sic* in MS

45 This section contains names from Coventry, Shrewsbury, Stafford, and Derby archdeaconries.

De vicario de Hampton	2m.
De Ricardo Anote	1/2m.
De Ada de Barre	8s.
De Roberto de Folkeshull	40d.
De exec(utoribus) vicarii de Longeford	20s.
De Johanne Gylbert et Roberto Gilbert	2m.
De Willelmo filio Willelmi Gilbert	2s.
De Ricardo capellano de Kyngeston	1/2m.
De Jordano capellano de Whytacre	1/2m.
De Philippo de Eginton	1/2m.
De Galfrido Bercar(io) de Tamworth	20d.
De Ricardo Garcione Margerie ad Crucem	20d.
De Waltero de Hauekesford	1/2m.
De Thoma de Wadiloue	40d.
De eodem	1m.
De Ricardo serviente rectoris de Irton	1/2m.
De Johanne filio Johannis de Swancote	4s.
De domino Galfrido capellano de Sheldon	1/2m.
De Thoma capellano de Byruntham	12s.
De Willelmo capellano de Hunesworth	1/2m.
De Ada Lune	40d.
De vicario de Erdynton	1/2m.
De domino Willelmo de Lich'	20s.
De Willelmo Bertram	10s.
De Henrico le Barber	1/2m.
De vicario de Dunchirch	1/2m.
De vicario de Merton	40s.
De Willelmo capellano de Hullemerton	1m.
De Rogero Beauveismer	1m.
De Andrea capellano de Stretton	10s.
De Johanne Brodebrok'	10s.
De Nicholao Scorti	10s.
De vicario de Wylughby[46]	1/2m.
De domino Ricardo Sauvage	10s.
[Membrane 4]	
De domino Thoma ad Crucem	10s.
De domino Nicholao de Morlee	1m.
De domino Stephano capellano de Stok'	30s.
De exec(utoribus) Radulphi de Thiknes	1/2m.
De exec(utoribus) Willelmi porcionarii de	1/2m.

46 The vicar of Willoughby may have been Nicholas called Benet, who died on 5 Mar. 1311/12. The vicarage was in the patronage of the hospital of St John the Baptist, without the east gate of Oxford: Hughes, 'Episcopate', no. 644; Knowles & Hadcock, 329, 383-4; *VCH Oxford*, ii, 158-9.

Conedovere[47]

De domino Radulpho de Besages rectore de Walton	40s.
De Ricardo de Glascote	1/2m.
De Marthino de Irton	40d.
De Nicholao de Morlee	1/2m.
De Thoma filio Walteri de Shukkebergh	1m.

Summa £29 3°s. 8d. probavit

De probacionibus testamentorum

De testamento Henrici le Ferour de Ronton	4s.
De testamento Willelmi Cresset de Shauebur'	2s.
De testamento Sarre domine de Boulewas	1/2m.
De testamento Ricardi Pride	40d.
De testamento Willelmi rectoris de Harle[48]	20s.
De testamento Henrici le Gaunter de Novo Burgo	1m.
De testamento domine Nicholae de Wyngerworth	40d.
De testamento Agnetis Cantel de Horsele	5s.
De testamento Gerardi Waldyme de Allespath	40d.
De testamento Johannis Brun de Essheburn	1/2m.
De testamento Emme relicte Henrici de Upton	12[?d.][P]
De testamento Walteri Fabri	1/2m.
De testamento Henrici Ballard de Coventr'	1/2m.
De testamento rectoris de Esshovere[49]	1/2m.
De testamento Johannis Upegrene de Aldustr'	2s.
De testamento Ade Vyman de Cesterfeld	2s.
De testamento Siwardi de Aston	1/2m.
De testamento magistri[q] Michaelis de Ormesby	20s.
De testamento Johannis le Venour de Middelton	40d.
De testamento Alicie uxoris Roberti le Blound de Allespath	20s.
De testamento Reginaldi Ballard	1/2m.
De testamento Roberti de Hales	2s.
De testamento Johannis de Gourton de Derb'	1/2m.

o *3* written over an erasure
p MS unclear
q *gistri* written over an erasure

47 William de Wesenham died as portionary of Condover before 28 Feb. 1298/9 and Thomas de Charnes was eventually instituted to the vacant benefice: Hughes, 'Episcopate', nos. 327, 69; see n. 35.

48 William, rector of Harley, died before 24 Mar. 1300/1, when Richard de Kyn-redeleye was instituted: Hughes, 'Episcopate', no. 334.

49 The rector of Ashover died before 31 Mar. 1301 when custody of the sequestrated fruits of the church were granted to Roger Deyncurt, rector of North Wingfield (Derb.), during pleasure. On 26 Apr. 1301 Roger was granted Ashover church in commendam for half a year: Hughes, 'Episcopate', nos. 433, 442; see n. 62.

De testamento Roberti de Say	1/2m.
De testamento Matildis uxoris Ricardi de Barton	1/2m.
De testamento Gene uxoris Johannis de Knyveton	40d.
De testamento Is(abelle) uxoris Nicholai de Sekkyndon	40d.
De testamento Henrici le Yonge de Douberigge	1/2m.
De testamento Nicholai Lyot	1/2m.
De testamento Gunolde uxoris Thurstani de Pitcheford	1/2m.
De testamento Nicholai de Thyknes de parochia de Audeley	1/2m.
De testamento Willelmi de Oldefeld de Hodenet	4s.
De testamento Willelmo le Hore de Leghton	4s.
De testamento Radulphi rectoris^r Tinctor(is) de Cesterfeld	4s.
De testamento Roberti Bacun rectoris de Normanton	1/2m.
De testamento Johannis Prepositi de Throule	20s.
De testamento Alicie uxoris Johannis de Rydeware	1/2m.
Summa £12 10s. probavit	

Terminus Pasche

Archidiaconatus Coventr'

De sinodalibus decanatus de Merton	16s.
De perquisiciis ejusdem decanatus	13s. 6d.
De sinodalibus decanatus de Ardena	20s.
De perquisiciis ejusdem	13s. 8d.
De sinodalibus decanatus de Stonlee	1m.
De perquisiciis ejusdem	10s. 10d.
De sinodalibus decanatus de Coventr'	8s.
De perquisiciis ejusdem decanatus	13s.
Summa 108s. 4d. probavit	

Archidiaconatus Salop'

De sinodalibus decanatus Salop'	20s.
De perquisiciis ejusdem decanatus	40d.
De sinodalibus decanatus Novi Burgi	1m.
De perquisiciis ejusdem decanatus	3s.
Summa 39s. 8d. probavit	

Archidiaconatus Staff'

De sinodalibus decanatus de Alveton	10s.
De perquisiciis ejusdem decanatus	6s.

[Membrane 5]

De sinodalibus decanatus de Lappeleye	13s.
De perquisiciis ejusdem decanatus	3s. 6d.
De sinodalibus decanatus de Staff'	1m.

r *rectoris* deleted

De perquisiciis ejusdem	4s. 8d.[s]
De sinodalibus decanatus Tamworth	8s. 8d.
De perquisiciis ejusdem	40d.

Summa 62s. 6d. probavit

Archidiaconatus Derb'

De sinodalibus decanatus Derb'	61s.
De perquisiciis ejusdem decanatus	24s.
De sinodalibus decanatus de Essheburn	25s.
De perquisiciis ejusdem	17s. 6d.
De sinodalibus decanatus de Repyndon	22s. 8d.
De perquisiciis ejusdem	10s.
De sinodalibus decanatus Castellar	34s.
De perquisiciis ejusdem	16s. 8d.[t]
De sinodalibus decanatus de Alto Pecco	16s.
De perquisiciis ejusdem	6s.
De sinodalibus decanatus de Scarvesdal'	62s.
De perquisiciis ejusdem decanatus	1m.

Summa £15 8s. 2d. probavit

Archidiaconatus Cestr'

De pensione archidiaconatus Cestr'[50]	£20

s *d.* interlined
t *d.* interlined

50 M. Robert de Redeswell, archdeacon of Chester from at least 3 May 1289 until his death before 17 Jan. 1314/15, paid the bishop an annual pension of £20 in accordance with an agreement which lasted for their respective lives only. This agreement was presumably similar to that made on 26 Mar. 1315 between Langton and M. Richard de Havering, Redeswell's successor. Then, in order to avoid 'the toils of litigation', both parties agreed that, for their lives only, the archdeacon should have the primary hearing of causes, the probate of wills, and that he should receive there all synodals, Peter's Pence, and the perquisities of his chapter throughout his archdeaconry, while the bishop was to receive £20 yearly from the archdeacon, and retain all rights of sequestration and 'other matters' which pertained to him by custom. The need for such an agreement stemmed from the Palatine status the county of Chester enjoyed, which made it difficult for bishops of Coventry and Lichfield to cite Cheshire offenders to the consistory court in Lichfield, or elsewhere, without royal support. To overcome this, successive bishops granted the archdeacon exclusive primary jurisdiction, enabling all Cheshire offenders to be tried within the county. Here, as elsewhere in the diocese, the bishop devolved custody of some of the sequestrated benefices to the archdeacon, before granting temporary custody of them to clerks of his choosing; as this account and fragments of later account rolls show, the bishop received revenue from them. As to the 'other matters' which pertained to the bishop by custom, these included the right of institution and visitation, and the granting of absolution and the enjoining of penances in cases reserved to him in the archdeaconry, for which he appointed two penitentiaries in Jan. 1310/11: P. Heath, 'The medieval archdeaconry and Tudor bishopric of Chester', *JEH*, 20 (1969), 244–9; Lichfield Cathedral Library MS *Magnum Registrum Album* (register of the dean and chapter) fos. 262v-263r; Savage, *Magnum Registrum Album*, no. 587; Hughes, 'Episcopate', i, 91, 96, 98–100, 287–8; nos. 441, 826, 835, 897, 809, 901, 853; LJRO MSS D30 M9, D30 M5, D30 M7.

Summa patet
Terminus Michaelis
Archidiaconatus Coventr'

De denariis Beati Petri[51] decanatus de Merton	40s.
De sinodalibus ejusdem diaconatus[u]	16s.
De perquisiciis ejusdem diaconatus[v]	10s. 2d.
De denariis Beati Petri decanatus de Stonle	45s.
De sinodalibus ejusdem diacanatus[w]	1m.
De perquisiciis ejusdem diacanatus[x]	6s. 11d.
De denariis Beati Petri diacanatus[y] de Ardena	60s.
De sinodalibus ejusdem diacanatus[z]	20s.
De perquisiciis ejusdem decanatus	27s.
De denariis Beati Petri decanatus Coventr'	46s. 4d.
De sinodalibus ejusdem decanatus	8s.
De perquisiciis ejusdem decanatus	14s.

Summa £15 6s. 9d. probavit
Archidiaconatus Derb'[52]

De denariis Beati Petri decanatus Derb'	47s. 4d.
De perquisiciis ejusdem decanatus	19s. 1 1/2d.
De denariis Beati Petri decanatus de Essheburn	35s. 4d.[aa]
De perquisiciis	7s.
De denariis Beati Petri decanatus de Castellar	26s. 4d.
De perquisiciis	14s.
De denariis Beati Petri decanatus de Repindon	22s. 8d.[bb]
De perquisiciis ejusdem decanatus	1m.
De denariis Beati Petri de Alto Pecco	26s. 4d.
De perquisiciis ejusdem	7s. 4d.
De denariis Beati Petri decanatus de Scarvesdal'	£4 5s. 8 3/4d.[cc]
De perquisiciis ejusdem decanatus	9s. 4d.

u *Sic* in MS
v *Sic* in MS
w *Sic* in MS
x *Sic* in MS
y *Sic* in MS
z *Sic* in MS
aa *d.* interlined
bb *d.* interlined
cc *8 3/4d.* interlined

51 For Peter's Pence see W. E. Lunt, *Financial relations of the papacy with England to 1327* (Cambridge, Mass., 1939), 3–84; and for a discussion of the amounts collected in Coventry and Lichfield diocese see Swanson, 'Episcopal income', 3–4.

52 No synodals are listed for the archdeaconry of Derby at Michaelmas Term, suggesting that there may have been an agreement between the bishop and the archdeacon for the archdeacon to retain these payments. An archdeacon's account of 1533 suggests that he then received a proportion of the synodals paid within his archdeaconry: LJRO MS B/A/17/1, fos. 19–23; Swanson, 'Episcopal income', 3–4.

Summa £15 13s. 10 1/4d. probavit

Archidiaconatus Salop'

De denariis Beati Petri decanatus Salop'	£4
De sinodalibus ejusdem decanatus	20s.
De perquisiciis ejusdem	1/2m.
De denariis Beati Petri[dd] decanatus Novi Burgi	40s.
De sinodalibus ejusdem decanatus	1m.
De perquisiciis ejusdem	2s. [?6d.][ee]

Summa £8 2s. 6d. probavit

Archidiaconatus Staff'

De denariis Beati Petri decanatus de Alveton et Leek	48s.
De sinodalibus ejusdem decanatus	15s.
De perquisiciis ejusdem	6s.
De denariis Beati Petri decanatus Staff' et Novi Castri	75s.
De sinodalibus ejusdem	20s.
De perquisiciis ejusdem decanatus	1/2m.
De denariis Beati Petri decanatus Tamworth et Tottebur'	42s.
De sinodalibus ejusdem	13s.
De perquisiciis ejusdem	11s.
De denariis Beati Petri decanatus de Lappele et Tresel	63s.
De sinodalibus ejusdem	19s. 6d.
De perquisiciis ejusdem decanatus	10s. 5d.

Summa £16 9s. 7d. probavit

[Membrane 6]

Vacacio Archidiaconatus Staff'[53]

De Nicholao Pollard	9s. 9d.
De Jacobo Apparitore	10s. 10d.

Summa 20s. 7d.[ff] probavit

---

dd *Petri* interlined
ee MS unclear
ff *20s.* corrected from 22s.; *7d.* written over an erasure

53 The archdeaconry of Stafford was vacant between about 22 May and 6 June 1301. The archdeacon of Stafford, M. Rayner de Vichio, a papal chaplain in priest's orders, was granted papal licence to make a will on 22 May 1301. He died shortly afterwards, and on 6 June 1301 John de Brunforte was provided to the vacancy by Boniface VIII. John also succeeded Rayner as prebendary of Gaia Minor. John was granted papal dispensation to hold the archdeaconry and prebend as he was twelve years old and had received only his first tonsure; he was ordered to proceed to higher orders at the proper age. John was the son of Octavian de Brunforte, a member of Boniface VIII's household, and nephew of Reginald de Brunforte, knight. In Apr. 1309 a prebend in the diocese of Fermo was reserved for him, to be held in addition to his archdeaconry and prebend in Coventry and Lichfield diocese. He resigned his archdeaconry on 19 Jan. 1321/2, and exchanged his prebend of Gaia Minor for that of Pipa Parva on 9 Feb. 1324/5: *CPL*, i, 514, 561, 596; ibid, ii, 76; Jenkins, 'Lichfield cathedral', apps. E, F; *Fasti*, x, 18–19, 42; Hughes, 'Episcopate', i, 119–20.

Denarii Beati Petri de prebendiis[54]

De denariis Beati Petri de prebenda de Colewych[55]   10s.

De denariis Beati Petri de prebenda de Eccleshal'[56]   20s.

De denariis Beati Petri de prebenda de Berkeswych[57]   3s.

De denariis Beati Petri de prebenda de Brewode[58]   8s.

De denariis Beati Petri de prebenda de Longedon[59]   10s.

54 At the time of Langton's episcopate there were 30 prebendal churches in the diocese, eleven of which were acquired in the 13th century and remained subject to ordinary jurisdiction (Bolton le Moors, Bubbenhall, Dasset, Darnford, Flixton, Pipa Parva, Ryton, Sandiacre, Tarvin, Wellington, Wolvey). The other nineteen prebends (listed in *Fasti*, x), including the five listed in this section of the roll (Colwich, Eccleshall, [Whittington and] Berkswich, Brewood, and Longdon) were all in the peculiar jurisdiction of the prebendary, and the chapter of Lichfield heard matrimonial causes and other causes coming before it on appeal, although the dean was allowed to visit the prebendal parishes every three years: Jenkins, 'Lichfield cathedral', 160–2, 164, app. C; Hughes, 'Episcopate', i, 130–1.

55 Colwich was a Saxon prebend, its vicarage and its chapel of Fradwell in the gift and jurisdiction of the prebendary. The *Taxatio* assessed it at £26 13s. 4d. p.a. It is unclear who held the prebend at this date. Bogo de Clare had been presented to it by John de Colwich when Peter de Comite was provided by the pope. On 24 Nov. 1289 the pope ordered Bogo's removal but as Peter was engaged in litigation about the prebend of Whittington and Berkswich and, being unable to obtain possession of it, he may have re-occupied Colwich: Jenkins, 'Lichfield cathedral', app. C; *Taxatio*, 244a; *Fasti*, x, 24; *CPL*, i, 509–10. Was Bogo the rector of Frodesley listed on the account roll above?, see p. 122.

56 Eccleshall was a Saxon prebend, its vicarage also in the gift and jurisdiction of the prebendary. The *Taxatio* assessed it at £66 13s. 4d. p.a. M. Elias de Napton held the prebend from an unkown date until his death at Eccleshall on 12 July 1311. He was prominent in the diocesan administration, being archdeacon of Derby from at least July 1281 until his death, and on 30 Mar. 1302 he was appointed one of three administrators of the diocese when the see was placed under sequestration by the pope. He was a pluralist, holding also the rectory of Warmington (Warw.) and prebends in Derby and Chester: Jenkins, 'Lichfield cathedral', apps. C, F; *Taxatio*, 243b; *Fasti*, x, 16, 34; Bodleian Library MS Ashmole 794, fo. 71v; Hughes, 'Episcopate', i, 108–9, 188–9; nos. 635, 866.

57 The full title of this prebend was Whittington and Berkswich; Berkswich was a Saxon prebend and Domesday manor of the bishop, while Whittington was an appropriated parish, its curacy in the jurisdiction of the prebendary. The *Taxatio* assessed it at £20 p.a. The prebendary was another leading diocesan administrator, M. Thomas de Abberbur', having been collated by Langton on 17 Dec. 1298. Although Peter de Comite claimed the prebend for himself in Jan. 1299/1300 by virtue of a papal provision, Thomas remained in possession until he was collated precentor of Lichfield on 1 Sept. 1303: Jenkins, 'Lichfield cathedral', apps. C, F; *Taxatio*, 243b; *Fasti*, x, 7, 66; *BRUO*, i, 2; Hughes, 'Episcopate', i, 139–50, 186–9; nos. 18, 384, 392, 397.

58 The prebend of Brewood was granted to the dean of Lichfield cathedral in 1176, and it was augmented by the parish church of Adbaston in 1192. The *Taxatio* assessed the prebend at £26 13s. 4d. p.a. M. John de Derby was elected dean in Apr./May 1280 and his appointment was confirmed by Bishop Meuland later that year. He died on 12 Oct. 1319: Jenkins, 'Lichfield cathedral', app. C; *Taxatio*, 243b; *Fasti*, x, 7.

59 Longdon was a Saxon prebend, its vicarage in the gift and jurisdiction of the prebendary. The *Taxatio* assessed it at £20 p.a. Luke de Fieschi was provided to the prebend on 11 Oct. 1297 and he held it until his death on 31 Jan. 1336: Jenkins, 'Lichfield cathedral', app. C; *Taxatio*, 243b; *Fasti*, x, 45; *CPL*, i, 572.

Summa 51s. probavit

Derb'

De sequestro vicarie de Langeford[60]	23s.
De sequestro medietatis ecclesie Stavele[61]	21s. 4 1/2d.
De sequestro de Esshovere[62]	9s.
De sequestro vicarie de Cesterfeld[63]	27s. 10d.

60 The *Taxatio* assessed Longford church at £14 13s. 4d. p.a. with a pension of £2 10s. paid to the prior of Kenilworth; no vicarage is listed. The church had been granted to Kenilworth Priory before 1161, and Bishop Stavensby confirmed the grant; but in 1283 the advowson was said to have pertained to Oliver de Langeford, deceased, tenant in chief. Longford vicarage was presumably sequestrated after the death of the last vicar; the account roll notes above that 20s. was received from his executors. The vicarage must have been vacant for at least six months prior to 18 Apr. 1301 when Bishop Langton collated William de Retford, a priest, to it, in order for the presentation to have devolved to him through lapse of time, by authority of the Third Lateran Council of 1179. When the next institution took place in June 1304 the patron of the vicarage was M. John de Cressi, then rector of Longford: *Taxatio*, 247a; BL Harl. MS 3650, fo. 70; *VCH Warwicks.*, ii, 86; *CPR 1281–92*, 59; *Cal. Fine Rolls 1272–1307*, 181; Hughes, 'Episcopate', nos. 389, 257; 'Decretalium Gregorii Pape IX compilatio' in *Corpus Juris Canonici*, ed. E. Friedberg (Graz, 1955), iii, 8, 2; *Councils and Synods with other documents relating to the English Church*, ed. F. M. Powicke, C. R. Cheney (Oxford, 1964), II, i, 566.

61 This moiety of Staveley church became vacant on 22 Dec. 1300 and Thomas de Querle was instituted rector on 9 Feb. 1300/1, having been presented by Edward I, custodian of the land and heir of Nicholas Musard, the last rector of the moiety. The church was in Scarsdale deanery of the archdeaconry of Derby; it has been listed as 'Stanely' by the *Taxatio*, which assessed it and its chapel at £10 p.a.: Hughes 'Episcopate', nos. 468, 243; *CPR 1292–1301*, 560; *Taxatio*, 246b.

62 The rector of Ashover died before 31 Mar. 1301 when custody of the church's sequestrated fruits was granted to Roger Deyncurt, rector of North Wingfield (Derb.), during pleasure; he had been presented to Ashover church by Margery de Rerisby and Simon de Rerisby. As Roger de Eyncourt he was granted Ashover church in commendam for half a year on 26 Apr. 1301. He had vacated North Wingfield by 12 Nov. 1301 and he probably became rector of Ashover at about that time, although no record of this has survived; an incumbent with the same name has been independently recorded in 1303, and again in 1337. Roger was a member of the secondary branch of the Deyncourt family established on land in Derbyshire before 1135. North Wingfield and Tupton were soke of their manor of Pilsley, and North Wingfield church provided a living for the younger sons. John Deyncourt (4th baron) held one fee in Ashover. Roger's reason for changing churches is unclear, but it was not for financial gain; the *Taxatio* assessed Ashover church at £23 6s. 8d. and North Wingfield at £20 p.a.: Hughes, 'Episcopate', nos. 433, 442, 249; I. H. Jeayes, *Descriptive catalogue of Derbyshire charters in public and private libraries and muniment rooms* (London, 1906), nos. 115, 123; T. Foulds, *The Thurgarton Cartulary* (Stamford, 1994), table 2 (p. cxvii), pp. xxx, xlv, lxxvi, xcviii, cviii-cix, cxiii-cxiv; *Taxatio*, 246a.

63 Chesterfield vicarage became vacant on 18 Dec. 1300 either by the death or resignation of Thomas de Welton, priest, who had been instituted vicar on 19 Apr. 1298. His successor was Walter de Suthleyrton, who was instituted to the benefice on 3 Feb. 1300/1. Although no patron was recorded on this occasion, Chesterfield church was appropriated to the dean of Lincoln. The church was wealthy; with its chapel it was assessed at £73 6s. 8d. p.a. and the vicarage at £6 13s. 4d.: Hughes, 'Episcopate', i, 129–30; nos. 222, 242, 268, 465, 1083; *Taxatio*, 246a.

De sequestro vicarie de Ettewall[64]	32s. 11 1/2[gg]d.
De sequestro ecclesie Sutton in Dale[65]	4s. 4 1/2[hh]d.
De sequestro vicarie de Sutton[66]	38s. 8d.[ii]
De sequestro ecclesie de Normanton[67]	21 1/2d.
De sequestro ecclesie de Castro Pecci[68]	3s. 6d.

gg *1/2* interlined
hh *1/2* interlined
ii *8d.* interlined

64 Etwall vicarage presumably was sequestrated when it too became vacant and Br. Robert de Sutton, canon of Welbeck (Notts.), was instituted vicar on 5 Aug. 1301, having been presented by the abbot and convent of Welbeck, by the authority of a privilege they had to present one of their canons. St Helen's church, Etwall, had been granted to the abbey as part of its original foundation (1154–60) by Thomas of Cuckney. When the abbey's appropriation of the church was confirmed by Bishop Geoffrey Muschamp of Coventry (1198–1208) it was stated that on the death or resignation of the first vicar the abbot and convent were to receive two-thirds of the tithes, with the remainder forming the endowment of the vicarage. The *Taxatio* does not mention the vicarage, but it assessed Etwall church at £16 p.a., and it records additionally that the church was charged with a pension of £1 16s. to Tutbury priory, which may have been granted because the church had formerly been appendant to the manor of Etwall which was held of the honour of Tutbury: Hughes, 'Episcopate', no. 248; A. Hamilton Thompson, *The Premonstratensian abbey of Welbeck* (London, 1938), 13, 49–50; A. Hamilton Thompson, *The English clergy and their organization in the later Middle Ages* (Oxford, 1947), 120; BL Harl. MS 3640, fos. 38, 124v; *Taxatio*, 247a.

65 The reason for the sequestration of Sutton Scarsdale church is unclear. If it was vacant, no institutions to it have been recorded before 23 Sept. 1304, when the patron was Thomas, earl of Lancaster, then custodian of the heir of Richard de Grey, a minor. The church was valued at £4 13s. 4d. p.a.; Hughes, 'Episcopate', no. 259; *Taxatio*, 246b.

66 Sutton on the Hill vicarage may have been vacant; the first record of an institution to it is that of Adam de Novo Castro subtus Lymam, a priest, on 1 Dec. 1301. He had been presented by the prior and convent of Trentham (Staffs.), to whom the church had been granted by Ralph de Boscherville during the episcopate of Bishop Peche (1161–82). The church was appropriated to the priory and a vicarage ordained after the compilation of the *Taxatio*, which valued the church at £10 13s. 4d. p.a.: Hughes, 'Episcopate', no. 250; *Collections for a history of Staffordshire* (Wm. Salt Arch. Soc., 11, 1890), 315–6; *VCH Staffs.*, iii, 257, 258; *Taxatio*, 247a.

67 Why Normanton church was sequestrated is again unclear. The first record of an institution is dated 13 Nov. 1307, when the patron was Lady Denise le Wyne. It was valued at £6 13s. 4d. p.a.: Hughes, 'Episcopate', no. 501; *Taxatio*, 246a.

68 The church of Castleton in the Peak may have been vacant. William Notekyn, priest, was instituted to the newly ordained vicarage there on 6 Apr. 1302, having been presented by the abbot and convent of Vale Royal (Ches.), to whom the church had been appropriated. Langton's vicar-general, M. Thomas de Abberbur', had ordered an inquiry to be made of the portions and revenues of the church, which had been assessed at £12 p.a. With the bishop's authority, he then summoned the abbot and convent and the priest they had presented to the benefice to hear his ordination of the vicarage. Half the manse which had been the rector's and in which the barn was situated was to pertain to the religious and their successors, with the benefits and profits of the moiety. In addition, the religious were to have the tithes of corn and hay, of the mine, of the foals from the king's stud (*pullanorum de haracio domini regis*), and of the king's water mill, and also the mortuary animals. The other half of the rector's manse was to pertain to the

De sequestro de Tybeshulf[69]   £8
Summa £16 2s. 6 1/2[ij]d. probavit
Coventr'
De sequestro ecclesie de Lalleford[70] 4s. 10d.
De sequestro ecclesie de Grendon[71] 13s. 7d.

jj *Sic* in MS; *1/2* added in the same hand as probavit

vicar of Castleton and his successors, together with the church's demesne land and demesne park, the tithes of lambs, wool, milk and other small tithes, and the revenues, oblations and income of the church, except the tithes and revenues assigned to the religious. There were many poor wastes and woods in the area and the burden of hospitality was expensive, but the vicar was to bear the cost of archidiaconal synodalia, and maintain the books, vestments, and ornaments of the church, and all ordinary charges, saving only the charge of building a new chancel, which, if this was necessary, was to pertain to the religious, while two parts of the extraordinary charges were to pertain to the religious, and a third part to the vicar: Hughes, 'Episcopate', no. 476; *Taxatio*, 246b.

69 Tibshelf church was assessed at £8 p.a., the amount sequestrated. Presumably it too had been vacant prior to William de Weston being instituted rector on 9 July 1301, having been presented by the prioress and convent of Brewood (Salop.). The nuns of Brewood subsequently received the king's licence for the appropriation in mortmain of Tibshelf church on 1 Nov. 1315, and they paid a fine of £10; the church was then appropriated to them on 14 Jan. 1318/19, and Langton ordained a vicarage there on 9 July 1319, when some interesting details emerged. The vicar was to have all the fruits and revenues of the church, except the tithe of sheaves. He was also to have half the land of the church, equally divided from both the better and inferior, together with the headlands containing the meadow or pasture lying at the head of the selion, half the hay of the church from the headlands assigned to him and from the tithe of the parishioners, and also a small church-yard (*aream*) opposite the church containing half an acre of land for a manse [to be built there]. The nuns were to pay 40s. to the vicar and his successors from the fruits of the church in equal parts at Michaelmas and at Easter and they were to maintain the extraordinary charges of the church, while the vicar was to pay the procurations and other ordinary charges pertaining to the bishop or the archdeacon: *Taxatio*, 246b; Hughes, 'Episcopate', nos. 247, 1170, 1171; *CPR 1313–17*, 364; Savage, *Magnum Registrum Album*, no. 326; Knowles & Hadcock, 278, 279.

70 John de Berevill, priest, was instituted rector of Church Lawford on 11 June 1300, and Thomas le Bretoun replaced him on 24 Dec. 1300, both having been presented by Thomas Boyn, proctor-general in England of the abbot and convent of St Mary, Saint-Pierre-sur-Dives, Normandy. The church was presumably sequestrated when it fell vacant between the dates of their institutions, as Thomas le Bretoun appears to have remained in office for the rest of Langton's episcopate. He received a one-year licence to study on 22 Apr. 1301, and he was ordained priest on 23 Dec. 1301. Church Lawford church was assessed by the *Taxatio* at £6 13s. 4d. p.a.: Hughes, 'Episcopate', nos. 107, 112, 440, 1287; *Taxatio*, 241b.

71 Grendon church was sequestrated when it fell vacant sometime after 17 Dec. 1300 when M. William de Swepston, then rector, was ordained priest. Although the record of his institution has not survived, William had been presented to Grendon church before 6 Jan. 1298/9, when it was noted that an appeal had been made to Archbishop Winchelsey against a sentence imposed by the Dean of the Arches depriving Matthew de Spaldinge of the benefice; the archbishop obviously ruled in William's favour. William was thus probably the unnamed rector of Grendon ordained subdeacon at the ordination service held on 4 June 1300; the record of his ordination

De fructibus autumpnalibus ecclesie de Burthingbur'[72] 5 1/2m.
De sequestro ecclesie de Burmyngham[73]   12s. 11d.
Summa 104s. 8d. probavit
Staff'
De sequestro ecclesie de Wolstanton[74]   £86 13s.[kk] 4d.[ll]
Summa patet
Salop'
De sequestro porcionis Nicholai de Trokuesford[75]

kk *s.* interlined
ll *d.* interlined

to the diaconate has not been found. William had been Langton's sequestrator-general from Nov. 1297 to Nov. 1298, and it is probable that he continued in that office until at least 5 Nov. 1299. Grendon church remained vacant until 23 Mar. 1300/1 when William de Edrichesleye was instituted rector, having been presented by Ralph de Grendon. Edrichesleye too was ordained priest at the following ordination service held on 23 Dec. 1301. Grendon church was assessed at £10 13s. 4d. p.a., besides a pension of 6s. 8d. due to the rector of Overton: Hughes, 'Episcopate', nos. 81, 86, 114, 1285, 1286, 1287; *Reg. Winchelsey*, i, 297–8; *Taxatio*, 242a.

72 St Nicholas' church, Birdingbury, was under sequestration when Ingram de Yerdele, chaplain, was presented to it by Sir John Paynel. Ingram was granted custody of the church on 23 Aug. 1301, during pleasure. As he was instituted rector shortly afterwards on 31 Aug. 1301 the bishop seized the autumn fruits in accordance with the grant made to him by Boniface VIII. The church was valued at £4 p.a.: Hughes, 'Episcopate', nos. 451, 116, 841; *Taxatio*, 244a.

73 Birmingham church fell vacant on 4 Dec. 1300, and it remained so until 14 Feb. 1300/1 when Thomas de Hinkelegh, acolyte, was instituted rector, having been presented by Lady Isabella, widow of Sir William de Bermingham. This church was valued at £5 p.a.: Hughes, 'Episcopate', nos. 466, 113; *Taxatio*, 242a.

74 The reason for the sequestration of Wolstanton church is unclear, but it too may have been vacant. The *Taxatio* assessed the church at £26 13s. 4d. p.a., and it was said to be worth 20 marks in 1317, so the very large sum of £86 13s. 4d. entered on the account roll presumably included its autumn fruits. No institutions to the church have been recorded in Langton's register, but M. John le Brabazon was rector on 1 June 1303 when he was ordained priest by letters dimissory at a service taken by Archbishop Winchelsey at Elmstead by Colchester, having first received papal dispensation for illegitimacy of birth. John received three licences for absence to study; initially for a three year period on 29 Dec. 1308, followed by two one-year terms on 4 Oct. 1313 and 29 Oct. 1319. He had vacated the church by Apr. 1332: *Reg. Winchelsey*, ii, 964; *BRUO*, ii, 1117; *CPL*, ii, 119, 139, 158, 161, 169, 337; Hughes, 'Episcopate', nos. 692, 744, 1265.

75 No record of Nicholas de Trokuesford's institution to St Chad's church, Shrewsbury, nor any other reference that he held a prebend in this secular college has been found, but (as de Troughford) he held the third part of Wroxeter church (Salop.) before 29 June 1301. Then, M. Walter de Clune was presented to the portion and its sequestrated fruits were granted to him during pleasure: thus either 'portion' is a scribal error for 'prebend', or more probably, St Chad's church has been mistakenly recorded instead of Wroxeter. St Chad's had a dean and ten prebendaries and was valued at £19, while the third part of Wroxeter church was then assessed at 5 marks p.a.: Hughes, 'Episcopate', nos. 444, 348; *VCH Salop.*, ii, 63, 66, 115; Knowles & Hadcock, 418, 438; *Taxatio*, 247b.

in ecclesia Sancti Cedde Salop'	40s. 6d.
De sequestro porcionis domini Bellingar' de Qwillino[76]	37s. 1d.[mm]
De sequestro ecclesie de H[nn]arleye[77]	13d.
De sequestro ecclesie de Langeford[78]	2s. 6d.
De sequestro ecclesie de Sheyngton[79]	11d.
De sequestro prebende J[ohannis] de Caleys[80]	40s.

mm *1d.* interlined
nn *H* interlined

76 Bellingar de Qwillino (or Berenger de Quiliano) held one of the two remaining portions of Wroxeter church which had been assessed at a higher valuation by the *Taxatio*; the first portion was then valued at 20 marks and the second at 10 marks p.a. Bellingar was portionary of Wroxeter by 17 Dec. 1295 when he was ordained priest by letters dimissory at a service held at Huntingdon. On 18 Oct. 1300 Langton granted him licence to travel to the Roman Curia until 2 Apr. 1301. Presumably he resigned his benefice, which then was placed under the bishop's sequestration, and on 18 Apr. 1301 Roland de Vinquiria (or de Viquiria) was granted custody of it; he was instituted to the portion on 31 May 1301. Bellingar, however, was still rector of Clipston (Northants.), having been instituted to that church on 26 July 1297, and he remained rector there at least until Nov. 1317. Bellingar was closely associated with Boniface son of Thomas Marquis de Saluzzo (or de Saluciis), who became archdeacon of Buckingham, in Lincoln diocese, on 10 Mar. 1299/1300, after his provision by Boniface VIII; Bellingar was his proctor and attorney on a number of occasions. Bellingar himself received protection while engaged on the king's business in June 1315 and July 1316: *Taxatio*, 247b; Hughes, 'Episcopate', nos. 335, 437, 414; *Reg. Sutton*, ii, 141; vii, 74; viii, 220 (*bis*); *CPR 1301–7*, 66, 366; *CPR 1307–13*, 278; *CPR 1313–17*, 295, 519; *CPR 1317–21*, 49.

77 Harley church was vacant for an unknown period until Richard de Kynredeleye was instituted rector on 24 Mar. 1300/1, having been presented by Sir Richard de Harle. The church was assessed at £3 6s. 8d. p.a.: Hughes, 'Episcopate', no. 334; *Taxatio*, 244b.

78 The sequestration of the vacant church of Longford similarly ended when John de Foresta was instituted rector on 29 Jan. 1300/1, having been presented by Sir Adam de Brimpton. John was then an acolyte, and he was ordained subdeacon by letters dimissory at a service conducted by Archbishop Winchelsey at Chedworth (Worcs.) on 27 May 1301. He received the priesthood at a service taken by John Halton, bishop of Carlisle, at Derby on 23 Dec. 1301; the record of his ordination to the diaconate, however, has not been found. Longford church was assessed at £2 p.a.: Hughes, 'Episcopate', nos. 333, 1287; *Reg. Winchelsey*, ii, 945; *Taxatio*, 245a.

79 On 18 July 1301 Langton granted custody of his sequestration on Sheinton church to the archdeacon of Shrewsbury, during pleasure, on condition that he would support the under-age presentee, John de Sheynton, in the schools. When John was eventually instituted to the church on 22 Sept. 1303 the patron was Hugh de Sheynton. John was in subdeacon's orders at that time, and he was ordained priest on 17 Dec. 1306; the record of his ordination to the diaconate, too, has not been found. Sheinton church is not listed by the *Taxatio*: Hughes, 'Episcopate', nos. 447, 338, 1297.

80 The prebend which M. John de Caleys held in the diocese has not been identified. He was presented to Edmondthorpe church (Leics.) by Edmund, earl of Lancaster. He was ordained subdeacon and instituted on 25 Feb. 1289/90, but he had resigned this living by 23 Aug. 1292. John was appointed notary public by William Gainsborough, bishop of Worcester, on 22 Apr. 1303, by authority of a faculty granted to him by

Summa £6 2s. 6d. probavit
Cestr'

De sequestro ecclesie de Thornton[81]	£22 4s. 2 1/2d.[oo]
De sequestro ecclesie de Tatenhal'[82]	3s. 2 1/2d.
De sequestro ecclesie de Mottrum[83]	4s. 5d.

oo *2 1/2d.* interlined

Boniface VIII on 24 Nov. 1302. He was collated to the church of St Martin, Eastleach (Glos.), on 3 Mar. 1303/4, and instituted to it on 15 July 1304. John was active as Bishop Gainsborough's notary and clerk, and he was appointed his proctor for the consecration of John Langton as bishop of Chichester at Canterbury on 19 Sept. 1305. He later became registrar and chancellor of John Ketton, bishop of Ely, 1310–16, and he was rector of Hartest, Suffolk, from Feb. 1314 until at least 1340: *Reg. Sutton*, viii, 43, 51, 60; *The register of Bishop William G[a]insborough, 1303 to 1307*, ed. J. W. Willis Bund (Worcestershire Historical Society, 1907), 3, 14, 24, 79, 82–4, 95, 114, 118, 131, 133, 136, 142, 179, 199, 209, 210, 231, 235; Haines, *Administration of Worcester*, 134, 152; *CPR 1301–7*, 533; A. B. Emden, *A biographical register of the University of Cambridge to A.D. 1500* (Cambridge, 1963), 117.

81 Robert de Askeby was instituted rector of Thornton le Moors on 7 Dec. 1301 following a bitter dispute over the patronage of the church which had lasted almost six years: as the account roll shows, the church had been placed under the bishop's sequestration for at least some of that time, from which he received the considerable sum of £22 4s. 2 1/2d., more than double its assessment by the *Taxatio* of £10 13s. 4d. p.a. Robert had been presented to the church by Edward I on 3 Jan. 1295/6, by reason of his custody of the lands and heir of Ranulph le Ruter, deceased, tenant in chief. However, the king's right to present had been contested by William de Venables, Katherine his wife, and Peter, the late Ranulph's son and heir. John Droxford (keeper of the Wardrobe) had consulted the justices of King's Bench, the barons of the Exchequer and John Langton, the chancellor, and both Droxford and John Langton then wrote to Bishop Langton's vicar-general, M. Thomas de Abberbur', advising him to admit Robert de Askeby without any obstruction in order to avoid being in contempt of the king, and his son Edward, earl of Chester, who favoured Robert de Askeby, and to prevent loss to the bishop. Nevertheless, Robert was still unable to enter the church and assume his duties after his institution, and on 26 Jan. 1301/2 the king wrote to the earl of Chester ordering him to remove the 'lay force and resistance of rebels' from the church which was preventing the vicar-general from exercising his spiritual office there, and to protect Robert in his possession of the benefice: Hughes, 'Episcopate', no. 177; *Taxatio*, 248a; *CPR 1292–1301*, 181; *CCR 1296–1302*, 579.

82 Tattenhall church fell vacant on 24 Jan. 1300/1 and remained so until 12 Feb. 1300/1, when M. Richard de Birchek was instituted, having been presented by the abbot and convent of St Werburgh, Chester. He then also received letters dimissory for all holy orders and, a day later, a licence to study for one year, although when a copy of this licence was later added to the record of his institution it was said to be for a three year period. Tattenhall church was valued at £6 13s. 4d. p.a.: Hughes, 'Episcopate', nos. 467, 175, 430; *Taxatio*, 248b.

83 M. Jordan de Macclesfeld was instituted rector of the vacant church of Mottram in Longdendale on 17 Dec. 1300, following his presentation by Thomas de Burgo. Although no licences allowing Jordan to be absent from his church have been recorded, he did receive a seven year licence to study; he was at Oxford in Feb. 1307/8, and he was granted papal dispensation on 10 May 1308 to study canon and civil law for a further three years. When another incumbent was instituted to Mottram church on 4 Feb. 1315/16 and it was noted that Jordan had freely resigned his benefice following the bishop's visitation of the archdeaconry of Chester earlier that year when legal proceedings

De sequestro ecclesie de Bankerbur'[84]	2m.
De sequestro vicarie de Acton[85]	4s.
De sequestro ecclesie de Wermyngham[86]	10 1/2d.
De sequestro ecclesie de Stanedissh[87]	38s. 4d.[pp]
De sequestro ecclesie de Prestwych[88]	79s.
De sequestro ecclesie de Tilstan[89]	18s. 2 1/2d.[qq]

pp   *d.* interlined
qq   *d.* interlined

(*processus*) were begun to deprive him of his office; unfortunately, no explanation is given as to why this course of action was taken. Mottram church was assessed at £10 p.a.: Hughes, 'Episcopate', nos. 174, 901; *BRUO*, ii, 1200; *CPL*, ii, 39; *Taxatio*, 248b.

84 On 25 Apr. 1301 Langton ordered the archdeacon of Chester to deliver custody of his sequestration on Bangor church to Walter Reginaldi, priest, to whom he had granted it during pleasure. The bishop wished Walter to support the under-age presentee, William son of Sir John de Sancto Johanne, in study from the revenues of the church. Walter was instructed to ensure the church was adequately served. No subsequent institutions to the church have been recorded. Bangor church too was assessed at £10 a year: Hughes, 'Episcopate', no. 441; *Taxatio*, 248b.

85 The reason for the sequestration of Acton vicarage and its autumn fruits of £13 6s. 8d. listed below, is unclear. Thomas de Prestecote, deacon, was instituted vicar on 6 Oct. 1300. He was ordained priest on 17 Dec. following. There is no indication that he had died or resigned his benefice, suggesting the sequestration was employed as a means of canonical coercion on the appropriators, Combermere Abbey (Ches.). In 1301 custody of Acton may have been granted to Henry le Waleys, rector of Standish (Lancs.). He was bound to pay £20 to the bishop for the fruits of the church in 1302, and he had been bound to the bishop for 20 marks (£13 6s. 8d.) to be paid at Michaelmas 1301, the exact sum receipted for the autumn fruits here. Acton church was assessed at £48 and its vicarage at £5 p.a.: Hughes: 'Episcopate', nos. 171, 1286; *VCH Cheshire*, iii, 151; *Taxatio*, 248b.

86 M. John de Havering was instituted rector of Warmingham on 29 June 1300, having been presented by the Edward I, by reason of the minority of the heirs of Warin de Mainwaryn, deceased, tenant in chief. The next institution to the church was recorded in Jan. 1306/7. John may have been the nephew of M. Richard de Havering, who became archdeacon of Chester in 1315. Warmington church was valued at £6 13s. 4d. p.a.: Hughes, 'Episcopate', nos. 170, 213; *CPR 1292–1301*, 518; *BRUO*, iii, 2181; *Taxatio*, 248b.

87 Standish church was assessed at £13 6s. 8d. p.a. Its sequestration ended on 25 May 1301 when Henry le Waleys, priest, was instituted rector, having been presented by William de Standissh. Henry may have been granted custody of Acton church (Ches.) in 1301: *Taxatio*, 249a; Hughes, 'Episcopate', nos. 176, 371, 373; see n. 85.

88 On 9 Feb. 1300/1 the rector of Prestwich, M. Matthew de Sholure, was granted a licence to serve Roger de Pilkinton until Whitsun following (21 May). He had vacated the church by 4 May 1301 when M. William de Marklan was granted it *in commendam* for half a year, and on 23 Oct. 1302 he was granted custody of the benefice, during pleasure, having been presented on both occasions by Adam de Prestwych. The church was valued at £18 13s. 4d. p.a.: Hughes, 'Episcopate', nos. 428, 443, 461; *BRUO*, iii, 2195; *Taxatio*, 249a.

89 On 10 July 1301 custody of the bishop's sequestration on Tilston church was granted to John de Sancto Petro, during pleasure, having been presented by Urian de Sancto Petro. However, another clerk, Henry de Bleccheleye, was instituted rector on 26 Jan. 1301/2, following his presentation by the same patron. Tilston was valued at £6 13s. 4d. p.a.: Hughes, 'Episcopate', nos. 450, 179; *Taxatio*, 248b.

De sequestro fructuum autumpnalium de Acton   £13 6s.[rr] 8d.[ss]
Summa £44 5s. 7d. probavit
[Membrane 6 dorse]
Summa totius £598 13 3/4d.[tt] probavit

rr *s.* interlined
ss *d.* interlined
tt *Sic* in MS

IV

Morley vs. Montagu (1399): A Case in the Court of Chivalry

Edited by M. H. Keen and M. Warner

CONTENTS

PREFACE

In 1991 Mark Warner presented his doctoral thesis in the Department of History at University College, London, on the Earls of Salisbury of the Montagu family, 1337–1428. I was privileged to be one of his examiners. One of the most interesting sections in the thesis dealt with the case of Morley vs. Montague, heard in the Court of Chivalry in 1399, the proceedings of which are here presented. Some time after the *viva voce* examination, I wrote to Dr Warner, suggesting that he should publish the text, which for both our researches had a special interest. He asked me to collaborate with him, and I agreed: we have since worked on it together. It should however be made clear that it was he, guided by his supervisor, who had gone to the record of the case and identified its significance, that it was from his transcript for purposes of his thesis that we started work, and that the relevant chapter in the thesis provided the base out of which our introduction grew. For remaining shortcomings we are of course equally responsible.

We should acknowledge a number of debts of gratitude. First and foremost to Dr Lisa Jefferson who guided past many misreadings two people neither of whom had editorial experience and neither of whom would claim the instinct for accuracy and consistency that is the key to good editing. We are also indebted deeply to Mr D.A.L. Morgan, Dr Warner's supervisor: to Dr Nigel Ramsay: to Dr Robert Ireland of University College, London: and to Dr Nigel Saul. Crown copyright material in the Public Record Office is reproduced by permission of the Controller of Her Majesty's Stationery Office, to whom we are deeply grateful.

M. H. Keen

INTRODUCTION

The text here reproduced records the proceedings in the appeal of treason brought by Thomas Lord Morley against John Montagu, Earl of Salisbury, heard before the Court of Chivalry in 1399, just after the succession of King Henry IV. The case is of interest for the light that it sheds, first, on the procedures of that Court, and secondly on some of the events surrounding and preceeding Henry's usurpation. The text is taken from a transcript made by Sir John Borough in the reign of Charles I, now preserved at the Public Record Office. Borough copied it from a manuscript then in the possession of the great lawyer, Sir Edward Coke.[1] This was presumably a copy (or a copy of a copy) of the official record of the proceedings in the Register of the Court of Chivalry, which we know to have been carefully maintained in the early fifteenth century.[2]

Borough was prompted to make his transcript by an incident which concerned him in his capacity as secretary to the Earl Marshal: the

1 The case forms a documentary preface to Sir John Borough's own commentary on Thomas of Woodstock's regulations for judicial combat. The transcript is to be found in the State Papers – a seventeenth century collection compiled by Charles II's secretary of state, Sir Joseph Williamson (Public Record Office, State Papers 9 (Miscellaneous), 10). The original from which Sir John made the copy can no longer be traced, but was catalogued in the seventeenth century under the title of 'A rolle of the proceedings before the Constable and Marshall anno 1. H : 4. in case of treason betweene the lord Morley and the Earle of Salisbury' (*A Catalogue of the Library of Sir Edward Coke*, ed. W. O. Hassall (Yale & London, 1950), p.25, no. 323; we are grateful to Dr Nigel Ramsay for this reference). A second transcript of the case survives in the British Library (Additional MS. 35821) which was purchased in 1730 in an auction of Peter Le Neve's books. This copy, however, is less accurate than the one reproduced here : the date of the privy seal letters, for instance, wavers between 9, 10 & 11 November; the Duke of York (d'Euerwyk) is on occasion mistaken for a Duke of Warwick; and a number of words are carelessly anglicized, e.g. 'adversary' for 'adversaire', 'judges' for 'juges'. We have not attempted a full collation of the two texts, but have compared them and have used the BL manuscript in one or two places (which we have noted) to supply missing words or letters in Borough's text.

We would like to give particular thanks to Dr Lisa Jefferson for her very generous help. Her expertise in the Anglo-Norman of the period has been invaluable in the preparation of this text. Not only has Dr Jefferson corrected many faults in our original transcript, but we have also benefitted from her advice on a great number of points of editorial finesse. In short, she has brought a much needed dose of professionalism to our often erratic tentatives at editing this MS.

2 We know something of the proceedings in the case of Scrope vs. Keighley (1401) from a letter of Henry Percy as Constable, based on a careful scrutiny of 'tous les actes ... et toutz les processes devers nostre Registre du Court de Chevalrie' (BL Add. MS. 9021, f. 123). A transcript of the sentence passed on Henry Boynton in 1405 is similarly based on the record in the Registers of the Court (M. H. Keen, 'Treason Trials under the Laws of Arms', *Transactions of the Royal Historical Society*, 5th series xii (1962), 85).

dispute between Donald Lord Rea and David Ramsey which arose in 1631.[3] The case, which concerned treasonable words, generated considerable legal interest at the time. Ramsey, embittered with the court of Charles I, had allegedly informed Rea, whilst on board the latter's ship off the port of Elsinore in May 1630, that 'matters of church and state was so out of frame as must tend to a change, if not desolation.' On account of his disaffection with this state of affairs, Ramsey had chosen to live in the Low Countries with sufficient resources to last him three years at the rate of £6 per day. When Lord Rea replied, sympathetically, that the Lord would amend these evils, and that there was no remedy but patience, Ramsey rejoined, 'By God, Donald...we must help God to amend it.' Rea's subsequent appeal of Ramsey revolved around these and other words spoken by the latter in favour of a conspiracy to invade England *via* Scotland. Since the Marquis of Hamilton, Ramsey's patron, had been granted the sum of £10,000, together with the revenues from the wine customs in Scotland for 16 years, to raise an expeditionary force of 6,000 men, Ramsey could claim that 'the only stay was for want of arms, ammunition, and especially powder.' As Lord Rea then had two regiments under his command in the army of Gustavus Adolphus, Ramsey requested that he should 'put in hard' with the Swedish ambassador to obtain the required ordnance. Enticing Ramsey to speak further, Rea was later to mention a promise from King Charles of the reversion of the Orkneys; Ramsey immediately asked whether there were any good harbours there, and on receiving a positive reply exclaimed, 'by God, it was to be thought upon.'[4]

The prosecution of this particular case was to present certain difficulties. There were no witnesses to the supposed treasonable advances made by Ramsey; and additionally, the conversations themselves had taken place outside the realm. Furthermore, Ramsey had offered combat to clear his name – a challenge which Lord Rea had readily accepted. A memorial made by Justice Whitelock shows that the justices of the King's Bench were consulted on the best way to proceed in the affair, and that in their opinion, given the peculiarities of the case and since treason was involved, the trial should be held 'after the manner of the civil law, and we were not to meddle in it.'[5] The implication of the reference to civil law was that the proper tribunal to try this case was the Court over which the Earl Marshal usually presided. But the Earl Marshal alone had no authority to hear such an appeal as this, and it was deemed necessary to appoint a

3 For this case, we have relied upon the accounts given in Howell's *State Trials* vol iii (London, 1816), cols. 483–519.

4 Ibid., cols. 487–9, 503.

5 Ibid., col. 495.

Constable *durante bene placito* to sit with him.[6] The Rea vs. Ramsey case thus occasioned a revival of the criminal jurisdiction of the Court of the Constable and Marshal, otherwise known as the Court of Chivalry.

This seventeenth-century judicial dilemma raised two particular issues, the first being a question of the historical and legal precedents for the hearing of the appeal. The case that most obviously resembled the Rea vs. Ramsey trial was the Duke of Hereford's appeal of the Duke of Norfolk in 1398; a case which had similarly concerned spoken treason and in which the only witness had been the appellant himself. Unfortunately there was no adequately detailed record of proceedings. It was the need to fill this gap that drew Borough's attention to Coke's manuscript recording the trial of Lord Morley's appeal of the Earl of Salisbury in 1399, and his transcript was intended as a guide for the trial of 1631. The second question that arose was, by what law should the case be tried ? The answer appeared to be, by civil law and the law of arms. As we have seen, the Justices of the King's Bench had recommended that the trial should be 'after the civil law', which had traditionally governed proceedings in the Court of Chivalry. Similarly, the civil law advocate Dr Arthur Duck would justify the Court's revival for this kind of case, by referring to the

> records of our own chronicles and examples herein, as the duke of Hartford in Henry 4, his time; Jo. Ely and William Scroop against Ballamon at Burdeaux, the king being there; the lord Morley impeached Mountague earl of Salisbury; and that Thomas of Walsingham and Thomas of Woodstock in their learned writings, expressed sundry precedents for this manner of proceeding...[7]

The origins of the law of arms, the basis of the Court of Chivalry's jurisdiction, lay in the development and extension of the traditional authority exercised by the Constable and Marshal over the royal host.[8] The law of arms, which the Court administered, was deemed to be founded in the *ius gentium*, as defined by Roman law, and in the late middle ages formed the basis of an international code of behaviour for Christian knights and men at arms.[9] The civil and canon laws supplied the jurisprudential principles, in the light of which contemporary knightly custom and common military usage (the law of arms) were interpreted. In practice, from the mid fourteenth century the Court of

6 Ibid. There had been no permanent Constable of England since the execution of Edward Stafford, Duke of Buckingham, in 1521, 'the authority and charge, both in war and peace, being deemed too ample for a subject'. The Earl of Lindsay was appointed *pro hac vice* for the duration of the case.

7 Ibid., col. 487.

8 Keen, 'The Jurisdiction and Origins of the Constable's Court', *War and Government in the Middle Ages* ed. J. Gillingham & J.C. Holt (1985).

9 Keen, *The Laws of War* (1965), pp.11–22.

Chivalry could take cognizance of a wide range of matters which were deemed to be outside the competence of the common law: armorial disputes, where two knights claimed the same coat of arms; complicated ransom disputes, involving rights in prisoners; the judgment of rebels taken in time of open war, when the king's banner had been unfurled, and the ordinary course of law was therefore suspended. Its jurisdiction was formally defined by a statute of 13 Ric. 2 c2, which gave it cognizance of contracts touching deeds of arms and of war out of the realm, also of matters touching arms or war within the realm which could not be determined or discussed by the common law.

The second half of the fourteenth century also saw the rise to prominence as advocates in this Court of civil lawyers, trained in the universities, such as the chronicler Adam of Usk, who brought a more legalistic approach to the interpretation of knightly traditions and customs.[10] But the Court of Chivalry, or *curia militaris* in latin, was above all, as its name suggests, a Court of knighthood. Veteran knights were the men who were usually appointed to preside in the Court as deputies when the Constable was absent, men such as Sir William Farendon and Sir William Fulthorp, both of whom acted for them in a number of Court of Chivalry cases in this period.[11] In the case of Morley vs. Montagu we find that when counsel was assigned to the parties, with royal approval, it included in each case the lawyers who were to act as their advocates; but veteran knights who knew the customs of arms outnumbered them and were more prominent. Among others of Morley's counsel were Hotspur, Sir Thomas Erpingham and John Norbury; among Montagu's John Lord Lovel, Sir John Roches and Sir Ralph Eure – all experienced soldiers.[12] Significantly, the two civil law advocates, Thomas Stokes (for Morley), and Lawrence Stapelton (for Montagu) petitioned the court at the beginning of the case that they should be allowed to stand corrected should they say anything 'otherwise than seemed good' to their principals and their fellow counsel.[13] Clearly they understood that they might need expert guidance on matters of knighthood.

The particular significance in legal history of the case between Lord Morley and the Earl of Salisbury is the light that it throws upon the

10 Idem, 'The Jurisdiction and Origins of the Constable's Court', p.168.

11 Farendon, who had served as Marshal of the army in Bishop Despenser's crusade of 1383, was active in numerous Court of Chivalry cases, such as Copyn vs. Snoke and Saxlingham, and Gerard vs. Chamberlain (*CPR 1391-6*, 42, 68 & 340). Fulthorpe deputed for the Constable in Morley vs. Montagu in 1399. For his rôle in the judgment and execution of Archbishop Scrope, he was condemned, according to a popular tradition, to wander the streets of York for eternity, a leper as white as snow (L. W. Vernon Harcourt, *His Grace the Steward and Trial of Peers* (1907), p.375).

12 PRO, SP 9 (Miscellaneous), 10, fos. 6r–6v.

13 Ibid., f. 7r.

procedure followed by the Constable and Marshal in determining trial by combat on an appeal of treason. This is the only such case of which a complete and detailed record survives, although such appeals and challenges to judicial combat seem to have been relatively common. A martial aristocracy cherished the right, in matters affecting personal honour, to be permitted in the last resort to prove one's cause by the judgment of battle.[14] The petition of the commons in 1379, against appeals of treason being heard before the Constable and Marshal, is an indication of how commonly men did seek recourse to this right.[15] Their petition notwithstanding, such appeals continued to be heard by the Constable and Marshal as a regular procedure. That was probably what prompted the composition, on behalf of the Constable, Thomas Duke of Gloucester, of the tract on the 'order and form of battle within the lists', an adaptation to English usage of an edict of Philip the Fair, which was presented to Richard II *circa* 1390. The tract, intended to regulate the judicial duels which were presumably flourishing at the time, gives several precise details on the procedure to be followed in adjudicating an appeal of treason, and also the grounds on which combat could be judged:

> In the first the quarrel and the bills of the appellant and defendant shall be pleaded in the Court before the Constable and Marshal, and when they may not prove their cause by witnesses, nor by any other manner, but determine their quarrel by strength...the Constable hath power to join battle.[16]

Appeals of treason could be on various grounds. In 1380, for example, Sir John Annesley appealed Sir Thomas Caterton of having sold the castle of St. Sauveur to the French.[17] During the course of a protracted duel, fought before Richard II at Westminster, Caterton was vanquished, later expiring from exhaustion. Treason of a serious nature was also at issue in the case between the Dukes of Hereford and Norfolk; Hereford claimed that Norfolk had confided to him that the king's intention was 'to do with them (both) as he had done with the

14 Olivier de la Marche, for example, in advising Duke Philip the Handsome on who should be permitted to fight a judicial duel equated this right with noble status itself: 'And so, my lord, it is needful both in this regard and others that you should know who they are whom you should hold for gentlemen (gentils hommes), who for nobles, and who for non-nobles' (Cited by Keen in *Chivalry* (New Haven/London, 1984), pp. 149–50).

15 *Rotuli Parliamentorum*, ed J. Strachey et al. (1767–77), iii, 65.

16 For Gloucester's ordinances, see *The Black Book of the Admiralty*, ed. T. Twiss (Rolls Series, 55, 1871), i, 301–30.

17 For an analysis of this case and duel, see J. Bellamy, 'Sir John de Annesley and the Chandos inheritance', *Nottingham Mediaeval Studies*, 10 (1966).

others already', on account of 'what was done at Radcot Bridge'.[18] Since the appellant could not prove his charges, and the defendant denied any knowledge of the treasonable conversations, the court's rôle, as it was put in the seventeenth century, was to sift the truth between the two parties (in the case of Hereford vs. Norfolk the court was not the Court of Chivalry, but the Parliamentary Commission of 1398). As is well known, the duel did not take place as expected since before the combat could even begin both Dukes were unchivalrously banished by Richard II. A very comparable case (and one that has close parallels, too, with Morley vs. Montagu) was that of Sir Stephen Scrope vs. John Keighley (1400/1). Keighley appealed Scrope of treason, alleging that he had been privy to the conspiracy to restore Richard II in December 1399 and had traitorously concealed his knowledge of it; Scrope denied the charge, claiming that Keighley was motivated by rancour over disputed lands, and counter-charged that Keighley had sought to ambush and kill him 'encontre loialté d'armes'.[19] Other cases confirm the suggestion here that appeals of treason could be, and perhaps often were, a cover for the pursuit of more private quarrels (this may be what lay behind the objection of the Commons to them in 1379). A good instance is the appeal brought by the Navarrese knight, Matigo de Vilenos, against John Walsh in 1384. According to the chronicler Walsingham, Vilenos charged Walsh with treason to the king and kingdom (presumably collusion with the French) when he had been lieutenant of Cherbourg. However, when vanquished and overcome by remorse, the appellant confessed that he had really wanted to revenge himself on Walsh who had insulted his wife. In accordance with the law of arms, Matigo was subsequently disarmed, drawn by horse from the lists to the place of execution and hanged.[20] As Gloucester's ordinances had laid down in cases of false appeals, 'good faith and right and law of arms will that the appellant incur the same pain that the defendant should do if he were convicted and discomfited'.[21] Similar evidence of the often surprisingly trivial matters of such appeals, reminiscent of later seventeenth- and eighteenth-century duels, is provided by the case of Bolomer vs. Usana in 1407; here the defendant, whose nationality is unknown, was accused of having let slip certain unflattering remarks regarding the iniquity of Englishmen. The appeal nonetheless went to combat.[22]

The Morley vs. Montagu case had its roots in political events. It was during the course of the first Parliament of Henry IV's reign in October 1399, in the early days of which charges and counter charges of

18 *Rot. Parl.*, iii, 382.
19 BL Add. MS. 9021, fos. 123–5.
20 T.Walsingham, *Historia Anglicana*, ed. *W. Hardy* (Rolls Series, 1868), ii, 118.
21 Cited by Vernon Harcourt, *His Grace the Steward*, p.367.
22 *Foedera*, viii, 538-40 for a description of the combat.

disloyalty were flying thick, that Thomas Lord Morley appealed and challenged John Montagu, Earl of Salisbury, of treason. The basis of Morley's charges against the Earl was that he had been simultaneously of the Duke of Gloucester's and King Richard's counsel, and that he had ridden as a false knight and spy between the two, revealing the Duke's counsel to Richard. Salisbury had thus traitorously deceived the Duke, later adding to the seriousness of this treasonable crime by appealing him of treason in the Parliament of 1397. In maintenance of these charges Morley then threw down his gauntlet as a pledge. In reply, the Earl of Salisbury denied that he had ever betrayed Gloucester, and he too 'getta son gaunte en gage'. The gauntlets of the parties were then delivered to the Constable of England, Henry Percy, Earl of Northumberland, whilst both men were arrested by the Marshal, Ralph Neville, Earl of Westmorland.[23]

Thomas Lord Morley was a Norfolk landowner of some standing, and he had been been closely connected to Richard II's uncle, Thomas of Woodstock, Duke of Gloucester. Born *circa* 1360, Morley first served under Gloucester during the *chevauchée* of 1380, at some point in the course of which he was knighted by the Duke. In 1391 he also took part in the crusade which Gloucester had hoped to lead to Prussia – due to inclement weather, the expedition was blown off course off the Scottish coast and forced to return to England.[24] Despite this obviously close association with the Duke, Morley experienced little difficulty in switching political allegiance following the murder of his lord at Calais in 1397: in the same year he acted as the deputy of the Marshal, Thomas Mowbray, Duke of Norfolk, in supervising the execution of the Earl of Arundel.[25] He accompanied Richard II to Ireland in 1399, although his activities subsequent to Bolingbroke's invasion are unknown. It is probable that Morley followed the example of two other Norfolk landowners and former Gloucester retainers, Thomas Lord Bardolf and Robert Lord Scales, who deserted Richard by joining Bolingbroke at Shrewsbury.[26] In the light of the recent past, one cannot help suspecting that Morley, himself not spotless in respect of things that happened in 1397/8, may have had it in mind when he appealed Montagu that this was no bad way, among other things, of demonstrating that he was now back in the right camp. He was no stranger, it may be added, to the Court of Chivalry, having disputed there in a long running case commenced in 1386 the right to the arms *argent un lion rampant sable couronné et enarmé d'or* with John Lord Lovel, who in

23 SP 9/10, fos. 3v–4r.
24 A. Goodman, *The Loyal Conspiracy: The Lords Appellant under Richard II* (1971), pp.38, 75, 101–2.
25 *The Complete Peerage of England*, ix, 216.
26 Goodman, *The Loyal Conspiracy*, p.102.

1399 was prominent, perhaps not accidentally, among John Montagu's counsel in Morley vs. Montagu.[27]

In contrast with Morley, John Montagu had been a long standing member of the Ricardian circle. He inherited the earldom of Salisbury only late in life, in 1397 (he was born *circa* 1350), succeeding his uncle Earl William, who had accidentally killed his only son and heir in a tilting match in 1382.[28] John's father, also Sir John, did not die until 1390, and John the younger's pre-comital career as an under-endowed cadet had naturally gravitated toward the court (his father had been steward of King Richard's household from 1381-6). He was described as a king's knight in 1383.[29] Following his inheritance of the comital title, he was appointed steward of the newly created principality of Chester – a sure sign of his closeness to Richard II.[30] When he was not engaged in the king's business, John Montagu passed his time with such typically curial pursuits as composing French verses : he was also one of those knights of Richard II's entourage who was rumoured to have Lollard leanings. The parallel with those two other Lollard knights, Sir John Clanvowe and Sir Lewis Clifford, both authors in their own right, emphasizes the decidedly literary flavour of Richard's court.[31] Nevertheless, John Montagu was the only tried and tested soldier among the peers closest to Richard II at the end of the reign. Froissart had earlier commented upon his prowess at Bourdeilles in 1369, where he had been knighted by the Earl of Cambridge;[32] in 1399, he was appointed Marshal for the Irish campaign of that year due to the exile of the Duke of Norfolk; when news of Bolingbroke's landing reached the king, it was Earl John who was entrusted with the considerable responsibility of leading the advance guard of Richard's army from Ireland.[33] The appeal of 1399 thus pitted one who had been personally close to Richard and loyal to him to the last against one who had important connections with King Richard's former enemies and who had been swift (and perhaps had needed to be swift) to rally to the rising star of Lancaster. In the circumstances of the autumn of that year, the affair was, to put it mildly, heavily loaded in political terms.

The case between Morley and Salisbury opened on Sunday 11 November in the great chamber of the palace of Westminster. Proceedings began with the recitation of the king's letters under the privy

27 PRO C47 (Chancery Miscellanea), 6/1.

28 *Complete Peerage*, xi. 391.

29 K. B. McFarlane, *Lancastrian Kings and Lollard Knights* (Oxford, 1972), p.168.

30 R. R. Davies, 'Richard II and the Principality of Chester, 1397-99', in *The Reign of Richard II*, ed. F. R. H. du Boulay & C. M. Barron (1971), p. 266.

31 J.C. Laidlaw, 'Henry IV, Christine de Pisan and the Earl of Salisbury', *French Studies*, 36 (1982).

32 *Complete Peerage*, xi. 391.

33 Ibid., p.392.

seal of 10 November, empowering the Constable and Marshal to determine the case in accordance with the laws and customs of arms. Both appellant and defendant were then summoned before the Court, while the clerk of the crown, James Billingford, read out the records relevant to the case : namely, Morley's initial challenge of 29 October, Montagu's subsequent denial, and the assignment of counsel to both parties on 3 November.[34] Following these preliminaries, Lord Morley reminded the Court that he had ended his original appeal with the proviso that he might amend or change his appeal as often as he saw fit. Acknowledging that the original bill had lacked proper form, he now delivered an additional bill, beginning, 'Jeo, Thomas, sire de Morlee, alliee a Thomas, Duc de Gloucester'.[35] This new bill (hereafter referred to as the 'pretense addicion') was careful to specify that Salisbury had been simultaneously of the Duke of Gloucester's counsel and of Richard II's counsel in the twenty first year of the reign (i.e. 1397), before going on to repeat his original charge that the Earl had gone many times, falsely and traitorously, between the king and the Duke in this year, later appealing Gloucester of treason, 'qe feust cause de sa morte'. Furthermore, Morley took this opportunity to add further to his allegations, claiming that the Earl of Salisbury had been of 'conseil covigne' ('covigne' with its overtones of coven and the unholy) from 1397-8, and that he had not simply consented in the king's false and evil purposes, but had also actively counselled the same king to destroy the lords and community of the realm by various ransoms and extortions contrary to the public good and common profit.

The charges contained in this second bill form, not just legally but culturally and ideologically too, the most complete expression of Morley's objection against the conduct of John Montagu. Of particular interest in this respect was Morley's insistence that Salisbury had acted against the community of the realm ('la chose publique') in misdirecting the king. The concept of a motherland as a higher public interest encompassing a range of collective and private interests with the king at its head may be traced back to the thirteenth century, although the origins of such ideas of the common good (*res publica*) lay in Roman law. The canon lawyer Guillaume Durand (d.1296), for example, had written that all should be ready to contribute to the defence of the country and the crown; similarly, the late Roman military strategist, Vegetius, in his enormously influential work of knightly reference, *De re militari*, laid particular stress upon the responsibility of not just the fighting man but also the whole community for the defence of the public good.[36] A king

34 SP 9/10, fos. 3r–6v.   35 Ibid., fos. 7r–8r.
36 C. T. Allmand, *The Hundred Years War: England & France at War c.1300–c.1450* (Cambridge, 1988), p.147.

who acted in contravention of the public interest was therefore not
fit to represent his subjects, and the section of the charges in
Morley's additional bill which claimed that Richard II had acted
against the community of the realm and the public good may be
considered as reflecting the standard definition of a tyrant during
this period. The king, the sanction of whose authority was God's
natural law and who was the fount of its interpretation and
expression in terms of positive human law, had gone astray; rather
than governing in respect of the common weal of the people, in
whose name he ruled and whose interests he represented, he had
instead governed according to the selfish interests of a minority. In
medieval political culture, such a breakdown of the natural order
could only be explained in terms of either the wickedness of the
ruler, or to the influence of evil counsel, or both. But Morley's
allegation that Salisbury had actively led Richard II to destroy the
common good needs to be considered not only in terms of
contemporary constitutional thinking but also in practical terms of
the political context of 1399. As Caroline Barron has demonstrated,
some seventeen of the thirty-three deposition articles of that year
were concerned with aspects of Richard's government which had
touched upon his subjects' possessions during the period 1396-9.
One particular article is highly reminiscent of Morley's charge against
Salisbury, claiming that King Richard had extorted the goods of his
subjects to his own personal interest and contrary to the common
good ('bona sic levata non ad commodum et utilitatem Regni Anglie
convertendo, set ad sui nominis ostentationem et pompam ac vanam
gloriam prodige dissipando').[37] In thus adding to the charges against
the Earl of Salisbury, therefore, Morley was deliberately trying to
identify himself more closely with the new king.

　A further study of the 'pretense addicion' confirms the suspicion that
Morley, in appealing the Earl of Salisbury, was also attempting to
further his own personal interests in the context of Henry of Lancaster's
usurpation of Richard II's throne. Thus, the decision to specify 1397
as the year in which Salisbury had been simultaneously of the Duke of
Gloucester's counsel and the king's counsel, and also the new accusation
that the Earl had been of 'conseil covigne' from 1397-8, reinforce the
impression that Lord Morley's appeal had been largely inspired by the
political events of October/November 1399. In this respect, the opening
developments of Henry IV's first Parliament in October would have
already supplied Morley with ample indications of the way in which
the political tide was turning since the Commons petitioned the new
king to the effect that Richard II could not have committed the

---

37　C. M. Barron, 'The Tyranny of Richard II', *Bulletin of the Institute of Historical Research*,
41 (1968), 1.

considerable faults of government for which he had been deposed without the counsel of those who had been 'entour sa personne'.[38] The petition went on to claim that the bill of appeal levelled against the Duke of Gloucester and the Earls of Warwick and Arundel in the 1397 Parliament was the very summit and epitome of King Richard's misgovernment, and that it revealed at the same time 'des nouns de ceux q'avoient la coulpe'. The Commons requested, therefore, that the signatories of this bill of appeal, Edward, Duke of Aumale, Thomas, Duke of Surrey, John, Marquis of Dorset, Thomas, Earl of Gloucester and finally John Montagu, Earl of Salisbury, should appear before Parliament to account for their conduct during the previous reign.

When he was summoned before the Parliament on 30 October 1399, the Earl of Salisbury did his best to minimize the significance of his part in the events of 1397-8, stressing that he had in no way been the 'fondour, ordeigner, ymaginour, controvour, ne enditour' of the misdeeds of King Richard's rule. For instance, the Earl claimed that he had known nothing of the 1397 appeal until the king had commanded him to pursue it, 'lequel commaundement de son faux coeur il n'osa disobeier, mes applia a son dit commandement'. Thus, although Salisbury acknowledged that he had not acted loyally, he declared that he was ready to exercise his right as a gentleman to defend himself by combat should any claim that he had been anything more than merely an obedient accomplice in policies which originated with Richard II personally.[39] In thus disclaiming any responsibility in the formulation of Richard's misdeeds, Salisbury's defence was typical of the group reaction of the other lords summoned with him to account for themselves before Parliament.[40] Lord Morley who was present in Parliament that day, and heard Salisbury's defence, was clearly not prepared to accept it in his regard. His subsequent contention that Salisbury had counselled both King Richard and the Duke of Gloucester during the period 1397-8 formed the essence of his 'pretence addicion'; far from a

38 *Rot. Parl.*, iii, 449-51.

39 Ibid.

40 For example, Aumale similarly denied complicity in both the murder of Gloucester and the formulation of the 1397 bill of appeal. In the case of the latter he recounted how he had been ordered by King Richard in person 'de faire cel jour une chose pur qelle chose a faire il fuist pluis dolent que unques ne fust'. The Duke of Surrey asked the new King to take into account his youth and 'la petite reputation de qi il fuist' at the time of the appeal. On the occasion of Henry's exile, Surrey claimed that he had been commanded 'de venir au dit nadgairs Roy sur le scaffold et adonqes la dite Ordinance luy fuist premierment monstré, de qoi il fuist dolent en son coer'. The Marquis of Dorset recalled his own circumstances when he first was made aware of the bill of appeal : 'Et quant le Markys fuist sys a maunger en la sale deins la chastell de Nottyngham, le dit nadgairs Roy...envoia a dit Markys un home que luy commanda de par le roy de lever et aler hors del porte de dit chastell. Et il demanda, Pur quy ? Et il luy disoit, que a son venue il saveroit, et q'il ferroit come ses compaignons feroient' (*Rot. Parl.*, iii, 449-51).

mere signatory of the 1397 appeal, Lord Morley claimed that the Earl was its inspiration and instigator. It seems likely that only political prudence stayed Henry IV from permitting similar charges to be pursued against all the five appellants of 1397. He was dissatisfied with their initial replies, and adjourned the proceedings to the following morning, when the accused were again interrogated individually in his presence 'none of them waiting or hearing the other', so that the truth might be discovered. Unfortunately their statements this time are not recorded, although we know that shortly afterwards a sentence was pronounced 'par commandment du roi et par avis et assent des seigneurs de Parlement'. These sentences involved the degradation of the three Dukes arraigned (Surrey, Exeter and Aumale) to comital status, whilst the Earl of Gloucester and the Marquis of Dorset were relegated to lords.[41] The sentences are a clear indication that the king wished to censure these lords for their conduct in the previous reign.

Lord Morley's new allegation that the Earl of Salisbury had been of 'conseil covigne' from 1397-8 was thus carefully calculated to strike a chord with the new king. Henry had already shown himself keen, even before the usurpation, to settle old scores with those of the late king's counsellors whom he held responsible for his banishment and disinheritance. Shortly after Henry's return to England, in August 1399, he summarily executed William Scrope, Earl of Wiltshire, together with the courtiers Bushey and Greene at Bristol, following a trial purporting to be in accordance with the law of arms, for the treasonable crime of having misguided the king and kingdom.[42] Among those who escaped their fate, it is clear that Henry bore a particular grudge against the Earl of Salisbury in consequence of his part in certain events of 1398. Following his banishment in that year, Henry (at the time Duke of Hereford) had repaired to Paris where he was received with considerable hospitality. During his stay, he entered into negotiations for the hand of Marie, daughter of the Duke of Berry.[43] The implications of such a marriage were considerable since John of Berry's only son and heir had died in the previous year. In order to foil these negotiations, Richard despatched the Earl of Salisbury to deliver a message, stating

41 Vernon Harcourt, *His Grace the Steward*, pp. 370–1.
42 'Existebat tunc in castro eodem (Bristol) dominus Willelmus Scrope comes Wilts-chiriae et thesaurarius Angliae, dominus Henricus Grene et dominus Johannes Busch locutor ultimi parliamenti milites, qui fuerunt maxime consiliarii dicti regis Ricardi ad mala praemissa perpetranda. Tandem capti sunt et inviti ducti extra castrum in campum ad ducem Lancastriae. Et primo quidem arrestati sunt, deinde in crastino coram judicibus, viz. constubalario et marescallo, judicio sistuntur. *Et de proditione et mala gubernatione regis et regni convicti,* dampnati et decollati sunt' (Quoted by Vernon Harcourt, *His Grace the Steward*, p.368 n.1).
43 F. Lehoux, *Jean de France, duc de Berri: sa vie, son action politique (1340–1416)* (Paris, 1966), ii, 406–7.

not only the king's objections to the proposed match, but also impugning the character and reputation of Duke Henry. It was this affront to his honour which particularly offended Henry. 'He knew' recorded Froissart 'of the Earl of Salisbury being at Paris; but they never saw each other; and the Earl of Salisbury returned to England without speaking to him'; and 'Duke Henry was much displeased that the Earl of Salisbury should leave Paris without seeing him'. Henry's friends, according to the same chronicler, voiced similar feelings of resentment:

> The Earl of Salisbury has done very wrong to carry such a message to France, and make so heavy a charge against the most honourable man in the world. The day will come when he shall repent heavily of this and say 'it weighs heavily on me that I ever carried a message to France against Duke Henry'.[44]

Froissart's testimony is supported by the metrical history of the deposition written by the French courtier Jean Creton. Creton had accompanied Richard II to Ireland only to find himself caught in the middle of the dramatic events of August 1399.[45] When news of Henry's invasion broke, he decided to accompany the Earl of Salisbury, a fellow poet, to Conway 'for the sake of song and merriment'. On Richard's betrayal by the Earl of Northumberland and his capture at Flint, Creton vividly portrayed the fear of both the king and his entourage. The Earl of Salisbury's despondency was particularly acute: 'Now see I well that I am certain to be a dead man, for Duke Henry surely beareth a great hatred towards me...May Jesus, in whom I believe, vouchsafe to help us all'. When Richard and his followers were received at the castle of Flint, the Earl was brutally shunned, being greeted with this message:

> Earl of Salisbury, be assured that no more than you deigned to speak to my lord the Duke of Lancaster (i.e. the future Henry IV) when you and he were at Paris Christmas last-past, will he speak unto you...then was the Earl of Salisbury much abashed and had great fear and dread at heart, for he saw plainly that the Duke mortally hated him.[46]

That Henry IV was covertly supportive of the accusations made by Morley against the Earl of Salisbury may be deduced from the list of counsellors appointed by the Constable to advise Morley in the case.

44 J. Froissart, *Chroniques*, ed. K. de Lettenhove (Brussels, 1867–72), xvi, 141–4.

45 J. Creton, 'A Metrical History of the Deposition of Richard II', ed J. Webb, *Archaeologia*, 20 (1824). The historical validity of Creton's account has been upheld by J.J.N. Palmer in 'The Authorship, Date and Historical Value of the French Chronicles of the Lancastrian Revolution', *Bulletin of the John Rylands Library*, 61 (1978–9).

46 Creton, p.60.

John Norbury had served under Henry during his first crusade to Prussia in 1390; after the usurpation he was appointed to the important posts of Treasurer of the Exchequer and Keeper of the Privy Wardrobe.[47] Thomas Erpingham had also accompanied Henry in 1390, and then on pilgrimage to Jerusalem in 1392. In addition he had been in Henry's company during his Parisian exile of 1398.[48] The names of those assigned to counsel Morley thus confirm clearly that his adversary was a man who was regarded with particular and personal antipathy in the intimate Lancastrian circle.

Nevertheless, the charges that Salisbury had betrayed the Duke of Gloucester and sanctioned the destruction of the realm could not be defined as treason in the terms of the 1352 common law statute. To understand why such charges constituted treason in Morley's opinion, we should recall Salisbury's own admission in Parliament that in pursuing the 1397 bill of appeal he had not acted as a loyal man, and in repentance of which he asked for the forgiveness of not only of King Henry but also the crown and the persons whom he had wronged.[49] The Earl had of course been only too loyal to Richard II, and to make any sense the charge that Salisbury was guilty of treasonable conduct must be supposed to relate rather to the obligations in honour of knighthood. A parallel to this notion that a knight might betray both himself and his calling is provided by the story that Henry V in 1417/8 ordered the execution of Jean d'Anguennes, captain of Cherbourg, for having surrendered his charge to the English whilst the garrison still enjoyed adequate supplies and ammunition to endure a longer siege.[50] The supposed treason could hardly be construed as having been committed against Henry V (as king of France) or his rival Charles VI, but contrary to the accepted precepts of honour and knighthood then in force. A way of expressing that a traitor had been false not only to his lord but to the principles of chivalry was the addition to the death penalty of the punishment of degradation from the order of knighthood. Sir Ralph Grey in 1464 for example was condemned to have his spurs struck off by the hand of a master cook and his coat of arms torn off and reversed by the heralds.[51] His offence was not only to have resisted his sovereign lord; but as a member of the chivalric order of the Bath he had also broken his oath of fidelity as knight. Lord Morley's charge

47 M. Barber, 'John Norbury (c.1350–1414): an Esquire of Henry IV', *English Historical Review*, 68 (1953).

48 McFarlane, *The Nobility of Later Medieval England* (Oxford, 1973), pp.145–6; T. John, 'Sir Thomas Erpingham, East Anglian Society and the Dynastic Revolution of 1399', *Norfolk Archaeology*, 35 (1970).

49 *Rot. Parl.*, iii, 449–51.

50 J. de Wavrin, *Recueil des croniques et anchiennes istories de la Grant Bretagne a present nomme Engleterre, 1399–1422, 1422–31*, ed. W. & E. L. C. P. Hardy (Rolls Series, 1864–91), ii, 244.

51 Keen, 'Treason Trials', pp.90–1.

that Salisbury had acted as a false knight in both betraying the Duke of Gloucester and misguiding the king by his 'conseil covigne' surely has at its heart the infringement of a chivalric code of honour.

On Thursday 20 November, Salisbury duly launched into a detailed criticism of Morley's two bills of appeal. In his opinion, both were vague and insubstantial and many points required clarification; in addition to this, Salisbury argued that the second half of the additional bill lacked precision and was unconnected to the first part of the 'pretense addicion'; since both bills lacked any legal coherence and validity, the defendant claimed that they should be rejected on that basis.[52] Following the reading of the defendant's bill, the Constable agreed that many of the appellant's charges were indeed 'generalls et obscures' and granted term to Morley to supply more information on certain points, so that the defendant might know more clearly his intent, and the Court whether such charges could indeed be proved by judicial combat. The charges specified for clarification were thus : the manner in which Morley had been connected ('allié') to the Duke of Gloucester, and how this relationship gave the appellant an interest in pursuing charges relating to the injury and death of the Duke; how Montagu had been of Gloucester's counsel, and then of both Gloucester's and the king's counsel simultaneously; what counsel had been betrayed by the Earl, and how this had been connected to the appeal of the Duke in 1397; finally the Constable requested that the months and locations of these imputed treasons should be stated.[53] These requests aggravated Morley beyond measure. His main point in challenging the Court's request for further information was that as Salisbury had already denied the charges levelled against him and thrown his gauntlet down (referred to as the 'contestation' during the trial) it was now too late for either the Earl or the Court to put up obstacles to the judicial combat. Morley claimed that Salisbury's bill should not have been accepted as valid since it had been submitted after Salisbury's contestation and acceptance of the challenge to duel of 11 November.[54] The Court however did not accept that the defendant's contestation and acceptance relieved it of its obligation to sift matters further so as to make certain that the case could not be resolved otherwise than by battle. As the Constable put it, it was more in accordance with the 'corage et honesté de chivalrie' that the charges should be discussed and clarified wherever possible.[55]

Morley's eventual reply to the questions posed by the Constable on 26 November forms the most detailed and informative statement of his

52 SP 9/10 fos. 11v–17r.
53 Ibid., fos. 18v–20r.
54 Ibid., f. 17r–v.
55 Ibid., f. 19r.

case and permits two checks upon the veracity of the accusations against the Earl of Salisbury.[56] In the first of his clarifications – how Montagu had been of Gloucester's counsel – Morley took the Court back to 1387. He claimed that at this time, whilst a case was pending in the Court of Chivalry between William Montagu, then Earl of Salisbury, and his brother Sir John Montagu the elder, the latter's son, Sir John the younger (Earl of Salisbury in 1399), had gone to the Duke of Gloucester (at the time Constable of England), to ask for his assistance in his father's case and offering his service in return. The Duke agreed, and afterwards Montagu was retained as a member of the Duke's company for his projected Prussian crusade, so that he was 'allors et après privé de son conseill'. Salisbury, claimed Morley, therefore knew of the 'loyal' counsel of the Duke in 1387, and in particular his intention to resist the machinations of Robert de Vere, Duke of Ireland. As Montagu then went directly to the king to reveal these plans, he thus became simultaneously of Richard II's and the Duke's counsel. 'Counsel' in this sense did not imply a formal, institutional connection such as that between an indentured retainer and his lord; but it seems that in Morley's eyes the verbal commitments and personal associations involved were not much less binding in terms of honour (and so, if irreconcilable, of dishonour). As for the connection between the two seemingly separate charges, Morley argued that as the Earl of Salisbury had been of both counsels, that is counselling Gloucester whilst at the same time counselling the king in the destruction of the realm, this common factor provided the unifying theme between the two charges. Finally, months and locations for the evil counsel were supplied only approximately: June 1397 to September 1398, at London, Windsor, Nottingham and other places. Thus although Morley's 'pretense addicion' had been entirely concerned with Salisbury's treasonable conduct in 1397–8, the only real details provided by him in his bill concerned the period 1387–91. In this sense, it is once again difficult to escape the conclusion that Morley had to a large extent tailored his additional bill to fit the political situation of October 1399. As we shall see, however, although Morley's appeal may well have been inspired by motives of opportunism and self-interest, he may well have had grounds for suspecting John Montagu's conduct during the 1380's, and on that basis his original accusation of 29 October (which charged Montagu with being of 'both counsels' but was unspecific) was at least not entirely without foundation.

The details of the litigation in the case between the Earl of Salisbury and his brother, Sir John the elder, which spanned the years 1383–90 are obscure. The information which we have is mostly concerned with Sir John's appeal of November 1384 against the sentence of the

56 Ibid., fos. 22v–24v.

Constable and its repercussions, and is not sufficient to give a clear picture of the points at issue. We know that the quarrel arose out of a 'statute merchant' (a form of bond) registered by the Earl for £10,000 in favour of Sir John before Sir William Walworth, Mayor of the Staple, in December 1382.[57] It would appear that the case was one of *de fide lesa*, and pertained to the Court of Chivalry because one of the parties involved had broken his word as a knight.[58] We know that in November 1387 Richard II personally intervened in the case and that the sentence against Sir John was upheld; also that he failed to appear on 2 January 1388 and was fined for his disobedience; and that thereafter, until his death in 1390, he continued to resist the king's will and the enforcement of the sentence.[59] In May 1389 Richard II reprimanded Gloucester, the Constable (and his fellow appellant, Mowbray, the Earl Marshal) for having neglected in his official capacity to enforce the sentence of 1387 against Sir John.[60] In the light of these details, Morley's allegation that Gloucester had been asked to give assistance in the case, and that Sir John the younger had been the intermediary between the two, offering his service in return for assistance, sounds entirely plausible. That is about as much as we can say about this case, which was ultimately settled in 1394, when in Richard II's presence Sir John the younger surrendered the 'statute merchant' (which was torn up), and the Earl of Salisbury agreed to repay him 4,000 marks which he had received from Sir John the elder.[61]

That Sir John the younger (the future Earl of Salisbury), may have been his father's instrument in seeking aid from the Duke of Gloucester may be inferred from other sources. At an inquisition held in 1409 to prove that John's son and heir Thomas had attained his majority, various witnesses were asked to recall Thomas's christening some 21 years before in the church of St Botulph's at Shenley, Hertfordshire.[62] A certain Thomas Sharp could place the event by the attendance of 'Thomas of Wodstok', at the time Earl of Buckingham, whose horse he held at the entrance of the church, and continued to hold by the reins for the duration of the ceremony until the great man rode off again. Similarly, John Swaffham remembered that Gloucester had acted

---

57 *CPR 1396–99*, 172.

58 A petition of the Earl of Salisbury (28 November 1385), asked for the enrolment of certain records pertaining to the case, particularly the agreement of both parties two years earlier to submit themselves to the jurisdiction of the Court of Chivalry, and referred to a decision taken in Parliament to settle the dispute by the law of arms (*Foedera*, viii, 67–8).

59 BL Cotton MS. Titus CI, fo. 158r (we are grateful to Dr Robert Ireland for his help with this document) ; PRO C49 (Parliament & Council Proceedings), 47/21.

60 BL Cotton MS. Titus CI, fo. 158r.

61 *CCR, 1396–99*, 210.

62 PRO C137 (Inquisitions Miscellaneous), 75, under the return for Hertfordshire.

as Thomas's godfather, presenting the infant with a golden table, painted with images of the Trinity and covered with precious stones.[63] The Duke's attendance at the christening of Sir John's eldest son, in March 1388, indicates that a strong connection existed between the two men at the time. As a former retainer of the Duke, Lord Morley would have been in a position to know of contacts between Gloucester and Sir John Montagu. His testimony that Salisbury had been a member of Gloucester's retinue for the Prussian expedition may be verified by letters of protection enrolled in 1391 since John Montagu heads a list which also included Morley himself.[64]

Another godfather at the ceremony at Shenley was Sir Richard Stury. Stury no doubt knew Montagu well, for both were among the close associates of Richard II who were suspected of Lollard sympathies.[65] He had enjoyed a long career at court stretching back to the 1340's when he had served as a valet. In 1376 he had been expelled from court following accusations in the Good Parliament that he had gone between the king and the Commons misinforming both as to their respective intentions; his selection to stand as Thomas's godfather was thus ironic given the similar charges which would be levelled against Earl John in 1399. Stury continued to serve as a chamber knight to Richard II, being in constant attendance upon the king up to his resumption of power in May 1389. It was Sir Richard who briefed Froissart in 1395, giving the chronicler a hostile account of Gloucester's character and policies.[66] The attendance of both Gloucester and Stury at the ceremony at Shenley in 1388 indicates John Montagu's ambivalent position during this period.

When the Court reconvened on 2 December, the Earl of Salisbury was quick to point out the glaring omissions in Morley's bill of clarification. Citing the Court's own decree of 24 November, the defendant was able to catalogue various points which had been deliberately ignored by Lord Morley : such as the relationship between Gloucester and Morley, as well as specific examples of the supposed treasons which the Earl had counselled the king to perpetrate.[67] In reply, Lord Morley maintained the truth of all the charges contained in his three bills and that Salisbury was guilty of treason. At this point Morley cast down his gauntlet once more, declaring that he would prove his appeal in the combat with the aid of God and Saint George, and that the 'jour et lieu' should be assigned to him for this purpose.[68]

63 Ibid.
64 PRO C76, m. 12.
65 McFarlane, *Lancastrian Kings and Lollard Knights*, p.211.
66 Ibid.
67 SP 9/10, fos. 25Av–32r.
68 Ibid., fos. 32v–33r

The following Friday, 5 December, both sides were summoned to hear the Court's final will in a ceremony performed in the king's bedchamber at Kennington. The Constable began by addressing the defendant with only the charges contained in the second part of the additional bill : that Salisbury had been of 'conseil covigne' in conspiring with the king to destroy the lords and the community of the realm. The defendant's counsel was then told to hold silence, whilst Salisbury answered to the charges 'par parole de sa bouche'. With remarkable calm and grasp of the situation, the Earl pointed out that as the first part of the additional bill – that he had known Gloucester's and the king's counsel simultaneously – had been dropped, the essential link between the two bills of appeal was now non-existent and the charges consequently void.[69] In reply, however, the Constable maintained that in the Court's opinion, according to the law of arms a man might accuse another in a bill of appeal of various and diverse matters; in this sense Morley's earlier accusations regarding the betrayal of Gloucester had not been dismissed, but as the second charge was more serious other matters of less grave nature would be kept in suspense. Continuing to protest, Salisbury now switched his line of attack to the charge of which he was now accused, maintaining that if there was no demonstrable connection between the original appeal of 29 October and the additional bill of 11 November, the determination of the appeal no longer pertained to the Court's jurisdiction as its authority derived from the royal letters issued on the previous day and so could not relate to matters raised in the additional bill. Nevertheless, these objections were quickly overruled by the Constable who seemingly contradicted his earlier ruling by flatly declaring that in the Court's opinion the charges were connected and its authority therefore valid. Forced to rest upon his defence, Salisbury, and then Morley, sealed their respective bills. The Constable then ceremoniously took first the appeal and folding it, slipped the bill into the original gauntlet cast down by Morley. With the appellant's gauntlet and bill in his right hand and the defendant's in his left, the two were then twisted together as the Constable adjudged judicial combat in the name of God – the one and only judge of such important matters. The duel was then assigned for St Valentine's Day, 14 February 1400, at Newcastle upon Tyne.[70]

Despite these elaborate preliminaries, the combat between the Lord Morley and the Earl of Salisbury did not take place as planned. By the date set the Earl had in fact been dead for over a month. Conspiring with other disaffected lords, the Earls of Kent, Huntingdon, Rutland and Lord Despenser, he had planned to capture Henry IV and his

69 Ibid., fos. 33v–35r.
70 Ibid., fos. 36v–37r.

family at a tournament at Windsor, which had been planned for the Epiphany (January).[71] The conspirators planned to meet at Kingston before moving on to Windsor, where armed men were to be introduced into the town concealed in carts. But forewarned of their intentions by the Earl of Rutland, Henry retreated to London to avoid the plot. Consequently, the rebels elected instead to head across country with the intention of raising forces in Chester. However, whilst at Cirencester, Salisbury, together with the Earls of Kent and Huntingdon, were captured by the townspeople and imprisoned in the abbey there. At the same time a fire seems to have broken out in the town and in the panic which resulted, both Salisbury and Kent were dragged from the abbey and beheaded on the night of 8 January. Their heads were presented to Henry IV the next day at Oxford, as one chronicler was to put it, 'like fish in a basket'.[72]

Nevertheless, the case between Morley and Montagu produced an interesting posthumous epilogue. Adam of Usk, ecclesiastic and civil lawyer, recorded in his chronicle how he had represented Morley in a suit of April 1400, before the king at the Tower of London, in which he had pleaded that the Earl of Salisbury should be adjudged a traitor, according to the appeal levelled against him due to his failure to appear for the combat at Newcastle on the day assigned.[73] In addition, Morley and his counsel claimed that the Earl's sureties for his attendance should be condemned in costs. The sureties themselves took the logical line that as the Earl was dead, and since his death had occured before the appointed day, they could not be held responsible for his non-attendance. But Adam rejoined at this point that the Earl had caused his own death by his treasonable rebellion, strengthening his case with the citation of the law 'si decessit' and other passages from Justinian's *Digest*. As he concluded, 'And in short my side had colour against the pledges of the said Earl, and paid me a fee of over one hundred shillings and twelve yards of scarlet cloth'.[74]

Would the duel have been fought had the Earl of Salisbury lived to see the appointed day ? In this context, it is important to realize that the judicial combats of this period were essentially royal occasions, normally paid for by the king and fought in his presence. In 1400, for instance, it was Henry IV who covered the cost of the erection of a

71 J. H. Wylie, *A History of England under Henry IV*, (1884), i. 92–3.

72 Ibid., p.100.

73 *Chronicle of Adam of Usk*, ed. E.M. Thompson (Oxford, 1905), p.205. To have been able to make this point, Morley must have turned up on the appointed day at Newcastle despite the impossibility of meeting his adversary. In 1445, the Prior of Kilmaine appeared fully armed at Smithfield to demonstrate the justness of his cause even though his duel with the Earl of Ormonde had been annulled ('Gregory's Chronicle', in *The Historical Collections of a Citizen of London*, ed. J. Gairdner (Camden Soc., 1876), pp.186–7).

74 *Chronicle of Adam of Usk*, p.205.

scaffold at Newcastle upon Tyne.[75] In 1445, Henry VI went so far as to meet the expenses of the Prior of Kilmaine who needed a course of fencing lessons to prepare for his duel with the Earl of Ormonde.[76] It was therefore the king who decided whether the combat should go ahead, or whether it should be stopped and at which point. On two occasions Henry IV decided to intervene after a duel had got off to a lively start. In Usana vs. Bolomer, fought before the king at Nottingham on 12 August 1407, the two parties began bravely, until Henry, wishing to preserve both from an unfortunate end and traitor's death, stopped the fight with the traditional words of peace: Ho! Ho! Ho![77] In 1409, Henry again put an end to a duel, this time between two esquires 'the one called Gloucester, apppellant, and the other Arthure, defendant', after a similarly valiant beginning.[78] It was thus in no way incompatible with chivalric custom that a lord might intervene in the middle of a duel to impose a settlement on the two parties. Whilst discussing the general topic of wagers of battle, Nicholas Upton recounted how he had often seen such duels of honour fought before his lord, Thomas Montagu, Earl of Salisbury (Earl John's son and heir), in France during the 1420's,

> whyche sayde lorde hathe oftentymes be holde from the begynnyng to the ende bothe paretys so fyghtyng, and at the last fful honarably hathe browhte them to a good concorde and agreement, retornyng eche of them home ageyne rewaredyd bowntyously with large gyftes to ther gret worchyp and renowne.[79]

But as we have seen with duels such Annesley vs. Caterton and Villenos vs. Walsh, both of which resulted from Court of Chivalry cases, fatalities could and did occur. It should nevertheless be emphasized that none of the above duellists were of the same political and social rank as either Morley and Montagu. The sole example of the death in judicial combat of a lord of such elevated status in this period appears to have been Otto de Granson, a Savoyard nobleman accused of involvement in the murder of his lord, Duke Amadeus VII of Savoy, who was killed during the course of a duel in 1397; that such an outcome was rather atypical may be deduced from the sensation that this case created in Europe.[80] The reason for the rarity of fatal

75 F. Devon, *Issues of the Exchequer* (1837), pp. 275–6.

76 *Proceedings and Ordinances of the Privy Council of England*, ed. N. H. Nicolas (Record Commission, 1834–7), vi, 57–9.

77 *Foedera*, viii, 540.

78 J. Stow, *The Survey of London*, ed. H. B. Wheatley (London, 1929), p.341 (Ward of Faringdon extra).

79 *The Essential Portions of Nicholas Upton's* De Studio Militari, ed. F. P. Barnard (1931), p.13.

80 J. Huizinga, *The Waning of the Middle Ages* (English trans., 1927), p.93.

duels amongst the great was entirely political. The greater the social importance of the lords involved in such challenges to combat, the more serious was the risk that an actual confrontation would generate dangerous political repercussions. We may therefore project that a duel between Morley and Salisbury would not have ended in the death of either lord due to the very obvious resemblance between Morley's appeal and King Henry's own cause against Richard II and his followers. Had Salisbury vanquished Morley on the appointed day during the duel the embarrassment would have been particularly acute for the new king in the political context of 1399–1400. It is thus entirely possible, but by no means certain, that Henry IV would have thrown down his baton on 14 February to put an early end to the duel, perhaps even intending that this gesture might symbolize the calming of dissension and restoration of harmony amongst the lords of his army on the eve of his first campaign as king. But this potential scenario does not necessarily substantiate Huizinga's celebrated dismissal of the challenges and duels of this period as no more than chivalric fiction.[81] The overwhelming weight of contemporary evidence surely dictates rather the conclusion that the aristocracy of this period did believe that in personal causes involving the honour of men of high birth appeal to the judgment of God in battle was justified, in the last resort and when other means of settling their dispute could not be found. The opening words of the Constable's judgment in Morley vs. Montagu bring home that point, and in a very striking phrase: 'en noun de Dieu, qi de fyn force est juge a si haute chose come bataille et nulle fors luy, nous vous admittons, au bataille, come vicair a luy en cest place'.[82] The Morley vs. Montagu case also shows that this cultural attitude could be intimately linked to practical political realities and serves to underline once again what has been called 'the union, not the disjunction of chivalry and politics'.[83]

81 Ibid., p.95.
82 SP 9/10, f.36v.
83 D. A. L. Morgan, 'From a Death to a View: Louis Robessart, Johan Huizinga, and the Political Significance of Chivalry', in *Chivalry in the Renaissance*, ed. S. Anglo (1991), pp.104–5.

[f.1r] **'A True copy of the Roll of Proceeding in an Appeale of Treason before the Conestable and Marshall between Thomas Lord Morley, appellant, and John de Montague, Earle of Salisbury, defendant, Anno Primi Henrici Quarti'.**

[Public Record Office, State Papers Miscellaneous 9/10[84]]

[f. 2r] Lunedy, le unszime jour de novembre l'an du regne nostre tresredouté seigneur le roy Henry quart aprés le conquest primer,[85] devant mes treshonurés seigneurs, le count de Northumbre, Constable d'Angleterre, et le count de Westmurland, Marshall d'Angleterre, seantz judicielment en Court de Chivalrie, en tant come a chescun d'eux appertient par vertue de lour offices, en la Grand Sale de Westmoustier, ové diverses sages du counseil du court, c'est assavoir Monsieur William Heron, Johan Cheyne, chivaler, et autres, une lettre desoubz le privé seal nostre dit seigneur le roy feust presenté a mes ditz seigneurs, de par nostre dit seigneur le roy, sur la tenure q'ensuyt:

> Henry, par la grace de Dieu, roy d'Angleterre et de France et seigneur d'Irlaund a nos treschiers cousins, Henry, count de Northumbre, Constable d'Angleterre, et Rauf, count de Westmerland, Mareshall [f.2v] d'Angleterre, saluz; vous faceons assavoir qe nous, confiantz en voz grandes loialté et circumspeccion, vous avons assignez a oier, conusser et proceder en la cause de appelle que feust mue devant nous en nostre plein Parlement par Thomas,

---

84 The edition below follows the normal conventions for the expansion of abbreviations, the addition of the acute and cedilla accents, the use of apostrophe, the differentiation of u/v and i/j according to pronunciation, and the modification or addition of punctuation. A few problems arise from the fact that this is a seventeenth-century transcript of a document of c.1400 (or perhaps even a copy of a copy): the scribe's use of the word 'per', for example, is most probably the result of his expansion of the abbreviated 'p' in his exemplar, rather than an exact rendering of the original. Both 'per' and 'par' do appear unabbreviated in the text, the former more frequently; but a problem arises with the words 'perole' and 'Perlement'. These are quite clearly so spelt in the text, but we have corrected to 'parole' and 'Parlement' as this was almost certainly the original reading and is the consistent reading of the other transcript of the text (BL Add. MS. 35821). These cases, however, are very few, and in general the claim made that this 'a true copy' can be accepted, the language having all the appearance of Anglo-French of that period. The text is written carefully and clearly; the scribe has occasionally corrected himself in the course of his writing (these instances have not been noted as none have any significance); very occasionally he has missed a word such as 'et', and if it has been felt necessary to amend, then any editorial addition is indicated by the use of square brackets, and any rejected reading has been placed in the notes. Those familiar with the Anglo-French language of the time will meet here all the usual ways in which this language differs from that of continental France, and those unfamiliar with it should perhaps be warned not to be surprised if the grammatical rules of the latter are not followed.

85 That is, in first year of the reign of King Henry IV.

sire de Morley, partie appellant d'une part, et Johan Montague, count de Sarum,[86] partie defendaunt d'autre part, de certeins matiers comprises en les actes ent faites, come en mesmes les actes est contenuz plus au plein, et mesme la cause d'appell ové ses emergentz, incidentz, et connexez, discusser et finalment determiner et mettre en execution en maner qe a chescun de vous appertient par vertue de voz offices solonc les leyes et custumes de nostre court de chivalerie; et ausi a substituer et deputer et en voz lieux autres a faire terminer et mettre en execucion les choses avantdites, en le maner suisdit, a tantz de foiz come vous [f.3r] plerra; et pur ceo vous mandons qe appellez devant vous les dictes parties, soiez entour les premisses diligentement entendantz, et icelles facez, terminez et mettés en execucion par vertue de voz offices en le manere suisdit. Don[é] souz nostre privé seal a Westmoustier le x jour de novembre l'an de regne nostre primer.

Aprés la lecture de quele lettre, par vertue et auctorité d'icelle, les dictes parties nomez en mesme la lettre, c'est assavoir Thomas, sire de Morley, partie appellant d'une partie, et Johan, count de Sarum, partie defendant d'autre partie, furent publiqement preconizez, et chescun de eux comperust adunqes illoeqes en court personelment pur soi mesmes; et comperust ausi adunqes personelement en court James Billingford, clerc du corone, et myst et exhibist en court touz les actes et processes par lui heuz et fait en la dicte cause d'appele parentre les parties suisdictes, solonc ceo qe luy estoit commandez par nostre [f.3v] dit seigneur le roy par lettres desoubz son privé seal come le dit James disoit adunqes illoeqes; les queux actes et processes furent luez overtement en court adunqes en audience des dictes parties sur la fourme q'ensuyt:

Fait a remembrer qe le xxix jour d'octobre l'an du regne le roy Henry quart puis le conquest primer, Thomas, sire de Morley, devant le roy en plein Parlement appella Johan Mountagu, counte de Sarum, de ceo q'il fuist del counsaill de Thomas, duc de Gloucestre, et chivacha parentre Richard, nadgairs roy d'Engleterre, et le dit duc come une espie, et conust le counseill d'ambideux parties, et puis come un faux chivaler discovera son counsaill et traiterousement disceyva le dit duc, et puis luy appella; et sur ceo le dit sire de Morley metta son gage, faisant protestacion de adder et amenuser a tant [f.4r] de foitz come luy bosoignera, tout foitz tenant la substance de son dit appell, et pria de counseill, qe luy fuist graunté; et le dit counte de Sarum responsdy q'il unqes ne traia le dit duc en discoverant son counseill, et metta son gage;

---

86 We have expanded 'Sar' in the text to 'Sarum' despite the fact that 'Saresbery' does appear on f.23r. 'Sarum' is the more usual form of the title, and we have therefore preferred to follow *Rotuli Parliamentorum* and BL Add. MS. 35821 in expanding thus.

et sur ceo les ditz gages furent baillez al Constable d'Engleterre,
et le Mareschall d'Engleterre aresta les ambideux parties; et le dit
sire de Morley trova seurté, c'est assavoir le duc d'Euerwyk,
Monsieur Henry Percy le fitz et Monsieur Thomas Erpingham, a
pursuer son dit appell; et le dit counte de Sarum pria d'estre lessé
au maynprise en mesme le maner, a qi fuist dit qe le roy luy
vorroit aviser s'il serroit lessé a mainprise ou noun; et en le mesme
temps le dit counte demurereoit en garde. Et aprés commandé fuist
as parties suisditz par le dit Conestable de garder lour jour devant
les ditz Conestable [f.4v] et Mareschall en le Blank Sale deinz le
paleys de Westmoustier le lunedy proschein ensuant al noef del
clok.

Item, le tierce jour de novembre proschein ensuant en le dit
Parlement, le dit sire de Morley rehersa coment le mesquardy
devant il avoit oy[é][a] le dit Johan Montagu, counte de Sarum, luy
excuser de certeins matires, et entre autres del morte del dit duc
de Gloucestre; et sur ceo le dit sire de Morley avoit prié au roy
qe luy plerroit luy granter licence de faire une protestacion sur
certeines paroles q'il dirroit illoeqes en sa presence, qe luy fuist
graunté; et coment il avoit appellé le dit count souz certein fourme
comprise en l'act ent fait en le dit Parlement, et pria de counsaill;
et q'il serroit prest de prover son dit appell par son corps envers
le dit counte; et le dit count, alors present [f.5r] en le dit Parlement,
rehersa coment il avoit doné une respounce a dit appell, quel est
en acte de record en le dit Parlement, et q'il ne fuist home apris
de la ley, et pria de counseill; et le dit sire de Morley pria qe la
ou le dit count a temps q'il dona sa responce il ne fist ascun
protestacion, et q'il n'averoit counseill; et le dit count pria d'avoir
copie del acte de dit appell et counseill et q'il purroit estre lessé a
maynprise; et sur ceo fuist dit a dit sire de Morley q'il metteroit
en escript ceo q'il vorroit dire touchant son dit appell ; et le dit
counte pria que la ou le dit appel fuist en acte en le dit Parlement
qe le dit sire de Morley ne ferroit autre bille; et sur ceo sibien le
dit appell come la respounce a ycelle furent luez en le dit Parlement
par commandement du roy; et aprés fuist demaundé des ambideux
parties s'ils avoient [f.5v] mainprise, c'est assavoir le dit sire de
Morley a pursuer son dit appel tanque al outre determinacion de
mesme l'apel, et le dit count a defendre le dit appel tanque al
outre determinacion de l'appel avantdit. A quel temps le dit duc
d'Euerwyk pria au roy q'il purroit estre dischargé de sa mainprise
avantdit; et sur ceo le dit sire de Morley trova seurté, c'estassavoir
William, sire de Wilughby, Thomas, sire de Berklé, Thomas, sire

a *MS*, oyer.

de Bardolf, et Robert, sire de Scales, chescun corps pur corps, en
la fourme suisdit; et le counte trova seurté, c'est assaver le count
de Kent, Monsieur Raufe Euere, Monsieur Johan Roche et
Monsieur Johan Drayton, chescun corps pur corps, en la fourme
avantdit; et sur ceo jour fuist doné a les parties suisditz en la Blank
Sale le vendredy proschein venant devant [f.6r] les ditz Conestable
et Mareschall.

Aprés le letture de queux actes et processes, le dit sire de Morley,
partie appellant, prie le juge de luy declarer le counseill a luy
assigné pur son dit appell par nostre dit seigneur le roy a sa propre
denominacion et request; et en mesme le manere le dit counte de
Sarum, partie defendant, pria le juge de luy declarer le counseill
a luy assigné en sa dicte defense a sa propre denominacion et
request par nostre dit seigneur le roy; sur quoy mon dit seigneur
le Conestable mesmes par avise de mon dit seigneur le Mareschall
et autres declara as ditz parties lour dit conseil a lour dit request;
et primerement le conseil du dicte partie appellant, c'est assavoir
Monsieur Henry Percy, le sire Despencer, le sire de Bergeveney,
Monsieur Thomas Erpingham, Johan Northbury, tresorer d'An-
gleterre, Monsieur Thomas Rameston, Monsieur Thomas Grey,
Robert Waterton, Raulyn Ramsey, Janico Esquier, Thomas Stokes,
Multon, sergeant d'armes [f.6v], Lytelton esquier, Peryn Lohern
et Robert Northlod; le counseil du dit partie defendaunt, Monsieur
Johan, sire de Lovell, Monsieur Rauf Euere, Monsieur Johan
Roche, Monsieur William Hoo, Monsieur Johan Drayton, William
Newsam, Johan Mareshall, Thomas Rukby, Thomas Coupelond,
Lawrence Stapilton et William Lethe.

Aprés quel declaracion del assignement des ditz conseils, le dit sire de
Morley, partie appellant, protestast par parole d'avoir en temps avenir
plusours sages a luy assignez de son conseil, si luy semble expedient ou
necessarie a le pursuit de son dit appell; et en mesme la manere, la
dicte partie defendant protestast par parole d'avoir conseil egalement
a lui assigné en temps avenir en encresse de son dit conseil si lui semble
expedient et necessarie en sa dicte defense. Aprés queux protestacions
ensi faitz, la dicte partie appellant fesoit Thomas Stokes son advoket
avowé en ceste cause; [f.7r] et en mesme le maner la dicte partie
defendant, par licence del juge, fesoit Laurence de Stapilton son advoket
avowé en cest cause; les queux advoketz fesoient adunqes protestacion,
chescun pur sa part, par parole, qe si riens ils dient autrement qe bon
semblera a lour ditz mestres et a lour counseil q'ils soient par eux
correctez et lour conseil suisdit, chescun pur sa part; et adunqes, aprés
la dicte partie appellant myst avant en court une escript par voie
d'addicion a son primer appele, contenant la tenure q'ensuit:

Jeo, Thomas, sire de Morley, allié a Thomas, duc de Gloucestre, die qe vous, Johan Montagu, counte de Sarum, l'aan du regne roy Richard, nadgairs roy d'Angleterre, vyngt primer, estoiez de conseil du dit duc, et alastes plusours foitz entre le dit Richard, qe feust roy, et le dit duc, et descoverastes le conseil de dit duc a celuy qe feust roy, faucement et treiterousement, et aprés ceo vous [f.7v] appellastes le dit duc de treison, qe feust cause de sa morte, et sur ceo jeo vous apelle; et outre ceo, par voie d'addicion a la matere auterfoitz par moy devant nostre seigneur le roy en Parlement purposé, jeo die qe vous estoiez le dit aan et l'aan adunqe prochein ensuant de conseil covigne, et consent en plusours purpos malveis et fauces ovesque le dit roi encontre le roialme et commune profitt d'ycelle, c'est assavoir conseillant, pursuiant et consentant a dit roy a destruier les seigneurs et la comunalté de roialme par raunson des graundes summes et par autres voies de extorcions et autrement encontre chose public et commune profit del roialme, de qoy jeo die qe en cestes materes vous estoiez et estez faux et treitour, et avee fait faucement et treitorousement, et ceo jeo provera ové l'aide de Dieu, nostre dame et Seint George, par mon corps encontre le vostre, protestant [f.8r] d'amender, amenuser, accrestre ceste bille quanqe busoigne serra; et sur la matere par moy moevé en Parlement ay mys mon gage le xxix jour d'octobre l'an du regne nostre seigneur le roy Henry quart puis le conquest primer, devant luy, come appiert par record de dit Parlement, fesaunt protestacion d'amender, amenuser, accrestre cest addicion quanqe mester serra.

Aprés la lecture de quele bille, la dite partie appellant myst son gaunte a gage pur meyntenir la dicte bille et les contenuz en ycelle; et adunqes la dicte partie defendaunt respondist par parole de sa bouche propre en maner q'ensuit:

Jeo, Johan de Mountagu, count de Sarum, die qe tu, Thomas, sire de Morley, mentz faucement en tant qe tu moy surmettez treison en aucune matiere par toy purposé, et ceo je seeu prest a defendre solonc ley et custume d'armes [f.8v] al ordinance du court, et sur ceo jeo gette mon gaunte en gage,[87] faisant protestacion qe touz autres defences et benefices de ley et custume d'armes et du Court du Chivalerie a moi soient saufs ceste partie.

Les queux gages de tout deux parties remeynent en la courte; et adunqes aprés la dicte partie defendant demanda copies de toutz les

---

87 Sir Edward Hastings would use the same formula in challenging Lord Grey in 1408 : 'Thow lyest falsely, lewed knight, and yt I am ready to prove with my bodye against thy body, so therefore here is my glove to wedde and I ask day and place' (Quoted by R. I. Jack in 'Entail & Descent: The Hastings Inheritance 1370-1436', *Bulletin of the Institute of Historical Research*, 38 (1965), 15).

actes et actites et de toutz les exhibitz en la dicte cause pur avoir avisement d'icelles ovesqe son dit conseil. A quoy la dicte partie appellant repliast, en disant qe les matiers comprises en la dicte bille d'addicion touchent et concernent si hautes tresons qe solonc ley et custume d'armes la dicte partie defendant respondera a icelles sanz conseil, et sanz avoir copie d'icelles, et sanz estre lessez a meynprise en celle cause; et adunqes, aprés plusours altercacions heuz et [f.9r] faitz des ambedeux parties cest partie, finalment mon dit seigneur le Conestable, considerant les allegeances de tout deux parties, par avise de mon seigneur le Mareschall et autres, grauntast copies au dit partie defendant a sa request de touz les actes et actites et de toutz les exhibitz en la dicte cause, la dicte bille d'addicion soulement excepté, de quele bille et de les contenuz en ycelle mon dit seigneur le Conestable, par avise suisdit, disoit q'il vorroit soi aviser coment il doit estre outre procedé en la dicte cause celle partie et continua la dicte cause en mesme l'estat, et adjorna les ditz parties jesqes al samady proschein pur oier adunqes sa volunté celle partie.

Samady, le xv jour de novembre l'an du regne le roy Henry quart [f.9v] aprés le conquest primer, devant mes treshonurés seigneurs avantditz, les Conestable et Mareshall d'Engleterre, seiantz judicielment en Courte de Chivalrie, en tant come a chescun de eux appertient par vertue et autorité suisdictes, en la Grand Sale de Westmoustier, ové plusours et diverses sages du counseill du court, compareront personelement devant eux, chescun pur soy mesmes, Thomas, sire de Morley, partie appellant d'une part, et Johan Mountague, counte de Sarum, partie defendant d'autre parte; et adunqes aprés l'acte del darrein jour du courte devant cest partie overtement lue en audience des dictes parties, et meismes les parties a ceo assentuz, mon seigneur le Conestable demanda du dicte partie appellant s'il voedra declarer pluis avant son dit appele et l'escript par luy mys par voie d'addicion a icelle, ou s'il voet plus avant dire ou ajuster a icelle; et a ceo [f.10r] la dicte partie appellant respondist qe lui semble q'il ad assez dit et sufficeantement declaré son dit appele, et disoit q'il est illoeqes prest pur oier la volunté du courte solonc le terme a lui assigné le darrein jour devant; et puis aprés, monseigneur le Conestable demanda du dit partie defendant s'il voleit plus avant dire ou ajuster a sa dicte response sur sa defense; la quele partie defendant disoit que le darrein jour devant il demanda copie du dit escript mys par voie d'addicion par la dicte partie appellant a son primer appele et terme d'avoir deliberacion sur icelle, et qe terme luy fuist assigné adunqes pur oier cest jour la volunté du courte celle partie, come appiert par recorde del acte du dit jour come la dicte partie defendant disoit; sur quoy, aprés plusours altercacions heuz des ambedeux parties celle partie, finalement [f.10v] monseigneur le Conestable mesmes, par avise de monseigneur le

Mareschall et plusours autres chivalers presentz alors en courte, decreast et grantast copie du dit escript mys par voie d'addicion au dicte partie defendant a sa request; et outre ceo assigna terme a toutdeux parties a lour assent de outre proceder en la dicte cause selonc ley et custume d'armes et du dicte courte, c'est assavoir marsdy prochein venant; aprés quel decré et assignement, la dicte partie defendant protestast par parole q'il ne consent my, n'est son entent a consentier a proroger la jurisdiccion de mes ditz seigneurs en ceste partie par sa demande del copie del dicte addicion, ne par le resceit d'icelle, ne par sa apparance, ne aucune autre chose par luy fait a jour de huy; a quoy la dicte partie appellant repliast qe la dicte protestacion n'est point acceptable, ne doit par ley et custume d'armes estre accepté, pur tant que la [f.11r] dicte partie defendant ad responduz pleinement et fait contestacion en ceste cause, come la dite partie appellant disoit.

Marsdy, le xviii jour de novembre l'an du roy Henry etc. primer, devant Monsieur William Fulthorp, lieutenant monseigneur le Conestable d'Angleterre, et Monsieur Thomas Picworth, lieutenant monseigneur le Marshall d'Angleterre, seantz judicielment en Court de Chivalrie en la Grand Sale de Westmoustier, en tant come a chescun de eux appertient par vertue de lour offices, compareront personelement devant eux, chescun pur soy mesmes, Thomas, sire de Morley, partie appellant d'une part, et Johan Montague, count de Sarum, partie defendant d'autre part; et adunqes aprés le juge, par bone deliberacion, continua la dite cause en mesme l'estat et adjourna les dictes parties tanqe al joesdy prochein, par cause qe messeigneurs les Conestable et [f.11v] Mareshall ne purroient entendre a jour de huy entour l'esploit du dicte cause si avant, come as eux appertient en maner avantdit, pur diverses grandes bosoignes et charges q'ils ount affaire ové le conseil nostre seigneur le roy.

Joesdy, le vintisme jour de novembre l'an du regne nostre seigneur le roy Henry quart aprés le conquest primer, devant mes ditz seigneurs les Conestable et Mareshall d'Angleterre, seiantz judicielment en lour propre persones en Court de Chivalrie en la Grand Sale de Westmoustier, en tant come a chescun de eux appertient par vertue et auctorité suisdicte, ové plusours et diverses sages du conseil du court, compareront personelement, chescun pur soy mesmes, Thomas, sire de Morley, partie appellant d'une part, et Johan Montague [f.12r], cont de Sarum, partie defendaunt d'autre part; et puis aprés al request de toutz deux parties les retroactes du dicte cause furent overtement luez en lour audience; et aprés la lecture d'icelle le dicte partie defendaunt mist avant en courte une bille par voie d'enformacion ou d'exception sur la fourme q'ensuit :

Pardevant vous, mes treshonurez seigneurs, Henry, count de

Northumbre, Conestable d'Engleterre, et Rauf, count de Westm-
erland, Marshall d'Engleterre, ou voz lieutenantz, seantz judicielment par vertue et auctorité des lettres du privé seal nostre
tressoveraign seigneur le roy portantz la date le x jour de novembre
l'an nostre dit tressoverain seigneur le roy Henry quart aprés le
conquest primer, vous assignauns d'oier la cause desoubz escript,
come en les ditz lettres pluis pleinement appiert; la partie de Johan
Montagu, count de Sarum, partie defendant [f.12v], dist et en ley
purpose en terme competent a ceo faire par voie d'enformacion,
d'exception et autre manere queconque legal, selonc ley et custume
d'armes, encontre Thomas, sire de Morley, partie appellant sa
persone, et un le suen pretense appel devant nostre dit tressoveraign
seigneur en son Parlement le xxix jour d'octobre purposé, et
encontre une matere en escript par voie de pretence addicion par
le dit Thomas devant vous mes treshonurés seigneurs, seauntz
judicielment par auctorité des lettres suisdictes le xi jour de
novembre l'an suisdit, et encountre l'entencion du dit Thomas
total encountre la dicte partie defendant purpose, nondepartant
d'ascunes ses respounces devant nostre dit seigneur le roy en
l'avantdit Parlement et devant vous, judicielment seantz, come dit
est, autrefoitz donez, mes a icell firmement enherdantz selonc ley
et custume d'armes en la manere et forme q'ensuent :

[f.13r] Primerement, dist la partie du dit Johan, defendant, en
manere come desuis, qe le dit Thomas, partie appellant ne deduce,
ne monstre ascun enteresse en sa dicte pretense appel pur lui faire
legal partie, pur attachier, pursuer ou maintenir tiel appel de
pretence treson fait a Thomas, duc de Gloucestre, come la dicte
partie appellant pretendi en sa dicte pretence appel.

Et auxi dist la dicte partie defendant, en manere come desuis, qe
la dicte partie appellant en sa pretence appell ne monstre, n'expresse l'an, moys, ne lieu en les queux il pretende les ditz pretences
treson ou tresons estre faitz, les queux sont et devoient estre
substanciels au dit pretence appel et sanz queux la dicte pretence
appel est de nul value par la ley.

Et auxi dist la dite partie defendant [f.13v], en manere come
desuis, qe par null matere en la dicte pretence appell purposé ne
puist ascun tresoun encountre la persoun du dit Johan, defendaunt,
ensourdre, ne doit estre de droit supposé, et pur ceo la dicte
pretence appel, en manere come il est purposé, ne doit par vous
estre admis, depuis qe par la pruve de icell la partie appellant ne
poet estre relesé en ascun manere al effect de convictier le dit
Johan, partie defendant, d'ascun treson.

Et auxi dist la dite partie defendant, en manere come desuis, qe mesme la partie appellant en son pretense appel suisdit ne soy oblige ne soy enscrive a mesme la peyne qe la dicte partie appellant suppose estre dewe en cest cas, come la ley requiert,[88] pur quoy demaunde la dicte partie defendaunt qe la dicte pretense appel come inept et ineptement purposé et come de [f.14r] nul value soit par vostre decree rejecté pur les causes suisdites et pur chescun d'eaux; et la dicte partie defendaunt de cest pretence appell encountre lui purposé soit absolut, et qe la dicte partie appellant en les expences du dite partie defendant featz et affeare, ovesque ses damages et interesses, soit judicealment par vous condempné.

Et auxi dist la dite partie defendaunt, en manere come desuis, encountre la primere materes en escript par voie de pretense addicion devant vous purposé, q'ency commence *Jeo, Thomas, sire de Morlee, alié a Thomas, duc de Gloucestre etc.* tanqe a cest clause en la dite pretense addicion, *Et outre ceo, par voie d'addicion qe la dite partie appellant ne soi puet,* ne doit eider par cell primer partie de sa dicte pretense addicion, pur ceo q'il ne monstre riens en quell degree, n'en quel manere il est [f.14v] allié au dit Thomas, duc de Gloucestre, ne coment la pursuite du dit pretense appel a luy appertint de loy depuis qe aliaunce puet sourdre de diverses et plusours causes; et ency il ne deduce, ne specifie my clerement de son interesse, nomement depuis q'il pretende appell de treson; et ency la dite pretense addicion est inept et par vous mes seigneurs a estre rejecté.

Et auxi dist la dite partie defendant, en manere come desuis, qe coment qe la dicte partie appellant monstre et expresse l'an en quel il pretende qe la dicte partie defendant fuist del counseill du dit duc de Gloucestre, nepurquant il ne monstre, n'expresse le moys, ne le lieu quant et ou il doit avoir feat la dicte pretense treson, ne soy oblige n'enscrive a mesme la peyn que la dicte partie appellant suppose estre dewe en cest cas [f.15r], come la loy requiert; pur quoy requiert la partie du dit defendant qe la dit primer partie de la dicte pretense addicion soit come inept et de null value par vous rejecté.

Et auxi quant a la seconde partie du dite pretense addicion, la quell la partie appellant suppose une bille q'ency commence, *Et outre ceo, par voie d'addicion etc.* jesqes al fyn d'ycell, dist la partie du

<hr>

88 Salisbury was insisting upon a particular point of procedure; that Morley, as appellant should have declared that he was prepared to face the same punishment as the defendant – that is execution as a traitor – should he be vanquished in the combat, and his appeal thus prove to be false.

dit defendaunt, en manere come desuis, qe la dite secound partie del dit pretense addicion est ineptement purposé, pur ceo et de ceo q'il est matere estrange et seperate, non dependant, emergent, ne conexcé en ascun manere a la dite primer matere en la dite pretense appel, et est purposé par voie d'adduccion al primer matere du dite pretense appel, come overtement appiert en [f.15v] icell; et ency il est ineptement purposé par voie d'addicion, come la dite partie defendaunt serra prest a declarer si bosoigne serra.

Et auxi dist la dicte partie defendant, en manere come desuis, qe la dicte secounde partie de la dicte pretense addicion est ineptement purposé en tant q'il est expressement novell matere, come devant est dit, et n'est en icelle specifié moys, ne lieu en queux la dite partie defendant devoit avoir feat la dite pretense treason, ne soy enscrive a la paine, come la ley requiert, les queux sount substanciels et necessaries par loy, et ency la dicte secounde partie est ineptement purposé et demerit et droit a estre rejecté.

Et auxi dist la partie du dit defendaunt, en manere come desuis, qe depuis qe la dicte secounde partie de la dicte pretense addicion est un [f.16r] novell matere, et en null manere compris, dependaunt, emergent, ne connexé a le primer pretense appell, la conusance ne la determinacion de icell ne a vous mes seigneurs, ne a vostre cognicion appertint par vertue et autorité des lettres roials suisditz, n'en le forme come il est purposé par vous a estre admis ou determiné, mes est la partie du dit defendant, pur les causes premyses et avantdites, a estre demys de vostre jugement, et la dicte partie appellant en les costages du dite partie defendant ové ses expenses featz et affeare damages et interesses a estre condempné; les quelles choses et chescun de eux purpose et demande d'estre feat la dicte partie defendant, joyntment et severalment, le benefyce de loy a luy tout temps sauf, et sauf tout foitz al partie defendant avantdit en chescun temps ces [f. 16v] matere ou materes a les ditz appell [et] addicion pretenses, et auxi a le dite novel matere concernantz et touchantz pur justefier ses respounces par luy featz solonc loy et custume d'armes en cest partie, come bosoigne ou profit luy serroit en temps et lieu bosoignables.

Et auxi la dite partie defendant, adjoustant as premises, demaunde et requiert de vous mes seigneurs, en manere come desuis, qe depuis qe la matere pretense substancial continue en la primer pretense appel en nul de ses parties soit duement specifié, mes est waverant, generall, obscure et inept, et ineptement purposé, et les ditz pretenses addicions et novel matere en lour parties substancials pretenses ne sont duement specifiez, mes sont en manere waverant,

obscure purposez, qe les dites [f.17r] appelles et addicion pretenses
contenant la novell matere ineptes et ineptement purposés, soient
par vous a estre rejectez, decreez et realment et en feat rejettés
nomement come de les ditz generaltees, obscureteez et eneptitudes,
en manere come ils sont purposez, par l'enspeccion des ditz appell
et addicion pretensez overtement puet apparoir, reservé toutfoitz
al dite partie defendant benefice a monstrer et declarer, si bosoigne
soit, ou et en queux parties des ditz generaltees, obscuriteez et
eneptitudes[a] sont en les matirs suisditz oue sourdent de iceux, sauf
toutfoitz a dite partie defendant touz les autres defences et autres
benefices de loy et custume d'armes.

La quelle bille lue overtement en courte, aprés la lecture d'icelle, la
dicte partie appellant prie qe la [f.17v] dicte bille soit rejetté pur tant
qe la dicte partie defendant ad fait contestacion en la dite cause, come
la dite partie appellant allegeast, et la dicte bille d'exception duist avoir
esté mys devant contestacion, et nemye aprés, s'il serroit admissible; et
aprés plousours altercacions heuz de tout deux parties celle partie,
finalment mon dit seigneur le Conestable, par avise de mon seigneur
le Mareshall et autres sages, assigna terme a tout deux parties pur oier
sa volunté celle partie, c'est assaver lundy prochein a lour assent; et
outre ceo chargea mesme la partie appellant de mettre en escript les
ditz resons et allegeances par luy faitz par parole en cest partie, et luy
bailler parentre cy et le dit lunedy, si lui semble expedient.

Lunedy, le xxiiij jour de novembre l'an de nostre seigneur le roy
Henry [f.18r] quart puis le conquest primer, devant [mes][b] treshonurez
seigneurs les Conestable et Marshall d'Angleterre avantditz, seantz
judicielment en lour propre persones en Court de Chivalrie en la
Grand Sale de Westmoustier, en tant come a chescun de eux appartient
par vertue et autorité suisdites, soi presenteront personelement, chescun
pur sa partie, Thomas, sire de Morley, partie appellant d'une part, et
Johan Montague, count de Sarum, partie defendant d'autre parte; et
adunqes aprés l'acte del darrein jour du courte devant cest partie feust
lue en audience de les parties suisdites, et mesmes les parties a ceo
assentirent, demandantz entrechangeablement chescun pur sa partie le
volunté du courte selonc le terme as eux limité le darrein jour devant,
come en le dit acte est contenuz plus [f.18v] au plein, a ceo q'ils
disoient; et pur ceo mon seigneur le Conestable, par avise de mon
seigneur le Mareshall et plousours autres sages presentz alors en courte,
considerant les actes desuisditz par bone deliberacion, et pur tant qe la
dicte partie appellant ne ad baillé, ne mys en escript aucunes causes

a *MS*. eneptitutudes.
b *MS*. mon.

resonables pur quoy les ditz exceptions purposés en escript par la dicte partie defendant ne soient admisibles ou ne devont estre admys, et considerantz ausi en manere suisdit que les matires purposés par la dicte partie appellant en son dit appele et la pretense addicion a icell sont trop generalls et obscures en plusours ses parties, finalment mon dit seigneur le Conestable, par avise suisdite, commanda la partie appellant susdite et a lui assigna terme a declarer en escript [f.19r] les pointz desoubz escriptz compris en ses ditz appele et pretense addicion a icelle, c'est assavoir mesquerdy prochein, al effect qe la dite partie defendaunt purra clerement estre certifié et conustre l'entent du dite partie appellant, et auxi qe la courte purra savoir si sur les ditz matiers appertient bataille, et si ils purront autrement estre triez et provez qe par bataille, nonobstant qeconqes pretenses contestacions queux furent faitz, sicome il semble a mon dit seigneur le Conestable plus tost de corage et honesté de chivalrie que par autre due deliberacion; les tenures verraiement de les pointz comprises en l'appele et la pretense addicion d'icelle du dicte partie appellant, queux la dicte partie appellant ad terme a declarer et cy ensement et sont tiels :

Primerement [f.19v] etc., il conveint[89] declarer cest point, c'est assavoir de ceo *q'il feust de conseil de Thomas duc de Gloucestre:* coment il feust de conseil du dit duc, et de quell conseil.

Item, il conveint declarer cest point, c'est assaver *et conust le conseil d'ambideux parties:* quel feust le conseil q'il conust d'ambideux parties.

Item, il conveint declarer cest point, c'est assaver et puis *come une faux chivaler descovera son conseil et traiterousement deceiva le dit duc, et puis lui appella:* quel conseil il discovera du dit duc, et a quel persone il discovera le dit counseil, et coment traiterousement deceiva le dit duc, et coment lui appella, et sur quelx choses.

Item, il conveint declarer icy queux mois, an, et lieu il deceiva traiterousement le dit duc.

Item, il conveint declarer coment la matere [f.20r] contenuz en la dicte pretense addicion est dependaunt, emergent ou autrement connexé a la primere appele purposé en le dit Parlement par le dit Thomas, sire de Morley, encontre le dit cont de Sarum.

Item, il conveint declarer le primer point du dit pretense addicion q'est tiele *Jeo, Thomas, sire de Morley, allié a Thomas, duc de Gloucestre:* coment le dit sire de Morley est allié a Thomas, duc de Gloucestre.

89 Here and for the rest of this bill, the text clearly reads 'coment'. But we have altered this to 'conveint', following BL Add. MS. 35821, since the sense demands this reading which is certainly the correct and original one.

Item, il conveint declarer en la dicte pretense addicion queux mois et lieus il feust conseillant, pursuant et consentant au dit Richard, nadgairs roy, a destruire les seigneurs du roialme et la cominalté, par raunson des queux grandes sommes, et par queux voies de extorciouns, et coment autrement encontre chose public et commune profit du roialme.

Mesqerdy, le xxvj jour de novembre l'an du regne nostre seigneur [f.20v] le roy Henry quart puis le conquest primer, devant mes ditz seigneurs les Conestable et Mareschall d'Engleterre seantz judicielment en lour propre persones en Court de Chivalrie en le Blank Sale de Westmoustier, en tant come a chescun de eux appertient par vertue et auctorité suisdictes, ové plusours et diverses sages du conseil du court, compereront personelment, chescun pur soi mesmes, Thomas, sire de Morley, partie appellant d'une part, et Johan Montague, count de Sarum, partie defendant d'autre parte; et adunqes aprés la dicte partie appellant purposast et disoit par parole q'il ad mys et bailla a monseigneur le Conestable extrajudicielement sa declaracion en escript solonc le terme a luy assigné le darrein jour devant ceste partie, et fesoit protestacion q'il ne voet consentir qe la dicte partie defendant eit [f.21r] copie d'icelle, mes qe la dicte declaracion soit pris soulement pur enformacion de la court, et en null autre manere; et la dicte partie defendant priast adunqes q'il soit enactés qe la dicte declaracion est baillez extrajudicielement et nemye judicielement, et demanda qe les appele et pretense addicion du dicte partie appellant soient rejettez come trop generales et obscurez en plusours ses parties, en manere come il est contenuz plus au plein en lour exceptions suisdites; et adunques aprés plusours altercacions heuz des ambideux parties ceste partie, finalment le acte del darrein jour du court devant ceste partie feust overtement lue en audience des ditz parties, et aprés la lecture d'ycelle mon dit seigneur le Conestable, par avise mon seigneur le Mareschall et plusours [f.21v] autres sages chivalers presentz alors en court, considerant ové bone deliberacion les dictes actes et le decree du darrein jour devant, rebaillast au dit partie appellant la dicte declaracion pur rebailler mesme la declaracion judicielment en court selonc le decree du darrain jour devant, si lui semble expedient. A quoy la partie appellant respondist q'il feust commandez le darrein jour devant par la court soulement de office affaire la dicte declaracion pur lour enformacion, et pur ceo il poet bailler la dicte declaracion sibien extrajudicielment come judicielment a sa propre volunté, come il disoit, et sur ceo rebailla en courte la dicte declaracion, toutz foitz protestaunt come desuis qe la dicte declaracion soit soulement receue extrajudicielment, pur enfourmacion du [f.22r] courte, saunz grantier copie d'icell au dicte partie defendaunt; et puis aprés mon dit seigneur

le Conestable, par avise suisdicte, rebailla derechief la dite declaracion
au dit partie appellant, luy declarant expressement qe tout ceo qe serra
fait et baillé en la courte en yceste cause serra fait judicielment en
presence de toutz deux parties, et nemye en absence de nulle d'eux; et
pur ceo la dite partie appellant feust commandez sur son perile de moien
d'eslire s'il voet rebailler la dicte declaracion en court judicielement ou
non; et tantost mesme la partie appellant rebailla en courte la dite
declaracion, priant q'il soit receivé judicielment ou extrajudicielment al
eleccion du courte, sanz ceo que copie d'icell soit grantez au dit
partie defendant [f.22v], la quele declaracion receivé et lue adunqes
judicielment en courte en audience des dictes parties sur la fourme
q'ensuit etc.:[90]

> Ceux sont les declaracions faitz par Thomas le sire de Morley a
> la bille et addicion a lui fait en la Court de Chivalrie devant mes
> treshonorables seigneurs, Conestable et Mareschall, sur la matier
> d'appele fait parentre le dit Thomas de Morley, partie appellant
> d'une part, et Johan Montagu, count de Sarum, partie defendant
> d'autre part; et le dit Thomas proteste en cest escript q'il vous
> doigne cestes declaracions escritz taunt soulement par vostre
> enformacion.

> Primerement, quant a ceo qe vous demandez qe soit declaré par
> le dit Thomas coment le dit Johan Montagu fuist de conseill de
> Thomas, duc de [f.23r] Gloucestre, l'avantdit sire de Morley
> declare ceste matiere et dist qe come une querele estoit movee en la
> honourable Court de Conestable et Mareschal parentre Monsieur
> William Montagu, nadgairs count de Saresbery d'une part, et le
> pere de l'avantdit Johan d'autre part, le dit Johan Montagu vient
> au dit duc de Gloucestre pur avoir socour et aide de luy au son
> dit piere en la dite querele, et offrist son service en quanque il
> purroit faire, et fuist retenuz en son service pur aler ovesque luy
> en Pruys, et allors et aprés privé de son conseill; et ency le dit
> Johan estoit de conseil du dit duc.

> Item, quant a ceo qe vous demandez qe le dit Thomas doit
> declarer coment le dit Johan conust le conseil d'ambedeux [f.23v]
> parties, c'est assavoir de Richard, nadgaires roy d'Engleterre, et
> le dit duc, coment le dit defendant fuist del conseil du dit duc est

---

90 Morley's reluctance to see the defendant given his 'declaration' is reminiscent of
the case of William Lord Latimer, who, during the Good Parliament of 1376, had
similarly demanded a copy of the charges against him. This was refused by the Chancellor,
Wykeham. Ironically Wykeham's reply was flung back at him in the following Parliament
after he had asked to see the charges against him in writing: *The Anonimalle Chronicle,
1333–1381*, ed. V. H. Galbraith (Manchester, 1927), pp.93, 98–9; G. A. Holmes, *The Good
Parliament* (1975), p.179 (both references which we owe to Nigel Saul).

desus declaré, et coment le dit Johan estoit del conseil du dit
Richard, le dit Thomas dist et declare qe le dit Johan conust le
loial conseil de dit duc et son purpos et ordinance pur resistier les
malices et malveys purpos ordeignez en destruccion du roialme
par Robert de Veer, nadgairs duc d'Irlaund, et cez complices, et
cest conseil il discovera au roy, par quell discoverance il devient
de conseil du dit roy, et ency est declaré q'il conust le conseil
d'ambedeux parties. Et depuis, luy conissaunt le conseil le dit duc,
come desus est escript, appella le dit duc faucement de haut treson,
la quell fuist cause de sa mort. [f.24r] Et quant a ceo qe vous
demandez qe le dit Thomas doit declarer coment la dicte addicion
est emergent, incident, dependent ou connexé a la matier principall, le dit Thomas dist et declare qe come en la matier principall
est contenuz qe le dit Johan conust le conseil d'ambez deux parties
suisditz, come devant est dit, il conseila et consenta au dit Richard
a destruire faucement les seigneurs et la comunalté du dit roialme
par raunsouns des grandes summes et par autres voies d'extorciouns et autrement encontre chose public et comune profit de
la dite roialme, come en sa dite addicion appiert pluis au plein.

Item, a declarer la ans, moyses et lieux en queux les ditz tresons
estoient faites, le dit Thomas dist qe le dit Johan fuist conseillant
[f.24v], consentant et pursuyant a destruire les seigneurs et la
communalté du roialme la anes du regnes le dit roi Richard vynt
primer et vynt secunde, en les moyses juyn, juyll, d'augst, septembre
et autres; et quant as lieux, a Loundres, Windsore et Notingham
et autres lieux.

Aprés la lecture de quele declaracion mon seigneur le Conestable, par
avise suisdicte, demanda du dit partie appellant s'il voet declarer icest
jour plus pleinement ses ditz appelle et la pretense addicion a ycelle
selonc le decree du darrain jour devant cest partie; et le dicte partie
appellant respondist qe noun, et disoit qe luy semble q'il ad assés dit
et sufficeauntement declaré celle partie, et de ceo soi mist en jugement
de court. Nientmeins mon seigneur le Conestable, par avise suisdicte,
luy commanda [f.25r] de prendre unqore bone deliberacion et avise
ové son conseil cest partie; et adunqes la dicte partie appellant soi mist
un poy apart pur avoir deliberacion ovesque son conseill ceste partie,
et tost aprés revient et disoit par avise de son conseil come desuis, qe
luy semble q'il ad sufficeantment declaré ses ditz appelle et l'addicion
d'icelle en tant come luy bosoigne, et ne veulloit aucunement plus
avant dire, ne declarer cell partie; et adunqes aprés la dicte partie
defendaunt pria la court de luy grauntier copie du dit declaracion, et
auxi luy assigner terme de respoundre a ycelle solonc ley et custume
d'armes come le cas requiert; et aprés plusours altercacions heuz de

tout deux parties ceste partie, finalment mon dit seigneur le Conestable, par avise de mon [f.25v] seigneur le Mareshall et plousours autres sages, graunta copie du dit declaracion au dicte partie defendaunt a sa request, et outre ceo lui assigna terme pur respoundre a ycelle solonc ley et custume d'armes, come le cas requert, c'est assaver lundy proschein; et en aprés mesme la partie appellant protestast par parole q'il ne consent mie, mes disassent overtement au dit decree. Nientmeins mon seigneur le Conestable, par avise suisdit, continua la dicte cause en estat suisdit et adjorne les ditz parties jesqes le lundy prochein; et tantost aprés la dicte partie appellant protestast par parole q'il ne consent mie au dit continuance et adjornement, mes soulement en tant come il est tenuz par ley et custume d'armes, et outre ceo, en meintenance de les matiers contenuz en sa dit [f.25Ar] declaracion jetta son gaunte en gage, la quele remeint devers la courte.

Marsdy, le secound jour de decembre l'an du regne nostre seigneur le roy Henry quart puis le conquest primer, devant mes ditz seigneurs les Conestable et Marshall d'Angleterre, seantz judicielment en lour propre persones en Court de Chivalrie en la Grand Sale de Westmoustier, en tant come a chescun de eux appartient par vertue et autorité susdictes, ové plousours et diverses sages du conseill du court, compareront personelment, chescun pur soi mesmes, Thomas, sire de Morley, partie appellaunt d'une part, et Johan Mountague, count de Sarum, partie defendant d'autre parte, le decree du darrain jour du court devant cest partie feust overtement lue en audience des dictes parties; et aprés la lecture d'ycelle la dicte partie defendant [f.25Av], en satisfiant au dit decree, myst avant en courte une bille par voie d'enformacion ou excepcion sur la fourme q'ensuyt:

> Pardevant vous, mes treshonurés seigneurs Henry, count de Northumbre, Conestable d'Engleterre, et Rauf, counte de Westmerland, Marshall d'Engleterre, ou voz lieutenantz, seantz judicielment, par vertue et autoritee des lettres du privé seal nostre tressoveraign seigneur le roy portauntz la date le xe jour de novembre l'an nostre dit seigneur le roy Henry quart aprés le conquest primer, vous assignauntz d'oier la cause dessouz nomee, come en les dictes lettres pluis pleinement appiert, la partie de Johan Montague, count de Sarum, partie defendaunt, a les choses deinz escriptz par luy a estre faitz par maner et voie [f.26r] d'enformacion, excepcion ou autre manere queconque legale, en la meillour maner et fourme q'il poet solonc loy et custume d'armes, encountre Thomas, sire de Morley, partie appellant en cest partie, et auxi encontre une le soen pretense enformacion par voie et manere de pretense declaracion par mesme la partie appellant devant vous le xxvj jour de novembre l'an suisdit

judicielment purposé, et encontre la force, fourme et effect d'icell, noun departant par ascune chose desoubz escrit de ascune chose par lui deducté ou purposé en une informacion ou exception par le dit partie defendant autrefoitz devant vous purposé, ne d'ascunes autres ses respounces queconqes autrefoitz par la dite partie defendant doneez, mais a yceux et chescun d'eux firmement enherdant solonc loy et custume [f.26v] d'armes, dist, allegge, et en ley purpose en terme a luy assigné, en manere come ensuyt, a tout effect de ley qe poet ou doit suyer de les choses dessouz escriptz pur le profit du dicte partie defendaunt, et encontre l'entent du dit partie appellaunt totale, et nemye autrement.

Primerement, dist allegge la dicte partie defendant al effect desuis escript coment par vostre decree par vous doné judicialment le xxiiij jour de novembre l'an suisdite, la dite partie appellant estoit par vostre decree moesté et commandé et terme peremptorie a luy assigné a declarer certeins articles ou pointz contenuz en ses pretence primer appell et pretense addicion. Nientmeins, la dicte partie appellant ad lessé et omys ascunes des ditz articles ou [f.27r] pointz contenuz en les ditz pretense appelle et pretense addicion nient declarez, les queux il doit avoir declaré a terme a luy limité a ceo faire, sibien pur vostre informacion come pur la legale respounse et defense du dicte partie defendant come par les actes et actites devant vous entre les parties suisdites ewes en cest partie evidentement appiert; as queux la dicte partie defendant soy refiert et voet avoir pur icy expressez les articles ou pointz queux la partie du dit appellant doit avoir declaree come dist est, et ne sont pas en lour nature declarez, ensuyent et sount tiels:

Primerement, il ne declare point coment ne en quell degree il est allié a Thomas, duc de Gloucestre, pur luy doner interesse [f.27v] par ley pursuyer tiel appell pur l'enjurie a dit duc pretense fait.

Item, il ne declare point queux moys, ne lieu, il deseyva le dit duc come il faucement pretende.

Item, il ne declare point des quelles hautes tresons il faucement appella le dit duc, ne coment la dicte appell estoit cause de sa mort, ne en queux moys, ne lieu, ne devant quell juge, n'en quell courte.

Item, il ne declare point en sa pretense addicion queux seigneurs il fuist consentant a destruier, ne coment consentant, conseillant et pursuiant, ne coment, ne par queux raunsouns des grandes sommes, ne par queux voies ou maneres d'extorcions, ne des queux persones, ne coment [f.28r] les ditz sommes et extorsions

furent levez ou faitz, ne coment autrement encontre chose public,
ne coment encountre comune profit du roialme.

Pur quoy demanda la dicte partie defendant, come del inspeccion
des ditz actes et de le noun declaracion des ditz articles, des queux
desuis est fait mencion, et saunz queux articles et la declaracion
d'iceux l'entencion del dite partie appellant a ascune effect par lui
demandé en sa primer pretense appell, n'en sa pretense addicion,
n'en ascun matere par luy deduct, ne poet de ley estre foundee,
ne luy eider a son entent, qe la dite partie appellant soit pronuncié
et declaré par vostre decree pur noun suffisauntment [f.28v] avoir
objecté ové effect, et ses pretensez declaracions par luy pretenses
faitz toutz et chescun d'iceaux a estre incompetentz, noun suffi-
sauntz et saunz effect, et a estre tenuz rejecteblez et realment par
vous a estre rejectez pur les causes suisditz, et l'excepcion du dite
partie defendant sur le ineptitude et noun suffisauntee des ditz
pretensez primer appell et la pretense addicion a icell par la partie
appellant purposez, les pretenses declaracions queconqes non
obstantz, pur les causes suisditz par vous a estre admys ové effect,
solonc la force, forme et effect queconqes en icell contenuz, queux
choses et chescun de eux purposés et demande a estre fait la partie
du dit defendant, jointement et severalment, le [f.29r] benefice de
ley a luy tout foitz saufe.

Et dist et allegge la dicte partie defendant, ajostant a les choses
pur luy devant purposés et en null manere departaunt d'icelles ou
ascun d'eux, mais enfortefiant sa dicte conclusion al effect d'icell
optiner par decree encountre la dicte partie appellant, come desuis,
sa persone et ses pretenses declaracions devant vous purposez, et
toute la force, fourme et effect d'icell et sa entent totale, en manere
et fourme q'ensuit, al affect desuis escript.

Primerement, qe la primere article ou point de pretense declaracion
par la partie du dit appellant devant vous purposé en quel le dit
appellant soy afforce coment que nient veritablement a declarer
qe le dit defendant estoit *del conseil de Thomas, duc de Gloucestre [f.29v],
de sa retenue pur aler ovesque luy en Pruce, et alors et aprés privee de son
conseil* come en le dit pretense declaracion pluis pleinement appiert,
la quelle la dicte partie defendant ne confesse mye, mais outrement
disconfesse, la dicte pretense declaracion en ceste primer point est
de null value en manere come le primer appell est inept et de null
value par loy, pur ceo et de ceo qe des ditz appell et declaracion
en icell partie ne poet null fauxtee, ne traiterouse desceite surdre
n'estre s[u]pposé[a] par loy encountre le dit defendant; et pur ceo

_____

a *MS smudged at this point.*

la dicte primer article del dicte pretense declaracion, de quell est fait mencion desuis, al effect par la dicte partie appellant purpose, est par vous a estre reputee de null value et demerit a estre rejecté.

Et quant a le seconde article ou point del dicte pretense declaracion par quel la dicte partie appellant [f.30r] soy afforce a declarer come qe nient veritablement qe la dicte partie defendant *conust le conseill d'ambedeux parties, et fausement pretende qe la dicte partie defendant conust le loial conseil du dit duc et son purpos et ordenaunce pur recistre les malicez et malveis purpose ordeignez en distruccion du roialme par Robert Veer, nadgairs duc d'Irlaund, et sez complicez, et cest conseil il discovera au Richard, nadgairs roy d'Angleterre, par quel discoverance il devient de conseil du dit roy, et puis luy conusant le counseill du dit duc appella le dit duc fausement de haut treson, la quelle appell fuist cause de sa mort* les quelles choses le dit defendant ne confesse my, mais outrement disconfesse; dist la dicte partie defendant qe le dit ii^{de} article del dicte secounde declaracion qe soy refiert a le matier del primere pretence appel come declaratif a icell. La quel appell est par vous a estre reputeez de null value pur ceo q'en le dicte appell n'est [f.30v] expressé null an, moys, ne lieu, n'auxi ne sount expressez en cest point de declaracion; et ency il est come dependant sur le principall appell a estre reputé pur null et de null value, et auxi pur ceo qe par la dicte declaracion n'est nemye expressé quel fuist le loiall conseil del duc de Gloucestre, ne quel ne fuist le malveis purpose de Robert Veer en destruccion del roialme; mais est trop generall en manere, come est le primer appell; et auxi pur ceo q'il ne declare point en sa dicte pretense [declaration coment le appel pretense]^{91} faite par le dit John, partie defendant, pretense purposé encontre le dit duc estoit cause de sa mort, ne coment il moriust par cause du dicte appelle, par juggement ou sanz juggement, ou si le dit appell estoit provee encontre le dit duc ou non, ne quell fuist la matiere du dicte appell, et ency est le dit point ou article del pretense declaracion a estre rejecté pur les causes suisdictes.

[f.31r] Et quant al iij pointe ou article de la dicte pretense declaracion, en quelle partie soi afforce a declarer qe la darrein partie de sa pretense addicion q'ency comence: *et outre ceo, par voie d'addicion* est emergent, incident, dependent ou connexé al principall, en pretendant q'ele est emergent de la matiere principale, pur ceo q'il dist en la principall appele *q'il conust le counseill d'ambedeux parties* la quell est un parole introductif et narratif de la matier principale touchant l'enjurie pretense fait a Thomas, duc de Gloucestre, et n'est mye parole de substance du dicte pretense

91 Here Borough missed out a phrase, which we have supplied (in brackets) from BL Add. MS. 35821.

appell; et en sa dicte pretense addiccion et pretense declaracion il dist qe la dicte partie defendant estoit counseillant et consentant ovesque le dit Richard, nadgairs roy, a destruier fausement les seigneurs et la comunalté du roialme par raunson des graundes sommes et autres voies d'extorcions et autrement encontre chose public et comune profit du roialme, la quell est novell [f.31v] matiere, divers et seperate, et en null manere dependaunt ne emergent de la matiere de la primer appell concernant l'enjurie fait a Thomas, duc de Gloucestre, n'en null manere poet estre par loy supposé de emerger ne dependre d'icest parole *il conust le counseill d'ambideux parties* la quell est parole narratif et introductif a introdure et monstrier qe le dit Johan Montague, partie defendant, estoit entre les deux parties come une espie, come la dicte partie appellant pretende en sa dicte primer appele, come par l'enspeccion des ditz appelle, pretense addicion et pretense declaracion pleinement poet appairor; et depuis qe la matier del principall appell est concernant l'enjurie pretense fait a un singuler persone, [et]ᵃ la matier pretense en la pretence addicion est pretense en destruccion del comunaltee encontre chose public, des ditz deux matiers ne puist par null loy estre supposé conjunccion n'ensemble par voie d'addicion, ne purrount conjoyner, mais sont tout foitz seperatez [f.32r], come desuis est dit. Pur quoy la dicte pretense declaracion est a estre rejetté et tenuz pur null et de null value pur les causes suisdictes; et sont toutz les ditz pretenses declaracions noun vaillables al effect par la dicte partie appellant purposé, mais sount a estre rejectez, et pur null reputez en forme et effect par la dicte partie defendant demandez.

Les queux choses purpos[és] demande la dicte partie defendant a estre fait ové effect jointement et severalment le benefit de loy toutz foitz a luy sauf.

Aprés la lecture de quelle bille plusours et diverses altercacions furont faitz de toutz deux parties de et sur les contenuz en la dicte bille, et ausi en les retroactes dudite cause; et finalment la dite partie defendant myst avant une bille al effect de affermer ses autres respounses sur la fourme q'ensuyt:

[f.32v] Jeo, Johan Montagu, count de Sarum, die qe mes respounses par moy donez en Parlement et devant vous mes seigneurs juggez, en manere come ils sont devant vous enactez, a queux actes jeo moy refer et voill aver pur icy expressés, sount loials; et sur ceo, jeo moy defendera come appertient a chivaler en manere come j'ay offré en les dites actes.

a *MS* a.

Aprés la lecture de quelle bille, la dicte partie defendant myst son gaunte en gage a meintener les contenuz en la dicte bille selonc tout force et fourme et effect d'icelles; et adunqes aprés la dicte partie appellant myst avant une bille al entent de affermer ses ditz appelle et pretense addicion et declaracion d'ycelles sur la fourme q'ensuyt:

> Jeo, Thomas, sire de Morley, devant vous mes treshonurez seigneurs, Conestable et Mareschall d'Engleterre, die qe mon appelle fait en Parlement [f.33r] encontre toy, Johan Montague, count de Sarum, ové l'addicion et declaracions ent fait devant vous mes seigneurs, sont verray, en affirmant ce qe j'ay purposé et alleggé devant; et en tant qe tu, Johan, as denyé les matires de tresons ou de treson encontre toy par moy purposez, jeo die qe tu mentz faucement, et sur ceo jeo mette mon gaunt a gage, et ceo jeo provera ové l'aide de Dieu et Seint George [par mon corps]^a encountre le teon, et sur ceo jeo demande jour et lieu.

La quell bille lue overtement en court, aprés la lecture d'icelles la partie appellant suisdit jetta son gaunte en gage sur la fourme contenuz en la dicte bille; les queux gages de toutz deux parties remeynent en la court; et adunqes aprés, mon seigneur le Mareschall et plusours autres sages dona terme as ditz parties pur oier sa volunté des materes suisdictes, c'est assaver vendredy prochein.

[f.33v] Vendredy, le quint jour de decembre l'an du regne le roy Henry quart puis le conquest primer, devant mes ditz seigneurs le Conestable et Mareschall d'Angleterre, seantz judicielment en Court de Chivalrie en la Graund Chambre deins la manoir de Kenyngton au cost du lit du roy, en tant come a chescun de eux appertient par vertue et auctorité suisdictes, ové plusours graundes seigneurs et sages chivalers du conseil du courte, compareront personelement, chescun pur soy mesmes, Thomas, sire de Morley, partie appellant d'une parte, et Johan Montague, conte de Sarum, partie defendant d'autre part; et puis aprés qe l'acte du darrein jour du courte devant cest partie feust overtement lue en audience des dictes parties, et mesmes les parties en ycell assentuz, mon seigneur le Conestable demanda du dit appellant s'il voet demurrer sur les actes et actites et sur les matires purposés et allegez par luy et son advoket en son dit appele ovesque l'addicion et declaracion d'icelles; [f.34r] et il respondist qe oy; et en mesme le maner mon seigneur le Conestable demanda du dit defendant s'il voet demurrer sur les actes et actites et sur les matires par luy et son advoket purposez et alleggez en sa defense; et il disoit qe oy, en maner come il est enactez; et adunqes aprés l'appell du dit appellant ovesque l'addicion et declaracion d'icell, et ausi la response du dit defendant a ycelles

---

a *Omitted in MS. We have added the words in brackets from f. 7v.*

furont overtement lues en court en audience de dictes parties. Et aprés la lecture d'icelles mon seigneur le Conestable, par avys de mon seigneur le Mareshall et plusours autres seigneurs et sages chivalers presentz alors en court, disoit au dit defendant en manere q'ensuyt:

Johan Montagu, cont de Sarum, pur tant qe Thomas, sire de Morley, vous appelle sur une crime compris en l'addicion de son appele, dont la tenure est tiele:

[f.34v] Et outre ceo, par voie de addicion a la matier autrefoitz par moy devant nostre seigneur le roy en Parlement purposé, jeo die qe vous estoiez le dit an et l'an adunqes prochein ensuant de conseill coveigne, et consent en plusours purpos malveys et fauces ovesque le dit roy encountre le roiaume et comune profitt d'icelle, c'est assavoir conseilant, pursuiant et consentant au dit roy a destruire les seigneurs et la comunalté du roialme par raunson des grandes sommes et par autres voies d'extorcion et autrement encontre chose pu[b]lique et comune profit du roialme, de quoi jeo die qe en cestz matiers vous estoiez et estez faux et treitour, et avez fait faucement et traiterousement:

Et pur ceo, il conveint qe vous respondez ore finalment si vous veullez demurrer sur vestre dit response fait au dit cryme, ou departier d'icell et le crime confesser, ou vostre dit responce justifier. Et sur ceo mon seigneur le Conestable comanda tout le [f.35r] conseil du dicte partie defendant a tenir silence.

Et tantost aprés le dit defendant respondist par parole de sa bowche propre en disant qe luy semble qe la primere matiere del appele surmys par le dit sire de Morley encountre luy en Parlement, le quell est originalle et substance de son appele, est wayne et voide, et pur ceo pria qe la dicte matire soit rejecté par decree, et luy mesmes demys ové ses costages et expenses cest partie. A quoy mon seigneur le Conestable, par bone deliberacion et avise suisdit, respondist au dit defendant en disant qe par ley et custume d'armes un homme poet dire et purposer encontre un autre en une bille diverses matieres de diverse nature et s'il y ad un qe comprehende en soy crime, la partie defendant serra constreint de respoundre au dit crime tanque al outre determinacion d'icelle, et les autres materes de [f.35v] plus bas nature serront mys en suspense. Et pur ceo mon dit seigneur le Conestable commanda derechief de respondre et dire sa final response et volunté ceste partie; et adunqes le dit defendant, ové bon deliberacion et avise sicome il sembloit, respondist par parole de sa bouche propre en disant qe le dit cryme compris en la dite pretense addicion est un novell matiere, diverse et seperate, et en null manere dependent, emergent, ne connexé a le primer pretense appele, et pur ceo la conusance, ne la determinacion d'icelle ne appertient a mes ditz seigneurs, ne a lour cognicion par vertue et auctorité des lettres roialx suisdictes; et pur ceo il priast d'estre demys de lour juggement ové ses costages et expenses cest partie. A quoy mon seigneur le Conestable disoit q'il semble a la court qe le dit crime est emergent et dependent de le primer appele, et pur ceo il commanda peremptoriement le dit defendant de dire sa responce sur quele il voet finalment demurrer cest partie; et adunqes le dit [f.36r] defendant, ové bon deliberacion et avise, respondist par parole de sa bouche propre en disant :

En noun du Pier, du Fitz, et du Seint Espirit, la treszeintisme Trinité que est soveraigne verité, jeo preigne tesmoigne a luy qe jeo ay fait ma diligence et mon poair par toutz voies legales qe jeo savoi pur eschiver la battaile; et pur ceo come actez et constreint a ceo faire, jeo die qe jeo veulle finalment demurrer sur ma dicte response en manere come il est mys en acte. Et adunqes le dit sire de Morley disoit par parole de sa bouche propre:

En noun du Pier, du Fitz, et du Seint Esperit, la tresseintisme Trinité, jeo die qe jeo veulle finalment demurrer sur le dit crime compris en la seconde partie de ma dicte addicion, et ceo jeo veulle proever en manere come jeo ay profré devant.

Et puis aprés, en tesmoignance des choses suisdictes, le dit appellant signa sa dicte bille de addicion desoubz son signet; et le dit defendant signa desoubz [f.36v] son signet une bille de sa dite respounse. Les queux billes mon seigneur le Conestable myst en lour gages, c'est assavoir la bille du dicte addicion en la gage du dit appellant et la dite bille de response en la gage du dit defendant et prist les ditz gages un en l'une mayn et l'autre en l'autre mayn. Et adonqes mon seigneur le Conestable suisdit, par avys de mon seigneur le Mareschall et autres, adjugeast bataille parentres les dictes parties, pliant lour gages ensemble sur la fourme q'ensuit:

En noun de Dieu, qi de fyn force est juge a si haute chose come bataille et nulle fors luy, nous vous admittons au battaile, come vicair a luy en cest place, sur le crime compris en la second partie du dicte bille de addicion et la responce a icell fait, dont les tenures sont tiels:[92]

> Et outre ceo, par voie de addicion a la matiere autrefoitz par moy devant nostre seigneur le roy en Parlement purposé, jeo die qe vous estoiez le dit an et l'an adunqes prochein ensuant [f.37r] de conseil coveign, et consent en plousours purpos malveys et fauces ovesque le dit roy encontre le roialme et commune profit d'icelle, c'est assavoir conseilant, pursuiant et consentant au dit roy a

92 This procedure was followed in the Rea vs. Ramsey case, the Constable advocating judicial combat 'In the name of God the Father the Son and the Holy-Ghost, the Holy and most Blessed Trinity, who is one, and the God and Judge of battels; we, as his vicegerents ... do admit you to a Duel ...', whilst similarly twisting the gauntlets together (*State Trials*, col.507).

destruire les seigneurs et la comunalté du roialme par raunsons des grandes sommes et par autres voies d'extorcions et autrement encontre chose publique et commune profit del roialme, de quoy jeo die qe en cestes matiers vous estoiez et estez faux et treitour, et avez fait faucement et traiterousement.

La responce:

Jeo, Johan Montague, count de Sarum, die qe tu, Thomas, sire de Morley, mentz faucement en tant qe tu moy surmettez treson en aucune matiere par toy purposé:

Et puis aprés, mon seigneur le Conestable assigna jour et lieu a toutz deux parties a faire lour devoir ceste partie, c'est assavoir le jour de Seint Valegntyn prochein a Noef Chastell sur Tyne en presence du roy, et ausi assigna terme as dictes parties [f.37v] de mettre en court lour protestacions, c'est assavoir lundy prochein; et outre ceo mon seigneur le Conestable commyst chescun des dictes parties en la saufe garde del autre. Et ausi adunqes illoeqes chescun des dictes parties trovast plegges a venir au dit jour as eux assigné, a faire lour devoir, et de porter pees ensemble pur lour mesmes, lour amys et lour servantz jesqes au dit jour, et riens faire l'un al autre en le moien temps autrement qe loy et custume d'armes demandent en cest cas; les plegges de Thomas, sire de Morley: Monsieur Henry Percy, le sire Despenser, Monsieur Thomas Erpingham, Monsieur Thomas Grey, Robert Waterton; les plegges de John Montague, count de Sarum : le count de Huntingdon, Monsieur William Hoo, Monsieur Adam Françoys, William Newsam et Thomas Rukby.

Lundy, le viij jour de decembre l'an du regne le roy Henry quart puis le conquest primer, devant les lieutenantz de mes ditz seigneurs les Conestable et Marshall d'Engleterre [f.38r] seantz judicielment en Court de Chivalrie, en tant come a chescun de eux appertient par vertue de lour offices en la Grand Sale de Westmoustier, compareront personelment Thomas, sire de Morley, partie appellant d'une parte, et Johan Montague, count de Sarum, partie defendant d'autre part, chescun pur sa part; et myseront en court lour protestacions et petitions, fesantz protestacion par parole, chescun pur sa parte, qe touz benefices de ley lour soient sauf celle partie; et ausi le dit defendant myst une bille en courte de certeins nouns de certeines persones queux il priast d'estre a luy assignez de conseil ; et en aprés le juge assigna terme as dictes parties et lour assent pur oier assignement de lour wepnes, et avoir respounse de lour protestacions, c'est assavoir lendemayn prochein.

A quell lendemayn, c'est assavoir marsdy, le ixe jour de [f.38v] december, l'an suisdit, devant mes ditz seigneurs le Conestable et

Mareshall d'Engleterre, seantz judicielment en lour propre persones en la Graund Sale de Westmoustier, en tant come a chescun de eux appertient par vertue et auctorité suisdictes, compareront personelment Thomas, sire de Morley, partie appellant d'une part, et Johan Montague, count de Sarum, partie defendant d'autre part, demandantz, chescun de sa part, d'avoir assignement de lour wepnes et responce de lour protestacions; et puis aprés monseigneur le Conestable, par avise de monseigneur le Mareshall et autres sages, assigna a chescun des dites parties lour weapnes, c'est assavoir lance d'assise d'une point, long espee d'une point, court espee d'un point et dagger d'un point; et qant a les protestacions des ditz parties, mon seigneur le Conestable, par cause suisdit, ad allowé et accept[é]ᵃ les dictes protestacions en la manere et fourme desouz escript; et ausi granta a chescun des dictes parties [f.39r] de avoir sys persones a chescun de eux assignez le jour del bataille en encresse de lour autre conseill ; et outre ceo le dit defendant demanda par parole qe la primer matier mys en court par le dit Thomas, sire de Morley soyt rejecté par decree.

Les Protestaciouns Thomas, Sire de Morlee, Appellant.ᵇ

Primerement, il demanda des juges qe ses armes a luy soient [assignés]ᶜ appellés wepnes pur soy eider encountre son adversarie as jour et lieu a luy assigné, ov en autres si luy soient assignez, et q'ilᵈ puisse avoir un wepne d'avantage; et q'il soit receiu dedeinz le dit champ closse ové mesmes les armes que luy serront assignez, et armez en quel manere que luy plerra, et avoir toutz ses autres choses a luy bosoignables et accustumez de droit pur luy eider a bosoigne encontre son dit adversarie, non obstant q'ils ne sount expressement [f.39v]escriptz, ne qe son dit adversarie eit null autre wepne, ne d'autre entaill qe la dit Thomas avera.

La courte semble q'est resonable q'il soit resceivé, armé et monté ové son escue, come [a] chivaler affiert en tiel cas, et qant a les pointz, vous averez come est suisdit : lance d'assise, long espé, court espé et dagger, chescun d'un point.

Item, le dit Thomas prie qe son conseil puisseᵃ estre receiu dedinz le champ ovesque luy pur luy conseiller a ceo qe mestier luy serra, et d'avoir myere ové ses oyntementz et instruementz pur luy servier quant mestier luy serra, et requert qe son dit conseil puisse

a *MS* accept.
b *Written in bold as heading.*
c *Omitted in MS but this is the reading of BL Add. MS. 35821.*
d *MS* qi. *We have again followed BL Add. MS. 35821 in altering to* q'il *since this reading is clearer.*
a *MS* puis. *We have followed BL Add. MS. 35821 which reads* puisse *at this point.*

demurrer ové luy tanque la parole de 'Lessé les aler' soit crié.[93]

La courte voet q'il avera sufficeant counseill, come dit est, un myre, ses oynetmentz et instrumentz deinz la dit champ, come appertient [f.40r] de reson en tiel cas, tanque la parole de 'Lessez les aler' soit crié.

Item, il demande q'il puisse avoir deinz le dit champ sige, pavilon, pur son reposer, ou autre coverture, standard pur mounter a chivall, payn, vyn et autre liquor, fers, clouez, martel, fil, aguylez, sizailles, voy de lin, laverz de lyn , caumbre de soy ou de quoer garniz ové tiel manere de metall qe luy plerra, armerer, suturer, ové lour instrumentz, et autres necessaries pur luy et son apparaill pur luy eider a bosoigne.

La courte voet qe vous eiez un seige et tiel coverture come vous plerra sanz rien fycher en terre, payn, vyn, ewe, ferres, clowes et toutz autres necessaries en tiel cas tanque la parole de 'Lessez les aler' soit cryé.

Item, il demande q'il puisse assaier son chival et son harnoys deinz le dit champ, sengler et [f.40v] desengler son chival, mounter et descendre, ferrer et deferrer, et toutz autres choses a luy bosoignables a son apparaile, boir et mangere, et faire tout sez autres necessariez.

La courte graunte tanque 'Lessez les aler' soit crié.

Item, le dit Thomas demanda qe aprés ceo q'il serra venuz [en] champ que son dit adversarie ne luy face delaye, ne trop attendre, sur peyne d'estre convict.

La courte vous ferra reson.

Item, le dit Thomas demanda as ditz juges de tenir ou fair tenir a luy l'avauntdit champ tanque al fyn de la bataille, sauve et sein, sibien de nuyt come de jour, tanque ové l'aide de Dieu il avera prové son entente.

La courte vous ferra reson.

Item, il demande que si Dieu nostre saveour face de luy sa volunté, come faire poet par sa benoit grace, q'il trespassa cest vie [f.41r] en pursuiant seuz droit qe ses amis, saunz ascun empeschement, puissent prendre son corps et porter en seint terre, et mettere la ou il ad divisé par son testament.

___

93 The usual manner of beginning combat, see Gloucester's ordinances in the *Black Book of the Admiralty* (p.325). The full formula appears to have been 'Lessez les aler, lessez les aler, lessez les aler et faire lour devoir' (*Foedera*, viii, 538).

Il faut qe soit a la volunté du roy.

Item, le dit Thomas demande et requert qe, noun obstant qe la custume d'armes voet qe le dit Thomas par droit deveroit porter certeins choses a luy bosoignables deinz la champ, qe les ditz choses puissent estre apportez par autres en ease de luy, et luy estre sauvez et reportez par les soens si Dieu luy doigne la victorie, come il poet par sa benoit grace.

La courte voet qe vous facez solonc custume d'armes usé en cas semblable devant ses heures.

Item, il demande que a mesme le jour a quell, ové l'eyde de Dieu, il provera son entent, q'il eit toutz autres choses a luy bosoignables [f.41v] et accustumez de droit qe ne sount mye expressez en cest presente escript.

La court lui ferra ceo qe lour semblera de reson.

Item, le dit Thomas demande qe ceste escript, ne la copie d'icelle, ne soit deliverez, ne a monstre a son dit adversarie, ne a null de son counseill, ne a autre par qoy son dit adversarie purra avoir conisaunce de les protestacions avauntditz et comprisez dedeinz ceste present escript, outre empriant et reqeraunt a vous mes graciouses seigneurs qe les ditz requestz et demandez soient a luy ottroiez come droit d'armes requert.

La court vous ferra reson.

Item, le dit Thomas demande q'il puisse avoir du counseill outre ceo qe luy est assigné des pluis sufficeantz chivalers et esquiers que serront trovez la journey q'il ad [a]ᵃ prover souez entent.

La court vous ferra reson.⁹⁴

---

a *Omitted in MS. We have inserted a from BL Add. MS. 35821 which reads thus.*

94 In 1631 Lord Rea copied almost word for word the details of Lord Morley's petition. Thus he requested that the court should allow him 'a seat or pavilion, or other coverture to rest himself; that he might have bread, wine, or other drink, iron-nails, hammer, file, scissars, bodkin, needle and thread, armorer and tailor with their instruments, and other necessaries to aid and serve him in and about his armour, weapons, apparel and furniture, as need required'. Similarly, Lord Rea also petitioned that 'he might have liberty to make trial of his arms and weapons within the field, to put them off, and to put them on, and change them at his pleasure; to nail, fasten, or loose his arms and apparel, and other things; to eat and drink, and to do all other his necessities'. Morley's rather typical request that the defendant should not be granted a copy of his protestation was similarly repeated (*State Trials*, col. 510).

V

The Chronicle of John Somer, OFM

Edited by Jeremy Catto and Linne Mooney

CONTENTS

ACKNOWLEDGEMENTS

The editors are particularly grateful to the staff of the Students' Room of the British Library and to the staff of the Bodleian Library for their help and patience in making these texts available. They are also very grateful for the help they have received on particular points from James Clark, David Dewhirst, Chris Given-Wilson, Jeremy Griffiths, Jonathan Hughes, Simon Kingston, Patrick Nold and Malcolm Parkes.

ABBREVIATIONS

BL   British Library

BRUO   A. B. Emden, *A Biographical Register of the University of Oxford to A.D. 1500* (Oxford 1957-9)

CCR   *Calendar of Close Rolls*

CPR   *Calendar of Patent Rolls*

CJC   *Chronique des règnes de Jean II et de Charles V*, ed. R. Delachenal (SHF 1900-20)

CUL   Cambridge University Library

GCF   *Grandes Chroniques de France*, ed. J. Viard (SHF 1920-53)

OHS   Oxford Historical Society

PRO   Public Record Office

RHS   Royal Historical Society

RS   Rolls Series

SHF   Société de l'Histoire de France

VCH   Victoria County History

INTRODUCTION

The chronicle commonly attributed to John Somer OFM survives in two roughly contemporary manuscripts of the late fourteenth to early fifteenth centuries, Oxford, Bodleian Library, Digby 57, ff. 24–31, and London, British Library, Cotton Domitian A.ii, ff. 1–7; and in one manuscript written later in the fifteenth century, British Library, Royal 13 C 1, ff. 43–51. While all three manuscripts include subsequent additions, the essential text is a single project, which is worthy of attention not only for the amount of new information – albeit not a large amount – which it contains but equally for the original chronological conception on which it is based: a table set out according to the current revolution of the Great Cycle of 532 years in which the dates of Easter repeat themselves, giving the year (anno domini), the year of the Metonic cycle,[1] the Golden Letter indicating which years are leap years,[2] and the date of Easter according to the Roman calendar.[3] Each line of the table therefore leaves space to record events of that year in each cycle: a minimal space, restricting information to the most succinct, though occasionally it continues on to another line, and in one version a note is added at the bottom of a page. The revolution of the Great

[1] In the fifth century BC a Greek astronomer, Meton, observed that the new moon fell on the same day of the year every nineteenth year, and established this reckoning by nineteen-year cycles (the Metonic cycle) to offer corresponding measurements between the sun's and moon's orbits. The year 1 BC was the first year of a Metonic cycle, AD 18 the nineteenth year, and AD 19 the first year of the next Metonic cycle. The golden number, prime or primacio, for each year, as noted in this second column of Somer's chronicle, indicated the place of a year in its Metonic cycle. Somer also noted these golden numbers on his Table of Bisextiles for the years 1367–1462 (later extended to 1500) that accompanied his *Kalendarium*.

[2] 1 January of each year was assigned the letter A, 2 January the letter B, and so on to 7 January, assigned the letter G. Then the letters began their sequence again with A on 8 January, and so on to A once again on 31 December. The Dominical letter, or golden letter, for any year was the letter which fell on Sunday, the Lord's Day, in that year. A problem arose in leap years, because the leap day, added at 24 February, was assigned the same number in the Roman calendar – it was called the Bis vi Kalendae Marcii, and in those years the 25th was the vi Kalendae Marcii (thus the name 'Bisextilis' for leap year) – and the same Dominical leter (F) as the day it doubled, which caused a change in the letter which fell on Sunday. Thus it was that in a leap year there were two Dominical letters, one for 1 January–24 February, and another for 25 February–31 December. Both letters are given in the third column of the chronicle, the one for the first part of the year to the left, that for the second part to the right in the column of letters assigned to common years.

[3] In the Cotton Domitian A.ii text, designated by 'y' for ides, 'n' for nones, and 'k' for kalends, and 'm' or 'a' for the months of March or April. Fuller spelling out of abbreviations is given in the Bodleian Digby 57 text.

Cycle on which the text is constructed is the years 1001–1532;[4] but it was intended to include events from the two previous revolutions, those of 65 BC–AD 468 and AD 469–1000, in the line for the corresponding year in the third revolution. Almost all events are preceded by the figures 1, 2, or 3 to denote the revolution in which they occurred, and some events of the first and second cycles also give the corresponding date from that cycle at the end of the entry (e.g. '2 Merlinus 476' on the line for 1008 in the third revolution).

The original text must have been close to that common to the two oldest manuscripts, Cotton and Digby, which are roughly contemporary. The Cotton MS. having been written originally in the early 1380s and extended by additions in the form of current events and new information discovered by the writer for past events until ca. 1402, the Digby MS. having been written at one time in the late 1380s. Both include additions by later scribes. The core of information common to these two suggests a common source, but that common source can no longer be deduced from the texts.

British Library, Cotton Domitian A.ii is a composite manuscript made up of the Somer chronicle and the Battle Abbey Chronicle.[5] The Somer chronicle was initially a separate parchment quire, in a different hand and decorated in another style, on the earlier history of which the remaining part of the manuscript can shed no light.[6] The first and last leaves of the quire are blank and somewhat dirty, indicating that this copy had circulated separately, and was originally intended to do so. In the volume as it presently exists, the eight-folio quire in which Somer's chronicle has been written comes first, preceded by a single folio, whose stub may be seen after folio 8. This single folio, numbered 'i,' is blank except for shelf numbers on its verso. The first folio of the quire has a table of contents for the whole volume on its recto, added in the seventeenth or eighteenth century; its verso is blank. The chronicle occupies most of this quire, filling folios 2 to 7. It is followed by astronomical tables and canons for their use by 'S. wyk' or 'liwyk,'[7] and by a last folio (f. 8), blank except for a note written top to bottom beside the gutter on the verso: 'Clement a nonne of S. Ursula in Lorayne.' There was originally at least one line more to this writing, further in the gutter, but it is now lost in the reconstruction of the folios at the gutter (as all four bifolia of the quire have been reconstructed at their centre-folds).

---

4 This periodicity differs from the usual, which begins the first cycle from the birth of Christ.

5 The latter ed. Eleanor Searle, *The Chronicle of Battle Abbey* (Oxford 1980).

6 This portion of the manuscript is briefly described by Searle, pp. 25–26.

7 These tables and the canon are written by the main hand of the chronicle, C1. The table in the lower left, beside the canon, is described by Searle as 'an astronomical table for the conversion of the transits of astronomical objects to time' (p. 26).

The original heading of the chronicle, in what appears to be the main hand of the text, simply described it as 'Chronica quedam brevis.' A later hand, possibly but not certainly that of William Worcester the antiquary, has qualified this with the added, 'fratris Johannis Somour ordinis sancti francisci de conventu ville Briggewalter'.[8] The original lack of specification about provenance in the heading suggests that this copy was produced for personal use, and that, if the later qualification to the heading was correct, as the references to Bridgewater noted below indicate, it was Somer's own copy, primarily in his own hand.[9]

Bodleian Library MS. Digby 57 is a collection of astronomical tables and excerpts from Greek and Arabic astronomical writings: a calendar of the median motions of the planets, calculated for 1374 apparently, the astronomical tables of William Rede, a table of eclipses for 1376–89, another table of conjunctions of the sun and moon calculated for Oxford in 1376–90, etc., written in an Anglicana hand or hands of the late fourteenth century, with a table of contents prefixed of the same date. It seems therefore to have been made as a single book, probably in Oxford, about 1376 or shortly afterwards. Later in the fifteenth century it belonged to Mr John Philipp, rector of Exeter, who sold it in 1468 to another master whose name has been erased, but who was identified by the cataloguer of the Digby manuscripts as Mr. John Jolyffe.[10] The annals occupy folios 21–31.

The author of the shared body of information in the Cotton and Digby manuscripts must have been responsible for the concept and format of the chronicle, as well as for those entries that appear in both texts. The grammar of these entries has sometimes been altered, but their substance is identical for most of the annals from the first two revolutions of the Great Cycle, and the majority of those from the third up to 1364 or perhaps 1368; the two manuscripts' entries for 1377 and 1381 are similar in matter but not wording, and may have been composed independently. The annalist was probably therefore conceiving his calendar chronicle and compiling the annals in the 1370s, though possibly a decade earlier or later. He was clearly writing in England, since he recorded the succession of most of the English kings from the Conquest. Besides royal successions, he took an interest in

8 It appears by signs of erasure and change of hand that some other words were originally written where 'ffratris Johannis Somour' are now, and were subsequently erased and replaced by the friar's name; and that 'ordinis sancti' originally read, 'ordinis istius', and was later changed by overwriting.

9 If this is Somer's hand, the note of inception as Doctor of Theology in Oxford in 1395 may refer to Somer's own inception; A. G. Little writes, 'It does not appear whether [Somer] was a doctor either at this time [1380] or afterwards.' (*The Grey Friars of Oxford* (OHS 1892), 244.)

10 William D. Macray, *Catalogi codicum manuscriptorum Bibliothecae Bodleianae ... pars IX, Codices a ... Kenelm Digby ... anno 1634 donatos, complectens* (Oxford 1883), cols. 59–62, esp. 59.

the origin of the major religious orders founded after 1080; and he noted, briefly, the incidence of weather, comets, and plague. Two references to the church of Salisbury, in 1085 (with bishop Osmund denoted *sanctus* as observed in Sarum practice) and 1220, suggest an interest in its affairs, but not enough to draw any firm conclusion. The conflict between Oxford scholars and townsmen in 1355 was too well known to indicate a university origin for the annals, but the reference to the making of the tables of al-Zarqālī (Arzachel), attributed to 600 (1132), does point to Oxford or some other centre of astronomical study. The impression is reinforced by the innovative concept of the chronicle itself, difficult to explain in a less learned and less speculative context.

The text as it appears in the Digby manuscript shows few additions to the common annals, but those few may be significant. Three further entries, for 1386, 1387 and 1388, the latest in the original hand, make it likely that the compiler of this text was writing in the late 1380s. Joachim (of Fiore) is dated under 1172, and the birth of Gilbert de Clare, last Clare earl of Gloucester, under 1291. There are more specific references to Salisbury: the dedication of the cathedral in 1258, and the beginning of the 'fourth' plague there in 1374; and to Oxford, in 1355, where the town and gown riots were dated 'in vigilia Frideswide' (referring to the translation of the saint, a feast observed apparently only in Oxford), and in 1361, where the damage done by a thunderstorm to the towers of St Frideswide's Priory and the church of St Cross was noted. The compiler added two details to the account of the rising of 1381, the time of execution of Archbishop Sudbury and Prior Hales, and the burning of the Savoy 'per communitatem de sacia'. His final additions were brief notes of the king's breach with his leading subjects in 1387 and the Merciless Parliament in 1388; and preceding that, a mention of the death of 'Katerina domina de Wotton', clearly Katherine, Lady Berkeley, under 1386. At a later stage, presumably about 1417, another hand (D2) inserted notes of Henry V's victories of 1415 and of the capture of Sir John Oldcastle in 1417.

There is not enough evidence for anything more than speculation as to who may have been responsible for the annals in the Digby version. It is noticeable that two indistinct features of the common annals, their interest in Salisbury and their Oxford perspective, are more clearly delineated in the additions to this text. One explanation for that might be that the Digby text is simply a more elaborate version of the original annals, written up, though not greatly altered, some time after 1388 and thus after the Cotton text had been copied, i.e. about 1382–88. On the available evidence that can only be surmised. The entry, *obitus katerine domine de Wotton*, entered as an addition under 1386, seems to provide a clue. She must be Lady Katherine Berkeley, widow of Thomas Lord Berkeley (died 1361), whose dower lands included Wootton-under-

Edge, where she founded a school in 1384. A master of the school would be an obvious person to record her death, and we know that Mr John Stone was master there from 1384 to after 1390.[11] One William Seward, an apparently favoured dependent cleric of Sir Thomas Berkeley, was priest of the living of Wootton-under-Edge until alienated from it by Richard II in 1387.[12] Unfortunately nothing is known of the intellectual interests or training of these men.

It is perhaps more fruitful to note that Digby 57 appears to have been conceived as a coherent body of tables, of which the annals constitute one item, and that the tables and other contents include both those of the Merton astronomer Mr William Rede about 1340, and the more original tables of about 1348 attributed (uncertainly, and not in this text) to Mr William Batecombe. The brief note of Mr John Ashenden of Merton on the 1365 conjunction of Jupiter and Saturn is included, without ascription. Of later origin, presumably, are the Oxford planetary tables calculated for 1374, the Oxford table of conjunctions and oppositions for 1375-90, and the table of eclipses for 1376-90. Mertonian astronomers are at least prominent in this collection. One fellow of Merton, Dr John Turk, would certainly fit the conditions already deduced for authorship both of the common annals and the Digby text. Fellow of Merton about 1352-55, he remained a trusted associate even thirty years later, and probably lived at least partly in Oxford in the 1360s and 1370s, briefly acting as chancellor in 1376-77. From 1376 until his death about 1397 he was a canon of Salisbury, and from 1384 warden of De Vaux College there. On the other hand, nothing whatever is known of his intellectual interests, and his authorship must remain for the moment little more than an idle speculation.

The features peculiar to the Cotton text are quite different. The compiler frequently varied the wording of those annals to which he added nothing of substance. He was also a scholar: he sought exact dates for events such as the coronations, deaths, and other particulars of kings; and he recorded in a note in the lower margin the descent of Edward the Confessor from King Egbert. He seems to have erased an original entry for the death of Bede in 731 (1263) and to have entered it, correctly, under 735 (1267). His interest in calendars is evinced by his notice of the inauguration of the Arabic and Persian calendars in 622 (1154) and 632 (1164) respectively. He recorded three comets, in 678 (1210), 1261 and 1402, and one eclipse, in 664 (1196). He added to the political information of the common annals, especially about more recent events; details of Richard II's movements in 1394-96 suggest personal knowledge. An interest in the Franciscan houses in the west

11 See A. F. Leach's account in *VCH: Gloucestershire*, ii.396-9.
12 See Ralph Hanna III, 'Sir Thomas Berkeley and his Patronage', *Speculum* 64 (1989), 888-9.

country, at Bridgewater, Exeter and Cardiff, appears in 1241, 1280 and 1300, and in other friars minor in 1381, where the execution of Fr William Appleton is inserted with the other prominent murders of that year. Equally local is the notice on weather in Taunton (1402), perhaps the mention of the ports of Richard II's embarkation and reentry, Haverford and Bristol, in 1394–95, and, in a sense, given the Irish commerce of the port of Bristol, the notice on the University of Dublin in 1358. A personal detail is the reference to the vesperies and inception at Oxford of an unnamed doctor, presumably the compiler, on 24 June 1395. These features are at least compatible with the authorship of this version asserted in the addition to the heading, by John Somer OFM of Bridgewater.

The latest notice in the principal form of the original hand in this version refers to events of 1402; the latest in a secondary form distinguishable by variations in ink colour, presumably making further entries at a subsequent date, is for 1403. This main hand (C1) was responsible for the chronological data and Easter table on the left sides of the pages, for the canon which explains the use of the table written in the bottom margins of folios 6v and 7, and for all the entries dated in the first two revolutions and the great majority of the entries in the third before 1402. Variations in ink colour, including a greenish-brown, light brown, a very pale and rusty-tinged colour, a grey-brown with a greenish tinge, and a rusty brown, indicate that the entries were not all made at the same time, and indeed must have been made on several occasions. The additions were frequently made to an original text identical with the Digby version, or varying from it only in syntax. To take as an example the annal for 1312:

Digby text: Gauston decollatus / Nativitas Edwardi tertii

Cotton text: (Petrus *superscript addition*) Gaveston decollatur / Edwardus 3us (Rex Anglie *superscript addition*) nascitur (in ffesto sancti bricii *?later addition by main hand*).

The main hand originally copied, but varied, the entry in the common annals, as given in the Digby text. This was later glossed, probably by the same hand, with the entries Petrus and Rex Anglie. The main hand then added a specific date, the feast of St Bricius. These additional entries seem to be fairly homogeneous in matter. For instance, specific dates, 1 August (1100), 3 September (1189), 17 May (1220), and royal events such as the coronation of Queen Joan (1403) are inserted in the greenish-brown ink. Notices of births and deaths, comets, and the Arabic and Persian eras are entered in the rusty-tinged ink. More recent royal births and deaths, from 1330 to 1394, are added in the grey-brown ink. These probably represent the compiler's passing concerns or new access to information. In any case, he appears to have ceased making entries before, or not too long after, the battle of

Shrewsbury on 21 July, 1403, the earliest important event not to be recorded.

Thereafter, it seems, the compiler laid aside the Cotton text; but other hands made some further entries. They can be classified as four hands who made multiple entries; three more who made single but significant additions; eight who added only one entry or part of an entry; and one who simply darkened the presumably faded ink of an earlier entry.

C1 The main hand of the manuscript, probably John Somer's, which wrote all of the date and Easter information and most of the notes of events to 1402. Variations in ink colour indicate several times of making entries, possibly spaced over a number of years. The last event from the third cycle recorded in this hand is the double entry for 1402 noting the appearance of the comet and the bad weather in May at Taunton. Thereafter, entries by this hand are notes for events that occurred in the first or second cycles, parallel with third-cycle dates 1403, 1409, 1440, 1448, 1451, 1473, 1474, 1481, 1491, 1513, 1528, and the lengthy explanation of the cycles in the bottom margins of folios 6v and 7.

Entries probably by this hand are as follows:

Additions to entries, written with greenish-brown ink: the supralinear date to the entry for 1100 ('1 die Augusti', on line for 1099) and the rest of entry for 1100 ('Et coronacio...augusti'); the middle entry for 1189 ('30 die septembris'); the date to the entry for 1199 ('27 die May'); the supralinear date for 1216 ('19 die octobris,' on line for 1215); the supralinear date for 1220 ('17 die mayy'); the supralinear date for 1307 ('7° die Julii'); and possibly 'deponsacio margarete...' for 1299 and 'Johanna regina coronatur' for 1403.
An entry written by a more cramped version of the main hand: the entry for 1215.
An addition to an entry written by a crowded version of the main hand: the first part of entry for 1221, '12 kalendae mayy...rome.'

Entries possibly by this hand are as follows:

Entries written with light brown ink and slightly larger script, recording 'caristia' in 1347, 1351, and 1370.
Entries written with very pale, slightly rusty-tinged ink, recording several astronomical entries and entries relating to royal births and deaths. These include entries for 1128, for the second part of the entry for 1154 ('2 Anni arabum...Julii'), for 1196, for the first part of the entry for 1210 ('2 cometa...678'), for 1261 (2 comete apparuunt), for 1291, for 1300, for the second part of the entry for 1312 ('Edwardus tercius' and 'nascitur...bricii'), for the second part of the entry for 1354 ('nascitur Thomas Wodestok'), for 1372, for 1394, and for 1395.

Entries written with grey-brown ink, sometimes greenish, recording several entries related to royal births and deaths, including entries for 1330 and 1376 (birth and death of Edward, the Black Prince), 1367 (birth of Richard II), 1377 (death of Edward III), and 1394-5 (death of Queen Anne).

Entries written with very pale, rusty-brown ink, recording dates and battles, mostly as additions to other entries, including the added date for 1265 ('4 die augusti'); the added date '1284' in entry for 1285; the entire entry for 1298 regarding the Battle of Falkirk; the added dates for the entry for 1307 ('25 die Januarii...augusti'); the added 'bellum stirelyn' for 1314; the entire entry for 1353 ('captio berwici per scoces'); and the second part of the entry for 1356 ('bellum de paytiers').

C2 A large script, writing in dark ink. This hand adds the second part of the entry for 1248 ('Conversio britonum 184'); and probably the second part of the entry for 1264 regarding the comet; and, in paler ink, the entry for 1460 recording the first-cycle founding of the order of Augustinian canons in 396.

C3 A large but fine Anglicana script, in dark black ink, very vertical, and sometimes shaky. This hand adds 'rex filius imperatricis' to the note on Henry II's death in 1189; and records the dearths of 1284 and 1319, the death of Queen Philippa at the end of the entry for 1370, and the deposition of Richard II in 1399.

C4 A distinct hand in black ink using mixed secretary and Anglicana letter forms, with a somewhat angular look. This writer was interested in Henry V, recording his birth (1387), his accession (1413) and his victories of 1415 and 1417 ('3 victoria...hareflut'); together with the second part of the entry for 1420 ('3 de quodlibet...xiij').

C5 A very small secretary script, writing with rusty brown ink. This hand writes the entries relating to popes for 1003, 1004, 1009, 1012, 1227 and 1271 (a longer note on the friars); to the Danes in 1002; to the fifth jubilee of Canterbury at the end of the entry for 1420; and to political and ecclesiastical events for 1422, 1429, 1431, 1450, 1455, and 1457.

C6 A pale Anglicana, who inserted a notice on the laying of the foundation stone of the Bridgewater convent of friars minor in 1411 (1412 by new reckoning).

C7 This is evidently the hand of William Worcester; it inserted the notice of the hour of death of Sir John Fastolf in 1459, and conceivably the gloss *rex anglie* to the entry on Edward III's birth (1312). This hand may also be responsible for adding the attribution to Somer in the heading.

C8 A secretary hand writing in dark greyish-brown ink. In this hand the notice of the eclipse of 1433, and its attribution to Somer, is recorded.

C9 A medium sized Anglicana script, in brown ink. It adds '3 haraldus regnavit 9 mensibi' to the entry for 1066.

C10 A medium-sized script, in brown ink. This hand adds the year '622' to the second-cycle entry for 1154.

C11 A medium-sized hand, writing in pale brown ink. This hand adds 'episcopus' to the entry for 1199.

C12 A medium-sized secretary hand, writing in pale brown ink. It adds to the entry on Richard of Cornwall's birth in 1210 the place of his eventual burial: 'qui sepelitur...postea'.

C13 A large, loose secretary hand, writing in light brown ink. It glosses 'comes sarum' to the entry for 1250.

C14 A cramped, very vertical, Anglicana hand, writing in very rusty-red ink. It enters the notice 'bellum hispanie' in 1367, and possibly that on Edward III's coronation in 1327.

C15 A loose secretary hand, writing in pale grey ink. This hand adds 'bellum' twice to the entry for 1417.

C16 An upright, compact Anglicana hand, writing in pale grey ink. It writes the first part of the entry for 1420, 'Jeronimus transtulit bibliam'.

C17 A hand of indeterminate date, probably more recent than the others, writing over earlier text, '16 die,' to darken it at the end of the entry for 1377.

The independence of many of these hands, given the short entries they made, must remain in doubt, but the main lines of this history of the text are fairly clear. It is based on a text of the common annals which was presumably written not long after 1381. Its original title, *Cronica quedam brevis*, indicates that it was copied for private use, and its compiler then added a considerable body of historical information which helps to pinpoint his own interests. The inference from the annal for 1411 that it was then at the Bridgewater Franciscans, combined with the fifteenth-century attribution of it to John Somer in the title, and the congruence of its detail on Richard II's movements with his known court affiliations in the 1390s, make it likely that this well-known compiler of a calendar for 1387–1462 was indeed the compiler, and presumably the main hand in the manuscript. We have no record of Somer's birth or origins, but he must have been at least thirty, more probably nearing forty, by 1380 when he had achieved such a reputation as an astronomer that he was asked to write the new kalendar. He is believed to have entered the order of Franciscan friars at its Bridgwater convent, based on the attribution in this chronicle. Sometime in the late 1370s or early 1380s he may have held the office of Warden of the

Franciscan priory at Bodmin, Cornwall.[13] In or just before 1380 his provincial superior Thomas Kingsbury, asked him to write the new kalendar requested or commissioned by Joan of Kent, the Princess of Wales, mother of the boy King Richard II, for the four Metonic cycles covering the years 1386 to 1462. Thirty-two complete and eight fragmentary copies of the *Kalendarium* survive.[14] By the time he composed the *Kalendarium* he was certainly resident at the Oxford convent, since its astronomical tables were computed for Oxford. By the early 1390s his name as an Oxford astronomer was well known, being cited by Chaucer in his *Treatise on the Astrolabe* and by the compiler of the manuscript containing the *Equatorie of the Planetis*, Cambridge Peterhouse 75.I (identified by some scholars as Chaucer).[15] He may have incepted in theology at Oxford in 1395, based on the entry in this chronicle. His connections with the royal court may have begun with the writing of the *Kalendarium* for the Princess Joan, but apparently did not end with her death in 1385, for he was in attendance at court in 1394 and 1395 to receive the royal alms for his Oxford convent.[16] He seems to have survived the 1399 change in dynasty, for in the first year of his reign the new King Henry IV granted him eight ells of russet and eight ells of blanket per annum.[17] Somer continued writing astronomical and astrological treatises, and updating the charts accompanying his kalendar, through the 1390s at least.[18] He last collected his royal grant in

13 One of the early copies of his *Kalendarium*, BL Add. MS 10,628, identifies the author as '*quidam frater Minorum in Cornubia, Bodminne Gardianus*', or 'A certain Franciscan friar in Cornwall, warden of Bodmin' in the prologue to its canons (f. 10).

14 See *The Kalendarium of John Somer*, ed. Linne R. Mooney, Chaucer Library series (Athens Ga: University of Georgia Press, forthcoming). The earliest MSS of the *Kalendarium*, BL Add. 10,628 and Vatican Library, Regina Sueviae, Lat. 155, probably date from 1383 and 1384, respectively.

15 For Chaucer's reference, see Chaucer's *The Treatise on the Astrolabe*, Prologue, where Chaucer states that the third part is to contain various astronomical tables taken from 'the kalenders of the reverent clerkes, Frere J. Somer and Frere N. Lenne'. For *The Equatorie of the Planetis*, see D.J. Price, *The Equatorie of the Planetis* (Cambridge 1955); Price argues for Chaucer's authorship, as does J.D. North, *Chaucer's Universe* (Oxford 1988), pp. 157–181. But see also A.S.G. Edwards and Linne R. Mooney, 'Is the *Equatorie of the Planetis* a Chaucer Holograph?' *Chaucer Review* 26 (1991), 31–42.

16 A.B. Emden, *A Biographical Register of the University of Oxford to AD 1500*, 3 vols. (Oxford 1957–9), ii.1727.

17 Ibid.

18 The BL Sloane 282 copy of his *Kalendarium*, written ca. 1410, contains a table of moveable feasts revised since the 1380 writing of the *Kalendarium*, according to its heading: *Ad honorem dei & virginis gloriose necnon sanctorum confessorum francisci, Antonii & episcopi lodowyci. [In hoc opusculo] tabularum festorum mobilium quam posui succincte in kalendario domine iohanne, principisse Wallie, matris domini nostri regis Ricardi secundi post conquestum iam per annos singulos usque annum domini millesimum quingentesimum excedere curavi ad solacium plurimorum* ... (To the honour of God and the glorious virgin and also of the Holy Confessors Francis, Anthony, and Bishop Louis. [In this little work] of the Tables of Moveable Feasts, which I set forth briefly in the Kalendar of the Lady Joan, Princess of Wales, mother of our lord King

October, 1409, and may have died soon after that; though Worcester, on the evidence of a Franciscan martilogium, assigned his death to 1419.[19]

Somer's court connections must have won for him considerable status within his order and considerable wealth, incongruous with his fraternal vows. William Worcester mentions a friar John Wells (whom he spoke to as an old man in 1478, then a tanner in Bridgewater) who had been servant to John Somer ('*quondam servientis Fratris Johannis Somour*').[20] Worcester also notes that at his death, according to a chronicle of the Norwich friars, Somer left 200 marks for the building of the new friary church at Bridgewater (whose ground-breaking in 1411/12 is noted by another hand in the chronicle) and 40 marks for books at the friary.[21]

Beyond the references to him as a learned astronomer in the 1390's, he continued to be cited after his death as if he had been one of the leading astronomer/astrologers of his day. In the fifteenth century, William Worcester copied Somer's texts into his own book, Oxford, Bodl. Laud Misc. 674, noting that they were taken from copies written by Somer's own hand;[22] and he also noted that another star catalogue he copied into that manuscript was compiled by Friar Ralph Hoby, Professor of Theology at Oxford, who was a '*discipulum librorum fratris Johannis Somour ordinis Minorum*', 'a student of the books of John Somer, Franciscan friar' (folio 99[v]). In the fifteenth century, too, Thomas Cory of Muchelney Abbey and Lewis Caerleon of Cambridge included excerpts from his works in their collections of astronomical and astrological texts;[23] and his reputation survived even into the sixteenth century, when an unknown compiler of astrological figures ascribed to him a horoscope figure.[24]

Richard the Second after the Conquest, I have now taken care to proceed year by year up to the year of Our Lord 1500, for the solace of many.)

19 See Emden, i.1727 for date of last collection of his grant. Cf. William Worcester, *Itineraries*, ed. John H. Harvey (Oxford 1969), pp. 78–80 and 124–6 for references to his death in 1419. If he left money at his death for the building of the new friary church at Bridgewater, begun in 1411 (see below), it seems more likely that he died in 1409–10, shortly before the building began, than that he died eight or nine years after it began.

20 Quoted by Harvey in his edition of Worcester's *Itineraries*, p. 125, n. 4, from Worcester's medical collection, BL Sloane 4, f. 57. This date seems much too late for a man who had served Somer before 1409.

21 William Worcester, *Itineraries*, ed. Harvey, pp. 78–80.

22 Folios 24[v], 42[v], and 100; e.g. on f. 100 is a star catalogue, adjacent to which is the marginal note, '*1438. 25 die Octobri. Has stellas extraxi de libro ac manu Johannis Somour*', literally, 'I have extracted these stars from the book and hand of John Somer'.

23 '*Canones Johannis Somour pro veris motibus habendis planetarum*' was copied by Thomas Cory of Muchelney Abbey in 1440, in Oxford, Magdalen College 182, folio 37, column b; and a '*Tabula proportionis diversitatis aspectus extracta de copia manus proprie ffratris Sommour*' was copied by Lewis Caerleon in 1482 in CUL Ee.3.61, f. 152.

24 Cambridge, Corpus Christi College 420, f. 57, dating from the sixteenth century. In the centre of the horoscope figure the original scribe notes, '*figura fratris Johannis Somer*'.

The chronicle was apparently in Somer's possession in the years preceding 1403, the date of the last third-cycle entry probably written by the main hand. From the most site-specific entries in these years we can map his movements from Bridgewater and the west country to Oxford and to the court. In the mid-1390s in particular he seems to have been occasionally attached to the court: in 1394 he records the date (29 September) and place (Haverford) of the King's embarkation for Ireland, and in 1395 the date and place of his return (9 May in the evening, at Bristol). In 1396 he must have accompanied the King and court to Calais where Richard went to sue for the hand of Isabella, first, as he records, on 7 August and again on 27 September until the 4 November wedding abroad, since he records in his chronicle the otherwise unremarked collapse of the walls of Calais in that year.[25] In 1395, he records an inception in theology at Oxford, possibly his own; and in 1402 he was in Taunton, Somerset, to witness the heavy rains, thunder, and hail on 2 May.[26]

After Somer's death the manuscript appears to have been returned to Bridgewater, where hands C6 and C8 made entries specific to Bridgewater or Somer, including the laying of the first stone in the foundation of the convent's new church on 4 March 1411 (1412 by modern reckoning). Two other hands, C4 and C5 – also probably members of the Bridgewater convent – recorded events of political importance for the years 1413–1420 and 1422–1457, respectively.

By 1459 or shortly thereafter the manuscript had come into or passed through the hands of William Worcester, who added the note on Sir John Fastolf's death in that year, and possibly also the specificity as to authorship and provenance in the heading, as noted above. Worcester had also had access to scientific manuscripts in Somer's hand in 1438, when he copied texts into his miscellany, Bodleian, Laud misc. 674. In 1438, Worcester also had access to a copy of John Somer's *Kalendarium*, of which he made a copy at the request of Richard Roper of Bristol, as noted at the bottom of folio 1[v] of the kalendar.[27]

After Worcester's possession, the Cotton manuscript of the chronicle seems to have remained in Norfolk, possibly among Worcester's other

The figure is referred to, also with attribution to '*ffryer John Somer*', at the end of an English summary of the Latin explanation of the horoscope figures, at the bottom of the facing page, f. 56[v].

25 See explanatory note for the year 1396.

26 See explanatory notes for these years.

27 The *Kalendarium* is written at the front of the Tiverton Horae, now at St. Peter's Church, Tiverton, Devon. Worcester's note reads, '*Explicit kalendarium secundum laborem fratris Johannis Somour scriptum Bristollie per manum Willelmi Wercestre ad instanciam Ricardi Roper anno domini 1438 inconpleto et anno regni Regis Henrici 6 post conquestum 16° 14° die Augusti in meridie. Deo gracias.*' See N. R. Ker, *Medieval Manuscripts in British Libraries*, 4 vols. (Oxford 1969–92), iv.494–5.

books and papers, and among men of similar antiquarian interests: in the sixteenth century Robert Talbot (c. 1505–58), prebendary of Norwich Cathedral in 1547–58, added notes to Worcester's Itineraries, including, beside Worcester's record of the death in 1440 of '*Frater Galfridus Pollard...contemporaneus Fratris J. Somour*' the query, '*An hic scripsit chronica.*'[28] At the least this note demonstrates that Talbot knew of the existence of the chronicle, and more likely that he had seen a copy of it. Before another century had passed, the manuscript had been acquired by another antiquarian, Sir Robert Cotton; and it was probably Cotton who first had it bound with the manuscript of the Battle Abbey chronicle.

The copy of the chronicle to which Talbot's note bears witness may, on the other hand, have been the third text of the chronicle, which occurs in Royal MS 13.C.i, ff. 43–50[v].[29] The manuscript is a collection of historical materials apparently put together by or for William Worcester. As we have seen, Worcester had either owned the Cotton text of John Somer's annals or at least had had access to it about 1459, when he inserted the note on the death of his master Sir John Fastolf; it was a minor item in the indefatigable antiquary's historical collections, put together it seems to justify a new call to arms to reverse in the name of chivalry the defeat of the English cause in France. This had already been the theme of his *Boke of Noblesse*, of which the first version may have been written about 1453.[30] The materials pressed into service in his collections as *preuves* for his argument were characteristically various: old chronicles, accounts of recent events, the example of ancient heroes, commonplaces on public morality, *exempla* on the hope of victory in adversity and modern military and political papers. The Royal manuscript was a composite volume of 22 quires, of which the sixth encompasses folios 42–51. The manuscript includes both notes in Worcester's hand and texts by other authors; his own contribution includes lists of archbishops of Canterbury and bishops of Bath and Wells for depiction in a new window in Wells Cathedral, moral *exempla*, notes on Roman history and historical abstracts. Among them he incorporated a part of Higden's *Polychronicon* with the continuation

28 Although we believe Somer wrote the Cotton copy of the chronicle, Talbot may have had other information about Pollard, and Pollard, a friar of Bridgwater who outlived Somer by at least 20 years, may be responsible for some of the post-1409 entries in the chronicle.

29 See *British Museum Catalogue of Western Manuscripts in the Old Royal and King's Collections*, ed. G. F. Warner and J. P. Gilson (London 1921), ii.101–2. On Worcester see K. B. McFarlane, 'William Worcester: a preliminary survey' in *Essays in Memory of Sir Hilary Jenkinson*, ed. A. E. J. Hollaender (Oxford 1957), 196–221, reprinted in his *England in the Fifteenth Century* (London 1981), 199–224.

30 The passages on Roman history were compiled in November and December 1453, according to Worcester's marginal note, f. 143.

termed D by John Taylor, the apparently autograph version of Giles's Chronicle written perhaps about 1459, Elmham's Life of Henry V and the present text.

Though the cataloguers state that the text of these annals is in Worcester's hand, it differs widely from the examples of his writing both in this collection and elsewhere. The hand of the annals is a standard mid-fifteenth-century secretary script which, given the cancelled sentences and revisions, is likely to be that of the author. Like John Somer in the Cotton MS, he was apparently writing at several distinct times, as evidenced by changes in ink colour and by the way later additions are squeezed between lines of original text. It may be noted, for instance, that an original dark ink, usually at the top or in the middle of the space left for each year, rarely extends beyond the right margin of the frame, while a lighter and a second dark ink regularly do. Note, too, that the lighter ink entries sometimes extend beyond the lower edge of the space left for each year, and when they do so, are written to the right of dark-ink entries in the following year. The annals are written out from the year 1000 to 1532, the final twenty years squashed into the lower right hand corner of the last page. The historical material was then added in the same hand as the tables. After it had been completed, the same or another hand inserted in roundels on f. 43 a separate text, brief notes on the seven days of creation, without however altering the text of the annals. The only other part of the collection which may be written in the same hand is that of folios 52–61ᵛ, which contains some notes on the taking of bribes and some historical collections on English bishops, Saxon kings, French kings, Norman dukes, kings of Rome and Persia, and notes on biblical history; but the hand is not certainly the same as that of the annals.

In contrast to the comparatively spare appearance of the Cotton and Digby versions, the Royal manuscript's text is altogether fuller. It has numerous additions in the same hand, which had first written in a version not much expanded from the Cotton text and then in a lighter ink put in further information and a few cancellations, made usually to correct an erroneous chronology. The last entry of the third and base cycle, 1000–1532, summarises the events of the Coventry parliament of 1459. However there is no doubt that the basis of the Royal annals is a text of the original version of the chronicle before either John Somer or the editor of the Digby annals had made their contemporary additions. All three versions were dependent on the same body of material as far as the entry for 1364; thereafter, though Cotton and Digby coincide in reporting the "third pestilence" in 1368, the brief entries might still be independent; no entry was made in the Royal version. The author of this version, therefore, had a copy more or less identical to the texts in front of the other annalists.

He added to it considerable material from other sources, frequently putting the same events in under slightly different dates with the note *in alio libro* or *in veteri libro*. It is not possible to identify the immediate provenance of these entries, which may have come from epitomes and extracts rather than from original chronicles. However, a number of the substantial works from which the entries derive can be recognised. Probably the basic text, at least for entries before 1325, was the Westminster compilation *Flores Historiarum*, a source both for the history of Christendom in general and for English history in particular.[31] The entries were expanded up to 1265 by reference to one of the sources for the *Flores* themselves, the *Chronica Majora* of Matthew Paris,[32] which was particularly full for the late twelfth and early thirteenth centuries. Occasional material or isolated items from Bede's *Historia Ecclesiastica*, the *Historia Anglorum* of Henry of Huntingdon, the *Annales Londonienses* and Higden's *Polychronicon* are also included.[33] For the mythical history of Britain up to the coming of the Saxons, the compiler makes extensive use of the *Historia Regum Britanniae* of Geoffrey of Monmouth.[34] More surprising are the thirty or so entries on events in France, particularly in the fourteenth century, but ranging from the death of the crowned heir of Louis VI in 1131 to the building of the Bastille in 1383 (recorded under 1382). Most of them are paraphrases of episodes mentioned in the St Denis chronicles, either the Latin chronicle of Guillaume de Nangis (up to 1300) and his continuator (up to 1358), or the French *Grandes Chroniques de France*, including its own continuation through the reigns of John II and Charles V. The account of events of 1382–3 may even be derived from the Latin *Chronique* of the Religieux de St-Denis, which continues the series with the history of Charles VI's reign.[35] In addition, there are a few episodes which seem to derive from the *Speculum Historiale* of Vincent of Beauvais.[36] But in this case too it is likely that the immediate source is a French compilation which had already incorporated these materials. Compilations of this kind, such as the French translation of the *Flores Historiarum* of Bernard Gui (itself

31 *Flores Historiarum*, ed. H. R. Luard (RS 1890).

32 Matthew Paris, *Chronica Majora*, ed. Luard (RS 1872–83).

33 Bede, *Historia Ecclesiastica Gentis Anglorum*, ed. C. Plummer (Oxford 1896); Henry of Huntingdon, *Historia Anglorum*, ed. T. Arnold (RS 1859); *Annales Londonienses*, ed. W. Stubbs in *Chronicles of the Reigns of Edward I and Edward II* (RS 1882); Ranulf Higden, *Polychronicon*, ed. C. Babbington and J. R. Lumby, 9 vols (RS 1865–86).

34 Geoffrey of Monmouth, *Historia Regum Britanniae*, ed. A. Griscom (London 1929). Since there are numerous editions of this text reference is made only to book and chapter.

35 Guillaume de Nangis, *Chronique latine de Guillaume de Nangis avec les continuateurs*, ed. H. Géraud (SHF 1843); *Grandes Chroniques de Francee*, ed. J. Viard (SHF 1920–53); *Chronique des règnes de Jean II et de Charles V*, ed. R. Delachenal (SHF 1910–20); *Chronique du Religieux de Saint-Denys*, ed. L. Bellaguet, *Documents inédits relatifs à l'histoire de France* (Paris 1839–53).

36 Vincent of Beauvais, *Speculum Historiale* (Venice 1591 and Douai 1624). The chapter divisions vary in these editions; we have used the former.

too early to be our compiler's source) were common in France, and much read at the court of Charles VI.[37]

Equally notable is the compiler's interest in events in Ireland, from the conquest of Henry II onwards. There are numerous entries on English affairs which include a reference to Ireland: the specification of the Irish element in King John's tribute to the Papacy for instance, or the incidence of the plague of 1361 in Ireland as well as England. An entry on the French famine of 1318 was first applied to Ireland, but then corrected to specify France instead. These entries have not been traced in any particular source, though they can be confirmed generally either from Anglo-Irish sources or from chronicles in Irish. They become more numerous up to 1401, after which they are almost entirely limited to dates of birth in the family of the Butler earls of Ormond.

Only a few of the entries can have any claim to add to historical knowledge. The annals are the only source for the place and date of birth of James, fourth earl of Ormond (died 1452), of the date of birth of John Holland, duke of Exeter (died 1447), William Beauchamp, Lord St Amand (died 1457), John, Viscount Beaumont (died 1460) and Elizabeth Butler, Countess of Shrewsbury (died 1473). It gives a time of birth for Henry VI which is within the time given in his several horoscopes, but which is unique to this version. The battle in the district of Bree between the Dubliners and the native Irish may be the same as a raid reported in the Annals of Connacht; if so, its location and the number of Irish casualties are new information. The warm summer of 1442 is not otherwise recorded; nor is 14 September 1459 as the date when Henry VI took the field against his Yorkist opponents. This in itself, particularly in a set of annals which frequently records inaccurate dates, is no guarantee of the truth of this information. However they are in most cases within the bounds of probability and in some more or less contemporary.

There are therefore some indications of the compiler's circumstances, if not of his identity. The last event recorded in the first Easter cycle is in the autumn of 1459; the battle of Northampton on 10 July 1460 and the death of James Butler, fifth earl of Ormond and earl of Wiltshire shortly after 1 May 1461 are not noted. It is likely therefore that the annals were completed between October 1459 and July 1460. The compiler notes his own birth on 2 February 1403 or 1404, and a serious fever in 1441. His Irish connexions and evident association with the Butler family, together with his obvious sympathy with the Dubliners, indicate an origin among the Anglo-Irish of the Pale; but the absence of Irish material apart from the dates of birth of James and Elizabeth Butler after 1417 suggests that he was domiciled in England, and perhaps in the Butlers' service, by the 1420s. His collection of 'nativities'

37 Paris, Bibliothèque Nationale de France, MS nouvelles acquisitions françaises 1409.

or dates of birth of the leading nobility of the court and foreign princes in the 1440s points to an interest in making horoscopes, an activity which could be dangerous, as the fate of Eleanor Cobham duchess of Gloucester and her astrologers (duly noted) illustrated. The relevance of a calendar of dates of Easter and other chronological information to a man with such interests in the 1440s and 1450s is as easy to understand as his interest in filling out the information from historical sources and his own experience. Nor is it surprising that he should have access to a French chronicle or epitome, some of which undoubtedly reached England among the spoils of Lancastrian France. Several historical texts were in the library of Charles V, the bulk of which passed to the regent John, duke of Bedford and was dispersed after his death in 1435; others passed to Sir John Fastolf and were used by his secretary, William Worcester.[38] James, the fourth earl of Ormond had served in France in 1419, at the siege of Rouen, and was present at Henry VI's French coronation in Paris in 1431; his well attested learning in matters of chivalry and deeds of arms would have found such material of interest. It has not, however, so far proved possible to identify any individual in the Ormond circle who might have written the annals in the Royal manuscript.[39]

The concept of the base chronicle from which all three versions were made is unique and intriguing: its format suggests that the author – and possibly those who copied him like Somer, the scribe of Digby 57, and possibly even the scribe of Royal 13.C.i – used his chronicle to test whether historical events repeat themselves in a pattern related to the Great Cycle in which the conjunctions of the sun and moon repeat themselves. Marking historical entries as belonging to the first, second, or third Great Cycle, the compiler and his copiers recorded events that portended evil, like the appearance of comets or the aurora borealis, and events whose coincidence with positions of the heavenly bodies might be construed as indicating influence of those bodies over terrestrial catastrophies, like the deaths of rulers or popes, storms, famine, and pestilence. These coincidences in astrological cycles might have been intended to convince a sceptic of the astrological influence of the heavens upon terrestrial events. Whether it was so used, or even whether this was the intent of the unique format of this chronicle, is merely matter for speculation.

---

38 See L. Douët d'Arcq, *Inventaire de la bibliothèque du roi Charles VI, fait au Louvre en 1423* (Paris 1867); J. Stratford, *The Bedford Inventories* (London 1991), 96–99, 119–123, and McFarlane, 'William Worcester' repr. 1981, 208.

39 The rich collection of deeds in the archive of the Marquess of Ormonde, calendared by E. Curtis, *Calendar of Ormond Deeds* (Dublin 1932–43) do not include household accounts or other material which could help to identify possible authors of the annals.

EDITORIAL PRINCIPLES

The text of the chronicle as it appears in Cotton Domitian A.ii, is edited below, with notes of variants from the Digby 57 manuscript, followed by a separate list of the historical entries in the Royal 13.C.i manuscript. Cotton was chosen as base text because it is the fullest of the two early versions that survive. Historical notes from Royal are printed in full because they were too extensive for textual notes. Royal includes the Easter tables in columns between the year and the historical annals, but we have not reprinted them in with the historical notes since they are identical to those in Cotton and Digby.

Given the limited space, the entries in the chronicles are necessarily highly abbreviated and sometimes run over one another. Further, especially in the cases of the Cotton and Royal manuscripts, wear to the manuscript or pale ink has rendered some entries almost unreadable, even with the assistance of ultra-violet light; some readings in the editions below are therefore conjectural, and for a few we have had to give partial readings because nothing more could be clearly discerned in them. Expansions of abbreviations are indicated by italic script, and omissions or conjectural readings are enclosed in square brackets. Supralinear additions are enclosed in pointed brackets, and text deleted by erasure, expunction, or cancellation in rounded brackets. We have not been able exactly to maintain the manuscripts' lineation; blank lines in the year-tables and Easter-tables are editorial, to allow space for the longer notes of events.

[*London, British Library, Cotton. Domitian A.1*]

f. 2

Cronica quedam brevis ffratris *Johannis Somour* ordinis sancti ffrancisci de conuentu ville Briggewalter

1001	14	e			
2	15	d	.	3	[dani inter*fec*ti in Anglia **C₅**]
3	16	c	5ka	3	[Joh*annis* 18 sed*it* p*a*pa me*n*sibus 6 **C₅**]
4	17	ba	16km	3	[Joh*annis* 19 sed*it* p*a*pa annis 5 **C₅**]
5	18	g	ka		
6	19	f	11km		
7	1	e	8ya		
8	2	dc	5ka	2	Merlin*us* 476 & br*e*ve pr*ius* e*r*at adv*en*tus saxonu*m* in angliam
9	3	b	15km	3	[Sergi*us* 5 sed*it* p*a*pa annis 3 **C₅**]
1010	4	a	5ya		
1	5	g	8ka		
2	6	fe	ya	3	[Ben*e*dict*us* 8 sedit p*a*pa annis 12 **C₅**]
3	7	d	Na		
4	8	c	7km		
5	9	b	4ya		
6	10	ag	15ka		
7	11	f	11km		
8	12	e	8ya		
9	13	d	4ka		
1020	14	cb	15km		
1	15	a	4Na		

Heading. *om.* D.
1002. *om. entry* D.
1003. *om. entry* D.
1004. *om. entry* D.
1008. 2 M*e*rlin*us* 476 **D**
1009. *om. entry* D.
1012. *om. entry* D.

1002 Massacre of St Bryce's Day, cf. Higden, *Polychronicon* vii.84.
1003 John XVII (1003)
1004 John XVIII (1003–09)
1008 Cf. Geoffrey of Monmouth, *Historia Regum Britanniae* vi.15–18 for the association of Merlin with the *adventus Saxonum*, though the original entry, preserved in the Digby MS, referred only to Merlin.
1009 Sergius IV (1009–12)

2	16	g	8ka
3	17	f	18km
4	18	ed	Na
5	19	c	14km
6	1	b	4ya
7	2	a	7ka
8	3	gf	18km
9	4	e	8ya
1030	5	d	4ka
1	6	c	3ya
2	7	ba	4Na
3	8	g	10km
4	9	f	18km
5	10	e	3ka
6	11	dc	14km
7	12	b	4ya
8	13	a	7ka
9	14	g	17km
1040	15	fe	8ya
1	16	d	11ka
2	17	c	3ya
3	18	b	3Na
4	19	ag	10km
5	1	f	7ym

Nota quod per istam cronicam habetur annus incarnationis christi ciclus solaris & lunaris cum bisexto dies etiam pasche & per consequens omnia ffesta mobilia pro semper

*f. 2*ᵛ

1046	2	e	3ka		
7	3	d	13km	3	berengarius
8	4	cb	3Na		
9	5	a	7ka	2	boethius 2 brigida 517
1050	6	g	17km		

1023. 18 kl aprili **D**.
1037. f. 16ᵛ **D**.
After 1045. Nota quod per istam cronicam ... *written in lower margin by the main scribe* **C**. *Same text follows 1075 in* **D**.
1049. *Before* 'brigida' *add* 'sancti' (*sic*) **D**

1047 Cf. *Polychronicon* vii.206, s.a. 1059.
1049 Cf. *Polychronicon* v.322 s.a. 520–1 places the death of St Brigid after a notice of Boethius.

1	7	f	2ka	1	beata virgo nata est
2	8	ed	13ka		
3	9	c	3ya		
4	10	b	3Na		
5	11	a	16km		
6	12	gf	7ya		
7	13	e	3ka	2	benedictus sanctus prestes 525
8	14	d	13km		
9	15	c	2Na		
1060	16	ba	7ka		
1	17	g	17km		
2	18	f	2ka		
3	19	e	12km		
4	1	dc	3ya		
5	2	b	6ka	1	Nativitas domini
*6	3	a	16km	3	obiit beatus edwardus In vigilia epiphanie [3 haraldus regnavit .9. mensibus C$_9$]
7	4	g	6ya	3	adventus normanorum Coronacio bastardi 25 die decembris
8	5	fe	10ka	1	Johannis ewangelista nascitur
9	6	d	2ya		
1070	7	c	2Na		
1	8	b	8km	3	translacio sedis schireborne ad sarum
2	9	ag	6ya		
3	10	f	2ka		
4	11	e	12km		
5	12	d	Na		
6	13	cb	6ka	3	terre motus magnus

1057. 2 sanctus benedictus prestes 525 **D**

1066, *third cycle.* 3 obitus beati edwardi regis / adventus Willelmi bastardi **D**. *Asterisk in left margin beside 1066 corresponds in this entry to asterisk beginning the note in the lower margin, by the main scribe* **C**.

1067. *Om.* 'Coronacio ... decembris' **D**.

1068. 1 Nascitur Johannes evangelista **D**

1076. f. 17 **D**.

1057 Cf. *Polychronicon* v.346–8, s.a. 553.

1066 Higden gives the date of Edward the Confessor's death, *Polychronicon* vii.224–6; he does not recite the king's ancestors given here at the bottom of the page, though they could have been reconstructed from his text. The omission of Aethelwulf (not paralleled in Higden's text) is presumably just a mistake.

1067 Cf. *Polychronicon* vii.248–50 for the date of William I's coronation.

1071 The transfer of the see was authorised by the Council of London in 1075. Cf. *Polychronicon* vii.292.

1076 Cf. Matthew Paris, *Chronica Majora*, ed. H. R. Luard (RS 1872–83) ii.16; *Flores Historiarum*, ed. ibid. (RS 1890) ii.9.

7	14	a	16km		
8	15	g	6ya		
9	16	f	9ka		
1080	17	ed	2ya		
1	18	c	2Na		
2	19	b	8km		
3	1	a	5ya		
4	2	gf	2ka		
5	3	e	12km	3	sanctus Wlstanus
6	4	d	Na	3	obiit Willelmus bastardus
7	5	c	5ka		
8	6	ba	16km	3	coronacio Willelmi Roufei 27 die septembris
9	7	g	ka	3	ordo cisterciensium & cartusiensis incepit
1090	8	f	11km	3	sanctus osmundus constituit canonicos

*anno domini 1066 edwardus confessor filius elredi filii egdari filii (sic) edmundi filii edwardi senioris filii alfredi filii egberti primi regis anglorum legavit regnum anglie Willelmo bastard consobrino suo

f. 3

1091	9	e	ya		
2	10	dc	5ka		
3	11	b	15km		
4	12	a	5ya	3	sanctus anselmus consecratur
5	13	g	8ka	1	baptizatur christus
6	14	fe	ya		
7	15	d	Na		
8	16	c	5ka		
9	17	b	4ya	1	christus passus est 3 ordo cisterciensium incepit

1088. om. entry **D**.
After 1090. Om. footnote **D**.
1095. 1 baptizatus est christus **D**
1099. om. '3 ordo ... incepit' **D**.

1085 Wulfstan, bishop of Worcester 1062–95.
1086 William I's death is dated 1086 in *Polychronicon* vii.312.
1088 William II was crowned on 26 September, but *Polychronicon* vii.318 gives the feast of Cosmas and Damian (27 September) as here.
1089 Higden, *Polychronicon* vii.304 recounts the origin of the Carthusians s.a. 1085, and vii.394 that of the Cistercians s.a. 1098. See the possibly correcting entry s.a. 1099.
1090 Osmund, bishop of Salisbury issued his institution charter (*Register of St Osmund*, ed. W. H. R. Jones, RS 1883–4, i.212–15) in 1091.
1099 See the note to 1089 above.

1100	18	ag	ka	3	*obitus willelmi* rufi fil*ii* bast*ardi* <*1 die Augusti*> *Et coronacio* henrici p*rimi* fra*tris* sui 5 die aug*usti*
1	19	f	11km		
2	1	e	8ya		
3	2	d	4ka		
4	3	cb	15km		
5	4	a	5ya		
6	5	g	8ka		
7	6	f	18km		
8	7	ed	Na	3	hugo de *sancto* victore ordo te*m*plarior*um* incep*it*
9	8	c	7km	3	*obiit* anselm*us* & Rober*tus* fil*ius* h*enrici* p*rimi* comes glou*cestriensis* cr*eatur* q*ui* cast*ellum* br*ist*olli*e* fe*cit* cuius fil*ius* fe*cit* Keynysham
1110	9	b	4ya	3	Matilda filia h*enrici* p*rimi* duci*tur* i*n* ux*orem* i*m*p*er*atoris 5 a*n*nor*um*
1	10	a	4Na		
2	11	gf	11km		
3	12	e	8ya	2	anglici fide*m* accep*erunt* s*ub* g*re*gorio 581
4	13	d	4ka	3	Tamisia exsiccata e*st*
5	14	c	14km	1	assu*m*p*tio* be*ate* vir*ginis*
6	15	ba	4Na		
7	16	g	8ka		
8	17	f	18km		

1100. *om.* '<1 die Augusti> Et coronacio ... augusti' **D**.
1105. 5 N api D.
1109. *om.* 'obiit; *and* '& Robertus ... Keynysham' **D**.
1110. *om. entry* **D**.
1112. f. 17ᵛ **D**.
1115. *For* 'virginis' *substitute* 'marie' **D**

1100 William II died on 2 August; in *Polychronicon* vii.410, 3 August.

1108 Hugh of St Victor's death is noted by *Polychronicon* viii.10-12, s.a. 1148; the beginning of the Templars at vii.464, s.a. 1122.

1109 Robert FitzHenry was made Earl of Gloucester in 1122; he built the keep of Bristol Castle in 1136-7. His son William FitzRobert founded Keynsham Priory, Somerset in 1169.

1110 This presumably means that Matilda was five on marriage to the Emperor Henry V in this year. She was born about February 1102 and married in January 1114; but *Polychronicon* vii.436, s.a. 1107 reports her marriage *vix quinquuennem*, 'at not more than five'.

1113 Subsequent annals s.a. 1121 (presumably for 589), 1125 (593) and 1128 (596) on Pope Gregory I and the conversion of the English show that the compiler was using more than one discrepant source and chronology, and inserting entries at various times.

1114 Cf. *Polychronicon* vii.446-8, s.a. 1114. On the drought of this year see C. E. Britton, *A Meteorological Chronology to A.D. 1450*, Meteorological Office: Geophysical Memoirs 70 (London 1937), 53-4, with references to earlier sources.

9	18	e	3ka		
1120	19	dc	14km	3	ordo pr*emonstratensium* incep*it* & castr*um* de Wyndesore man*erium* de Wodestok & Abba*ti*a de redyng
1	1	b	4ya	2	*obiit* b*eatus* gregor*ius*
2	2	a	7ka		
3	3	g	17km		
4	4	fe	8ya		
5	5	d	8ka	2	Conv*er*sio anglor*um* 593
6	6	c	4ya		
7	7	b	3Na	3	despon*sati*o matild*ae* i*m*peratricis galfrido co*mi*ti andegavie. Abba*ti*a de Wav*er*ley p*ri*ma [cisterciensis?]
8	8	ag	10km	2	Augu*stinus* cu*m* mo*n*achis m*ittitur* a beato gregorio i*n* ang*liam* 596. hoc a*n*no po*stquam* fu*er*ant i*n* ang*lia*
9	9	f	18km		
1130	10	e	3ka		
1	11	d	13km		
2	12	cb	4ya	2	Tabule Arza*ch*el fac*te* s*un*t 600
3	13	a	7ka	3	He*n*ricus fi*lius* I*m*peratricis nasci*tur* & p*ri*mus epi*scop*us karlioli crea*tur*
4	14	g	17km		
5	15	f	7ya	3	Ordo cist*erciensium* ven*it* in anglia*m* Obiit

1120. *Om.* '& castrum ... redyng' **D**

1121. **D** *incorrectly numbers cycle* 1:1 O*bitus* bea*ti* gregorii.

1127, *third cycle.* Cisterciensis, **C**, *conjectural, squeezed at edge of page. Slash in this entry and the following one, in* **C**, *is scribal, dividing two entries. Om. both entries* **D**.

1128. *Om. both entries* **D**.

1132. 2 Tabu*le* Arza*ch*el fac*te* s*un*t 600**D**

1133. *om. entry* **D**.

1135. *Om.* 'Obiit henricus ... decembris' **D**.

1120 Cf. *Polychronicon* vii.458, s.a. 1119. Henry I enclosed the park at Woodstock in 1110, according to *Eulogium Historiarum*, ed. F. S. Haydon (RS 1858–63), i.269. Henry of Huntingdon, *Historia Anglorum*, ed. T. Arnold (RS 1879), 237, asserts that he built New Windsor shortly before 1110. Reading Abbey was founded in 1121.

1121 See note to 1113 above.

1125 See note to 1113 above.

1127 Matilda was married to Geoffrey, count of Anjou in 1128. Cf. *Polychronicon* vii.468, s.a. 1126. Waverley Abbey was founded in 1128 or 1129.

1128 See note to 1113 above, and for the arrival of the English the entry for 1513 (449) below.

1132 See introduction [p. 206]. This is the name (al-Zarqālī) under which the well-known Toledan tables circulated from the twelfth century onwards.

1135 The foundation of Waverley (see note to 1127 above) brought the first Cistercians to England. The dates of Henry I's death and Stephen's coronation are correct, but they are not included in Higden's account.

henricus primus primo die decembris Et
coronacio Stephani 22 die decembris

f. 3ᵛ

6	16	ed	11ka		
7	17	c	3ya		
8	18	b	3Na	1	Petrus & Paulus martirizantur
9	19	a	9km	2	institutio ffestivitatis omnium sanctorum a bonifacio papa 4ᵗᵒ 607
1140	1	gf	7ya		
1	2	e	3ka		
2	3	d	13km		
3	4	c	2Na		
4	5	ba	7ka	3	anglici iuraverunt fidelitatem matildi (*sic*) imperatrici
5	6	g	17km		
6	7	f	2ka	2	ysidorus machometus exaltacio crucis 614
7	8	e	12km		
8	9	dc	3ya		
9	10	b	3Na		
1150	11	a	16km	3	gelu vehemens decreta a gratiano compilantur
1	12	g	6ya		
2	13	fe	3ka	3	henricus filius matilde duxit elianoram ducissam aquitaniae
3	14	d	13km	3	obiit bernardus
4	15	c	2Na	3	henricus filius cepit regnare 19 die

1139, *second cycle. just* Institutio [ ] **d** (*incomplete entry*).
1144, *third cycle.* matildi, **C**, *scribal; should be* 'Matilda.'
1148. f. 18 **D**.
1150. *Om.* 'decreta ... compilantur' **D**.
1153. *Om. entry* **D**.
1154. *Om.* '19 die decembris' *and* '2 Anni arabum ... 622' **D**.

1139 Boniface IV (608–15) dedicated the Pantheon to the Blessed Virgin and All the Martyrs; cf. *Polychronicon* v.416 (referring to All Saints). The Digby MS seems to have lost the substance of the entry.

1144 This seems to be a displaced reference to the oath sworn to Matilda at Henry I's behest in 1126; cf. *Polychronicon* vii.468, s.a. 1127.

1146 Evidently a combination of early seventh-century references, perhaps from *Polychronicon* v.468, s.a. 622 (Exaltation of the Cross at Jerusalem), vi.14–50, s.a. 637 (Mahomet) and vi.50, s.a. 638 (death of Isidore of Seville).

1150 On the frost, not noted in *Polychronicon*, see Matthew Paris, *Chronica Majora* ii.84, and *Flores Historiarum* ii.69. Gratian's *Decretum* was compiled about 1140.

1152 Cf. *Polychronicon* viii.28, s.a. 1155.

1153 Bernard of Clairvaux, 1090–1153; cf. *Polychronicon* viii.16, s.a. 1151.

1154 Henry II was crowned on 19 December; the date is not mentioned in *Polychronicon*.

decembris   2 Anni arabum inceperunt 15
die Julii [622 **C**₁₀]

5	16	b	6ka		
6	17	ag	17km		
7	18	f	2ka		
8	19	e	12km		
9	1	d	2ya		
1160	2	cb	6ka		
1	3	a	16km		
2	4	g	6ya		
3	5	f	9ka	3	pontificatus sancti thome cantuariensis
4	6	ed	2ya	2	anni persarum inceperunt 16 die Junii 632
5	7	c	2Na		
6	8	b	8k[a]		
7	9	a	6ya	1	obitus Johannis ewangeliste
8	10	gf	2ka		
9	11	e	ya		
1170	12	d	Na	3	sanctus thomas passus est [sanctus benedictus **D**]
1	13	c	5ka		
2	14	ba	16km	3	dominium anglorum incepit in hibernia [3 Joachim circa hoc tempus & dominium anglorum incepit in ybernia **D**]
3	15	g	6ya		
4	16	f	9ka		
5	17	e	ya		
6	18	dc	2Na	3	petrus comestor moritur [secundum alios **D**]
7	19	b	8k[m]		
8	1	a	5ya		[erased entry]
9	2	g	Na		

1163. *Om.* 'cantuariensis,' *substitute* 'martiris' **D**.
1164. *Om. entry* **D**
1166. 8 k a *with* 'a' *erased* **C**
1167. *Add* 'beati' *before* 'Johannis' **D**.
1170. *Add* 'sanctus benedictus' **D**.
1172. 3 Joachim circa hoc tempus & dominium anglorum incepit in ybernia **D**
1176. *Add* 'secundum alios' **D**.
1177. 8 k m *with* 'm' *erased* **C**; 5 yd aprili **D**.
1178. *Entry in* **C** *irretrievably erased; probably relating to the death of Thomas Becket.*

1162 Thomas Becket was consecrated archbishop of Canterbury on 6 June 1162.
1172 Joachim of Fiore (c.1135–1202). On the English in Ireland cf. *Polychronicon* viii.44,
s.a. 1168.
1176 Peter Comestor died about 1179.

1180	3	fe	12km		
1	4	d	Na	3	sanctus gilbertus ordo de simphringham
2	5	c	5ka		
3	6	b	15km		[petrus commestor **D**]

f. 4

4	7	ag	ka		
5	8	f	11km		
6	9	e	ya	3	Jerusalem destructa Sanctus hugo consecratur 1187
7	10	d	4ka		
8	11	cb	15km		
9	12	a	5ya	3	Ricardus rex coronatur <3° die septembris> obiit henricus [<rex filius imperatricis> **C₃**] sponsus alianore
1190	13	g	8ka		
1	14	f	18km	3	Ricardus rex capit acon
2	15	ed	Na		
3	16	c	5ka		
4	17	b	4ya		
5	18	a	4Na		
6	19	gf	11km	2	eclipsus solis 3 die May hora 10ᵃ & pestilencia venit 664
7	1	e	8ya		
8	2	d	4ka		
9	3	c	4km	3	Ricardus rex interficitur <6 die aprilis> Johannes coronatur 27 die May / obiit sanctus hugo [episcopus **C₁₁**]

1183. [ ] petrus commestor **D**.
1184. f. 18ᵛ **D**
1186. *Om.* '1187' **D**.
1189. *Om.* '<3° die septembris>' *and* '<rex filius imperatricis>' **D**.
1196. *Om. entry* **D**
1199, *third cycle. Om.* '<6 die aprilis>' *and* '27 die May / obiit ... episcopus' **D**. *Slash,* **C**, *scribal, dividing two entries.*

1181 St Gilbert of Sempringham (1083?–1189) had founded his order before 1147.
1183 See note on 1176 above.
1186 Jerusalem was captured by Saladin on 2 October 1187; St Hugh bishop of Lincoln was consecrated on 21 September 1186.
1196 See Bede, *Historia Ecclesiastica* iii.27, ed. C. Plummer, *Baedae Opera Historica* (Oxford 1896), i.191–2. The editors are grateful to Dr David Dewhirst for confirmation of the correct timing, as the tenth unequal hour after sunrise (about 5.00 p.m.), of the eclipse as seen in England.
1199 Hugh bishop of Lincoln died 16 November 1200.

1200	4	ba	5ya	3	ordo predicato*rum* i*n*cepi*t*
1	5	g	8ka		
2	6	f	18km		
3	7	e	8ya		
4	8	dc	7km	3	abba*n*a belli loci
5	9	b	4ya	3	*sanctus* do*m*i*n*icus ordo pred*icatorum*
6	10	a	4Na	3	*sanc*tus ff*r*anciscus ordo mi*n*o*r*um [3

Conversio beati francisci **D**]

7	11	g	10km	3	[henricus filius Johannis nascitur & **D**]

stepha*n*us de langtou*n* *con*sec*ratur*

8	12	fe	8ya	3	interdi*ctum* angli*e* <24 die ma*n*> henri*cus*

in *fes*to o*m*ni*u*m s*a*nc*tor*um nasci*tur*
wynton*nie* p*r*oge*n*itu*s* Joha*n*ni*s*

9	13	d	4ka		
1210	14	c	14km	2	cometa app*aruit* 678 Ric*ardus* rex

alema*n*nie nasci*tur* [q*ui* sepeli*tur* ap*u*d
haylys postea **C₁₂**]

1	15	b	3Na		
2	16	ag	8ka		
3	17	f	18ka		
4	18	e	3ka	3	Relax*atio* interdi*cti*
5	19	d	13km	3	alex*ander* necqu*am* abbas

cir*en*cest*r*ie   *con*sili*u*m late*r*ane*n*se

1200. *Om. entry* **D**
1204. *Om. entry* **D**
1206. 3 Co*n*ve*r*sio bea*ti* f*r*ancisci **D**
1207. 3 h*en*ricus fi*lius* Johannis nasci*tur* & lange*ton* *con*secratur **D**
1208. *Om.* '<24 die maii>' *and* 'henricus ... Johannis' **D**
1210. *Om. both entries* **D**
1215. *Om. both entries* **D**

1200 See the note on 1205 below.

1204 Beaulieu Abbey, Hants, founded in June 1204.

1205 St Dominic founded a convent for nuns in 1206, but his order was not approved before 1217. The compiler must have had discrepant materials for this annal and that for 1200.

1206 The Franciscan Order's first Rule was approved in 1210, but a notice of them is in *Flores Historiarum* ii.134, s.a. 1207.

1207 On the birth of Henry III, see note on following entry.

1208 The interdict was promulgated on 24 March; cf. *Flores Historiarum* ii.136. Henry III was born on 1 October 1208.

1210 Cf. Bede, *Hist. Eccl.* iv.12, ed. Plummer i.228. Richard earl of Cornwall and king of the Romans was born 5 January 1209.

1215 Alexander Neckham, abbot of Cirencester 1213–17. Though the Fourth Lateran Council forbade the foundation of new religious orders, the Dominican and Franciscan orders were approved.

6	1	cb	4ya	3	*obiit* Johannes rex <19 d*ie* octob*ris*> h*en*ricus filiu*s* eiu*s* ungi*tur* glou*cestrie* 28 die *octo*bris coronat*ur*
7	2	a	7ka		
8	3	g	17km		
9	4	f	7ya		
1220	5	ed	4ka	3	h*en*ricus rex coron*atur* <17 d*ie* mayy> ap*u*d westm*onasterium* tra*n*s*lacio sanct*i tho*me* Ecc*lesia* saru*m* fundat*ur* *obitus* Sanct*i* edmundi Ar*chi*episco*pi*
1	6	c	3ya	2	12 kal*endas* mayy *obitus* cadwaladris rome Et angli regn*a*veru*n*t hi*c* 689 *cristi*
2	7	b	3Na	3	O*biit* sanc*tu*s dominicus
3	8	a	9km		
4	9	gf	18km	3	h*en*ricus rex cep*i*t cast*ellu*m bedfordi Minores i*n*traba*n*t in angl*iam* & intraba*n*t i*n* oxon*iam*
5	10	e	3ka		
6	11	d	13km	3	O*biit* beatus fra*n*ciscus
7	12	c	3ya	[3	Gregori*us* non*us* sed*it* p*a*p*a* a*n*nis 14 **C**₅]
8	13	ba	7ka	3	O*biit* step*han*us langton*us* Nove decretales *com*pilate su*n*t
9	14	g	17km		
1230	15	f	7ya		
1	16	e	10ka	3	O*biit* sanc*tu*s a*n*toni*us* de ordine minoru*m*

f. 4ᵛ

2	17	dc	3ya
3	18	b	Na

1216. 3 Rex Johannes O*biit* & filiu*s* eiu*s* unct*us* e*st* glou*cestrie* **D**
1218. d & m **D**
1220. f. 19 **D** *Om*. '<17 die mayy' **D**
1221. *Om. both entries* **D**
1227. *Om. entry* **D**
1231. *Om.* 'de ordine minorum' **D**

1216 *Coronatur* was a later gloss, but accurate: Henry III was crowned twice, first on 28 October 1216 and again on 17 May 1220, as stated in the following annal.

1220 See note to 1216 above. Thomas Becket's remains were translated on 7 July 1220; the foundation stone of the new cathedral at Salisbury was laid on 28 April. Edmund of Abingdon archbishop of Canterbury died 16 November 1240.

1221 Cf. Bede, *Hist. Eccl.* v.7, ed. Plummer i.292, giving the day of Caedwalla's death (20 April 689).

1222 St Dominic died in 1221.

1228 The Decretals were published in 1234.

4	19	a	9ka	3	comes marescallus interficitur [& sanctus edmundus consecratur **D**]
5	1	g	ya		
6	2	fe	3ka		
7	3	d	13km		
8	4	c	2Na		
9	5	b	6ka	3	Rex Edwardus nascitur 14 kalendas Julii
1240	6	ag	17km		
1	7	f	2ka	3	minores primo intrabant locum quem nunc habent brugewaltere prius enim erant ultra pontem [3 Obitus sancti Edmundi **D**]
2	8	e	12km		
3	9	d	2ya		
4	10	cb	3Na		
5	11	a	16km		
6	12	g	6ya		
7	13	f	2ka	3	terre motus 10 kalendas marcii
8	14	ed	13km	3	alius 10 kalendas Januarii [1 Conversio britonum 184 **C₂**] [Escambium monete **D**]
9	15	c	2Na		
1250	16	b	6ka	3	longispe occiditur [comes sarum **C₁₃**]
1	17	a	16km		

1234. [ ] kl api D. Add '& sanctus edmundus consecratur' **D**
1241. Om. entry; substitute '3 Obitus sancti Edmundi' **D**
1250. 3 longespe occisus est **D**

1234 Richard Marshal earl of Pembroke died 16 April 1234. Edmund of Abingdon was consecrated 2 April.

1241 Thomas Eccleston, *De Adventu Minorum in Anglia* (ed. A. G. Little, Manchester 1951, 45) noted that the site of the Bridgewater convent had been changed in the time of Br. William (1240–54). A new site had been found by January 1246 (*CPR 1232–47*, 470). There had been an earlier house, which must have been situated 'over the bridge' in the suburb of Eastover. The site is mentioned in the ministers' accounts of the Mortimer part of the manor (PRO SC.6/968/19–22), referring to 'nine burgages where the Grey Friars used to dwell'. The reference here to the earlier house is probably trustworthy, but the friars' occupation of the new convent may be misdated. See VCH *Somerset* ii.151-2, vi.203; *Bridgewater Borough Archives*, i, ed. T. B. Dilks (Somerset Record Society 1933), xlvi-xlii; P. Ellis and I. Burrow, 'Excavations in Friar Street and West Quay, Bridgewater', *Somerset Archaeological and Natural History Society Proceedings*, cxxi (1985), 69-80. On Edmund of Abingdon's death see note to 1220 above.

1247 Cf. Matthew Paris, *Chronica Maiora* iv.603 and *Flores Historiarum* ii.329; see Britton, *Meteorological Chronology* 97, noting the discrepant dates in various sources. The date given here (20 February) does not agree with any of them.

1248 Presumably 23 December 1248 is intended. No other source mentions an earthquake on this date. On the conversion of the Britons see Geoffrey of Monmouth, *Historia Regum Britanniae* iv.20. On the recoinage of 1248 see *The De Moneta of Nicholas Oresme and English Mint Documents*, ed. Charles Johnson (London 1956), xxvi–xxix.

1250 William Longespee, who had claimed the earldom of Salisbury unsuccessfully in 1237, died in Egypt on 7 February 1250. Cf. Matthew Paris, *Chronica Maiora* v.76.

2	18	gf	2ka	3	ffredericus imperator moritur 3 estas calida
3	19	e	12km	3	O*biit sanct*us Ri*cardus* et Ro*bertus* grostest mori*tur* E*piscopus* lyncoln*iensis*
4	1	d	2ya		
5	2	c	5ka		
6	3	ba	16km		
7	4	g	6ya	3	magna fames in Angl*ia*
8	5	f	9ka	[3	p*rovide*ncia oxonia & dedicacio ecc*lesie* sar*um* **D**]
9	6	e	ya		
1260	7	dc	2Na		
1	8	b	8km	2	comete app*a*ruunt 729
2	9	a	5ya		
3	10	g	ka		[erased entry **C**] [3 O*bitus* ven*e*rabil*is* bede **D**]
4	11	fe	12km	3	bellu*m* de lewis [cometa an*te* ortu*m* sol*is* a *f*esto margar*i*te usque in *f*estu*m* michaelis **C₂**]
5	12	d	Na	3	bellu*m* de evesham 4 d*ie* augu*s*ti
6	13	c	5ka		
7	14	b	15km	2	o*büt* ven*e*rabil*is* beda 735 7 k*a*l*endas* Jun*ii* in d*o*m*i*n*i* festo
8	15	ag	6ya		
9	16	f	9ka		
1270	17	e	ya		

1252. O*bitus* f*r*ederici *i*mperator*is* **D**; *om.* '3 estas calida' **D**
1253. O*biti* san*ct*i Ri*cardi* & Ro*be*rti grosseteste **D**; *Om.* 'Episcopi lyncolniensis' **D**
1256. f. 19ᵛ **D**
1261. *Om. entry* **D**
1263. *Entry in* **C** *irretrievably erased; probably relating to the Venerable Bede, as in* **D**.
1264. *Om.* 'cometa … michaelis' **D**
1265. *Om.* '4 die augusti' **D**
1266. f. 19ᵛ **d**
1267. *Om. entry* **D**

1252 The emperor Frederick II died 13 December 1250. On the warm summer of 1252 cf. Matthew Paris, *Cronica Maiora* v.279 and 317.

1257 Cf. Matthew Paris, *Chronica Maiora* v.630 and 728, recording crop failure in the autumn of both 1257 and 1258.

1258 The Provisions of Oxford, 1258. Salisbury Cathedral was consecrated in 1258.

1261 Cf. Bede, *Hist. Eccl.* v.23, ed. Plummer i.349, giving the date 729.

1264 Not generally noticed in contemporary chronicles, but the occasion for a treatise by Giles of Lessines, *Tractatus de essentia, motu et significatione cometarum* (Cambridge, Pembroke College MS 227, fos 250–282). See L. Thorndike, *Latin Treatises on Comets between 1268 and 1368* (Chicago 1950), 94–101.

1267 Bede died on the evening of 25 May 735, which was reckoned to be 26 May (Ascension Day).

1	18	d	Na		[3 Gregorius decim*us* sed*it* p*a*p*a* *a*nni 4 pr*e*dicator*es* & mi*n*ores approbavit, Augustine & car*melit*e tolleravit, sacci q*ui* intr*a*nt*ur* de p*a*rma sive de valle viridi repr*o*bavit **C**₅]
2	19	cb	8km	3	O*biit* h*e*nricus rex 16 die *novem*bris sep*ultus* 20 d*ie* e*i*usdem
3	1	a	5ya		
4	2	g	ka	3	Consiliu*m* g*e*n*e*rale Ed*w*ardus pr*imus* coronat*ur* 19 d*ie* Augusti
5	3	f	18km	3	t*e*rre mot*us* in *septem*bre
6	4	ed	Na		
7	5	c	5ka		
8	6	b	15km	3	p*e*ccham ar*chi*epi*s*copus creat*ur*
9	7	a	4Na	3	Escambiu*m* monete

f. 5

1280	8	gf	11km	3	ff*e*ria 4ᵃ infra oct*av*am assu*m*pci*o*nis intr*a*ver*unt* vj ffr*a*tres aream kerdi*v*e eis c*o*ncessam
1	9	e	ya		
2	10	d	4ka		
3	11	c	14km		

1271. *Om. entry* **D**
1272. *Om.* '16 die ... eiusdem' **D**
1274. *Om.* '19 die Augusti' **D**
1278. '*peccham* ar*chi*epi*s*copus' *cancelled* **D**
1280. *Om. entry* **D**

1271 Cf. W. Rishanger,*Chronica*, ed. H. T. Riley (RS 1865), 81. The Friars of the Sack, or of the Penitence of Jesus Christ, and the Friars of the Blessed Mary, or Pied Friars, sometimes called *de Valle Viridi*, were no longer permitted to recruit members after this decree; see R. W. Emery, 'The Friars of the Sack', *Speculum* xviii (1943), 323–34, and 'The Friars of the Blessed Mary or the Pied Friars', *ibid.*, xxiv (1949), 228–38.

1274 The Second Council of Lyons.

1275 Cf. *Flores Historiarum* iii.46, which states that the earthquake occurred on 11 September between the first and third hours of the day.

1278 John Pecham was consecrated archbishop of Canterbury on 19 February 1279.

1279 The first recoinage of Edward I; see *The* De Moneta *of Oresme*, ed. Johnson, xxxi–xxxiv and M. C. Prestwich, 'Edward I's monetary policies and their consequences', *Economic History Review* 2nd series, xxii (1969), 406–7.

1280 Wednesday 21 August 1280. There seems to be no other evidence for the date of occupation of the Cardiff Greyfriars, the buildings of which were 'completed by the late thirteenth or early fourteenth century'; see W. Rees, 'The suppression of the friaries in Glamorgan and Monmouth', *South Wales and Monmouthshire Record Society* iii (1954), 9–11.

4	12	ba	5ya	[3	*erant* te*m*pora messiu*m* mala plu*v*iosa frigida m*agis* & nive ac gelu repleta *hoc* a*n*no & t*ri*bus seque*n*tibus ita quod p*ri*mo a*n*no vendere*tur* modi*us* fru*c*ti p*ro* 2 s*olidos*; s*e*c*undo* 40 denar*iis*; terci*o* 80 denar*iis* **C**₃]
5	13	g	8ka	3	E*d*wardus fili*us* Reg*is* nasci*tur* in die s*anc*ti marci 1284
6	14	f	18ka		
7	15	e	8ya		
8	16	dc	5ka	3	Nicho*l*us 4 creatur 1 origenes s*anc*ta cecilia
9	17	b	4ya	3	exiliu*m* Judeoru*m* de Anglia
1290	18	a	4Na	[3	Regina ux*or* ob*iit* **D**]
1	19	g	10km	3	O*biit* pet*rus* qu*i*vel ep*iscopus* Exon*ie* p*ri*mo die octobris [*substitute* '3 Regina mate*r* ob*iit* G*i*lbertus de clare fili*us* nascitu*r*' **D**]
2	1	fe	8ya	3	O*biit* pe*c*cham Judeoru*m* expulsio
3	2	d	4ka	[3	Inchoacio discordie fr*anc*ie & angl*ie* **D**]
4	3	c	14km		
5	4	b	3Na	3	ulti*m*a guerra in Wallia
6	5	ag	8ka	3	s*u*bjuga*c*io scotie
7	6	f	18km	3	cap*c*io berwyk & dunbar
8	7	e	8ya	3	bellu*m* de fawkyrke p*er* E*d*wardum p*ri*mum 22 di*e* Julii

1284. *Om. entry* **D**
1285. *Om.* '1284' *at end of entry; substitute* 'si*m*ul Edwardus <de> O[t---?]' **D**
1289. *Om. entry* **D**
1292. f. 20 **D**. *Add* 'ar*chi*episcopus' **D**
1298. *Om. entry* **D**

1284 There is no similar report in other sources, which report dry summers (1284, 1285, and 1287) and a mild winter (1285); cf. Britton, *Meteorological Chronology*, 120–24.

1288 The first cycle equivalent date (224) is an approximation for the career of Origen and the supposed era of St Cecilia's martyrdom.

1289 The Jews were expelled from England by Edward I by an edict of 18 July 1290. The *expulsio* noted in the annal for 1292 below seems to refer to the same event. This entry, though more accurate, is only in the Cotton MS.

1291 Bishop Peter Quivel or Quinel's death, the date of which is given correctly here, may have been noticed because he was believed to have been a firm opponent of the Franciscans' occupation of their new site (see below s.a. 1300), and to have died by divine intervention accordingly; see A.G. Little and R.C. Easterling, *The Franciscans and Dominicans of Exeter* (Exeter 1927), 14–16. Gilbert de Clare, earl of Gloucester was born 10 or 11 May 1291.

1292 See the note on 1289 above.

1295 The revolt of Madog ap Llewelyn lasted from September 1294 to July 1295.

1297 Berwick was captured by Edward I on 30 March 1296, and Dunbar castle surrendered after the battle of Dunbar, 27 April 1296.

	9	8	d	13km	3	desponsacio margarete regine 8 die *septembris*
1300	9	cb	4ya	3	In vigi*lia* pasche i*n*travit c*ommuni*tas ff*ra*tr*um* pr*im*o aream novam Exonie.
	1	10	a	4Na	
	2	11	g	10km	
	3	12	f	7ya	
	4	13	ed	4ka	
	5	14	c	14km	
	6	15	b	Na	3
	7	16	a	ka	3	O*biit* Ed*wardus* pr*imus* <7° die Julii> Edwardi se*cundi* uxoracio 25 *die* Jan*uarii* coro*n*atus 26 *die* febr*uarii secundum* al*ios* 19 d*ie* a*ugusti*
	8	17	gf	18km	
	9	18	e	3ka	
1310	19	d	13km	
	1	1	c	3ya	
	2	2	ba	7ka	3	petrus Gav*e*stone decollat*ur* E*dwardus* *tercius* [<rex anglie> C_7?] nascit*ur* in ff*es*to *sancti* bricii
	3	3	g	17km	[3	bellu*m* de stevelyn i*n* die *sancti* joha*nn*is bapt*iste* **D**]
	4	4	f	7ya	3	Gilbert*us* Comes glou*cestrie* i*n* scotia inte*r*ficit*ur* & m*ulti* capiu*ntur* confusibilit*er* bell*um* stirelyn
	5	5	e	10ka	
	6	6	dc	3ya	
	7	7	b	[3]Na	
	8	8	a	9k[a]	

1299. *Om. entry* **D**

1300. *Om. entry* **D**

1306. *Om.* '3' *of base MS.* **D**

1307. *Substitute* '3 Obit*us* E*dwardus* pr*im*i A*nn*o regni sui 34to   Coronacio E*dwardi* secundi & uxoracio sim*ul*' **D**

1312. *Om.* '<rex anglie>' *and* 'in ff*es*to sancti bricii' **D**

1314. *Om.* 'Gilbertus'; *for* '& multi ... stirelyn' *substitute* '& capc*io* m*ultorum*' **D**

1317. 2 n a **C**

1318. 9 k a *with* 'a' *erased* **C**

1300 9 April 1300, apparently the only record. See G. Oliver, *Monasticon Diocesis Exoniensis* (Exeter 1846), 330–1 and additional supplement 28, and Little and Easterling, *Franciscans and Dominicans of Exeter*, 16–19, where evidence for a much longer period of building is assembled.

1307 Edward II was crowned on 25 February 1308.

1314 Gilbert de Clare, earl of Gloucester died at the battle of Bannockburn (24 June 1314).

| 9 | 9 | g | 9ya | [3 | hoc anno & sequenti fuit morina taurorum vaccarum bovum & vitulorum per totam angliam tanta quod in regno toto anglie fuit illa species animalium quasi de\<leta\> **C₃**] |

1320	10	fe	3ka		
1	11	d	[13]km	3	Thomas lancastrie comes occiditur
2	12	c	[3]ya		
3	13	b	6ka		
4	14	ag	17km	2	karolus magnus & alquinus magister anglicus
5	15	f	7ya		
6	16	e	10ka		
7	17	d	2ya	[3	Edwardi tercii coronacio in conversione sancti pauli **C₁₄**?]

f. 5ᵛ

8	18	cb	[3n]a	1	laurencius
9	19	a	9km		
1330	1	g	6ya	3	Edwardus princeps Wallie 15 die Junii nascitur
1	2	f	2ka		
2	3	ed	13km		
3	4	c	2Na		
4	5	b	6ka		
5	6	a	16km		
6	7	gf	2ka		
7	8	e	12km		
8	9	d	2ya		

1319. *Om. entry* **D**
1321. 12 k m **C**
1322. 2 y a **C**
1324. *Substitute* 2 *circa* hec tempora karolus magnus & alquinus anglicus' **D**
1326. *Substitute* '3 Coronacio Edwardi *tercii in* Purificacione *sancte* marie' **D**
1327. *Om. entry* **D**
1328. 2 y a **C**. fo 20ᵛ **D**. *Add date* '264' **D**
1330. *Om. entry* **D**

1319 See *Flores Historiarum* iii.343 and Britton, *Meteorological Chronology* 133.
1324 The equivalent year of the second Easter cycle is 792. Alcuin was at Charlemagne's court from 782 until his death in 804.
1327 Edward III's reign was reckoned from the feast of the conversion of St Paul (25 January 1327), but he was crowned on 29 January, not 2 February as in the Digby MS.
1328 The equivalent year of the first Easter cycle is 264. St Laurence was martyred in 258.

9	10	c	5ka		
1340	11	ba	16km	3	bellum navale apud scluse in ffesto Johannis baptiste
1	12	g	6ya		
2	13	f	2ka		
3	14	e	ya		
4	15	dc	2Na		
5	16	b	6ka		
6	17	a	16km	3	bellum de cressy 26 die augusti 3 bellum dunelmie 17 die octobris
7	18	g	ka	3	caristia Capcio kalisii 4 die Augusti
8	19	fe	12km	3	pestilencia generalis incepit in partibus australibus anglie circa ffestum Johannis baptiste & duravit per annum & plus
9	1	d	2ya		
1350	2	c	[5]ka		
1	3	b	15km	3	caristia
2	4	ag	6ya		
3	5	f	9ka	[3]	captio berwici per scoces
4	6	e	ya	3	conflictus inter scolares & laicos in oxonia nascitur Thomas Wodestok
5	7	d	Na	2	Rabanus & Strabus discipulus eius 823

1341. 6 kl api **D**

1346. *Om.* '26 die augusti'; *substitute* 'in die sancti firmini episcopi'; *om.* '17 die octobris' **D**

1347. *Om.* 'Capcio ... Augusti' **D**

1350. 15 k a **C**

1353. *scribe of* **C** *omits* '3' *for third cycle. Om. entry* **D**

1354. *For* 'conflictus ... oxonia,' *substitute* 'conflictus inter scolares oxonie & laicos in vigilie frideswide'; *om.* 'nascitur Thomas Wodestok' **D**

1355. *Om. entry* **D**

1346 The battle of Crécy was fought on 26 August 1346, as stated in the Cotton MS. St Firmin's day, to which it is attributed in the Digby MS, is 25 September.

1347 The shortage referred to was probably the result of the rains noted by the St Albans continuator of the *Polychronicon*, printed as a continuation of Adam Murimuth, *Chronica*, ed. T. Hog (London 1846), 178, s.a. 1348, and may be displaced from the following year, since the chronicle states that the rains began at the same time as the plague. On this text see J. Taylor, *The Universal Chronicle of Ranulf Higden* (Oxford 1966), 117–19. Calais capitulated on 3 August 1347.

1351 Probably this is the shortage mentioned by the St Albans *Polychronicon* continuator (Murimuth, *Chronica*, ed. Hog, 182, s.a. 1352).

1353 Berwick was captured by Scottish forces in November 1353, but lost again before 20 January 1356.

1354 The riot of St Scholastica's Day, 10 February 1355. Thomas of Woodstock duke of Gloucester was born 7 January 1355.

1355 Rabanus Maurus was elected abbot of Fulda in 822, and later taught there Walafrid Strabo, future abbot of Reichenau.

6	8	cb	8km	3	Johannes Rex francie capitur 19 die septembris bellum de paytiers
7	9	a	5ya		
8	10	g	ka	3	Ysabella mater Edwardi tercii obiit universitas diflinie in hibernia incepit
9	11	f	11km		
1360	12	ed	Na	3	Johannes Rex ffrancie solvebatur & pax inter Anglia & ffrancia proclamatur
1	13	c	5ka	3	tonitruum vehementer horribile 13 die J[unii] & pestilencia fortium & robus[torum]
2	14	b	15km	3	ventus horribilis frangens domos prosternens ecclesias circiens campanilia & ar[bores]
3	15	a	4Na		
4	16	gf	9ka	3	gelu a ffesto micheli ad ffestum gregorii [Johannes rex francie mortuus est in Anglia D]
5	17	e	ya		
6	18	d	Na		

1356. *Om.* 'Johannes'; *add* 'in' *before* 'bello' **D**

1358. *For* 'Ysabella' *substitute* 'Regina Francie'; *om.* 'universitas ... incepit' **D**

1360. *For* 'solvebatur' *substitute* 'liberatus est'; *for* 'proclamatur' *substitute* 'facta' **D**

1361. 'Junii' *and* 'robustorum,' *and* 'arbores' *in next entry,* **C**, *conjectural, ink very pale at left edge, along gutter* **C**. *Substitute* '3 tonitruum horribile quod fregit turrim fredeswide & sancte crucis oxonie & pestilencia forcium circa pentecostem' **D**. 'secunda pestilencia' [*in left margin*] **D**.

1362. *Substitute* '3 ventus horribilis qui fregit domos ecclesias & arbores 15 die Januarii' **D**.

1364. f. 21 **D**. *For* 'a ffesto' *substitute* 'ad ffestum'; *add* 'usque' *before* 'ad'; *add* 'Johannes rex francie mortuus est in Anglia' **D**.

1358 On the attempted foundation of a university in Dublin, of which this is a unique chronicle witness, see Linne R. Mooney, 'An English record of the founding of a university in Dublin in 1358', *Irish Historical Studies* xxvii (1993), 225–27.

1361 The version of this annal in the Digby MS shows that in its original form it referred to Oxford, where this destructive thunderstorm must have occurred. This is evidently the only record of damage to the churches of St Frideswide and St Cross (misread by the compiler of the Royal MS as the church of the Trinity). For other storms of this year see Britton, *Meteorological Chronology* 144.

1362 On this storm see the St Albans *Polychronicon* continuator (Murimuth, *Chronica,* ed. Hog 196, confirming the date as 15 January 1362), and other authorities cited by Britton, *Meteorological Chronology*, 144–5.

1364 25 December (1363) to 12 March 1364. According to the *Eulogium Historiarum* (ed. S. Haydon, RS 1858–65) iii.232 it lasted from 7 December to 14 March. See Britton, *Meteorological Chronology*, 146.

7	19	c	14km	[3	bellum hispanie in ffesto sancti Ricardi C₁₄] nativitas Ricardi Regis in festo epiphanie
8	1	ba	5ya	3	pestilencia tercia [in Anglia **D**]
9	2	g	ka		
1370	3	f	18km	3	Caristia iterum ut modius ffructi venderetur per 40 denarios [Obiit philippa 17 [Aprilis] **C₃**]
1	4	e	8[y]a		
2	5	dc	5ka	3	capcio comitis penbrochie apud rupeliam in vigilia Johannis baptiste
3	6	b	15km		
4	7	a	4Na	1	invencio sancte crucis 310 [<3> quarta pestilencia circa festum Johannis baptiste **D**]
5	8	g	10km	1	sancta katerina 311 [3 incepit Sarum **D**]
6	9	fe	ya	1	sanctus Nicholaus 312 Obiit princeps Wallie 8 die junii [in die sancte trinitatis **D**]
7	10	d	4ka	3	obiit edwardus tercius 21 die junii sepultus 5 die julii coronacio Ricardi secundi [16 die **C₁₇**] julii [filius Edwardi principis apud Westmonasterium **D**]
8	11	c	14km		

1367. *Om. entry* **D**
1368. *Add* 'in Anglia' **D**
1370. 'Aprilis' *conjectural, in gutter* **C**. *Om. entry* **D**.
1371. 8 k a **C**.
1372. *Om. entry* **D**
1374. *Add* '<3> quarta pestilencia circa festum Johannis baptiste' **D**.
1375. *Add* '3 incepit Sarum' **D**.
1376. *For* 'Obiit ... junii' *substitute* 'Obitus Edward[us] princeps in die sancte trinitatis' **D**.

1377. *Substitute* '3 Obitus Edwardus tercii in die sancti Albani Anno regni sui 51mo & coronatur Ricardus filius Edwardi principis apud Westmonasterium' **D**.

1367 The battle of Najera, 3 April 1367.
1368 This visitation of the plague occurred in 1369; see the St Albans *Polychronicon* continuator (Murimuth, *Chronica*, ed. Hog, 205).
1370 High prices were noted in 1369 by Thomas Walsingham, *Chronicon Angliae* (ed. E. M. Thompson, RS 1874), 65; and see Britton, *Meteorological Chronology*, 146. Queen Philippa died on 15 August 1369.
1372 The battle of La Rochelle, 23 June 1372.
1374 The Invention of the Cross is recounted in *Polychronicon* v. 136–38 s.a. 314. On the fourth visitation of the plague see its St Albans continuator (Murimuth, *Chronica*, ed. Hog, 217), s.a. 1375.
1375 St Catherine of Alexandria is not mentioned in *Polychronicon*.
1376 Nicholas bishop of Myra died 351 according to *Polychronicon* v. 158, but his true date of death is unknown. Another date, 464, is given in the annal for 1528 below.
1377 Edward III died on 21 June, not on St Alban's Day (22 June) as the Digby MS states.

f. 6

9	12	b	4ya		
1380	13	ag	8ka		
1	14	f	18km	3	decoll*atio* ar*chiepiscopi* cant*uariensis* Rob*er*ti hales p*ri*oris hospital*is* & ff*ratris* Will*elmi* Appelton i*n* c*r*astino cor*poris christi* londo*nie* 14 d*ie* [Junii] [in die s*ancti* basilii ep*iscopi ci*rca hor*am* nonam & saveye crema*tur* p*er* commu*n*itatem de sacia **D**]
2	15	e	8[y]a	3	21 die maii fu*it* te*r*re mot*us* in Anglia p*ost* me*ri*diem 3 uxoracio Re*gis* Ric*ar*di 20 d*ie* Jan*uarii* d*ie* do*mi*nic*e*
3	16	d	11ka		
4	17	cb	4ya		
5	18	a	4Na	2	den*arii* petri 853 3 *secundo* die maii ho*r*a 11 an*te* m*edium* noctem item 16 die ho*r*a 11 an*te* me*ri*diem fu*it* te*r*re mot*us* nocte prece*denti* fueru*n*t visi duo insig*num* ignes [obit*us* Kate*ri*ne do*mi*ne de Wottone [*added right margin*] **D**]
6	19	g	10km		

1381. 'Junii' *conjectural, ink smudged* **C**. *Substitute* '3 Archiepiscopus cantuariensis & Robertus hales decollati sunt londonie in die s*ancti* basilii ep*iscopi ci*rca hor*am* nonam & saveye crema*tur* per commu*n*itatem de sacia' **D**.

1382. 8 k a **C**. *For entry in* **C** *substitute* '3 uxoracio Ric*ar*di secund*i*' **D**.

1385, first cycle. **C** *incorrectly numbers cycle* '2'; **D** *correctly numbers* '1.' *Om.* '853' *and* '3 secundo die ... ignes' **D**.

1381 Fr William Appleton's murder was also recorded in the *Anonimalle Chronicle*, ed. V. H. Galbraith (2nd ed., Manchester 1970), 145. St Basil's day (MS Digby) is 14 June. The only other account to give the time of the murders is the *Westminster Chronicle*, where it is reported as the eleventh hour (ed. L. C. Hector and B. F. Harvey, Oxford 1982, 6). The meaning and indeed the syntax of the Digby manuscript's entry on the burning of the Savoy Palace *per communitatem de sacia* is not clear.

1382 Richard II was married to Anne of Bohemia on Monday 20 January 1382. On the earthquake see the *Westminster Chronicle*, which reports the time it occurred as 1.00 p.m. (ed. Hector and Harvey, 26).

1385 853 is the equivalent year in the second Easter table. For Peter's Pence see *Polychronicon* vi.316, s.a. 835, but implicitly from a later date in King Athelwulf's reign. The two earthquakes are not otherwise recorded, but a fiery shape in the sky was reported on 15 July in the *Westminster Chronicle* (ed. Hector and Harvey 122); the word *Julii* may therefore have been omitted after *16 die* in the Cotton MS.

1386 This entry in the Digby MS probably refers to Katherine Lady Berkeley, widow of Thomas Lord Berkeley (died 1361), part of whose dower was Wootton-under-Edge, and who died 13 March 1386 (not 1385 as stated in the *Complete Peerage*; see *Calendar of Inquisitions Post Mortem, Richard II 7–15*, 81, no. 213). She founded the school there in 1384; see A. F. Leach in VCH *Gloucestershire* ii.396–99.

7	1	f	7ya	[3	henricus quintus nascitur in meridie xvi° die septembris apud monmouth C_4] [3 gravis discensio oritur inter Regiis familiares & regni proceres **D**]
8	2	ed	4ka	[3	celebratur parliamentum apud Westmonasterium quod duravit a festo purificacionis usque pentecostem **D**]
9	3	c	14km		
1390	4	b	3Na	3	ventus magnus tertium 3 nonas marcii inchoando annum a circumcisione
1	5	a	7ka		
2	6	gf	18km		
3	7	e	8ya		
4	8	d	13km	3	Anna regina obiit 7 die Junii Sepulta 3 die Augusti transitus Regis ad hiberniam de haverfordia 29 die septembris
5	9	c	3ya	3	Reditus eius ad bristolliam 9 die Maii Vesperie & incepcio in theologia in ecclesia carmelitarum oxonie 24 die [Junii]
6	10	ba	4Na	3	Casus campanili kalisii opprimens ecclesiam & Casus muri kalisii ad longitudinem 100 hominum armatorum 28 [ ] primus transitus Regis ad Kalisium 7 die augusti 2 transitus 27 die septembris

1387. *Om. 'henricus … monemouth'* **D**.
1390. *Om. both entries* **D**.
1394. *Om. entries* **D**.
1395. *'Junii' conjectural, very pale ink* **C**. *Om. entry* **D**.
1396. *Unable to conjecture the date lost to pale ink in* **C**, since this event is not recorded elsewhere. Om. entry **D**.

1387 Henry V's date of birth is disputed, and 1386 is marginally more likely than 1387. The day and month are almost certainly 16 September; the time, according to his astrological *nativitas* in Bodleian Library, Oxford, Ashmole MS 393, fo 109^r, was 11.22 a.m. See Christopher Allmand, *Henry V* (London 1992), 8.

1388 The parliament of 1388 lasted from 3 February to 4 June; Pentecost fell on 17 May.

1390 5 March; also reported in the *Westminster Chronicle*, ed. Hector and Harvey, 414.

1394 Cf. T. F. Tout, *Chapters in the Administrative History of Mediaeval England* (Manchester 1920–33), iii.487n., for evidence from the chancery rolls that though he was at Haverfordwest from 16 to 28 September, he sailed from Milford Haven on 30 September.

1395 The precise date of Richard's return is only given in this source; but he had embarked at Waterford on 1 May, and was evidently at Salisbury on 15 May (Tout, *Chapters* iii.495n.). The inception and vesperies are presumably those of John Somer, who was in Oxford in 1394–5 (Emden, *BRUO* iii.1727).

1396 The collapse of the church tower is not otherwise recorded. On Richard's two crossings of the straits of Dover in 1396 see Tout, *Chapters* iv.3-5, the authorities for which confirm the dates given here.

uxorac*io* secunda 4 d*ie novem*bris

7	11	g	10km	3	Coro*nacio* Regine 7 d*ie* augusti Capc*io* duc*is* glove*rnie* 11 d*ie* Jul*ii* decapitac*io* com*itis* aru*ndell* 21 d*ie septem*bris
8	12	f	7ya		
9	13	e	3ka	[3	Dep*osicio* Ricar*di* Reg*is* i*n festo* micha*eli*s Coro*nacio* henrici 13° die *octo*bris **C₃**]
1400	14	dc	14km		
1	15	b	3Na	1	*Con*stantinu*s* dotav*it* ecc*le*siam 336
2	16	a	7ka	3	Comata app*a*ruit 18 die febru*arii* 6 ebd*omadie* du*r*avit 6 nonas maii feri*a tercia* apud tantou*n* plu*vie* toni*trus* & *gra*nde
3	17	g	17km	2	Edmu*ndus* R*ex* ma*rtir* 871. [3] Joha*nna* regi*na* coro*natur*
4	18	fe	3ka		
5	19	d	13km		
6	1	c	3ya		
7	2	b	6ka		
8	3	ag	17km		
9	4	f	7ya	1	hengistu*s* ven*it* in Anglia 345
1410	5	e	10ka		
1	6	d	2ya	[3	*quarto* die m*a*rcii lapis pri*mus* ecc*le*sie

1397. *Om. entry* **D**

1399. *Om. entry* **D**

1400. f. 21ᵛ **D**.

1401. *Substitute* '2 A*n*nus ab i*m*pe*rio Con*stantini a*ui* dotavit ecc*le*siam 869' **D**. **D**'s *cycle and date incorrect.*

1402. *Om. entry* **D**.

1403. *scribe omits* '3' *for third cycle,* **C**. *For two entries in* **C**, *substitute* '2 Marti*r*ium bea*ti* Edmu*n*di reg*is* 871' **D**.

1409. 1 Hengistus venit in Angliam 877 **D**. **D**'s *cycle correct, but date incorrect.*

1411. *Om. entry* **D**

1397 The Queen was crowned on 5 January 1397.

1399 Richard II ceased to reign on 28 or 29 September, the latter date being Michaelmas.

1401 The equivalent first Easter cycle year is 337, date of the death of Constantine; in the second it is 869, the figure given, confusingly, in the Digby MS presumably for the interval since his reign. The donation is perhaps referred to in *Polychronicon* v. 128–30, s.a. 314.

1402 On the comet cf. T. Walsingham, *Historia Anglicana*, ed. H. T. Riley (RS 1863–4), ii.248, and the English continuation of the *Polychronicon* viii.516. 2 (6 Nones) May was a Tuesday in 1402. There seems to be no other account of this thunderstorm at Taunton.

1403 871 is the equivalent second Easter cycle year; but *Polychronicon* vi.342 recounts the martyrdom of St Edmund under 869. Queen Joan was crowned on 26 February.

1409 345 is the equivalent first Easter cycle year. It is not clear why Hengist's arrival is assigned to this year; see the annal for 1513 (449) below.

1411 Presumably 4 March 1411, as the compiler seems to have been beginning his year, as in the next entry, on 1 January at this point. There is no other evidence for the

fra*tru*m mi*noru*m Brigg*water* erat po*situs pro*
fu*ndat*i*one* int*er* 9 & 10 cloc m*eridiem* **C**₆]

2	7	cb	3Na		
3	8	a	9km	3	morit*ur* h*enricus* qu*artus* 20 die marcii [Coronac*io* h*enrici quinti* do*minica* in pa*sche* **C**₄]
4	9	g	6ya		
5	10	f	2ka	[3	h*enricus* qu*i*nti (*sic*) applicu*it* apud kytycaus in norma*n*nya in assu*mpci*o*ne* & p*ost* ea obsed*it* harefliet que capta e*st* 22° die *septem*bris & bellu*m com*missum *est* 25 die *octo*bris apud dasyngcourth **C**₄]
6	11	ed	[13]km		
7	12	c	3ya	3	[victoria co*m*itis dorcetie & anglor*um* sup*er* francos i*n* vig*i*l*i*a g*re*gorii apud benyle Et ap*u*d kytycaus in **C**₄] [bellu*m* **C**₁₅] [Et navale i*n* assu*mpci*o*ne* v*i*rginis gloriose ap*u*d hareflut **C**₄] [bellu*m* **C**₁₅] [3 Cobha*m* sive old castel c*re*ma*tur* londo*ne* c*i*rca fi*ne*m h*uius* a*n*ni **D**₂]
8	13	b	[6]ka		
9	14	a	16km		
1420	15	gf	7ya	[1]	[Jeroni*m*us tr*a*nstulit bib*li*a*m* 356 **C**₁₆]

1413. *Om. entry* **D**

1414. 8 y d apr*i*l*i* **D**.

1415. *Substitute* '3 harflu capit*ur* a r*e*ge anglie. <3> bellu*m* de Agyncorth' **D**₂.

1416. 12 k m **C**.

1417. *Substitute* '3 Cobha*m* sive old castel c*re*ma*tur* londo*ne* c*i*rca fi*ne*m h*uius* a*n*ni' **D**₂.

1418. 2 k a **C**.

1420, *third cycle. scribe omits* '1' *for first cycle*, **C**. *Om. entries* **D**.

foundation of the new Franciscan church at Bridgewater, which must be the church seen by William Worcester (*Itineraries*, ed. J. Harvey, London 1969, 80).

1413 Henry V was crowned on Passion Sunday, 9 April.

1415 Henry V landed at Chef de Caux (*Kytycaus*) west of Harfleur on Wednesday 14 August.

1417 Thomas Beaufort earl of Dorset's raid through the Pays de Caux was checked near Valmont on 11 March 1416, the eve of St Gregory. *Benyle* is presumably cognate with Bienville, the name given to Ouainville, between which village and Valmont the engagement occurred, in the *Chronique de Normandie* (ed. B. Williams, *Henrici quinti Angliae regis gesta*, London 1850, 173.) Though more a narrow escape than a victory, it was reported in England as a successful feat of arms. The naval battle of the Seine (15 August 1416) was certainly a victory. Sir John Oldcastle, Lord Cobham was burnt on 14 December 1417.

1420 356 is the first Easter cycle equivalent year. Cf. *Polychronicon* v.182, s.a. 371, for Jerome's translation. The entry on the execution of thirty subjects, including thirteen friars minor, is evidently displaced from 1402; see the somewhat confused account in another Franciscan chronicle, the continuation of *Eulogium Historiarum*, iii.389–94 and Walsingham, *Historia Anglicana*, 248–9, confirmed by the writs for the arrest of friars,

[3 de quodlibet (sic) statu & gradu triginti
fuerunt interfecti & de ordine minorum
tracti & suspensi xiij **C₄**] [& 5 jubile
Cantuarie **C₅**]

	1	2	3	4	5
1	16	e	10ka		
2	17	d	2ya	[3 Nativitas henrici sexti & annus primus sui regni **C₅**]	
3	18	c	2Na		
4	19	ba	9km		
5	1	g	6ya		
6	2	f	2ka		
7	3	e	12km		
8	4	dc	2Na		
9	5	b	6ka	[3 coronacio henrici vi^{u} in anglia **C₅**]	
1430	6	a	16k[m]		
1	7	g	ka	[3 coronacio henrici vi^{u} in ffrancia **C₅**]	
2	8	fe	12km		

f. 6ᵛ

	3	9	2ya		
3	9	9	2ya	[3 eclipsis solis universalis 17° die Junii in ffesto sancti Botulphi secundum fratrem Somour **C₈**]	
4	10	c	5ka		
5	11	b	15km		
6	12	ag	6ya		
7	13	f	2ka		
8	14	e	ya		
9	15	d	Na		
1440	16	cb	6ka	2	Adelstone primus Rex tocius Anglie 908

1422. *Om. entry* **D**
1429. *Om. entry* **D**
1430. 16 k a **C**.
1431. *Om. entry* **D**
1433. 2 no api **D**. *Om. entry* **D**
1436. f. 22 **D**.
1440. *Substitute* 'Annus a regno Adelston primi regis Anglie 908' **D**.

dated 27 May to 3 June, in *CCR (1399–1402)*, 527–9. The Canterbury jubilee celebrated two hundred years since the translation of Thomas Becket.

1422 Henry VI was born 6 December 1421.

1433 Cf. John Somer, *Kalendarium ...*, an accurate prediction: there was an eclipse of the sun at 2.36 p.m. on 17 June 1433, though only partial in southern England; see T. v. Oppolzer, *Canon of Eclipses* (New York 1962), 252, no. 6284. The editors are grateful to Dr David Dewhirst for help on this point.

1440 908 is the equivalent second Easter cycle year. It is not clear how Aethelstan (924–939) can have been associated with this date.

1	17	a	16km		
2	18	g	ka		
3	19	f	11km		
4	1	ed	2ya		
5	2	c	5ka		
6	3	b	15km		
7	4	a	5ya		
8	5	gf	9ka	1	hengist*us* occidi*tur*
9	6	e	ya		
1450	7	d	Na	[3	Insurrexio Cade Capitan*i* Cancie **C**₅]
1	8	c	7km	1	Athanasiu*s* Jeron*ymus* Ambro*sius* crisostom*us* gregor*ius* nazanzenu*s* sanct*us* mart*inus* hill*arius* Julian*us* apost*a*ta arr*ius*
2	9	ba	5ya		
3	10	g	ka		
4	11	f	11km		
5	12	e	8ya	[3	Conflict*us* sanc*ti* Albani **C**₅]
6	13	dc	5ka		
7	14	b	15km	[3	translacio sanc*ti* Osmu*n*di saru*m* ep*iscopi* **C**₅]
8	15	a	4Na		
9	16	g	8ka	[3	obit*us* nobili*s* viri Joha*n*nis ffastolf milit*is* singul*aris* domi*n*i mei 5 die nove*m*bri*s* ho*r*a 6ᵃ mi*nute* 30 p*ost* me*ridiem* **C**₇]

1448. 1 hengist*us* occidi*tur* 916 **D**. **D**'s *cycle correct, but date incorrect.*
1450. *Om. entry* **D**
1451. *Substitute* 'circa he*c* tempo*r*a Athanasiu*s* Jeron*ymus* Ambro*sius* crisostom*us* nazare*n*us sanct*us* mart*inus* hill*arius* Julian*us* moriu*n*tur 368' **D**.
1455. *Om. entry* **D**
1457. *Om. entry* **D**
1459. *Om. entry* **D**

1448 384 is the equivalent first Easter cycle year. It has no obvious association with Hengist, who died in 468 in the version of *Polychronicon* v.296.

1451 387 is the corresponding year in the first Easter cycle: but there is no compelling reason to associate these figures of early church history either together or with this year. They were all mentioned in *Polychronicon* (Athanasius, v.150–58, s.a. 339; Jerome frequently, cf. v.182; Ambrose, v.186, s.a. 376; Chrysostom casually, v.214; Gregory of Nazianzus, v.88–90, s.a. 269; Martin of Tours, v.210, s.a. 389; Hilary of Poitiers, v.160–62, s.a. 357; Julian the Apostate, v.164–78, s.a. 365; Arius, v.150, s.a. 339). The Digby MS may or may not preserve the original text in reporting that they died about this time; its date, 368, is not of course the equivalent year.

1457 St Osmund of Salisbury was canonized after a long process in 1456; his relics were translated to a new shrine in the cathedral in 1457.

1459 This note is evidently in the hand of William Worcester. His account of the last illness of Sir John Fastolf is in BL, Sloane MS 4, fo 38ᵛ; the day was reported in several documents, but this is the only record that it took place at 6.30 p.m. On Fastolf's death see C. Richmond, *The Paston Family in the Fifteenth Century* (Cambridge 1990), 250-58.

1460	17	fe	ya	[1	ordo canonicorum a beato augustino inchoatur 396 **C₂**]
1	18	d	Na		
2	19	c	14km		
3	1	b	4ya		
4	2	ag	ka		
5	3	f	18km		
6	4	e	8ya		
7	5	d	4ka		
8	6	cb	15km		
9	7	a	4Na		
1470	8	g	10km		
1	9	f	18km		
2	10	ed	4ka		
3	11	c	14km	1	Roma a gothis capta est ex quo tempore romani in britannia regnare cessaverunt postquam 470 annis ibi regnaverant a tempore Julii a tempore condicionis rome 1164 annis
4	12	b	4ya	1	Obiit Ambrosius 410
5	13	a	7ka		
6	14	gf	18km		
7	15	e	8ya		
8	16	d	11ka		
9	17	c	3ya		
1480	18	ba	4Na		
1	19	g	10km	1	Obiit Jeronymus 417
2	1	f	7ya		
3	2	e	3ka		

1460. *Om. entry* **D**
1467. 8 kl api **D**.
1472. f. 22v **D**.
1473. *Om. entry* **D**
1474. *Substitute* 'Obitus beati Ambrosii 410' **D**.
1481. *Substitute* 'Obitus beati Jeronimi 417' **D**.

After 1483 (**C**) 'Nota quod instituto ciclo ...' *written in lower margin by the main scribe. These instructions continued in* **C** *in the lower margin of next folio. In* **D**, *one continuous prose note, following* *1532.*

1460 This is the corresponding year of the first Easter cycle. On the supposed foundation of the Austin Canons by Augustine see J. C. Dickinson, *The Origin of the Austin Canons* (London 1950), 8.

1473 These calculations were made by Bede, *Hist. Eccl.* i.11, ed. Plummer i.25; they are cited in *Polychronicon* v.218–20, s.a. 412.

1474 Not mentioned by Higden in the *Polychronicon*. Ambrose died in 397.

1481 Cf. *Polychronicon* v.230, s.a. 413. Jerome died in 420.

Nota quod instituto ciclo novemdecennali in ciclum solarem id est 19 multiplicatus 28 exurget ciclus magnus supra scriptus 532 annorum qui continet omnis varietes Kalendarii Sciendum tunc pro cronicando anno domini quod primus ciclus incepit 64 annis ante incarnationum. Secundus vero incepit anno incarnationis 469.

f. 7

4	3	dc	14km		
5	4	b	3Na		
6	5	a	7ka		
7	6	g	17km		
8	7	fe	8ya		
9	8	d	13km		
1490	9	c	3ya		
1	10	b	3Na		
2	11	ag	10km	1	Obiit beatus augustinus doctor 428
3	12	f	7ya		
4	13	e	3ka		
5	14	d	13km		
6	15	cb	3Na		
7	16	a	7ka		
8	17	g	17km		
9	18	f	2ka		
1500	19	ed	13km		
1	1	c	3ya		
2	2	b	6ka		
3	3	a	16km		
4	4	gf	7ya		
5	5	e	10ka		
6	6	d	2ya		
7	7	c	2Na		
8	8	ba	9km		
9	9	g	6ya		
1510	10	f	2ka		
1	11	e	12km		
2	12	dc	3ya		
3	13	b	6ka	1	Angli a britonibus accersiti adierunt

1489. 12 kl ma **D**.
1490. *Substitute* 'Obitus beati augustini doctoris 428' **D**.
1508. f 23 **D**.
1513. *Om. entry* **D**

1492 Cf. *Polychronicon* v.234, s.a. 425. Augustine died in 430.
1513 Cf. Bede, *Hist. Eccl.* v.24, the chronological *recapitulatio*, ed. Plummer, i.352.

britanniam 449

4	14	a	16km
5	15	g	6ya
6	16	fe	10ka
7	17	d	2ya
8	18	c	2Na
9	19	b	8km
1520	1	ag	6ya
1	2	f	2ka
2	3	e	12km
3	4	d	Na
4	5	cb	6ka
5	6	a	16km
6	7	g	ka
7	8	f	11km
8	9	ed	2ya
9	10	c	5ka
1530	11	b	15km
1	12	a	5ya
2	13	gf	2ka

8 9 ed 2ya   1   O*biit* sanctus Nicho*l*us 464

Tercius vero ciclus & presens c*iclus* annorum incarnationis per totum conscribitur incepit anno cristi 1001. *Quartus* vero incipiet anno cristi 1533. Si autem placuerit habere cotacionem primi cicli minuantur 64 de 3 primis figuris eiusdem loci & residuum est quostiens. Si vero secundi cicli libuerit habere cotacionem de toto numero conscripto minuatur unus ciclus id est 532 & patebit intentum. Et nota quod primus ciclus notificatur par 1 secundus per 2 tercius per 3 & quartus per 4 notificari debet & cetera. Et sic finitur cronica brevis & utilis.

After 1532. 'Tercius vero ciclus & presens …' *written in lower margin by the main scribe, a continuation of the note on the preceding page.* **C.** *Entire note,* 'Nota quod … utilis' *appears here* **D.**

1528 An alternative date is given in the annal for 1376, above.

THE BL ROYAL 13.C.i REDACTION OF SOMER'S CHRONICLE[1]

f. 43

Calendarium cum Rotulis cronicorum

Nota q*uod* p*er* ista*m* cronica*m* h*a*betur ann*us* incarnatio*nis* *chris*ti *et* cicli (solaris) lunar*is* cu*m* li*tte*ris do*m*i*n*ica*libus et* bissextili*bus et* dies pasche *et* p*er* *consequ*e*ns* alia festa mobilia. N*ot*a se*xt*a do*m*i*n*ica p*re*cedentes es*se*t p*ri*ma do*m*i*n*ica 40ᵃ a*li*a do*m*i*n*ica 50ᵃ *octav*a 60ᵃ *nona* 70ᵐᵃ Et 5ᵗᵃ do*m*i*n*ica post pascha Rogac*i*o*n*es *et* 7ᵃ p*en*teco*st*es.

left margin: cristum an*num* 63

1001
1002
1003
1004
1005
1006 [2] Aureli*us* cu*m* hengist*o* pug*n*avit *et* victoria h*a*buit   473
1007
1008 [2] M*er*lin*us* 476 vide 6ᵃ in fine
1009
1010
1011

[1] Heading. Another text, on the seven days of creation, is written in the blank spaces to right of the entries and continuing in lower margin of folio 43. Text of first five days enclosed in circles running down the right side of page. The text in first circle begins, 'In p*ri*nci*pi*o crea*v*it d*eus* to*t*am terram o*m*nes co*n*tine*nt*es co*n*tentes sc*il*icet o*m*ne*m* empireum *et* ang*e*licam creatura*m* terram id *est* mat*er*iam om*n*ium creatu*rum* corporu*m* id *est* 4 es*s*entia *et* mu*n*dum *sen*sibilem....'.

1001 Years for the second Great Cycle added to left margin on folio 43 recto only: '469' to left of '1001', '470' to left of '1002', etc, to '500' to left of '1032'. Continue sporadically in right margin thereafter; note also years of First Cycle added sporadically to left margin beginning with '2' in right margin beside entry for '1066'. '8' beside entry for '1072', etc.

1006. 2: 1
1008. 2: 1

1006 See Geoffrey of Monmouth, *Historia Regum Britanniae* viii.6. The equivalent year of the second Easter cycle is 474.

1008 The reference forward is to the entries for 1529 and 1530.

1012

1013

1014

1015   3   Urbanus papa apud cleremont in sinodo ordinavit matutinas
dicendas beate virgini et excommunicavit Philippum Regem
Francie propter adulterium

1016   3   christiani collocati ex omni parte occidentis ad numerum 600000
iuerunt ad terram sanctam et Godefridus dux Lothoringie fuit
unus capitaneorum et Robertus curthose alius
1 . 17

1018   3   ordo cisterciensis (de) de 21 monachis et abbate Roberto
intraverunt abbatiam de Molausmes in ffrancia

1019   3   die {veneris} idus capta fuit Jerusalem 30 die post obi-
sidionem Et Godfridus electus in Principem et Regem

1020

1021

1022

1023

1024

1025   1 3   obit beatus Patricius 494 Aurelius hengistum decollari man-
davit   489

1026

1027   1   certicius et kenrik filius eius cum 5 navibus applicuerunt
aput Certicheseyle qui fuit primus occidentalium   Regum
Saxonum cuius successio venit ad Alfredum regem qui primus
monarcha erat   494

1028

1029

1030   [2]   Aurelius veneno periit cui successit fratereius uter pendragoun

1030. 2: 1

1015 Displaced from 1095. Cf. Vincent of Beauvais, *Speculum Historiale* (Venice 1591)
xxv.102, from whom the claim that the Council of Clermont laid down that the Office
of the Blessed Virgin should be said on Saturdays is derived. Philip I, king of France
(1060–1108) was excommunicated at Autun (1094) for divorcing his first wife, and the
sentence was confirmed at Clermont.

1016 Displaced from 1096.

1018 Displaced from 1098. Robert of Molesmes founded the Cistercian order at
Molesmes in that year.

1019 Displaced from 1099, in which year on Friday 15 July (Idus Julii) Jerusalem was
stormed.

1025 The equivalent year of the second Easter cycle is 493, in which year the Annals
of Ulster (ed. S. MacAirt and G. MacNiocaill, Dublin 1983) place the death of St Patrick.
On the execution of Hengist see *Historia Regum Britanniae* viii.7.

1027 Cf. *Anglo-Saxon Chronicle* s.a. 495, the equivalent year of the second Easter cycle;
Henry of Huntingdon, *Historia Anglorum*, ii.11, ed. D. Greenaway (Oxford 1996) 92–4.

1030 See *Historia Regum Britanniae* viii.15.

et anno sequen*te* coronat*ur*

1031
1032

f. 43ᵛ

1033
1034
1035
1036
1037
1038
1039
1040
1041
1042   3   Coronacio Edwardi R*egis et con*fessor*is* ap*ut* Wynton*iam*
1043   1   Nativ*itas* chris*ti* secundum op*inion*em volentiu*m* pr*o*bare pas-
                sione*m* in plenilunio

1044
1045
1046
1047   3   berengariu*s* *left margin*: 'S. brigida 511 christi'
                1048   (2   boiciu*s* S. brigida 517)
1049   1 2   boeciu*s* S. brigida 517 / Uter pendragon p*er*iit veneno /
                Et arthur*us* filiu*s* eiu*s* sib*i* succ*essit* genitu*s* a filia duc*is*
                cornubie   516
1050   1   (Nata b*eata* vi*r*go maria) Arthur*us* petiit auxi*liu*m armo-
                ricor*um et s*ic po*st contr*a saxones tr*i*umpha*vit*   517
                1051   1   Nata b*eata* vi*r*go maria

1047–1060 Scribe originally wrote all Easter dates in this section with figures for the following years; thus the date for 1047 was originally written 3 Nonas Ap, that for 1048 originally written 7 kalendas Ap, etc. The original scribe has corrected his mistake by crossing out and/or rubbing out and adding new figures.

1043 The writer probably refers to the astronomer Richard Monk who in the 1430s wrote a new set of calendrical tables calculated for Oxford, preserved in Bodleian MS. Laud misc. 594 (f. 14ᵛ–21ᵛ). His reckonings of the age of the world, preserved in Bodleian Ashmole 369, f. viii, calculate the year of Christ's incarnation as 22 years later than that accepted by the Church, as indicated here. If this note does refer to Monk, this is the only evidence that he argued for dating Easter on the full moon. See J. D. North, 'The Western Calendar – "Intolerabilis, Horribilis, et Derisibilis"; Four Centuries of Discontent', *Gregorian Reform of the Calendar: Proceedings of the Vatican Conference to Commemorate its 400th Anniversary 1582–1982*, ed. G. V. Coyne, SJ; M. A. Hoskin and O. Pedersen (Vatican 1983), 90–93. Also Emden, *BRUO* ii.1294.

1049 The equivalent year of the second Easter cycle is 517. On Uter Pendragon see *Historia Regum Britanniae* viii.24.

1050 Cf. *ibid.* ix.1.

1052
1053
1054
1055
1056 2 Sanctus benedictus 525 // regno restaurato et pacificato duxit
Gwenhuiuaram ex genere wallianorum procreatam
1057
1058
1059
1060
1061
1062
1063
1064

f. 44

Kymbelinus regnavit in Anglia tempore ortus Christi. Tenacii filius anno
regni sui 5to. Et a morte brittii primi Regis brittonum usque ad predictum
kymbelinum regnaverunt 77 Reges per 1072 annos.

1065 1 Nativitas domini
1066 3 obitus beati Edwardi adventus Willelmi conquestoris coronacio
haroldi anno 2° nato domino magi adoraverunt dominum 2
1067 3 coronacio Willelmi conquestoris
1068 1 Nascitur Johannes Evangelista
1069 [2] Arthurus subjugavit gallias 536
1070
1071 3 translacio sedis de shirebourne ad Sarum
1072 1 Joseph cum maria et puero redit de Egipto in
Nazareth mortuo Herode 8
1073 9
1074
1075 (1 3 terre motus magnus / passio christi si passus fuit plenilunio)
/ Arthurus iter versus Romam arripuit 539
1076 1 3 passio christi si passus plenilunio / 3 terre motus magnus
Mordredus nepos arthuri eius uxorem Gwenhuiuaram cop-
ulavit 540

1069. 2: 1

1056 Cf. ibid. ix.9.
Kymbelinus Cf. ibid. i.18, iv.12. Brittius: presumably for Brutus.
1067 William I was crowned on 25 December 1066.
1069 The equivalent second Easter cycle year is 537. Cf. Historia Regum Britanniae ix.11.
1075 Cf. ibid. ix.18–xi.3.
1076 Cf. ibid. x.13.

1077   I   Arthur*us* ira inde mot*us* rev*er*sus e*st* et interfecit Mord-
              redu*m* 541

1078   I   Arthur*us* letalit*er* vuln*er*atus / Co*n*stantino cognato suo
              reg*num* dimisit 542

1079

1080

1081

1082

1083

1084

1085   3   S*anctus* Wlstan*us*

1086   3   obit*us* W*illelmi* co*n*questori*s* / Mortuo Ky*m*mbelino fili*us* ei*us*
              Guyderi*us* regnavit 22

1087 [3] obit*us* W*illelmi* conquestor*is* in alio vetusti*ssim*o li*b*ro 6 Id*us*
              octob*ris* 23

1088   3   coronacio Will*elmi* Ruffi ap*ut* Westm*onasterium*

1089   3   ordi*n*es cist*er*ciens*ium* et cartus*iensium* ince*perunt*

1090 8 3 S*anctus* Ed*mundu*s co*n*stituit cano*n*icos / advent*us* S*ancti* augu-
              stini in angl*ia*

1091

1092

1093

1094   3   S*anctus* anselm*us* co*n*secrat*ur*

1095   I   *christus* baptizat*ur*

1096

*f. 44*ᵛ

1097

1098

1099   I   *christus* passus est

1100   3   obit*us* W*illelmi* Ruffi et coronacio h*enrici* p*r*imi / Et obit*us*
              Godefredi R*egis* Jer*us*ale*m* et baudewyn*us* sibi successit

      I   passio p*r*othomartir*is* Stepha*n*i 3[ ]

1087. [3]: *om.*

1094. The scribe, correcting his error, draws the reader's attention to the entry at the bottom of the facing page, for 1192.

1077 Cf. *ibid.* x.13, giving the date 542. The dates of the two previous entries must have been extrapolated backwards from this entry's date.

1086 Cf. *ibid.* iv.12. The equivalent first Easter cycle year is 22.

1087 *Flores Historiarum* ii.17, where the coronation of William II is dated *sexto kalend. Octobris*, is perhaps the closest parallel.

1090 The equivalent second Easter cycle year is 558.

1101 3   Obitus Willelmi Regis et coronatur henricus frater eius per alium
          librum quia per sagittam interfectus fuit   1   conversio pauli
1102 1   Matheus apostolus Evangelium scripsit   3[   ]
1103
1104
1105 3   Henricus Imperator obiit et in diebus suis vicit in bellis
          campestribus   72
1106 3   conversio petri alfonsii Judei
1107 1   Petrus Cathedram tenuit antiochie et continuavit per sep-
          tennium   41
1108 1 3 Hugo de sancto victore et ordo temperalium incepit / bellum
          aput tenarthebury inter henricum Regem anglie et Robertum
          comitem Normannie in quo captus fuit comes
      1   Marchus Evangelista ewangelium petro narrante con-
          scripsit   42
1109 1 3 Sanctus anselmus // Petrus a compedibus liberatur // cor-
          onacio Baldewyni Regis Jerusalem aput betheleem quo anno
          omnes lampades circa sepulcrum a se illuminabantur mir-
          abiliter   43
1110 1   Claudius tiberius regnum invasit / et Gwiderius Rex eum in
          fugam coegit / Iste postea peremptus a principe militis
          Imperatoris / Arviragus frater eius sibi successit / et per 52
          annos negavit tributum Romanis quare Claudius intravit
          regnum et tandem pace firmata in pace quievit Arvir-
          agus   4[   ]
1111
1112
1113 2   Anglici fidem acceperunt sub gregorio pape 581 / Et sanctus
          bernardus 22 annorum etatis Intravit ordinem cisterciensium
1114 3   tamisia exsiccata fuit hoc anno
1115 1 3 Assumptio beate virginis / ffundatio abbatiarum de cleremont
          1108. temperalium: shd. be templariorum

1101 Cf. Matthew Paris, Chronica Majora, ed. H. R. Luard (RS 1872–83), ii.111–12, but
s.a. 1100.

1105 The Emperor Henry IV died on 7 August 1106.

1106 The Dialogi of Petrus Alphonsi, a converted Spanish Jew, are in Migne, Patrologia
Latina clvii, coll. 535-672.

1108 The battle of Tinchebrai, called Tenarchebrai in Flores Historiarum ii.38, was fought
on 28 September 1106.

1109 This is presumably displaced from 1100. Baldwin I was crowned at Bethlehem
on 25 December.

1110 The equivalent first Easter cycle year is 46. Cf. Historia Regum Britanniae iv.15-17.

1113 The equivalent second Easter cycle year is 581. St Bernard joined the Cistercian
order in 1112.

1115 Clairvaux (founded 1115), not 'Cleremont' is presumably intended; Pontigny was
founded in 1114. Both were mother houses of Cistercian congregations.

et ponteigny

1116

1117 18 k*a*l*endas* maii pascha matild*i*s reg*i*na angl*ie* 4 *octobr*is ob*iit*

1118

1119

1120 3 ordo pr*emon*stra*tensium* incep*it*

1121 2 obit*us* b*eati* g*regorii* 589

1122 1 mortuo Arvirago succ*essit* s*ib*i fili*us* ei*us* no*m*i*n*e Mari*us* 57

1123 (57)

1124 1 Petrus linu*m* *et* cletum Ep*iscop*os ordinavit 59

        1125 2 Conv*er*sio anglor*um* 593

1126

1127 1 Jacob*us* frat*er* dom*i*ni martire corona*tur* 62

1128 1 Maria magdalena mig*ra*vit ad dominu*m* 63

f. 45

1129

1130

1131 1 3 In fr*ancia* corona*tur* ph*ilip*us vivente lodowico p*atre* *et* modicu*m* post sicu*t* eq*u*itavi*t* p*ari*sie un*us* porcell*us* suppeditavi*t* equu*m* *et* cecid*it* un*de* moriebatur passio ap*o*stolorum petr*i* *et* pauli 66

1132 2 3 Imperator lothari*us* *con*duxi*t* Inno*cencium* *et* misit eu*m* in sede p*ap*ali *et* fugavit petru*m* leon*is* / Ta*bu*le arzachel fa*c*te su*n*t / 600 /

1133

1134

1135 3 ordo cist*er*c*iensium* in angl*iam* ve*n*it / obiit hen*r*icus p*ri*mus <3 Nonas octob*ri*s> *et* coronatur Stephan*us* / ob*iit* Will*elmus* cantuari*ensi* *et* succ*essit* theobald*us* et ob*iit* lodowic*us* R*ex* fr*ancie* *et* succ*essit* lodowic*us* fili*us* ei*us*

1136 2 consecra*tio* Westm*onasterii* in nocte Resur*rectionis* dom*i*ni *per*

1117 Easter occurred on 14 April (18 Kal. May) in 1118. Queen Matilda died on 1 May 1118.

1122 The equivalent first Easter cycle year is 58. Cf. *Historia Regum Britanniae* iv.16–17.

1131 Cf. Guillaume de Nangis, *Chronique*, ed. H. Géraud (Société de l'histoire de France 1843), i.22.

1132 The Emperor Lothair reached Rome with Innocent II in spring 1133. Peter Pierleoni, Anacletus II, remained in Rome until his death in 1138.

1135 Henry I died 1 December 1135. William of Corbeil died 21 November 1136; his successor, Theobald of Bec, was consecrated 8 January 1139. Louis VI king of France died 1 August 1137.

1136 King Stephen held an Easter (22 March) court in London, but there is no record of any consecration at Westminster.

sanctum petrum in spiritu

1137 1 3 maxima siccitas in francia quia omnes fontes et putei exsic-
          cabant et non pluvit per plures dies / Judea a tito capsa et
          dispersio Judeorum et subversio Jerusolomitarum 72

1138 1   petrus et paulus martirizantur 74

1139 2 3 Institutio festi omnium sanctorum a bonifacio 4to / 607 /
          Judei crucifixerunt in anglia unum puerum

1140 1 3 sacra synodus aput Renys sub papa Eugenio et condempnavit
          Gilbertum episcopum de poyters / Et bellum aput lincolniam
          inter Regem Stephanum et Comitem Robertum et rex capitur //
          Rodericus Rex pictorum applicuit et Marius eum interfecit et
          suis non peremptis dedit cathenesia dicitur que tunc fuit
          deserta in borea albanie 75

1141 76

1142 1 3 Nativitas Regis Ricardi filii Regis henrici / 1 picti in hibernensis
          repulaverunt quorum filii quia commixti scoti dicebantur quasi
          ex diversis nacionibus compatribus (et sunt) et sic mutabatur
          nomen albanie in nomen scotie 76

1143 1   defuncto Rege Mario successit filius eius Coilus Rome nutritus
          qui tributum solvens in pace permansit 78

1144 3   Anglici Jurauerunt fidelitatem Matildi Imperatrici
1145
1146 2   ysidorus et machometus et crucis exaltacio 614
1147
1148
1149 1   Johannes Evangelista a domitiano in pathmos exulatus et ibi
          composuit librum revalationum id est apocalipsium 84

1150 1 3 gelu vehemens / Johannes in ferventis olei doleo missus
          est 85
1151
1152 1 3 henricus filius matildis duxit alianoram ducissam aquitanie Et

1137. capsa: shd. be. capta

1137 Cf. Guillaume de Nangis, *Chronique*, ed. Géraud i.27.

1139 Perhaps a reference to the alleged crucifixion of St William of Norwich in 1144.

1140 The synod of Rheims, at which some of the teachings of Gilbert de la Porrée,
bishop of Poitiers were condemned, took place in March 1148; cf. Guillaume de Nangis,
Chronique ed. Géraud i.30-33, which however only mentions the condemnation of Peter
Abelard. The battle of Lincoln was fought on 2 February 1141. On Marius see *Historia
Regum Britanniae* iv.17, where Geoffrey of Monmouth calls the king of the Picts Sodric.

1142 Richard I was born 8 September 1157. The first cycle annal which follows it is a
continuation of that under 1140, dated 75, and may be intended for that year. It is
derived from the passage immediately following the material on Marius in *Historia Regum
Britanniae* iv.17.

1143 Cf. *ibid.* iv.18.

1152 Cardinal John Paparo was the papal legate who presided at the Synod of Kells
in February and March 1152. Lists of the Irish sees at this time differ on the number of

dominus Johannes paparonus legatus pape constituitur et 4
archiepiscopatus et 25 episcopatus in hibernia Sanctus Dionisius
marterizetur 87

1153 3   obitus bernardi (88)

1154 1 3 henricus secundus coronatur anno quo obiit Stephanus / 7
kalendas novembris / et ille henricus filius Imperatricis coronatur
in festo Nativitatis domini   Johannes Evangelista ad dominum
migravit 89

1155
1156

1157 3   obiit adrianus papa successit alexander tercius
1158

1159 3   Thomas Chancellareus factus est archiepiscopus
1160

f. 45^v

1161

1162 3   Imperator f[r]edericus destruxit Mediolanum et archiepiscopus
coloniam transtulit inde corpora 3 Regum qui ante oblati sunt
christo

1163 3   pontificatus sancti thome martiris
1164
1165

1166 3   Nascitur philipus filius lodowici in francia quo anno complentur
830 anni quod Anglici primo venerunt in angliam Et si eis
addentur 161 anni tunc sunt 989 anni quo primo venerunt a
saxonia Ista descriptio facta fuit anno christi 1383

1167 1   obitus beati Johannis Evangeliste
1168

bishops between twenty-two and thirty-four, with four metropolitan sees. See Aubrey
Gwynn, *The Irish Church in the 11th and 12th Centuries* (Dublin 1992), 221–24.

1154 King Stephen died 25 October (VIII Kal. Nov.), and Henry II was crowned 19
December 1154.

1157 Pope Adrian IV died 1 September and Alexander III was elected 7 September
1159.

1159 Thomas Becket was consecrated Archbishop 3 June 1162.

1162 The relics of the Magi, the Three Kings of Cologne, were transferred from Milan
to Cologne by Reinhold von Dassel, archbishop of Cologne, in 1162.

1166 Philip II Augustus, king of France, was born 21 August 1165; cf. Guillaume de
Nangis, *Chronique*, ed. Géraud i.60; *Grandes Chroniques de France*, ed. J. Viard (Societé de
l'histoire de France, 1920–53) (=*GCF*) vi.89. The calculations which follow are obscure:
830 years before 1166 gives the date 336 for the *adventus Saxonum*, whereas below, s.a.
1518, it is given as 454. 161 years after 1166 gives 1327, 991 years, not 989 after 336. None
of these figures relate to 1383, which might however be the year of this flawed calculation
or 'description'.

1169

1170   3   Sanctus thomas passus est tunc Sanctus benedictus / quo anno
           8 Idus Junii henricus 3 rex anglie Juvenis coronatur et hiberniam
           petiit in [mare?] transportato

           1171

1172   Joachim circa hoc tempus / Et dominium anglorum incepit
           in hibernia

1173

1174   1   Reconsiliati sunt pater et filius

1175

1176   3   petrus Comestor moritur secundum quosdam

1177

1178

1179   3   In festo omnium sanctorum aput Reynys coronatur philippus
           rex francie / henrico Rege anglie tunc precente / quo tempore
           grandis reverentia parisie facta fuit mulieri Enide qui non
           comedit in terra sciente gente

1180   2   obito alexandro papa eum successit lucius

1181   3   Sanctus Gilbertus et ordo de symphyngham // Aput Reynis
           corpus domini in sacra altare densit in sanguinem

1182   3   obiit dominus laurencius Archiepiscopus dublinensis / obiit
           henricus tercius rex Jerusalem .3. Idus Junii

1183   3   Petrus commestor moritur secundum alios / Et Salhadinus
           submisit sibi orientem et rehabuit Jerusalem /   in right margin:
           henricus tercius moritur et pater eius / henricus secundus iterum
           regnavit

1184

1179. Enid[e]: Enido

1170 There seems nothing to associate St Benedict with this year or its equivalents in earlier cycles. Henry 'the Young King' was crowned 24 May 1170 (IX Kal. Jun.). He never visited Ireland, but Henry II landed at Waterford on 18 October 1171.

1174 Henry II and his son were reconciled on 30 September 1174.

1179 Philip II of France was crowned 1 November 1179, during his father's lifetime and in the presence of Henry the Young King; cf. Ralph de Diceto, *Imagines Historiarum*, in *Opera Historica* ed. W. Stubbs (RS 1876) i.438–9. The cult of St Alpaidis ('Enide' in this text) is mentioned by Vincent of Beauvais, *Speculum Historiale* xxix.23.

1180 Alexander III died 31 August 1181, and was succeeded by Lucius III on 1 September.

1181 On this miracle see Vincent of Beauvais, *Speculum Historiale* xxix.24.

1182 Lorcán Ua Tuathail, sometimes called Laurentius, archbishop of Dublin, died 14 November 1180. Henry the Young King died 11 June (III Id. Jun.) 1183, but was never king of Jerusalem, an office offered to his father in 1185.

1183 Saladin captured Jerusalem in 1187. Henry III is the title conferred by some contemporaries on Henry the Young King, whose year of death is correctly given here. Henry II's rule had not been interrupted by his son's royal title.

1185 3   Johannes filius Regis venit in hiberniam / obito lucio eum
successit urbanus et baldewynus wigornensis sacratus est Archiepiscopus cantuarie

1186 3   Jerusalem destructa / Sanctus hugo consecratur / quo anno
philippus Rex francie decrevit nullo modo iubas nec premia
dari minimis joculatoribus nec adulatoribus sed pauperibus

1187 3   Natale domini capta fuit a saladino
1188

1189 3   Ricardus Rex coronatur / obiit henricus sponsus Alianore /
Mortuo Coillo successit lucius filius eius quo anno gracie 185
a papa eleutherio baptizatus est mortuo henrico secundo   in
left margin: 3 septembris 1189 coronatur Ricardus Rex et strages
Judeorum Imperator federicus Jerusalem petiit

1190 3   Inceptio ordinis beate virginis in prucia / per alium librum
obiit henricus Rex secundus secundo Nonas Junii et Ricardus
filius eius coronatur   in left margin: 1190 sub celestino papa
tercio ordo sancti dominici   124

1191 3   Ricardus Rex cepit Aconem // hugo Nonant episcopus coven-
trie expulsit monachos a prioratu et introduxit canonicos
seculares

1192 3   hoc anno Rex Ricardus accepit Insulam ciprie et principem
inde secum adduxit vinculis argenteis

f.46

1193 3   hoc anno Ricardus Rex fuit captus per ducem austrie et
deliberatus Imperatori et redemptus per Centum Mille librarum

1193. un[us] deliberat[us]: una deliberata.

1185 Baldwin bishop of Worcester was postulated archbishop of Canterbury on 16
December 1184. His translation but not consecration was recorded in the *Flores Historiarum*
ii.97 s.a. 1185.

1186 Cf. *GCF* vi.153–55. It is not mentioned by Guillaume de Nangis.

1189 Cf. *Historia Regum Britanniae* iv.19. 185 is presumably a mistake for 125, the
equivalent year in the first Easter cycle. On the slaughter of the Jews and the death of
the Emperor Frederick Barbarossa, see *Flores Historiarum* ii.104 and Matthew Paris, *Chronica
Majora* ii.358–59, 364–65.

1190 The Teutonic Order, dedicated to the Blessed Virgin Mary, was founded as a
hospital order before Acre in 1190. Its association with Prussia began only in 1225. Henry
II died 3 September 1189; the Dominican Order was founded in 1215, not under Celestine
III (1191–98).

1191 Cf. *Chronica Majora* ii.380 for the expulsion of the monks from Coventry.

1192 Richard I captured Cyprus in 1191. For his detention of its ruler Isaac Comnenus
see *Chronica Majora* ii.371.

1193 Cf. *Chronica Majora* ii.394–99 for Richard's capture, ransom and subsequent
taxation.

et calices arg*entei* si fu*erit* .2. *in* eccle*s*ia un[us] deliberat[us]
fuit et mo*n*achi cister*cienses* vendideru*n*t libr*os* suos p*ro*
redimendo ip*sum*

1194 3 (Ri*car*dus *primus* rex Angli*e* accep*it* Ins*ulam* cypri *et* vicit
Rege*m et* domin*os* *inde et* rediit in angl*iam*) error no*t*a i*n* fine
alt*erius* lat*er*is

1195
1196 3 (Ri*car*dus Rex capi*tur* p*er* duce*m* Austr*ie et* redimi*tur* 100000
libr*is* sterling*is*)

1197 3 hoc a*n*no R*e*x Ri*car*dus ven*it* in angli*am et* accep*it* castr*um* de
Notyngham *et* disher*edita*vit Johanne*m* fr*atrem suum et* iter*um*
fuit coronat*us* ap*ut* Wynchest*er* / Et Will*elmus* cum longa
barba h*er*eticu*s* fuit dampn*atus* sus*pensus et* tr*actus*

1198 3 ffundacio ord*inis* (*predicatorum*) <*sancti* tri*n*itat*is*> secundu*m*
quosda*m* / (alio li*bro* sub Inno*cencio terci*o ordo francisci) R*ex*
Ri*car*dus transivit in norma*n*iam *et* fuga*v*it R*e*gem fr*ancie*

1199 3 Ri*car*d*us* Rex inter*f*icitur <7 Id*us* ap*rilis*> *et* Joha*n*nes frater
ei*us* corona*tur* in die as*c*ensione do*m*ini *et* p*er*di*it* Norma*n*iam
et Andegaviam *et* a*ccep*it ab om*n*i caruca anglie 3 sol*idos*

1200 3 Ob*iit* hugo de lyncolnia / hoc a*n*no R*e*x Joha*n*nes tenuit
p*ar*liamentu*m et* petiit a clero exten*t*a b*e*n*e*ficia p*ro* a*n*no
et reacqui*re*ret Norma*n*iam *et* Andegaviam / ob*iit* hub*ertus*
Ar*ch*iepi*s*copus cantua*r*iensis c*ui* successit Stepha*n*us langton
/ Et ap*ut* vit*er*biam p*er* papa*m* co*n*secratur

1201 3 XXXV p*ro*bi ele*cti* Jure ad manutenenda*m* ass*is*am

1202 3 Rothomag*us* capi*tur* per philippu*m* Regem ffranc*ie* cum
residuo Normanie q*ue* ducat*us* stetit in manib*us* Rollonis
dani p*er* 315 annos // Et a*n*nus pluvios*us* to*n*itruosus gran-
di*n*os*us* vin*e*a *et* blada destr*uc*ta in angl*ia* cum corbell*is*
volacit*er* p*er* aera cum carbon*ib*us ig*n*it*is* combur*endo* plures
domos

1197 Richard I returned to England on 13 March 1194. He was crowned a second
time at Winchester, after his reduction of Nottingham Castle, on 17 April. William
FitzOsbert (*cum barba*) was condemned and hanged, as a demagogue but not as a heretic,
in 1196.

1198 The Trinitarian order was founded by St John of Matha and St Felix of Valois
in 1198.

1199 Richard I died 6 April (VIII Id. Apr.) 1199. King John was crowned on 27 May
(Ascension Day). On John's taxation see *Chronica Majora* ii.461, s.a. 1200.

1200 St Hugh bishop of Lincoln died 16 November 1200. The other events in this
entry are displaced from 1205; cf. *Chronica Majora* ii.490, 514–15.

1201 Cf. *Chronica Majora* ii.480–1, s.a. 1202, the Assize of Bread, where however the
thirty-five *probi* are not mentioned.

1202 Rouen and the rest of Normandy were occupied by Philip II of France in 1204.
The calculation of 315 years since Rollo's original conquest implies that it took place in
887.

1203 3 Normania tota cum civitatibus villis et castris subjugatur Regi francie // quarterium frumenti pro xv shillinges et sistema vini pro 4 *solidos*

1204 3 Interdicitur anglia in uno libro // 2ᵉ <plene>{lunio} vise fuerunt in celo / Et incepit ordo predicatorum Sancti dominici / E[t] glacies a circumsicione ad annunciacionem dominicam

1205 3 (3 Sanctus dominicus / secundum alios incepit ordinem predicatorum) <sunt veri> / quo anno perdebatur omnino Normania et proclamatur Interdictio regni

1206 3 Conversio sancti ffrancisci inceptor ordinis minorum   *in right margin*: Introitus henrici in sarum ad axonum die 13 / hora 18 / minuta 14 / secundo 0 / tercio 6 marcij

1207 3 Henricus filius Johannis Nascitur / Et langeton consecratur

1208 3 Interdicitur Anglia in alio libro

1209 3 Rex Johannes venit in hiberniam et eiecit filium hugonis de lacy (Et) in alio libro Nativitas filii eius henrici   et Relaxatio interdicti / In alio libro hoc anno interdicitur tota anglia nullo obstante privilegio / fundacio Ecclesie beate Marie de Overey   *in right margin*: hoc anno primus maior londonie fuit Henricus filius aldewyni et petrus duke et thomas Neele vicecomites

1210

1211 3 (ffundacio ecclesie beate) Marie de Overey   Relaxacio interdicti anglie   Et inceptio pontis londonie

1212

1206. inceptor: *shd. be* inceptoris

1203 Cf. *Chronica Majora* ii.482–3, not mentioning however the price of corn.

1204 The interdict was not pronounced until 24 March 1208. *Chronica Majora* ii.488 mentions a lunar eclipse; two moons are reported in 1106 (ii.132). On the foundation of the Dominican order see the notes to John Somer's Chronicle above s.a. 1205. The frost said here to have lasted from 1 January to 2 February (1205) was reported in *Chronica Majora* ii.490 to have occurred from 14 January to 22 March.

1205 On the interdict and the Dominican order see the note to 1204 above.

1206 Henry III was born 1 October 1207. The precision of this and other records of births suggests that the scribe had an interest in plotting nativities.

1209 These events seem to be displaced from 1210; cf. *Chronica Majora* ii.528, where it is reported that John's excommunication became generally known in that year, and ii.529–30, where John's arrival in Ireland on 8 July and his expulsion of Hugh de Lacy are recorded. Hugh, who had been made earl of Ulster in 1205 or before, was the son of another Hugh de Lacy, lord of Meath. The interdict was not relaxed until 1214. St Mary Overy had been founded in 1106; it was burnt down in the fire of 1212, and rebuilt in and after 1215. Henry fitzAilwyn had been mayor or the equivalent since about 1192; he died in 1212. Thomas FitzNeel and Peter le Duc were sheriffs in 1208.

1211 On St Mary Overy see the note on 1209 above. On the burning of London Bridge see *Chronica Majora* ii.536, s.a. 1212.

1213 3 Joh*ann*es Rex obtulit d*omin*o *et* S*anct*o petro *et* Innoc*encio* pape
Reg*num* angl*ie et* pr*o*misit 1000 m*a*rc*as* p*er* ann*um* 800 p*ro*
anglia *et* 200 p*ro* hib*er*n*i*a. discordia int*er* Rege*m et* baron*es*
et philipp*um* fili*us* R*egis fra*nc*ie* trans*ii*t uultr*a* mare *et* d*omin*us
R*ex* Joh*ann*is cum ex*er*citu eu*n*t contra eu*m* ad bramdoune

1214 3 Relaxacio int*er*d*ic*ti *in* alio libro / lodowic*us* fili*us* philippe
R*egis* fr*an*cie h*ab*uit victoria*m* contr*a* Joh*ann*em R*egem* anglie
/ Joh*ann*es Rex angl*ie* cruce sign*atur* / Destr*uc*tio castr*i*
baynardi   Incep*tio* ord*inis* s*anc*ti francisci min*orum* Et *in* *f*esto
gord*iani et* ep*im*achi baron*es* intraver*unt* civ*i*tatem london*ie et*
exulaver*unt* Roger*um* fili*um* alani *et* fec*er*u*n*t ser*l*onem le m*er*cer
maiorem

1215 3 d*omin*us Rex transfrettavit in vig*ili*a pur*ific*ationis v*er*sus pic-
tavia*m* / 3 R*egis* Joh*ann*is 18 a*n*no sui reg*n*o in crastin*o* S*anc*ti
luce dec*esit et* tran*s*l*atur* Wigorn*i*am

1216 3 Rex Joh*ann*es ob*ii*t Et h*en*ricus t*er*cius fili*us* ei*us* unct*us* *e*st (et
coronatur) glov*er*nie <in die s*anc*t*i*s simonis e[t] Jude> (*et*
gwallam legat*um* p*a*pe honorij t*er*c*ü* cum fuit 9 a*n*nor*um* *et* 4
ebd*om*ador*um* etat*i*s qui iter*um* coronabatur Westm*o*nasterie ab
arch*ie*p*is*c*o*po c*an*tuar*i*ensi Steph*en*o Langton a*n*no chris*ti* 1[21]9

1217 3 pax f*ac*tum fuit int*er* R*e*ges angl*ie et* ffranc*ie*

1218 3 Sanctus Will*e*lm*us* de Bourg canoniz*atur* // Hoc a*n*no Wallia
int*er*d*ic*ta fu*i*t / *et* m*o*nachi gallie qu*i* ven*er*u*n*t ad lodowicum
fil*ium* philippe R*egis* ff[rancie] in mare fuer*unt* capti   Et
Eustachi*us* eor*um* pr*in*c*i*p*a*lis decollat*us* fuit p*er* hub*er*tum
borgh *et* custodes 5 portuu*m* / Et lodowic*us* relic*tus* *e*st in

1218. Regis ff[rancie]: Text runs off right edge of page.

1213 Cf. *Chronica Majora* ii.544–6, where John's charter of resignation is quoted in full.
The terms of the payment specified 700 marks for England and 300 for Ireland. On
Philip II's plan to invade England and John's muster at Barham Down, Kent see *ibid.*
ii.538–9.

1214 On the interdict see note to 1209 above. Castle Baynard was destroyed on 14
January 1213; the invasion of Louis of France took place in 1216. Serlo le Mercer was
installed as mayor of London on 10 May; cf. Arnold FitzThedmar, *Liber de Antiquis Legibus*,
ed. T. Stapleton (Camden Society 1846), 4. The Franciscan order was approved in 1215.
There is no contemporary authority for King John's taking the cross.

1215 John set sail for Poitou on 9 February 1214. He died at Newark on 19 October
(the morrow of St Luke's Day) 1216.

1216 Henry III's second coronation took place in May 1220.

1217 The peace of Kingston was signed on 12 September 1217 and ratified at Lambeth
on 20 September.

1218 'St William de Bourg' may be a confused form of St William of York (*de Eboraco*),
who was canonized in 1227. There seems no authority for an alleged interdict in Wales
at this time. The death of Eustace the monk, on which cf. *Chronica Majora* iii.28–29, took
place on 24 August 1217. Louis of France received 4000 marks under the peace of
Kingston, though no chronicler records it; see D. A. Carpenter, *The Minority of Henry III*
(London 1990), 45.

*fra*ncia *et* h*a*buit mille marc*os* per qu*arterium*

1219 3 a*nno tercio* h*en*r*ici tercii* / pl*u*res barones capti f*uerunt* ap*u*t lincoln*iam* / et d*ominus* R*ex* h*a*buit ab *omni* caruca reg*ni* 2 s*olidos* Et in eodem a*n*no fuit tr*an*sla*cio* S*an*cti (Edward*i*) thome

1220 3 h*en*ricus Rex corona*tur* ap*u*t Westm*onasterium* / Tr*an*slac*io* S*an*cti Thome / Ecclesia Sar*um* funda*tur* / O*bitus* S*an*cti Edm*undi* ar*c*hiep*iscop*i

1221 3 In al*io* l*ib*ro transla*c*io S*an*cti thome

1222 3 S*an*ctus dom*i*nicus obiit

1223 3 hoc a*n*no baldewyn*us* p*or*tav*it* an*te* se un*am* {crucem} q*ui*a be*a*ta Elena fec*it* et un*us* presb*ite*r an*g*licus no*mi*nat*us* hugo borgh' eod*em* tem*pore* adduxit ad bromholm et obcessio castri bedferd*i* in*ter* ascensionem do*mi*n*i et* assum*p*cionem be*a*te v*ir*ginis Et ince*p*tio ord*in*is carmelitar*um* Vent*us* ter*ri*bil*is* cum draco*n*ibus in aere

1224 3 h*en*ricus Rex cep*it* castr*um* de bedford / Minores venerunt in angli*am et* tu*n*c i*n*gress*i* sunt oxon*ie* / in f*es*to s*an*cti bartho*lo*mei

f. 46ᵛ

1225 3 persecut*io* Jud*eorum* London*ie* p*er* suggestione*m* Walt*er*i Bok-erell Item q*uo*d const*an*tin*us* fili*us* Arnulfi i*n* cr*a*stino assum*p*-t*ion*is v*ir*ginis fuit i*n*terfect*us* et eodem a*n*no R*ex* p*ro*posuit frang*ere* muros civ*itatis*

1226 3 O*bitus* be*a*ti fr*an*cisci o*bitus* lodowici R*egis* francie in veter*e* l*ib*ro

1227 3 O*bitus* lodowici R*egis* fr*an*cie / funda*t*io carmelitar*um* ordin*is*

1228 3 O*bitus* Steph*an*i de lang*ton* / Et nove decre*tales* com*p*ilate sunt

1229

1219 The battle of Lincoln took place on 24 May 1217. The carucage of 2s. a plough was levied in 1220. The translation of Thomas Becket, given variously here in 1219 (and cancelled), 1220 and 1221, took place, as John Somer's Chronicle correctly has it, in 1220.

1221 See the note on 1219 above.

1224 The arrival of the Franciscans in England on St Bartholomew's Day (August 24), though not in Thomas of Eccleston's *De adventu fratrum minorum in Angliam*, is given in the *Lanercost Chronicle*, ed. J. Stevenson (Bannatyne Club, Edinburgh 1839) i.31.

1225 These events are displaced from 1222. Walter Bukerel's instigation of a persecution of the Jews is mentioned in *Annales Londonienses* in *Chronicles of the Reigns of Edward I and Edward II*, ed. W. Stubbs (RS 1882) i.24. The alderman Constantine FitzAlulf was hanged for sedition in 1222, after riots beginning on 1 August; cf. *Chronica Majora* iii.72–3. His death on 16 August is recorded in *Annales Londonienses* i.24, but neither source mentions the threat to break the London walls.

1226 Louis VIII, king of France died 8 November 1226.

1230

1231 3   *obitus* Sancti Anthonii

1232

1233

1234 3   Comes marescallus interficitur et Sanctus Edmundus consecratur

1235 3   Magna caristia in acquitania

1236 3   In francia magna siccitas a dominica proxima post festum Nativitatis domini usque ad exaltacionem Sancti crucis et tunc cecidit in pluvia lapis habendus in passionem crucis et in eo scripto Jhesu nazarenus rex Judeorum aput cleremont

1237

1238

1239 3   Rex Edwardus natus est 14 kalendas Julii

1240 1   Lucius munivit francesias et libertates ecclesiarum et specialiter Westmonasterii

1241 3   Obitus Sancti Edwardi cui apparuit IHC Nazarenus per nomen scriptum in fronte parisie (177)

1242 1   (lucius munivit franchesias et libertates ecclesiarum et specialiter Westmonasterii) lucius munivit franchesias ecclesiarum anglie 177

1243 3   Henricus tercius Rex (intravit in Vasconiam) / et reveniebat in angliam. Innocencius papa consecratus contra voluntatem Imperatoris henricus tercius (redivit) intravit Vasconiam circa festum Sancti Michaelis / Ricardus comes duxit in uxorem sororem Regine anglie

1244

1245

1246 3   terre motus perhorribilis fuit in hibernia

1247 3   terre motus 10 kalendas marcii

1248 3   Et alius 10 kalendas Januarii / Escambium monete <factum

---

1235 Cf. *Chronica Majora* iii.305.

1236 Cf. Guillaume de Nangis, *Chronique*, ed. Géraud i.187. There is no obvious source for the reported miracle at Clermont.

1240 Cf. *Historia Regum Britanniae* v.1; *Flores Historiarum* i.146–7.

1241 This is one of the miracles ascribed to St Edmund of Abingdon by Matthew Paris; see C. H. Lawrence, *The Life of St Edmund by Matthew Paris* (Stroud 1996), 120–21. He died 16 November 1240.

1242 See the note to 1240 above.

1243 Henry III landed in Gascony on 19 May 1242, and returned to England on 9 October 1243. Innocent IV was elected on 25 June 1243 with the initial approval of the Emperor Frederick II. Richard earl of Cornwall married Sancha of Provence on 22 November 1243.

1246 An earthquake in Ireland and Wales is mentioned in the *Annals of Inisfallen*, ed. S. MacAirt (Dublin 1951), 353 s.a. 1248 (corrected from 1249).

1248 Richard of Cornwall's attempt to use the new coinage is mentioned in *Chronica Majora* v.18–19.

per Ricardum comitem> / Rex francie intravit in partes
transmarinas

1249

1250 3   longspe occisus est

1251 3   Pastores collium in maximo numero fecerunt enormia et
          dixerunt quod transirent ultramare . burgenses Auriolanenses
          interfecerunt eorum magistrum et discipati sunt

1252 3   Obitus frederici Imperatoris / Magna discordia parisius inter
          religiosos et clericos

1253 3   Obitus Sancti Ricardi et Roberti grossetest

1254 3   bonefacius archiepiscopus fecit primam visitacionem / Et Hoc
          anno transfretavit henricus Rex in Vasconiam

1255
1256

f. 47

1257 3   Magna fames in Anglia

1258 3   providencia Oxonie Et dedicacio ecclesie Sarum

1259
1260
1261

1262 3   Reversio Iodowici Regis ffrancie a terra sancta et maritavit
          Philippum filium Isabelle filie Regis Arragonie

1263 2   Obitus venerabilis bede presbyteri

          1264 3   bellum de lewys die {mercurie} post festum sancti
          dunstani

1265 1 3 bellum de Ewesham die {martis} post festum sancti petri ad
          vincula. et eodem anno pax reclamata et ottobonus legatus
          intravit in angliam circa festum beate marie

1266 1 3 Karolus comes andegavie habuit bellum contra Malemfrey

1251 Cf. Guillaume de Nangis, *Chronique*, ed. Géraud i.207–8, *GCF* vii. 162–65 and
Chronica Majora v.246–52; the leader of the Pastoureaux was killed at Bourges.

1252 On the quarrel of secular and regular masters at the University of Paris cf.
Chronica Majora v.416–7.

1254 Boniface of Savoy, archbishop of Canterbury, made his first visitation in 1250;
cf. *Chronica Majora* v.119–27. Henry III sailed for Gascony on 6 August.

1262 The return of Louis IX has been displaced from 1254; cf. Guillaume de Nangis,
Chronique, ed. Géraud i.209; GCF vii.175–8. For the marriage of the future Philip III to
Isabella, daughter of James I king of Aragon on 28 May 1262 cf. GCF vii.226–7.

1264 The battle of Lewes was fought on Wednesday 14 May, not Wednesday 21 May
as implied here.

1265 The date here for the battle of Evesham (4 August) is correct. The legate
Ottobuono arrived in England on 29 October, not on any of the Marian feasts.

1266 Manfred, son of the emperor Frederick II, was killed at the battle of Benevento
on 26 February 1266. On Lucius and Severus cf. *Historia Regum Britanniae* v.1–2.

fil*ium* ffred*er*ici Imper*ator*i*s* ci*r*ca reg*na* Cicilie *et* Napulie.
Ob*üt* luci*us et* rema*n*sit reg*num* sine Rege us*que* adventu*s*
severi   201

1267   1   Severu*s* ve*n*it *et* regnavit   202
1268
1269   3   Rex lodowicu*s* cu*m* 3 filiis acce*p*it cruce*m* ad eund*um secund-*
*a*rio ad t*e*rram sa*n*cta*m*
1270   1 3   Mori*tur* ille lodowic*us et* phi*lipp*us filiu*s* eiu*s* succe*ssit* in reg*num*
fra*n*ci*e*. Et fames *et* pest*ilencia* in hib*er*nia. Et coronat*ur* ille
phi*lipp*us in die m*edie* augusti ap*ut* renys. Severu*s* fec*it* mur*um*
a mari us*que* ad mare   205
1271   3   henricu*s* rex ob*üt*. Severu*s* interemptu*s* e*st*. Et dux brito*num*
ffulgentiu*s* letalit*er* vuln*e*ratur. Qui severu*s* ha*b*uit 2 filios
vi*delicet* Getam *et* bassianu*m*. Geta int*er*fecto r*e*gnavit bassianu*s*
1272   3   Symon Comes de Montfort Int*er*imitur. Ob*üt* henricu*s* 3us
1273   3   Ed*w*ardus Rex fili*us* R*e*gi*s* h*e*nrici coronat*ur* 14 die *septem*bri*s*
1274   3   Consilium gen*er*ale. Ed*w*ardus 3us coronat*ur*
1275   3   t*e*rre mot*us* in *septem*bri. phi*lipp*us Rex nupsit maria*m* fili*am*
duci*s* brita*n*nie
1276   3   senior fili*us* di*cti* phi*lipp*i nom*in*e lodowicu*s* mori*tur*
1277   3   ob*üt* Ed*w*ardus 3us in vig*ilia* S*an*cti albani
1278   1 3   pecha*m* ar*chi*epi*scopus* creat*ur*. bassianu*s* interemitur   213
1279   3   Escambiu*m* monete. q*uo* a*n*no Judei su*s*pensi *et* de*tr*acti *pro*
tra*n*smu*tacione* mo*n*et*e*. Inhibitio *contra* Religiosos ne pos-
*s*essio*n*e*s* acq*ui*er*er*ent
1280   3   statuit*ur* q*uo*d religiosi no*n* ema*n*t t*e*rras
1281   3   civ*i*tas de acon capta fuit de sarace*n*is

1269 Louis IX's last crusade was directed against Tunis.
    1270 Cf. Guillaume de Nangis, *Chronique*, ed. Géraud i.240, s.a. 1271; *GCF* viii.38–39.
Philip III was crowned about 15 August 1271. An Irish famine is mentioned in the *Annals
of Inisfallen*, ed. MacAirt 371, s.a. 1271 (corrected from 1272). On the wall cf. *Historia Regum
Britanniae* v.2.
    1271 Cf. *ibid.* v.2.
    1272 Simon, son of Simon de Montfort earl of Leicester died in 1271 near Siena;
Henry III died 16 November 1272.
    1273 Edward I was crowned 19 August 1274.
    1275 Philip III married his second wife Mary, daughter of Henry III duke of Brabant,
on 21 August 1274; cf. Guillaume de Nangis, *Chronique*, ed. Géraud i.245; *GCF* viii.49–50.
    1276 Cf. *ibid.* i.247.
    1277 Edward III died 21 June (St Alban's Eve) 1377. The entry has been displaced by
a century.
    1278 Cf. *Historia Regum Britanniae* v.3.
    1279 Cf. *Flores Historiarum* iii.52 for penalties against debasers of the coinage; the
inhibicio refers to the Statute of Mortmain (1279) s.a. 1278.
    1280 Cf. The note on the entry for 1279 above; in *Flores Historiarum* iii.53 the Statute
of Mortmain was noted s.a. 1280.
    1281 Acre fell to the Mameluke sultan al A_s_hraf in 1291.

1282 3 Isto a*nno* Rex E*dwardus* diffidebat Regi fr*a*ncie. Neulin*us* fili*us* gr*i*ffini obsidebat castr*um* de Rotheland 9 Kl apr*i*lis *et* vi kl Maii a*m*motu*s* fuit

1283 3 Guydo comes fflandr*ie* sursu*m* reddi*t* R*egi* ffr*a*ncie fide*m* *et* homag*ium* *et* fu*it* ta*m* mag*na* Inunda*c*io in *decembri* q*uod* 2 pontes p*a*ris*ius* fracti fueru*nt* Ort*us* guerr*e* in vasconia

1284 1 3 In alio li*br*o h*oc* a*nno* nat*us* fu*it* E*dwardus* filius R*egis* E*dwardi*. Calixt*us* p*ap*a co*n*stitu*it* jejun*ia* *quattuor* te*mporum* pro te*m*pe*r*ie aere fr*umentorum* copia 219

1285 3 E*dwardus* fili*us* R*egis* nat*us* in die Sanc*ti* Marci

1286 3 transfr*etavit* E*dwardus* R*ex* in ffr*a*nc*ia* pro *concordiam* faci*endo* int*er* R*egem* fr*a*ncie ex p*a*rte una et R*egem* arragonie <ex alia> et hispan*os*

1287 3 comes de bar q*ui* nupsit fili*am* R*egis* angl*ie* devasta*vit* cam-p*a*ni*am.* cano*n*iza*tur* S*anctus* lodowic*us*

1288 3 Nich*olaus* 4^{tus} creatur. Origenes. S*ancta* Cecilia

f. 47^{v}

1289 3 p*ap*a bonefaci*us* fec*it* pace*m* int*er* Reges A*n*glie *et* ffr*a*ncie *et* ordi*na*vit Rege*m* angl*ie* nub*ere* Margrat sorore*m* R*egis* ffr*a*ncie in uxore*m* in sig*no* fed*er*is *et* amor*is.* 2 Id*us* aug*usti* rediit E*dwardus* R*ex* in anglia a p*a*r*t*tib*us* vasco*n*ie

1290 3 Regina ux*or* ob*iit* v*idelicet* Alianora v*idelicet* 4 kl. *decembri*s uxor E*dwardi* fil*ii* R*egis* H*e*nrici. et c*ir*ca f*estu*m omni*um* s*anc*torum exiliu*m* Judeor*um.* S*anc*ta cecilia martiriza*tur* *et* canoniza*tur*

1282 The defiance of Edward I probably refers to the deprivation of his French lands by Philip IV in 1294, reported in *Flores Historiarum* iii.87 shortly after the account of the fall of Acre. In *Flores* iii.56 the beginning of the siege of Rhuddlan is dated to the night of Palm Sunday (22–23 March), not 24 March as stated here.

1283 This appears to be displaced from 1297; cf. *Flores Historiarum* iii.106–7, and for the most likely source, Guillaume de Nangis, *Chronique*, ed. Géraud i.296–7, 311–12, and *GCF* vii.169–70, 188–9. The war in Gascony began in 1294.

1284 Edward II was born 25 April 1284. 220 is the equivalent year of the first Easter cycle; on the fasts established by Pope Callistus I see *Flores Historiarum* i.152, from which the wording is abbreviated.

1286 Edward I left England on 23 May 1286. For his mission, cf. *Flores Historiarum* iii.64–5.

1287 The raid of Henry III, count of Bar into Champagne took place in 1297; cf. Guillaume de Nangis, *Chronique*, ed. Géraud i.298; *GCF* viii.172–3. For his marriage to Eleanor, daughter of Edward I see *Flores Historiarum* iii.86. Louis IX was canonized in 1297.

1289 The first part of this entry is displaced. Pope Boniface VIII's arbitration award was sealed on 30 June 1298, and Edward I married Margaret of France on 4 September 1299. He had returned from Gascony on 12 August 1289.

1290 The Jews were expelled by an edict of 18 July.

1291 3 Regina mater obiit. Galfridus de clare filius nascitur. Acon destruitur

1292 3 Pecham archiepiscopus obiit. Expulsio Judeorum

1293 3 Inchoacio discordie inter reges anglie et ffrancie. bellum navale inter anglos et Normannos

1294 3 philippus Rex francie hoc anno per li[tem] ve[xativam] habuit seisinam in vasconia

1295 3 ultima guerra in wallia

1296 3 Scocie subjugacio

1297 3 capcio berwici et donbarre. combustio in westmonasterio. bellum de ffaukirk

1298 3 In cimiterio Sancti pauli occisi fuerunt 16

1299 3 In alio libro ea qui scribuntur de pape ordinanciis circa jurisdiccionem et concordiam regnorum hoc anno est. et 4 id. septembris Rex anglie duxit in uxorem Margaretam sororem philippi Regis ffrancie aput cantuariam.

1300 3 Insurreccio brugensium contra Jacobum de Sancto Paulo et omnes francigene cum eo ipso excepto fuerunt interempti quo anno totus quasi mundus occidentalis visitavit limina appostolorum

1301 3 descensio maxima inter papam bonefacium et philippum Regem ffrancie, annus Jubileus

1302 3 Comes dartoys cum magno numero francorum occiduntur per fflandrenses prope tournay

1303

1304 3 bertrandus archiepiscopus burdugalis electus est in papam clementem 5^m

1305

1293 The battle off Cap St-Mathieu was fought on 15 May 1293.

1294 Gascony was confiscated by Philip IV, king of France on 19 May 1294. The expansion given here for *li ve* is speculative.

1297 The fire at Westminster occurred on 29 March 1298, and the battle of Falkirk on 22 July. Cf. *Flores Historiarum* iii.104.

1298 There seems no obvious source for this episode.

1299 See the note on the entry for 1289 above. The marriage was celebrated in Canterbury as stated here.

1300 The rising of the citizens of Bruges against James, son of Guy III, count of St-Pol and governor of Flanders for Philip IV, occurred on 17 May 1302; cf. *Annales Gandenses*, ed. H. Johnstone (London 1951), 23–25. The remainder of the entry refers to the celebration of the Jubilee in Rome in 1300.

1301 The quarrel of Philip IV and Boniface VIII began in December 1301. On the Jubilee see the note on the entry for 1300 above.

1302 Robert II count of Artois was killed at the battle of Courtrai, about fifteen miles from Tournai, on 11 July.

1304 Bertrand de Got, Pope Clement V, was elected on 5 June 1305.

1306 3 Expulsio Judeorum a francia. Institucio nove solempnitatis corporis Cristi

1307 3 Obiit Edwardus. Et Edwardus 2us simul uxoratur <bolonie> et coronatur <Westmonasterie die I in festo sancti Mathie apostoli> . destruccio templariorum quorum possessiones date fuerunt hospitillariis

1308 3 Eleccio per papam Clementem henrici comitis de luxenbourgh in Imperatorem. Obiit Nonas Julii Rex Edwardus primus. Edwardus 2us duxit in uxorem filiam Regis lodowici francie et eodem anno coronatur per Episcopum Wyntonie

1309 3 Isto anno in alia cronica destructi sunt templarii

1310 3 Thamisia congelata. philippus omnium Imperator primus efficitur Cristianus)

1311 3 aput dartyngtone capcio petri de Gavestone comitis Cornubie, et eadem mense decollatus aput gaversage prope Warwick. (philippus omnium Imperator primus efficitur Cristianus)

1312 3 Causton decollatur, Nativitas Edwardi 3 13 die novembris

1313 3 unus cardinalis portavit Indulgencias maximas in ffranciam. Et Rex philippus fecit 3 filios milites in presencia Edwardi Regis anglie et acceperunt {crucem} ut venerent contra sarazenos. Et 4 milites sunt destructi pro adulterio videlicet Walterus et philippus davey

1306 Cf. the continuation of Guillaume de Nangis, *Chronique*, ed. Géraud i.355. The entry on the Corpus Christi feast probably refers to the promulgation of the decree making it universal in the *Clementina* (*Si Dominum*, Tit.3.16.1), the decretals collected by Clement V but only published by John XXII in 1317.

1307 Edward II was married to Isabella, daughter of Philip IV at Boulogne on 25 January 1308, and both of them were anointed and crowned at Westminster on Quinquagesima Sunday, 25 February (which was also, as 1308 was a Leap Year, the feast of St Matthias). The French Templars were arrested and their property seized on 13 October; cf. the continuation of Guillaume de Nangis, *Chronique*, ed. Géraud i.365; *GCF* viii.256-7.

1308 Henry count of Luxemburg was elected King of the Romans on 27 November 1308 and styled Henry VII, though he was not strictly Emperor before his coronation in Rome on 29 June 1312. On the remainder of the entry see the note to 1307 above; Louis X was brother, not father of Queen Isabella. On Edward II's coronation see *Flores Historiarum* iii.141-2, including the leading role of Henry Woodlark, bishop of Winchester.

1309 See the note on the entry for 1307 above.

1310 Cf. *Flores Historiarum* iii.146. The equivalent year in the first Easter cycle was 246; the Emperor Philip the Arab (244-49) was reputed to have been Christian.

1311 Piers Gaveston, earl of Cornwall surrendered at Scarborough to Aymer, earl of Pembroke on 19 May 1312, was taken by Guy, earl of Warwick at Deddington, Oxfordshire on 10 June, who had him beheaded at Gaversike near Warwick on 19 June; cf. *Flores Historiarum* iii.151-2.

1313 Cf. the continuation of Guillaume de Nangis, *Chronique*, ed. Géraud i.395-6, 404-6; *GCF* viii.288, 297-8. The two adulterous knights (four is evidently a mistake) were Gautier and Philippe d'Aunoy.

1314 3   comes gloucestrie interfectus in Scotia et plures capti cum
           confusione. et Episcopus Cantuarie in festo sancti Johannis
           baptiste

1315 3   Inundacio talis in francia quod per biennium destruxit sal
           vinum et bladum.

1316 3   Moritur lodowicus. sabbato post pentecostem cui successit
           philippus frater eius. Caristia per 3^{ennium} ab hinc inclusive et
           obiit Elizabet de bohunn comitissa hereford 3 Nonas Maii

1317 3   Robertus bruys cum scotis intravit hiberniam et anno post
           interemptus

1318 3   Post quadragesimam caristia vini et bladi fuit in (hibernia)
           francia per 2 annos . autem circa pentecostem copia creavit[?]
           ut per vilitatem

1319

1320 3   Collacio pastorum et ignobilium et dixerunt quod transmeaverunt
           et subito mutarunt proprium et transcenderunt vias suas

f. 48

1321 3   Thomas lancastrie occiditur. Omnes leprosi acquitanie fuerunt
           combusti. Rex philippus moritur et karolus frater eius coronatur.
           Scoti vicerunt in conflictu anglos

1322 3   decollacio comitis lancastrie in alio libro et obiit comes Herfordie
1323
1324 3   circa hec tempora Karolus magnus Et alquinus doctor anglicus

1314 Robert Winchelsey, archbishop of Canterbury died 11 May 1313.

1315 Cf. the continuation of Guillaume de Nangis, *Chronique*, ed. Géraud i.421–2.

1316 Louis X, king of France died on Saturday 5 June 1316. His brother Philip V only
succeeded after the four days' reign of Louis X's posthumous son John I, which ended
on 19 November. Edward II's sister Elizabeth, countess of Hereford died 10 June 1317,
not 5 May as stated here; cf. *Annales Paulini*, ed. W. Stubbs in *Chronicles of the Reign of
Edward I and Edward II* (RS 1882–3) i.279.

1317 Robert Bruce, king of Scotland arrived in Ireland in support of his brother
Edward in the spring of 1317. The attempt to establish Edward as king of Ireland ended
with his death in October 1318.

1318 Cf. the continuation of Guillaume de Nangis, *Chronique*, ed. Géraud, ii.12; GCF
viii.341–2. The reading *creavit* is uncertain.

1320 Cf. the continuation of Guillaume de Nangis, *Chronique* ed. Géraud ii.25–28.

1321 Cf. *ibid.* ii.31–32; *GCF* viii.357–8. Philip V died 3 January 1322; his brother
Charles IV was crowned 21 February. The Scots defeated the English forces near Byland
in Yorkshire on 14 October 1321.

1322 Thomas earl of Lancaster was beheaded on 22 March 1322. Humphrey earl of
Hereford was killed at the battle of Boroughbridge on 16 March.

1325 3 Regina angli*e* cu*m* E*dwardo* filio suo seniori i*n*tr*a*vit fr*a*nci*am* p*ro* tr*a*ctatu pac*is*. Quo a*nno* capi*tur* Comes flandrie p*er* co*m*mun*e*s

1326 3 Hugo de Spe*n*s*er et* fili*us* evisc*er*ati su*s*pensi de col*lo et* qua*r*tizati. O*büt* E*dwardus* 2ᵘˢ <depo*s*itus 25 Januarii> cui successit E*dwardus* 3ᵘˢ In vig*ilia* pur*ificacionis* coronatur

1327 3 Karolus Rex ff*r*anc*ie* mori*tur* in vigilia pur*ificacionis*. decolla*cio* pa*tris et* fili*i videlicet hugonis* de spens*er*

1328 1 Laurenci*us* 264. R*ex* ph*i*l*i*pp*us* de valoys coronat*ur et* in festo s*a*nc*te* kat*er*ine restituit lodowyc*um* Comit*em* ffl*a*ndr*ie* in Co*m*itatu*m*

1329 3 h*oc* anno orta *e*s*t* guerra int*er* Reges angl*ie et* ff*r*anc*ie* p*ro* ducatu acq*ui*tanie

1330

1331

1332

1333

1334

1335

1336

1337

1338 3 Rex E*dwardus* fecit guerra*m contra* p*hilippum* R*egem* ff*r*anc*ie et* misit obsidione*m* ad Cambray

1339

1340 3 R*ex* angl*ie* E*dwardus* in ffl*a*ndria ap*ut* lysle fugavit francos *et* dux brit*a*nnie mori*tur*

1341

1342 3 Godefrid*us* harcou*r*t fugit in angl*iam et* fuit ban*n*itus an*te* a

1325 Queen Isabella crossed to France early in March 1325, and her son Edward on 12 September. Louis of Nevers, count of Flanders was captured by the men of Bruges on 2 May. Cf. the continuation of Guillaume de Nangis, *Chronique*, ed. Géraud ii.60–62; *GCF* ix.41–42, 47.

1326 Hugh, Lord Despenser the elder was executed on 27 October; his son Hugh the Younger on 24 November. Edward II was deposed on 20 January 1327 and murdered on 21 September.

1327 Charles IV, king of France died on 1 February 1328.

1328 Philip VI, king of France was crowned 29 May. The feast of St Catherine was 25 November. Cf. The continuation of Guillaume de Nangis, *Chronique*, ed. Géraud ii.91–2, 97–103; *GCF* ix.81–82; 99–104.

1329 On the question of homage for Edward III's French territories cf. the continuation of Guillaume de Nangis, *Chronique*, ed. Géraud ii.107–8.

1338 This probably refers to Edward III's invasion of France in September 1339; he began to besiege Cambrai about 22 September.

1340 The battle at Lille on 11 April was in fact an English defeat. John III, duke of Brittany died 30 April 1341.

1342 Godefroi d'Harcourt, lord of Saint-Sauveur-le-Vicomte, was banished from

francia

1343

1344

1345　3　Rex Edwardus accepit Cadamum et deinde transivit ad Cambray

1346　3　bellum dunelmie. david de bruis capitur Rege scocie. Edwardus Rex fugavit in festo sancti lodowici fugavit philippum Regem ffrancie et obsessit calisiam et habuit eam 4 die augusti

1347　3　Caristia

1348　3　pestilencia generalis incepit in anglia in partibus australibus circa festum sancti Johannis baptiste et duravit per annum et plus tunc fuit in tota hibernia post intervallum temporis

1349　3　Philippus Rex francie moritur cui successit Johannes filius eius

1350

1351　1 3　caristia. Isto anno rumpebatur pax inter regna. Carausius venit a romanis et eorum nomine acquisivit regnum et cum coronatus fuit renuit dare tributum Rome　　　　　　　　　　286

1352

f. 48ᵛ

1353

1354　3　hoc anno conflictus inter scolares et laycos oxonie in vigilia sancte fredeswide

1355　2　circa hec tempora Rabanus et Strabus eius discipulus floru- erunt 823. Et papa fugatus ab avynione

1356　3　Rex francie Johannes captus 19 die Septembris

1357　1　Allectus venit a Romanis et interfecit carausium et recuperavit

France after his flight to Brabant in March 1343. He came to England in May 1345. Cf. the continuation of Guillaume de Nangis, *Chronique*, ed. Géraud ii.197; *GCF* ix.243.

1345 Edward III's army took Caen on 26 July 1346. He then marched into Picardy, but nowhere near Cambrai: perhaps Calais is intended.

1346 St Louis's Day is 25 August. The battle of Crécy was fought on 26 August. Calais surrendered on 3 August 1347.

1348 The plague in Ireland is recorded under 1348 in the annals compiled in or near Dublin some time after 1370, and printed in *Chartularies of St Mary's Abbey, Dublin*, ed. J. T. Gilbert (RS 1884), ii.287–398; cf. 390.

1349 Philip VI died 22 August 1350.

1351 The breach of the peace probably refers to the raids made by English captains from Calais in March and April 1351; cf. *Chronique des règnes de Jean II et de Charles V*, ed. R. Delachenal (Société de l'Histoire de France, 1910–20) (= *CJC*) i.34. On Carausius cf. *Historia Regum Britanniae* v.3–4.

1355 The equivalent year in the second Easter cycle is 823. The Pope (Innocent VI) did not flee from Avignon in this or any other year; but cf. the continuation of Guillaume de Nangis ii.316, s.a. 1360 for the danger to Avignon from routiers.

1357 Cf. *Historia Regum Britanniae* v.4.

     tributum Romanis   292

1358 3 Regitur ffrancia per Isabellam matrem Edwardi 3ⁱ. Isto anno et
    2 proximis sequentibus Anglici Navarri Normanni et picardi
    fecerunt guerram in francia inter aquas de Rosne et somme et
    tenuerunt faciliora. Dioclicianus primo gemmavit ipsum ves-
    tibus constantii   293

1359 1 Asclepiodotus dux cornubie in britonibus peremit londonie
    allectum et levium gallum eius collegas et residuos Romanos
    aput Walbroke   294

1360 3 Rex francie Johannes liberatus est. inter francos et anglos pax
    Inita fuit. Asclepiodotus regni dyadema suscepit 295
     1361 3 tonitruum vehemens et horribile qui fregit turres
    Sancte fredeswide et Sancte trinitatis oxonie 13 die Julii. leonel-
    lus filius Regis Edwardi 3ⁱ venit in hiberniam. et pestilencia
    fortium et robustorum in anglia et hibernia

1362

1363 3 ventus vehemens horribilis et inauditus qui fregit domos
    ecclesias et arbores 15 die Januarii

1364 3 gelu a festo Sancti Nicholai usque festum Sancti gregorii. Johannes
    rex francie mortuus est in anglia

1365
1366
1367 1 3 Nativitas Regis Ricardi 2ᵈⁱ burdigali 6 die Januarii. Et Nativitas
    Henrici 4ᵗⁱ in anglia 16 die marcii. Marcellus papa sedit annis
    5 mensibus 6 Et coel dux [illegible: cancelled] Colchestrie
    interemit asclepiodotum quo audito senatus constancium in
    angliam misit cum quo coel fecit [?] pacem et post mensem
    decesit. cuius filiam helenam duxit in uxorem a quo genuit
    constantinum Imperatorem   302

1368 1 Sanctus albanus martirizatur cuius percussor lumine privatur
                303
1369
1370 3 Urbanus papa moritur. Gregorius 11ᵘˢ eligitur. Robertus Knoll

  1358 Cf. the continuation of Guillaume de Nangis, Chronique, ed. Géraud ii.278–315
on the Anglo-Navarrese depredations of France. On Diocletian cf. Higden, Polychronicon
v.100, referring to his use of gemmatis vestibus, from which this passage seems to derive.
  1359 Cf. Historia Regum Britanniae v.4.
  1361 Sancte trinitatis is an error for sancti crucis, the reading of the Digby MS. There
was no church dedicated to the Trinity in Oxford.
  1367 Richard II was born 6 January 1367; Henry IV's date of birth is not known for
certain, but the most likely date is 4 April 1366. Pope Marcellus I's pontificate lasted
from November or December 306 to 16 January 308. The equivalent year of the first
Easter cycle is 303. On Coel cf. Historia Regum Britanniae v.6.
  1368 Cf. Bede Hist. Eccl. i.7, ed. Plummer i.21.
  1370 Urban V died 19 December 1370; Gregory XI was elected on 30 December. On
Sir Robert Knolles in France see CJC ii.143–6. On the plague in Ireland see the annals

viguit in francia. In hibernia pestilencia magna

1371	1	obiit constancius. Et constantinus dyadem suscepit. quo anno facta est 11ᵃ persequcio post Neronem 306
1372	1	constantinus creatur in Imperatorem
1373	1	Sanctus Nicholaus migravit a seculo
1374	1	Invencio Sancte crucis 310 et inferius per aliam cronicam 324
		308
1375	1	Sancta Katerina 311
1376	1	Sanctus Nicholaus 312. nota supra secundum alium librum. Melchiades sedit papa annis 3 mensibus 8 311
1377	3	Obitus Edwardi 3ⁱ 21 die Junii. coronatio Regis Ricardi 2ⁱ 16 die Julii. 19 Julii alio libro
1378	1	cessavit persecucio et pax fuit per 7 annos usque ad tempus Arriane vesanie. quo anno fundatur ecclesia sancti albani 313
1379	3 1	Karolus 5ᵗᵘˢ Rex francie moritur aput bastiam vincencii et habuit 2 filios Karolum et lodowicum. octavius Rex Gewiseorum invasit britanniam et sese insignivit dyadema. Et trahern awunculus venit a constantino qui fugavit octavium a regno 314
1380	1	Interfeccio Trahern per procuratores octavii et regnum recuperavit. Sanctus Silvester sedit annis 23 mensibus 10 diebus 11
		315
1381	3	tempore Insurrectionis anno regis Ricardi 2ᵈⁱ 4ᵗᵒ
1382	3	Karolus 6ᵗᵘˢ Rex francie interfecit 2600 flandrenses. eodem anno fecit le bastille parisius. et in anglia terre motus magnus 21 die maii
1383	1 3	Anglici with Episcopo Norwicensis Spenser devastaverunt partem fflandrie. constantinus a Sancto Silvestro baptizatur et

of Thomas Case printed in *Chartularies of St Mary's Abbey, Dublin*. ed. Gilbert, ii.241–86; cf. 282.

1371 Cf. *Historia Regum Britanniae* v.5–6.

1372 Cf. *ibid.* v.8.

1373 Presumably another speculative date for the death of St Nicholas.

1374 Pope Melchiades reigned from 2 July 311 to 10 January 314.

1377 Richard II was crowned on 16 July.

1378 Cf. *Flores Historiarum* i.177–8.

1379 Charles V, king of France died at Beauté-sur-Marne on 16 September 1380, not at the Château de Vincennes. His two sons were Charles VI and Louis duke of Orléans. On Octavius cf. *Historia regum Britanniae* v.8.

1380 Cf. *ibid.* v.8. Pope Sylvester I reigned from 31 January 314 to 31 December 335.

1382 The battle of Roosebeke, 27 November 1382. On the casualties cf. *Chronique du religieux de St-Denis*, ed. L. Bellaguet (Documents inédits de l'histoire de France, 1839–52) i.220. On the building of the bastille St.Antoine see *CJC* iii.41–2, s.a. 1383.

1383 The crusade of Henry Despenser bishop of Norwich in Flanders lasted from 25 May until October 1383. 'With' (wᵗ) is evidently a lapse into English. On the baptism of Constantine cf. *Flores Historiarum* i.179–80.

Christum vidisse *confitetur* et a lepra mu*n*detur. he*r*esis arriana
ori*tur. Contra* illud Ego *et* pater unu*m* sum*us* 318

1384   3   pestilencia mag*n*a in hibe*r*nia 319

f.49

1385   1   den*arii* pet*ri*   321   heresis arriana *con*fundi*tur* ap*ut* ci*v*itate*m*
arelate*n*se*m* 320

1386   3   Nati*v*itas he*n*rici 5 16 die *septem*bris.   he*r*esis donatistar*um* i*n*
affrica q*uod* fili*us* est mi*n*or pa*t*re *et* s*piritus* s*anctus* minor fil*io*

1387   3   Equitacio do*m*i*n*orum

1388   3 1   Nati*v*itas duc*is* Clarencie thome. co*n*sta*n*tin*us* vide*t* {*crucem*}
in ce*l*o *et* angel*us* dux*it* i*n* cruce vi*n*cendi 323

1389   3 1   Nat*v*itas duc*is* bedford 21 die Junii Joha*n*nis.   S*anct*a Elena
Inve*n*it {crucem} m*on*te clavis 324

1390   3   Nati*v*itas hu*m*fr*i*di duc*is* Glouc*estrie* 2 die *octo*br*is*

1391

1392

1393   3   Na*tiv*itas arthuri de brita*n*ia 22 augusti ap*ut* Nantes   Et
Na*tiv*itas J*acobi* co*mitis* Ormo*n*d 28 maii ap*ut* fruglasse

1394   3   Ric*ardus* 2us applicu*it* Wate*r*ford 2 die *octo*br*is*

1395

1396   3   Na*tiv*itas co*mitis* Suf*f*o*l*k 16 *octo*br*is*   Na*tiv*itas duc*is* b*u*rgundi*e*
30 d*ie* Julii *et* Na*tiv*itas Joha*n*nis duc*is* Exon*ie* 29 ma*r*cii

1397

1384 On the plague of 1384 see *Annála Connacht, The Annals of Connacht*, ed. A. M. Freeman (Dublin 1970), 350, and Kevin Down in *New History of Ireland, ii, Mediaeval Ireland*, ed. A. Cosgrove (Oxford 1987), 450: both however only incidental references.

1385 Cf. *Flores Historiarum* i.181.

1386 The date of Henry V's birth is disputed; the strongest evidence agrees with an early horoscope and with the claim made here, that it took place on 16 September 1386. See C. Allmand, *Henry V* (London 1992), 7–8. On the Donatists cf. *Flores Historiarum* i.181.

1387 Probably a reference to the battle of Radcot Bridge, at which the lords appellant defeated Robert de Vere duke of Ireland, on 20 December 1387.

1388 Thomas duke of Clarence was born 29 September 1388. On the vision of Constantine cf. *Flores Historiarum* i.181.

1389 John duke of Bedford was born on 20 or 21 June 1389. On the invention of the Cross cf. *Flores Historiarum* i.182.

1390 Humphrey duke of Gloucester was born on 2 or 3 October 1390.

1393 Arthur de Richemont, second son of John IV duke of Brittany, was born 24 November 1393. This entry is the only evidence for the place and date of birth of James, fourth earl of Ormond.

1394 Richard II arrived at Waterford on 2 October 1394.

1396 William earl (later duke) of Suffolk was born 16 October 1396; Philip duke of Burgundy on 30 June; John earl of Huntingdon (later duke of Exeter) on 29 March. The year of the latter's birth is either 1395 or 1396; this entry strengthens the case for 1396.

1398 3 Roge*rus* co*mes* ma*r*chie occi*ditur* Kenl*is* in ffothiut

1399 3 *primo* Junii Ri*car*dus 2^{dus} applicu*it* Waterfo*r*d. Et 13 die Octobr*is* corona*tur* henricus 4^{tus}

1400 1 3 Ri*car*dus 2^{dus} obiit ulti*m*o die febr*uarii* ap*ut* pontefract.   co*n*stantin*us* de*dit* eccle*sie* te*m*po*r*alia   337

1401 2 3 a*n*n*us* ab Impe*ri*o Constantini q*ui* dota*vit* eccle*s*iam   869. Et dux clar*encie* ve*n*it *in* hibe*r*niam 13 d*ie novem*br*is*

1402 3 Maior   *et*   commu*n*itas   dublin*ensis*   occi*dunt*   pr*o*pe   bree   487   hibe*r*nicos 11 die Junii

1403 2 3 ma*r*tiriu*m* bea*ti* Edmun*di* R*egis* 871. bellum de Shrewesbu*r*y 21 d*ie* Julii. Nati*vitas* mea[?] 2 febr*uarii*. Na*tivitas* delfini 21 eiu*sdem*

1404

1405 1 3 Nati*vitas* R*egis* castelle in aurora diei {veneris}. (Sil) S*anctus* Silves*ter* Et Co*n*stantin*us* obieru*n*t

1406 1 Marchu*s* sedit a*n*n*is* 11 me*n*s*ibus* 2 d*iebus* 20   340

1407 3 Nati*vitas* d*omini* W*il*le*lmi* beauc*h*amp d*om*i*n*i s*an*c*ti* amandi

                                                                              341

1408

1409 1 hengist*us* ve*n*it in angl*iam*   877

1410 3 die {saturni} in c*r*astino assu*m*ptio*n*is bea*te* vi*r*ginis. Nati*vit*as d*om*i*n*i de beaumont

1398 Roger earl of March was killed at Kells on 20 July 1398.

1399 Richard II left Milford Haven on 29 May; this is the only evidence for his arrival at Waterford on 1 June. Henry IV was crowned on 13 October 1399.

1401 The equivalent year of the first Easter cycle is 337, and of the second 869. The mention of 869 is perhaps an error for 337. Thomas duke of Clarence arrived in Dublin as lieutenant of Ireland on 13 November.

1402 This may refer to the retaliatory raid by the Dubliners on the forces of Art McMuchadha in 1401; cf. *Annals of Connacht* 380 and Cosgrove in Cosgrove, ed., *New History of Ireland*, ii.543. It seems that no other source mentions that it took place in the district of Bree (Brega) north of Dublin, or the number of the Irish dead.

1403 Edmund, king of the East Angles was martyred probably in 869. The battle of Shrewsbury was fought on 21 July; Charles VII, king of France was born on 22 February 1403. The reading *mea*, in large letters, is the most probable.

1405 John II, king of Castile was born Friday 6 March 1405. The Emperor Constantine died 22 May 337; Pope Sylvester I on 31 December 335.

1406 Pope Mark reigned from 18 January to 7 October 336.

1407 William Beauchamp, a cadet of the Beauchamps of Powick, was summoned to parliament as Lord St Amand in right of his wife from 2 January 1449. This is the only evidence of his date of birth; he was married in or before 1426.

1409 877 is the equivalent year of the second Easter cycle; the reason for the reference to Hengist, who reappears in the entry under 1514 (450), is not obvious.

1410 16 August 1410 was a Saturday; this is the only evidence for the date of birth of John Lord Beaumont, who is known to have been aged four at the death of his father Henry in June 1413.

1411   ysia patris filii et spiritus sancti aput arelatenses celebratur id est
           esse unius vere deitatis potestatis et virtutis   346

1412   3   Obitus henrici 4^{ti} 20 die marcii

1413   1 3   coronacio henrici 5 9 die aprilis. arrius purgans ventrem
           exieunt omnia viscera cum intestinis et sic cum heresi periit

                                                     349

1414

1415   3   13 augusti intravit mare et cito post applicuit kidycause 3°
           anno regni sui Et in festo crispini et crispiniani bellum de
           Agincourt

1416

f.49^v

1417   3   Obitus thome cranle archiepiscopi dublinensis aput ffaryngdon
           28 Julii et primo augusti henricus 5^{tus} applicuit towks anno 5to
           regni sui

1418

1419

1420   3   Nativitas Comitis de Wiltshire

1421   1 3   Nativitas henrici 6 post meridiem 6 diei decembris 3 hora 38
           minutis. Et Elizabeth comitissa salissopie in festo Sancti thome
           apostoli. liberius sedit annis 10 mensibus 7   356

1422   3   Obitus henrici 5^{ti} ultimo die Augusti

1423

1424

1425

1411 The equivalent year of the first Easter cycle is 345. Ysia: presumably ousia, being; cf. *Flores Historiarum* i.186–7.

1412 Henry IV died 20 March 1413.

1413 Henry V was crowned on 9 April 1413. Arius died about 336.

1415 Henry V's fleet arrived off the Chef de Caux on 13 August. The battle of Agincourt was fought on 25 October.

1417 Thomas Cranley, archbishop of Dublin died at Faringdon on 25 May 1417. The English army landed in Normandy at Touques on 1 August.

1420 James Butler, earl of Wiltshire and fifth earl of Ormond was born 20 November 1420.

1421 Henry VI was born 6 December 1421. The time, 3.38 p.m., is not given elsewhere and is presumably drawn from a horoscope similar to the seven horoscopes of Henry VI drawn up about 1442, two of which record the time of birth as 3.21 p.m. See J. D. North, *Horoscopes and History* (Warburg Institute Texts and Studies xiii, 1986), 141–7; H. Carey, *Courting Disaster* (London 1992), 254–56. The date of birth of Elizabeth, daughter of James, fourth earl of Ormond, 21 December is otherwise not recorded; she married John Talbot, second earl of Shrewsbury, probably in 1444. Pope Liberius reigned from 17 May 352 to 24 September 366.

1422 Henry V died 31 August 1422.

1426

1427

1428   3   h*oc* a*nno* pluv*i*ebat o*mn*i die plus v*el* min*us* a 28 m*a*rcii usq*ue* 3ᵐ diem *octo*br*i*s q*uod* cau*sat* maxim*am* morina*m et* caristia*m*

1429   3   Juli*us* ap*o*stata succ*essit* Co*n*stanti*no* mag*no* 369. coronacio h*enr*ici 6 in f*esto* S*ancti* leonardi

1430

1431   3   Nativ*i*tas R*egi*s Scocie. coro*natur* h*en*ricus 6ᵘˢ parisi*us* 9 die *decem*br*i*s

1432   3   Nativ*i*tas R*egi*s portugalie in f*esto* S*ancti* Mauri

1433

1434

1435

1436   3   In nocte cin*er*um opp*ressus* fuit Jacob*us* Rex Scotie in cloa*ca*. 3 die Januarii morieba*tur* Kat*er*ina regina angl*ie*

1437

1438   3   caristia incepit

1439   3   caristia enormis

1440   2 3 1 Ann*us* a Regn*o* adelstani p*rim*i R*egi*s reg*ni* anglie   908. mi*hi* gr*an*di*s* t*er*tiana. obiit octavi*us et* fuit sine herede masculo

                                                   375

1441   3   Elianora Cobh*am et* m*a*gist*er* Roge*r*us *et* m*a*gist*er* t*homas* Southwell

1442   3   Estas b*ene* ca*l*ida *et* sicca pr*o* maiori p*ar*te usq*ue* *septem*bre*m*

1428 Cf. J. Amundesham, *Annales Monasterii Sancti Albani* ed. H. T. Riley (RS 1870–71) i.26-27.

1429 The equivalent year of the first Easter cycle is 365. The emperor Julian succeeded Constans II on 3 November 361. Henry VI was crowned at Westminster on 6 November 1429.

1431 James II, king of Scotland was born 16 October 1430. Henry VI's French coronation took place in Paris on 16 December 1431.

1432 Afonso V, king of Portugal was born 15 January 1432.

1436 James I, king of Scotland was murdered hiding in the sewer of the Dominican convent at Perth on the night of Thursday 21 February 1437. Ash Wednesday that year fell on 13 February, but in 1436 on 22 February. Queen Catherine, widow of Henry V died 3 January 1437.

1438 On the famine of this year and 1439 see the Waltham Annals, ed. C. L. Kingsford in his *English Historical Literature of the Fifteenth Century* (Oxford 1913), 352.

1440 Cf. *Historia Regum Britanniae* v.11. 376 is the equivalent year of the first Easter cycle.

1441 Eleanor Cobham, duchess of Gloucester, her clerk Mr Roger Bolingbroke and Mr Thomas Southwell, rector of St Stephen Walbrook were arrested on and after 28 June, and were tried and condemned for conspiring to bring about the death of Henry VI by necromancy. Several favourable horoscopes of Henry VI were evidently drawn up in response to their prognostications of his death; see Carey, *Courting Disaster*, 138–49.

1442 Britton, *Meteorological Chronology* 162 cites no chronicler who mentions this warm summer.

1443
1444 I 3 treuga inter nos *et francos*. hoc anno incipit caducum imperii
           Regis. leolinus avunculus constantini duxit filiam octavii *et* sic
           habuit regni dyadema   379
1445 I 3 Rex hoc anno desponsavit Margaritam filiam Regis Sicilie *et*
           in festo Sancti trinitatis coronabatur. Maximianus subjugavit
           regnum armorice regno britanie *et* dedit regi conano nepoti
           octavii   390
1446
1447 I 3 Eugenius papa moritur. Nicholaus consecratur. humfridus dux
           gloucestrie <7 kl marcii> dux Exonie <6 die augusti> Et
           cardinalis <3 idibus aprilis> conanus misit ad dinotum ducem
           cornubie pro puellis ei *et* suis maritandis qui collegit 11000
           virgines circa   392
1448 I   Hengistus occiditur 916 (Mortuo octavio quia non habuit
           heredes masculos regnum fuit sine rege)   (375)

f.50

1449 3   treuge rumpuntur *et* tota Neustria intraditur *et* opprimitur
           concupiscencia *et* negligencia capitanorum *et* gubernatorum
1450 3   Insurrectio cancie per J. Cade anno regni 29
1451 I   circa hec tempora athanasius Jeronimus ambrosius crisostomus
           Nazarenus Sanctus martinus hillarius Julianus appostata *et* arrius
           moriuntur   386
1452
1453 3   In nocte Sancti laurencii Rex insanatur *et* continuat usque ad

1444 A truce was concluded between Henry VI and Charles VII, king of France on
28 May 1444. On Ioelinus or Leolinus, whom the compiler confuses with his son
Maximianus, cf. *Historia Regum Britanniae* v.9–11.

1445 Henry VI was married to Margaret of Anjou, daughter of René, duke of Anjou
and titular king of Sicily on 22 April; she was crowned on Trinity Sunday, 30 May. On
Maximian's conquest cf. *Historia Regum Britanniae* v.12–14. 390 must be an error for 380.

1447 Eugenius IV died 24 February 1447; Nicholas V was elected on 6 March. The
dates of death of Humphrey, duke of Gloucester (23 February) and Cardinal Beaufort
(11 April) agree with other sources; John, duke of Exeter died on 5 August. On Conan
see *Historia Regum Britanniae* v.15–16.

1448 See the entry for 1440.

1449 The truce between Henry VI and Charles VII ended on 31 July 1449. Neustria
is a poetic form for Normandy, used by Thomas Walsingham in the title of his *Ypodigma
Neustriae*. *Intraditur*: presumably for *traditur*, used here to mean betrayed as much as handed
over.

1450 The rebellion of Jack Cade lasted from 24 May to about 7 July.

1453 This date (10 August) for Henry VI's insanity is later than that given by any
other chronicler. Benet's Chronicle (ed. G. L. and M. A. Harriss, *Camden Miscellany* xxiv
(RHS, Camden 4th series 1972), 210 gives the date as about 1 August, but the later date
is marginally more likely, as is indicated by B. Wolffe, *Henry VI* (London 1981), 270. The
date of his recovery, 1 January, agrees with other authorities.

*cir*cumscitione*m* anni 1455 i*n*persona [?]

1454

1455 3   22 Maii affraia fuit ap*ut* Sanctum albanu*m*. i*bi* d*ux* s*o*merset
K*o*mes North*u*mberland *et* d*ominus* de clifford cu*m* aliis i*n*ter-
empti

1456 3   *obitus* d*o*mini thome liseux deca*n*i S*ancti* pauli londoni*e*

1457 3   cano*n*izatio S*an*c*ti* Osmu*n*di ap*ut* saru*m* te*m*po*r*e Kalisti p*a*pe
16 Julii

1458

1459 3   22 Junii capcio carracoru*m* Janu*e*nsium *et* navis hispani*e* p*er*
comitem Warwici. 14 *se*pte*m*br*is* Rex accepit campu*m* *et* in
nocte 12 d*ie* octobri *con*t*ra*rii Regi fugieru*n*t a ca*m*po pr*o*pe
ludlowe

1460

1461

1462

1463

1464

1465

1466

1467

1468

1469

1470

1471

1472

1473

1474 1   *obitus* bea*ti* ambros*ii*   410

1475

1476

1477

1478

1479

1480

f. 50[v]

1456 Mr Thomas Lisieux, keeper of the Privy Seal, died about 24 September.

1457 St Osmund was canonized on 1 January 1457. The feast of his translation was celebrated on 16 July.

1459 On the capture of these ships see *An English Chronicle of the reign of Richard II, Henry IV, Henry V and Henry VI*, ed. J. S. Davis (Camden Society 1856), 83–84; John Whetham-stede, *Registrum Abbatiae*, ed. H. T. Riley, *Registra Abbatum Monasterii Sancti Albani* (RS 1872), i.330, with the date. 14 September is an earlier date than is given elsewhere for Henry VI taking the field against the Yorkist lords. His confrontation with them at Ludford Bridge outside Ludlow took place on 12 October.

1481	2	*obitus* beati Jeronimi	417
1482			
1483			
1484			
1485	1	britones infestati per pictos scotos *et* norwigios peterunt aux- ilium a romanis	420
1486	1	Romani venerunt *et* expulerunt hostes ad mare *et* cum britonis fecerunt murum saxo solido a mari us*que* ad mare	421
1487			
1488			
1489	1	425 *Christi* mittitur Sanctus patricuus in hiberniam a celestino papa primo	
1490			
1491			
1492	1	*obitus* beati augustini 428. Sanctus patricius mittitur in hib- erniam ut puto	
1493			
1494	1	Sanctus paladius mittitur in hiberniam secundum gesta bede quamquam nihil proficuit	
1495			
1496			
1497			
1498	1	Scoti primo recipiunt fidem *Christi*	433
1499	1	Romani recedunt *et* scoti atque picti veniunt *left margin:* 435 Sanctus patricius revertitur glastoniam *et* sanctus fuit ibi abbas <div align="right">434</div>	
1500	1	constantinus frater aldroeni regis armorice eligitur in regem et a Romana genuit constantem aurelium *et* uterpendragon. et constantes [*sic*] monachus efficitur	435
1501			
1502			
1503			
1504			
1505			

1485 Cf. *Historia Regum Britanniae* vi.1. The equivalent year of the first Easter cycle is 421.

1486 Cf. *ibid.* 1.c.

1489 Cf. Higden, *Polychronicon* v.230. The date may have been deduced from this source.

1492 On Patrick, see the note on the entry above.

1494 Cf. Bede *Hist. Eccl.* i.13, ed. Plummer i.28.

1498 Cf. *Polychronicon* v.230, referring to Palladius converting the Scots.

1499 Cf. *Historia Regum Britanniae* vi.3, and on Patrick, *Polychronicon* v.305–6; the compiler amalgamates the greater and lesser Patrick, between whom Higden carefully distinguished.

1500 Cf. *Historia Regum Britanniae* vi.4–5.

1506
1507
1508
1509
1510 I Mortuo *constantino* constans filius eius *conve*hitur ex*tra*hitur a Win*tonia* cenobio *et* fit rex p*er* vortigernum *con*sulem gew-is*s*or*um* 445, quo inter*f*ecto vortig*ernus* ha*b*uit regnu*m* q*uia* tu*nc* aurelius i*n* armorica fuit

1511
1512
1513 I pi*c*ti cu*m* scot*i*s bellu*m* *contra* b*ri*tones 448 s*a*nctus ge*r*manus fec*it* omne*s* clamare una voce alba*num* *et* h*a*bue*r*unt victoriam *co*ntra suos 449
1514 I Vortige*rn*us voc*av*it anglos saxo*nes et* Jutos in 3 lo*ngis* navib*us* v*i*de*l*icet horsa *et* hingist 451
1515 Et sic a b*ri*to*ne* fluxe*ru*nt a*n*ni 1593 / Et fueru*nt* Reg*n*is 93
1516
1517
1518 I ang*l*ici ve*n*eru*nt* i*n* angl*i*am a saxo*n*ia *et* vortige*rn*us seduxit fil*i*am hingisti, qua depo*n*itur *et* vortimer*us* erigi*tur* 454

1519
1520
1521
1522 I defu*n*cto horso he*n*gist i*n* Regn*um* cancie erig*itur* 457
1523 I (he*n*gistu*s* sub fraude destr*ux*it b*ri*tones a*n*no 458 unde *con*-vener*unt* cum mult*is*)

1524
1525 I vortime*rus* per novercam i*n*terimitur *et* vortige*rn*us ite*rum* reg*it*
1526 I (q*uo*) he*n*gistu*s* cum subti*li* fraude interem*it* [*illegible: cancelled*] <de b*ri*to*n*ibus> 460 b*ri*to*n*ib*us* 464

1527
1528 I (o*bitus* s*a*n*cti* Nicho*lai* 464)
1529 I aureli*us et* ut*er*pendrago*n* remearu*nt* ab armorica. Vortige*rn*us i*n* tu*rr*e fortissi*m*o *et* tu*nc* m*er*linus [*illegible*]

1510 Cf. *ibid.* vi.6–8.
1513 This is evidently derived from *Historia Regum Britanniae* vi.9, with an attempt to insert the victory over the Saxons effected by St Germanus in Bede, *Hist. Eccl.* i.20, ed. Plummer i.38–39.
1514 Cf. *Historia Regum Britanniae* vi.10.
1518 Cf. *ibid.* vi.12–13.
1522 Cf. *ibid.* vi.13.
1523 Cf. the note to 1526 below.
1525 Cf. *Historia Regum Britanniae* vi.14.
1526 Cf. *ibid.* vi.15.
1529 Cf. *ibid.* 17–18. viii.1–2.

1530 I   merlinus vaticinatur sibi et prophetavit veritatem   465
1531 I   vortigernus a incendio periit et aurelius regnum suscepit 466
1532

1530 C f. *ibid.* vii., viii.1.
1531 Cf. *ibid.* viii.2.